Praise for *No Ordinary Joes*

"The book's content is fresh, and the narrative is superb."
— *The Oregonian* **(A Top 10 Northwest Book of 2010)**

"Colton ably re-creates the tension of submarine warfare on the high seas. . . . [His] real accomplishment, however, lies in the meticulous way he reconstructs the details, not just of combat, but of the four sailors' personal lives before, during, and after the two years they spend as POWs. . . . Ordinary or not, more [World War II veterans] deserve such a monument."
— *Willamette Week*

"Gripping . . . Colton tells their stories in unflinching detail. . . . A compelling glimpse into forgotten World War II history."
— *Kirkus Reviews*

"This meticulously researched and thoroughly well-written book adds much to the literature of the WWII generation."
— *Booklist*

"[I] am reading *No Ordinary Joes*. Should have had a medical checkup before I started it. Colton makes us fall in love with these guys, then puts our hearts in harm's way. It's lovely and ghastly and extremely powerful. His best yet."
— **Katherine Dunn, National Book Award finalist, author of *Geek Love***

"*No Ordinary Joes* is a marvelous treatment of a special time in American history, as well as an up-close and personal look at the devastating impact that war can have on the personal lives of those involved in it. Let's have a twenty-one-gun salute for Larry Colton!"
— **John T. (Jack) Ramsay, former Navy ensign, Underwater Demolition Team #30, and basketball analyst, ESPN TV and Radio**

"Larry Colton's Ordinary Joes are just like us, yet they endure what we could never imagine, and are ennobled in ways they themselves might not claim. Intimate and epic, unblinking and even-handed, Colton's engrossing story strips sentimentality and cliché from our notion of hero."
— **Ron Shelton, award-winning screenwriter and director of** *Bull Durham*, *White Men Can't Jump*, **and** *Tin Cup*

ALSO BY LARRY COLTON

Goat Brothers

Counting Coup

No Ordinary Joes

THE EXTRAORDINARY TRUE STORY OF FOUR
SUBMARINERS IN WORLD WAR II

Larry Colton

Broadway Paperbacks

New York

BROADWAY

Copyright © 2010 by Larry Colton

Published in the United States by Broadway Paperbacks, an imprint of the
Crown Publishing Group, a division of Random House, Inc., New York.
www.crownpublishing.com

Broadway Paperbacks and its logo, a letter B bisected on the diagonal,
are trademarks of Random House, Inc.

Originally published in hardcover in the United States by Crown Publishers,
an imprint of the Crown Publishing Group, a division of
Random House, Inc., in 2010.

Library of Congress Cataloging-in-Publication Data
Colton, Larry.
No ordinary Joes: the extraordinary true story of four submariners in World
War II / Larry Colton.—1st ed.
1. Grenadier (Submarine) 2. Submariners—United States—Biography.
3. World War, 1939–1945—Naval operations—Submarine. 4. World War,
1939–1945—Prisoners and prisons, Japanese. 5. Prisoners of war—United
States—Biography. 6. Prisoners of war—Japan—Biography. 7. Palmer, Bob.
8. Cox, Gordy. 9. McCoy, Tim. 10. Ver Valin, Chuck. I. Title.
D783.5.G75C65 2010
940.54'51092273—dc22   2010013572

ISBN 978-0-307-88845-7
eISBN 978-0-307-71724-5

Printed in the United States of America

Design by Leonard Henderson
Cover design by Dan Rembert
Cover photographs: Courtesy Barbara Palmer (sailor);
courtesy Bob Palmer (submarine)

Insert Photo Credits—COURTESY TIM McCOY: page 1, above left.
COURTESY BARBARA PALMER: page 1, top right; page 2, above; page 7, above
and below. COURTESY THE FAMILY OF CHUCK VER VALIN: page 1, bottom left;
page 2, below; page 6, below. COURTESY JANICE COX: page 1, below right;
page 3, above; page 5, below. COURTESY BOB PALMER: page 3, below;
page 4, above and below; page 5, above. OFFICIAL PHOTOGRAPH U.S. NAVY:
page 6, above.

Map by Jeffrey L. Ward

10 9 8 7 6 5 4 3 2 1

First Paperback Edition

To Dick Solomon,
friend and adviser

To Lieutenant William J. Yetter, a dedicated parent
and heroic World War II pilot

To Gordy Cox,
Tim McCoy,
Bob Palmer,
and Chuck Ver Valin

Any man who may be asked what he did to make his life worth-
while can respond with a good deal of pride and satisfaction:
I served in the U.S. Navy.

President John F. Kennedy

I saw the submariners, the way they stood aloof and silent, watching their pigboat with loving eyes. They are alone in the Navy.
I admired the PT boys. And I often wondered how the aviators
had the courage to go out every day and I forgave their boast-
ing. But the submariners! In the entire fleet they stand apart!

James Michener, Tales of the South Pacific

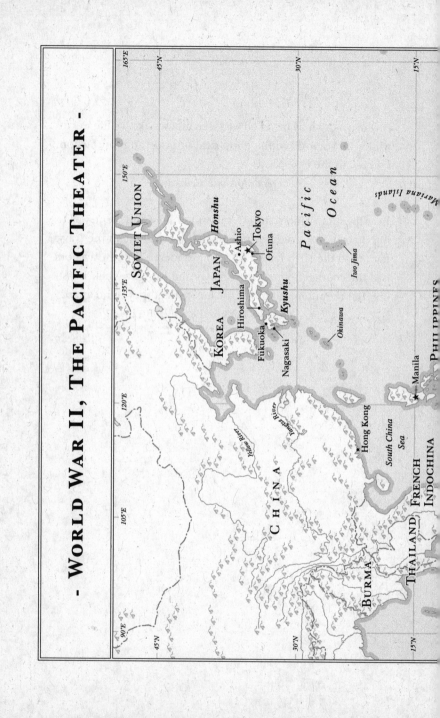

- WORLD WAR II, THE PACIFIC THEATER -

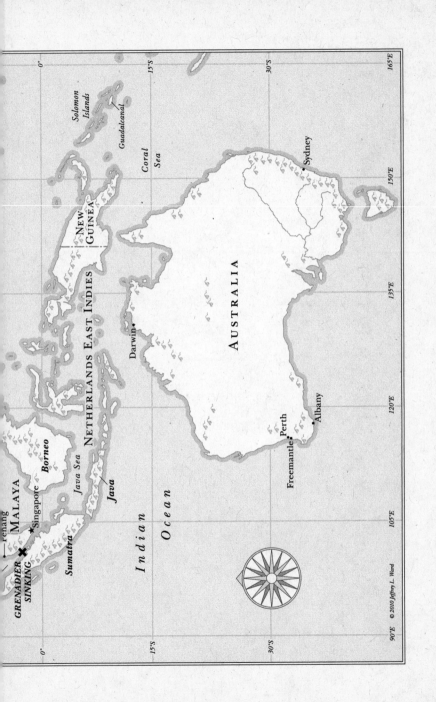

GRENADIER
SINKING ✕

Penang
MALAYA
Singapore

Sumatra

Borneo

Java Sea

Java

NETHERLANDS EAST INDIES

Solomon
Islands

Guadalcanal

Coral
Sea

NEW
GUINEA

Indian

Ocean

AUSTRALIA

Darwin

Sydney

Perth
Freemantle
Albany

0°

15°S

30°S

0°

15°S

30°S

90°E   105°E   120°E   135°E   150°E   165°E

© 2010 Jeffrey L. Ward

Contents

Prologue   3

Part One: Surviving the Depression   9

Part Two: Submariners   51

Part Three: Assignment: *Grenadier*   103

Part Four: Captured   133

Part Five: The Convent on Light Street   151

Part Six: From Bad to Worse   181

Part Seven: Saved by the Bombs   259

Part Eight: Going Home   287

Part Nine: Sixty Years Later   323

Epilogue   379

Author's Notes   385

Acknowledgments   394

Index   396

COMMANDER SUBMARINE FORCE
UNITED STATES PACIFIC FLEET

30 June 1944

My Dear Mrs. Palmer:

The Commander Submarine Force, Pacific Fleet, has the honor to award the Submarine Combat Insignia and to commend in absentia Robert Wiley Palmer, Yeoman first class, for service set forth in the following:

CITATION

The USS *Grenadier* on an offensive war patrol in restricted waters, heavily patrolled by the enemy, failed to return as scheduled. It is not known how many successful attacks the *Grenadier* made on this patrol; but, as she has had a splendid record since the early days of the war, it is believed that she was engaged in delivering the same relentless attacks against the enemy up until the time she was reported missing.

As Yeoman first class of the USS *Grenadier*, Robert Wiley Palmer's performance of duty materially contributed to the success of this vessel against the enemy. The Commander Submarine Force, Pacific Fleet, forwards this commendation in recognition of his splendid performance of duty, which was in keeping with the highest traditions of the Naval Service.

Please accept my deepest sympathy in your great loss, which I assure you I also consider a great loss to the Naval Service.

Most sincerely,
C.A. Lockwood, Jr.
Vice Admiral, U.S. Navy

Prologue

The waters felt unsafe to Bob Palmer. Too shallow. Too close to land. Too risky, given the ship's unreliable torpedoes. But who was he, a twenty-one-year-old, to question the strategy of his submarine captain, a graduate of the Naval Academy and respected by every man on the ship? Palmer worked hard as the sub's yeoman, but he was a high-school dropout, and he wasn't privy to the radio messages the captain received.

It was early evening, April 20, 1943, and the USS *Grenadier* was nearing the end of its sixth war patrol. Bob longed to get back to port in Fremantle, Australia; he was tired of the confinement, the foul smell of diesel fuel, and the constant stress of running deep in enemy waters. Back in Fremantle, there'd be large pints of Emu ale waiting in the bar at the Ocean Beach Hotel, as well as beautiful young Aussie women enamored of American sailors. Yes, he was recently married to his high-school sweetheart and loved her dearly. But this was war—a war on the other side of the world, and every time he and his crewmates left port there was the real possibility they'd be blown to bits.

As the *Grenadier* ran full speed on the surface through the Java Sea and the narrow Strait of Malacca between Malaysia and Sumatra, the lookout spotted two worthy targets—a pair of large Japanese freighters silhouetted on the horizon. The sea was calm, the sky bright from a full moon. Surprisingly, the vessels appeared to be unescorted, an opportunity almost too good to be true. The Japanese had recently taken Rangoon, and the Japanese ships plying the important supply route between Burma and Singapore were usually well guarded. But not these two.

The *Grenadier*'s captain, Missouri-born John Fitzgerald, a ballsy former boxing champ at Annapolis, was eager to confront the enemy, and he had decided to ignore warnings that these waters were much too easily guarded by Japanese planes from nearby bases for his ship to be running on the surface. A month earlier, a sub had been sunk, taking sixty-five men down with it. But Fitzgerald wanted a kill before heading back to port. At this point in the war, with the Japanese racking up victory after victory in the Pacific, American naval forces were desperate for any small victory.

Fitzgerald was one of a new breed of captain who had been hurried into battle; the top level of Navy leadership was now encouraging these newer graduates of the Naval Academy to "go in harm's way" and take the war to the enemy. His approach was more aggressive than that of the older and more conservative sub commanders in charge at the start of the war who believed the purpose of submarines was to scout for the Navy's surface fleet rather than to attack.

From long range and on the surface, Fitzgerald considered firing torpedoes, but at this stage of the war, the available torpedoes were notoriously ineffective, either running too deep or failing to explode on contact. Instead he closed to 2,500 yards.

The freighters discovered the ship's presence, possibly by radar, and turned searchlights in its direction. Fitzgerald ordered the men manning the three-inch deck gun to commence firing. Immediately, the two freighters returned fire, neither side scoring a hit.* Knowing the *Grenadier* had been spotted, Fitzgerald quickly turned direction, electing to make a surface end-around, which would put the sub in front of the enemy, in position to submerge and attack. But while the *Grenadier* moved twice as fast on the surface than it did when submerged, it would take the *Grenadier* all night—twelve hours—to accomplish this maneuver. The crew—eight officers and sixty-eight enlisted men—stood down from their battle stations.

Bob sat down at a table to write a letter to his wife, Barbara. He would post the letter as soon as the ship returned to Fremantle. Barbara was living in San Francisco, where they had gotten married a week after Pearl Harbor, six days before he'd shipped off to war. She'd gotten pregnant during

---

* Author's note: In researching this event, I found numerous conflicting reports of exactly what happened regarding the firing of torpedoes. In the end, I relied on Captain Fitzgerald's write-up.

those six days, but the excitement he'd felt when he'd gotten the news was soon offset by sadness when she lost the baby. He still had a year to go on his duty.

Seated at the table with Palmer were three other men just as anxious to get back to port—Tim McCoy from Dallas, Texas; Chuck Ver Valin from Dundee, New York; and Gordy Cox from Yakima, Washington. Tim and Chuck had met the women they thought were the loves of their young lives on their last leave in Fremantle, and both talked of marrying these young Aussies and taking them back to America after the war. Tim's girl was the reigning Miss Perth. Gordy, the fourth man at the table, had also met a girl, but he was the shy type and wasn't sure she liked him as much. Still, he hoped. He'd even written his mom about her. He'd never had a girlfriend growing up.

As the *Grenadier* made its long circle, Tim and Gordy had time to talk. The two sailors, neither yet twenty-one, were total opposites. Tim was extroverted, cocky, and full of Texas bravado; Gordy was slightly built, quiet, and not confident in his ability to learn the complex set of submarine skills necessary to advance beyond his rank of seaman first class. Despite the close confines of the sub and their shared experience in battle—which included being scared shitless—they barely knew each other. Gordy's initial impression was that Tim was a little too full of himself.

Chuck got up from the table and walked to his bunk, where he pulled a picture of Gwen, his nineteen-year-old girlfriend, out from under his pillow. He'd met her strolling through an arcade in Perth a few months earlier. Two nights before the *Grenadier* had shipped out on this mission, Gwen had given him a Saint Christopher's medal for good luck and protection. He promised he'd never take it off; she promised she'd wait for him. During their last night together, he confessed that he had an uneasy feeling about this patrol, much more than before the other four he'd been on. She asked why. "Because for the first time in my life I have somebody I really care about," he answered.

Throughout the night, the *Grenadier* sped along the ocean's surface at its top speed, 18 knots. Just before daylight it neared its attack position. As it closed on its targets, Fitzgerald ordered it to submerge and for everyone to man their battle stations. But the freighters had unexpectedly changed direction, and Fitzgerald watched through his periscope as they zigzagged out of sight, leaving only smoke plumes visible on the horizon.

More eager now than ever for a kill, Fitzgerald ordered the *Grenadier* back to the surface for a rapid pursuit, disregarding standard naval operating procedure, which advised subs to patrol on the surface only at night. The sun was now up, and so was a Japanese fighter plane sent to look for the *Grenadier*. For Bob Palmer, Gordy Cox, Tim McCoy, Chuck Ver Valin, and the rest of the crew, the war was about to take a terrible turn.

I first stumbled across this story when a cousin of Barbara Palmer's gave me a twenty-page story Barbara's husband Bob had written about his life. It was an earnest tale of war and survival, but that wasn't the part that sucked me in: the passionate love story Bob had written (he was eighty years old) brought tears to my eyes. A month later I flew from Portland, Oregon, to the couple's home on the Maryland shore. Their love was even more evident in person. As Bob was telling me about all Barbara did for him, unapologetic tears rolled down his cheeks and the lump in his throat was as big as a fist.

For me, that was the beginning of a quest to meet the surviving members of the *Grenadier*'s crew. Bob, Gordy, Tim, and Chuck all had clear minds and acute recall of things that had happened sixty years earlier. More than that, they shared a kind of "ordinariness." They were all enlisted men. They hadn't been to prep schools or fancy academies. They had come of age, like others on their ship, during the great Depression, their childhoods hardscrabble and austere. Even before the crucible of war, these guys were tough-ass survivors.

Following the war, they returned to an America far different from the one they'd left five years earlier, and were ill-equipped to deal with it. Over the next several decades, for the most part they went quietly about their business. But they all had troubles in their relationships with women and, later, with their sons. They all admitted to having drunk too much.

And these ordinary men all had great—extraordinary—stories to tell.

It wasn't just their heroic endurance in terrible captivity that intrigued me. The more I got to know them, the more I realized that the qualities that enabled these four sailors to survive unimaginable cruelties in war were the same ones that got them into trouble later in life. That's what made them so much more than abstract embodiments of the so-called Greatest Generation—and so real, men whose lives describe the lifetime burden of war.

Part One

SURVIVING THE DEPRESSION

1

Chuck Ver Valin

of Dundee, New York

It had been a wet spring in the western foothills of the Catskill Mountains in 1928, and the rivers ran dangerously high. Arthur Ver Valin told his wife not to let the kids anywhere near the water. People from those parts knew not to mess with the rivers.

Chuck, seven years old, heard his father's warning, but when his thirteen-year-old sister, Beulah, set out for the swimming hole, he tagged along anyway. His concern was not the danger—only that they might get the belt when they got home.

In Chuck's eyes, Beulah could do no wrong. All the Ver Valin girls were pretty, but she was the prettiest, with green eyes and chestnut brown hair that fell in ringlets to the middle of her back. She watched over him and took him into town to buy candy, never making him feel like a pest. He loved the way she sometimes carried him on her hip or let him lick the bowl when she made cookies. She also took him with her whenever she ventured down to the swimming hole at the Unidilla River. She was the best swimmer in the family.

At the river, Beulah told Chuck and a couple of friends to wait on the bank while she tested the water. Her plan was to swim out to the sandbar in the middle where they usually sunned themselves, and if it was safe, she would come back and escort Chuck across. She'd done it dozens of times.

Halfway across, she began to flounder, the current pulling her downstream, away from the sandbar and the bank. Flailing her arms, she yelled for help. A man standing nearby heard her scream and dove in after her. But the current was too strong, and he turned and struggled back to shore. Beulah disappeared under the water.

Chuck was still standing on the bank an hour later when several men carried his sister's body on a board across the field. He watched them load her into the back of a truck and disappear down the road. Three days later, he was sitting in a pew at the front of the Congressional Church, Beulah's pansy-covered casket nearby. Next to him, his mother and sisters wept, and his father fixed his cold glare straight ahead.

The Ver Valins were a close family, all the kids helping with the chores, but there was also an abusive edge to family life, even before Beulah drowned, mainly because of Arthur. An imposing 300-pound Dutchman who liked to drink, he often took his belt to the kids, including the girls. Sometimes there seemed to be no reason for his outbursts. Chuck, the oldest son, caught the greatest share of his wrath.

Arthur and his wife, Florence, scratched out a living on a 140-acre farm on the outskirts of Sidney, New York, with a couple of workhorses, a milking cow, pigs, chickens, vegetables, and an orchard with apples and pears. To help make ends meet, Arthur, an eighth-grade dropout, took an occasional job in town. Florence, an Irish redhead, worked from dawn to dusk, fixing meals, washing clothes, milking the cow, and feeding the pigs. Being pregnant, which she always seemed to be, didn't slow her down. After each birth, she'd be back at work the next day, picking potatoes and cleaning the barn.

Like her husband, she'd dropped out of school before the ninth grade, but she loved the written word and she read to her children every night, including the poetry of Longfellow. She sometimes wrote poetry herself but rarely shared it. Arthur thought it a waste of her time. She also read the Bible a lot, especially after two babies were stillborn. She found comfort in the Scriptures.

As the Depression spread across the country, the Ver Valins were unable to sell their milk, buy feed for their animals, or keep up with their taxes. They lost the farm in 1930 and moved fifty miles west to Binghamton. Some of their friends and neighbors suspected the move had as much to do with what had happened to Beulah that muggy day in June 1928 as it did with the Depression. Arthur couldn't stand looking at the river anymore. He never talked about it, but the kids knew that down deep he blamed his wife. If she'd heeded his warning, Beulah would still be alive.

After the move to Binghamton, Chuck missed the farm, especially the horses and riding on the tractor. There were now ten kids in the family, and times were tough. Even so, Chuck was energetic and quick to adjust. His mom signed him up for Boy Scouts, and he set his sights on making it all the way to Eagle Scout, earning half the necessary badges in his first two years. His other passion was baseball, and he and his friends cleared a makeshift diamond out of a farmer's pasture. They had only one ball and bat among them, the bat held together by screws and electrical tape.

He was also popular, in large part because he always took the dare. When a pal challenged him to shoot a rubber band at the backside of his teacher, Mrs. Sabercool, he did it and got caught. The principal took the belt to him. Even when he wasn't at fault, he was one of those kids that trouble seemed to find. If somebody threw a snowball and hit a passerby, Chuck got blamed. When a buddy threw a rock through a neighbor's window during a game of cowboys and Indians, Chuck got the belt.

In 1935, when Chuck was fourteen, the Ver Valins moved again, this time to a tenant farm just outside of Dundee, New York, in the Finger Lakes area, population 1,000. Dundee was only five miles from Seneca Lake, where summer yacht folks in fancy slacks vacationed, but to Chuck the lake seemed as distant as New York City. The family had moved to Dundee from Binghamton when natural gas was discovered in the area and Arthur got hired to head the purification plant, making him one of the lucky ones to have a job in the depth of the Depression. But his luck was short-lived—a coworker turned him in for drinking on the job and he got fired.

After that, Arthur worked a series of jobs for the Works Progress Administration (WPA), the largest New Deal agency, which employed millions across America during the Depression to work on buildings, roads, and other projects. Sometimes he'd go off to Binghamton or Elmira for weeks or even months at a time, sending part of what little money he made back home. Chuck wasn't up on politics, but he heard his mother give thanks many times to President Roosevelt and his New Deal.

To Chuck, it was his mother who held the family together. Although she was usually soft-spoken and gentle, she was resolute, and sometimes showed a glimpse of a fiery Irish temperament. She never took a day off from caring for her family, even when she was sick. Chuck loved the way she read to him and his siblings, especially the westerns of Zane Grey. It provided an escape from the hard times and his father's absences. He also appreciated the way she could stretch the little food they had, whether it was by making a big pot of soup out of milkweed or baking bread out of the buckwheat that grew on their property. She was adept at improvising, as when she brewed a home remedy for cuts from the leaves of plants that grew along the road.

Chuck did what he could to help. He especially liked going out to hunt or fish for food. He'd learned to shoot at an early age, and had a 16-gauge shotgun to go with his .22. He'd killed a lot of different animals for dinner—squirrels, woodchucks, rabbits, and even raccoons. He scrounged for whatever jobs he could find, such as selling magazines, but many nights he went to bed without anything to eat, or at best a bowl of beans and a little cornbread the neighbors had brought over. In school he'd get so hungry he couldn't concentrate.

Another job he had was picking berries. The Dundee area liked to think of itself as the berry capital of the world, with thousands of acres of blackberries, raspberries, and thimbleberries, and Chuck thought of himself as one of the best pickers around. He was a wiry 5 feet 6 inches, 120 pounds, and tireless, even on the hottest, muggiest days. On good days, he made a buck, turning all his earnings over to his mom.

Working so many jobs meant he had to quit the Boy Scouts. It was a hard decision. He loved earning his merit badges—he had thirty-four of them—but he knew he'd never make it all the way to Eagle Scout because he didn't have the time, and he knew he could never pass the lifesaving test. He could swim, but not well enough to haul somebody to safety.

One day, just after he'd turned fifteen, Chuck was walking home with his dog at dusk, feeling pretty proud of himself, his .22 rifle in one hand, two dead rabbits in the other. He knew his mom would make a good meal out of the rabbits, hopefully a stew. It had been a week since the family had had any meat on the table.

Chuck walked down the quiet main street of Dundee, passing the hardware store and lunch counter where two of his sisters worked. Down a side street, he saw a commotion at a WPA work site where construction workers were digging a water line. He figured his father most likely would be there. Approaching the small crowd gathered around the WPA work site, he heard his father's muffled voice. A friend of his father's pointed toward a ditch, four feet deep and two feet across. Chuck moved closer, peering down into the ditch. Mounds of freshly hoed dirt were piled to the side, and down inside the ditch, covered in dirt and wedged in too tight to move, was his dad, all 300 pounds of him. From the look of it, he had been drinking, had tried to jump over the ditch, and hadn't made it. In trying to extricate himself, he'd gotten so twisted around that it looked like it would take a major excavation effort to free him. Embarrassed, Chuck backed away from the crowd.

At dinner that night, everyone ate rabbit. Except Arthur, who didn't get out of the ditch until after midnight.

The family moved again in 1936, this time into town, with the ten kids squeezed together in two small bedrooms. The house was a big black box with chipped paint, no front yard, and a rotting outhouse out back. But the house didn't embarrass Chuck as much as his clothes did. Although none of the boys at school dressed like Ivy Leaguers, Chuck would wear the same shirt three or four days in a row, or until his mother did the laundry again. His only pair of shoes had holes in the soles, and he stuffed cardboard in them to keep his feet dry.

He got teased about his clothes, and he fought back. Fistfighting was a popular sport with the boys in Dundee, a town with not much to offer in the way of entertainment. Chuck was smaller than most boys his age, but he had a reputation as a scrapper, somebody who didn't go around picking fights but who wouldn't back down.

Chuck wasn't much of a student. Reading came hard for him, and he'd been held back a grade when he was nine. He frequently skipped school, usually to go fishing or hunting. But he was still popular, mainly because of his sense of humor and the pranks he pulled: hoisting an outhouse up a telephone pole; setting two skunks loose in a school restroom; coaxing a cow into the school and tying its tail to the school bell; dousing so much moonshine on another kid in class that the boy smelled like the town drunk—a smell Chuck knew well. Trouble was, he never learned the art of stealth.

He had, however, learned the art of being generous. On Christmas Eve 1938, Chuck, now seventeen, and his sister Ynez sat at the kitchen table using newspaper and yarn to wrap their presents to the family. Like every other Christmas at the Ver Valins', this would be a lean one. But unlike the other kids in the family, Chuck and Ynez at least had presents to wrap. Ynez had saved a few dollars from her job at the library, and Chuck had squirreled away money from his paper route. He'd bought each of his sisters a small dispenser of talc and a California orange.

Wrapping his gifts, he daydreamed, as he often did. He thought about traveling. He'd never been to New York City, let alone California, and except for the time he'd made it to Ithaca traveling with the town baseball team, fifteen miles from Dundee was the farthest he'd been from home.

Baseball was one of his escapes. Chuck had developed into a good third baseman, lettering on the varsity his sophomore year, one of only two kids from the team to be picked to play with the older guys on the town team. It had taken him months to save up enough to buy a glove. Sometimes he'd leave the house at seven in the morning to walk to an afternoon game in the next county. He still wasn't very big—5 feet 6 inches, 135 pounds—but he'd gotten strong from a summer job lifting seventy-pound bags of cement. He took special pride in having a good arm.

He fantasized about getting a tryout with a pro team, but his real dream, and he thought about it every day, was to be a harness race driver, and maybe even own his own pacer or trotter. Harness racing was a popular sport in New York, and his plan for the coming summer was to travel the racing circuit and hang around the tracks and stables, maybe getting hired to help with the horses. His father, on the other hand, told him he should start thinking about joining the service when he turned eighteen.

As he continued to wrap his gifts, his mind drifted to girls, especially one named Irene Damien. Not only was she really cute, she liked him too. They passed notes back and forth in class, flirting like crazy. But there was a problem. Her parents had forbade her to go out with him. They thought he was too unruly.

Undeterred, he had persuaded his friend Ernie, who was pleasant and polite, to go to Irene's house, make nice with her parents, and then escort her to the movie theater, where Chuck would be waiting. Ernie would hang around until the end of the date, then escort Irene back home, her parents never suspecting. The plan worked repeatedly, but other than a couple of harmless games of spin the bottle, Chuck never got past first base. But that was okay. The good girls of Dundee knew their boundaries, and the boys accepted them.

On Christmas morning, all of Chuck's sisters beamed as they opened their gifts. The last to open her gift from Chuck was Ynez. Peeling away the wrapping paper, she gasped. It was a doll he'd rescued from the doll graveyard, repainting its face and body and dressing it in a salvaged flowered cloth napkin. Ynez reached out to hug her brother. He shied away. Boys, he'd learned, weren't supposed to show affection.

Sitting on the hard wooden slats of the boxcar, Chuck was beginning to wonder if riding the rails across country was such a good idea. The hobo sitting across from him spit another chaw of tobacco on the floor. Chuck tried not to notice. He felt his stomach churn, not from the puddle of spit but from not having eaten in two days. The train rolled into Fort Wayne, Indiana.

It was September 1939 and German armies had just invaded Poland. Great Britain and France had declared war. According to Chuck's dad, America would also be in it soon. Chuck had dropped out of school after his junior year to make money. Not that he needed it to take his sweetheart Irene to the movies; she'd moved a hundred miles away. Despite letters back and forth, it might as well have been a million miles.

Riding the rails had seemed like a good idea when he and his new buddy Preston Dumar decided to hitch a ride to Seattle. He'd met Preston while working with the trotters and pacers at a county fair in Dundee, and when Preston invited him to his home in Erie, Pennsylvania, Chuck jumped at the chance, making the trip in the horse trailer with the animals, sulkies, and hay. Soon after he got to Erie, Preston claimed there was lots of work picking apples and pears out in Washington State, so Chuck signed on for that trip, too. It sounded like a great adventure. Not only would he get to see the country, he might just be able to save up enough in a couple of years to buy a horse to race himself.

As he'd hoped, Chuck had become known around the tracks, taking whatever odd jobs he could find. He cleaned stalls, shined the sulkies, washed the horses, bandaged their legs, and exercised them in their morning workouts. Some days he got paid 50 cents; some days he got nothing. At night he slept in the stalls with the horses. He had notions of becoming a driver, a job in which size, weight, and age were not restrictive factors. What counted was a driver's skill and courage to guide the horse and sulky in the tight quarters of a high-speed race, and he knew he could do it. It appealed to him that some drivers were also trainers, and some even became owners. He wanted to be all three.

As the train stopped in Fort Wayne, Chuck considered getting off and heading back to New York. Preston had failed to mention the hobos and the spit and the wind rattling through the boxcar. Or the hunger. They'd left Erie with no food and 25 cents between them.

This wasn't Chuck's first extended trip from home. When he turned seventeen, he'd been hired by the Civilian Conservation Corps (CCC), the New Deal public works program providing employment and training for men in projects related to conservation and natural resources. He'd spent the winter and spring working on a crew at Watkins Glen State Park, helping to haul rocks, build a retaining wall, and trim bushes. Out of his $33 monthly paycheck, $20 went home to his mom. Having money in his pocket and a guaranteed three square meals a day suited him. He even liked the Army-style regimen. Now, the way Preston told it, he'd make even better wages picking apples, and there was some good horse racing out west, too.

As they hopped off the train, a hobo warned them to watch out for the yard cop. It was too late. The cop had already spotted them. After a quick lecture on how stupid and dangerous it was for them to be riding the rails, he gave them a choice: they could spend two days in the dingy little jail on the yard with rats and hobos, or they could catch the next freight back east. Ten minutes later they were on a train heading east. Chuck was thrilled to be going home.

Chuck slipped his pipe into his pocket, grabbed his tattered suitcase, and stepped off the train at the Buffalo station. He was a baby-faced eighteen and a high-school dropout. He was also freshly enlisted in the Navy and on his way to boot camp. The pipe was meant to make him look older.

It was October 1940. President Roosevelt was running for an unprecedented third term against Republican Wendell Willkie and had just delivered on his promise of military aid to Winston Churchill, sending fifty used American destroyers, many that had served in World War I, to help replace the alarming number of British ships sunk by German U-boats. The president had pledged to make the United States the "great arsenal of democracy" in the fight against Hitler. At the same time, he'd imposed an embargo on oil and steel to Japan in response to its aggression against China, as well as its entering into the Tripartite Pact with Germany and Italy and its moving troops into Indochina to build air bases for possible attacks.

At home, the first peacetime conscription in the nation's history took place in 1940. Over 16 million men, ages twenty-one to thirty-six, signed up. The standards weren't high—an inductee had to be at least 5 feet tall and 105 pounds, had to have at least half his teeth, and could not have flat-feet, a hernia, or venereal disease. Nevertheless, almost 50 percent of the applicants were rejected, and hundreds of thousands of others were turned down because they could not read or write.

Chuck hadn't enlisted out of patriotic duty or the wish to be a hero. His father had convinced him that America would be pulled into the conflict, and the sooner Chuck enlisted, the better his chances of getting a good assignment. His father said that the military would make a man out of him and that it would be a good career. That made sense to Chuck. But what appealed to him even more was the money. His only hope of buying a horse was the steady paycheck the military offered. And the idea of eating three square meals every day—"three hots and a cot," as the saying went—seemed like a luxury. In the two weeks prior to enlisting, he'd eaten beans and cornbread every night, and nothing at all during the day.

Leaving the depot, he headed for a hotel in downtown Buffalo, where he would stay for three days while he was being processed before boot camp in Newport, Rhode Island. He checked his wallet to make sure his money was still there. Before leaving home, he'd sold his shotgun and several chickens he'd raised in the backyard. The $14 he'd gotten in exchange was his total net worth.

Originally he had tried to enlist in the Marines. More than anything, he liked the uniforms, especially the ones with the red stripes down the blue pants. But he was only 5 feet 7 inches and 135 pounds, and the sergeant said he wasn't big enough to be a Marine. "Go down the street and try the Navy," the sergeant suggested. Chuck passed the physical, and a couple of days later a Navy recruiter came to his house to tell him he had been accepted and would be called up in six months, maybe a year. The call came the next week.

Entering the hotel lobby in Buffalo, he noticed three young recruits sitting in a corner, passing around a bottle of wine in a brown paper bag.

They seemed much older. Chuck pulled his pipe from his pocket and headed to the desk to check in.

He didn't regret his decision to enlist, but he was nervous. Despite his mischievous ways in high school, he didn't drink alcohol or smoke cigarettes, and he was still a virgin. Smoking a pipe was just about the boldest thing he'd done until then.

The recruits in the corner motioned to him, offering him a swig of wine.

"Sure, why not," he said.

2

Bob Palmer

of Medford, Oregon

It was a Sunday morning in the summer of 1927, and eight-year-old Bob Palmer was playing with his new wagon in front of his grandparents' house in Ashland, Oregon, trying his best not to make too much noise. His grandfather, a deeply devoted Methodist, had warned him once already: "Don't make me come out here again."

But it was hard to play quietly. His father had made the wagon for his birthday out of wood carved from a southern Oregon pine, and Bob was excited. He'd spent the last two summers living at a construction site in the southern Cascades with his dad, Martin Palmer, a stern, taciturn man who worked on a crew building the road around the rim of Crater Lake. They lived in a stone cabin surrounded by sturdy mountain hemlocks and Shasta red firs. During the winters, snow piled up as high as the windows. Bob occupied his days during the summer picking wild berries, fishing for native trout, and hiking the rim of the lake. When his dad would allow it, he'd hang out in the shed, watching the men work on the equipment.

It was a magical setting, but Bob felt isolated from kids his age. His brother, Darrell, was four years older and rarely had the time of day for him except to use him as a punching bag. At night Bob often stayed alone in the cabin, with no books or radio, while his dad played poker with the crew. Discipline came from a leather belt. He liked coming down out of the mountains to town. On this day, his grandmother had promised to serve him apple pie and homemade ice cream later, and to read to him. He liked the attention she lavished on him.

His grandfather reappeared on the front porch and glared at him. Bob watched him walk to the shed at the side of the house and disappear inside, then reemerge carrying a big sledgehammer. He motioned for Bob to get out of the wagon. Then, with one mighty swing, he brought the head of the big hammer smashing down, shattering the wagon into a hundred pieces.

Bob stared up at him, his tear-filled eyes pleading for an explanation.

"There'll be no noise on the Sabbath" was all that his grandfather said.

Ten-year-old Bob Palmer sat in a chair at the foot of his mother's four-poster mahogany bed in their small, clapboard home in Medford, a town of 5,000 in southern Oregon, twenty-nine miles from the California border. Her skin was gray, her eyes barely open. He touched her hand and she felt cold. "Please don't die, Mama," he whispered. She struggled to speak, but the words wouldn't come. His father got up and closed the shades.

It was hard for Bob to see his mom like this. She'd always been the backbone of the family, the steadying, nurturing force during these hard times. His father hadn't said much about what was wrong, only that she'd had her appendix taken out and something had gone wrong, possibly an infection from a dirty instrument the doctor used.

To Bob, it seemed that his father was madder at the doctor for chopping off his mom's hair than for any medical mistake. His mother had not cut her hair for years in adherence to church rules, and it fell below her waist. But as she lay on her bed, twisting and turning in pain, she had become entangled in her hair, so the doctor cut it, incurring the wrath of Bob's father.

Keeping vigil at his mom's bedside, Bob and his brother were not allowed to leave her side. Her breathing was labored. Finally, she summoned Bob's father. He leaned in close to her, and in a voice barely above a whisper, yet loud enough for Bob to hear, she spoke: "Don't beat the kids."

Those were her last words.

For four unsettling days, Bob and his brother were made to sit next to her body, surrounded by grieving family—first while she lay on her death-bed, then when she was transferred to a cheap, gray casket. They watched their father take the hair the doctor had cut and clip it back on.

In the weeks following the funeral, Bob saw her cold, ashen face reflected in store windows, mirrors, and lakes. He couldn't escape it.

Bob stood in the corner, his punishment for not cleaning the pinecones off the porch as ordered. Cora, his new stepmother, glared at him, and he braced himself for the next verbal barrage. She and Bob's father had met when she was the cook for the Crater Lake crew, and they'd married less than a year after the funeral. She was always belittling Bob, always making him feel unwanted. His father did little to ease his discomfort.

"You're stupid!" Cora yelled. "Stupid and lazy!"

Bob tried to block out the words. He didn't think he was dumb, but maybe she was right. He struggled in school, disengaged, out of step, behind in his reading. Kids teased him.

He looked at Cora, her hair in a bun so tight that it pinched her face. He resented his father for marrying her; he resented her for not being his mother. Most days he avoided her as much as possible. His mind was made up. As soon as he'd served his penance in the corner he would take off.

The family was spending another summer in the stone cabin near Crater Lake. Now fourteen, Bob was supposed to move down to the Rogue River valley to go to Medford High next year, and he was dreading it because the plan was for Cora to go with him while his dad would stay at Crater Lake. When Bob questioned the move, his father ignored him.

Bob could go off into the woods for hours at a time without his father knowing or caring where he was. And that was what he was going to do now—disappear into the woods.

He picked up his hand-cranked Victrola and loaded it into a large canvas bag with straps, then hoisted it on his back. He had used the bag the previous summer for carrying large bottles of water up and down steep trails to players from the Chicago Cardinals pro football team. The Cardinals had come to Oregon for preseason training, and as part of their regimen, they cleared mountain trails, hauling large buckets of rocks. By carrying water to the men, Bob had earned enough to buy the Victrola. Listening to music was his favorite way to pass the time alone in his room.

Setting off down a trail, his Victrola strapped to his back and a fishing pole in his hand, he felt relief. He loved Crater Lake's dramatic cliffs and deep blue waters. Some days he hiked to the rim and sat on the edge for hours, watching the sunlight shimmer off the transparent water and the eagles riding the thermal breezes. He also loved to fish, hiking into Lightning Springs or Annie Creek, tributaries of the mighty Rogue River. He often caught twenty rainbows or Dolly Vardens a day using mealie worms for bait and selling his catch to the tourists for a nickel a fish. He didn't get an allowance, so whatever money he had was the result of his own initiative. Frequently, he hung out near the new tourist center and lodge, and he learned to get the black bears to come and eat right out of his hand while the tourists, the men dressed in white suits and the women in full-length dresses, stood beside their Hudsons and took pictures of their very own Huckleberry Finn. Sometimes they paid him a nickel. He kept his savings in a tin can, using some of the money to buy a new pair of shoes every year.

On this day, his destination was a small cave hidden off the trail. He came there often, his secret place of solitude. Slowly, he unpacked his Victrola and set it on the ground. Then he pulled out a record by his favorite recording artist, torch singer Ruth Etting, and placed it on the turntable. He cranked up the phonograph and, sitting alone in a cave deep in the woods, sang along to the record.

He returned home just before dusk without anybody noticing he'd been gone.

Bob headed out the back door of Beck's Bakery toward the truck, ready to make the afternoon deliveries around Medford with his buddy Fred Beck, the son of the owner. It was early spring 1937, Bob's junior year at Medford High. He was now living in town with Cora, their relationship unimproved.

His grades were barely passing and he didn't play sports or take part in school activities. He received no encouragement or help at home with his schoolwork from Cora. His dad, a fifth-grade dropout, was unconvinced of the value of an education, and anyway, he was still working up at Crater Lake.

Bob had started hanging around the bakery after school hoping to score day-old doughnuts and pastries. Cora rarely fixed him breakfast or lunch, and many days he hadn't eaten anything by the time he left school. When Fred asked if he'd like to drive along with him on his routes, Bob accepted. It wasn't a paying position, but snacks were guaranteed. He and Fred didn't socialize away from the truck, but it was something to do, a way to avoid going home.

As Fred started up the engine, Bob got back out. "Wait," he said, "I'll be right back." He returned with a hose and began washing down the dirty truck, which was covered with a layer of black soot emitted by the thousands of smudge pots in the nearby orchards. The Rogue Valley's major product was pears—Bartlett, Bosc, and Comice—and in the early springtime when temperatures dipped too low, "smudge crews" went into the orchards at 4:00 a.m. to hand-light pots of oil to heat the air around the trees to keep the pear buds from freezing. Bob worked on one of the crews, regularly getting up at 3:00 a.m. to go to work. He often came home with red eyes and a hacking cough, looking like a coal miner, but he always cleaned up before heading to school. He was fastidious about cleanliness and grooming. On weekends he worked part-time at Spencer's Clothing, even doing a little modeling at big sale events in exchange for shirts and pants.

As the truck headed into downtown Medford, Fred turned on the headlights. With almost no wind, the dense, suffocating black smoke of the smudge pots had blanketed the town, turning the afternoon into night and leaving a dark film on the streets and sidewalks.

Riding in the bakery truck, Bob and Fred were silent. There was something about Bob that Fred couldn't quite put his finger on. He didn't know anything about Bob's home life other than that the family was poor and Bob didn't like his stepmother. But he sensed that Bob was lonely and suspected that he rode along with him more for the companionship than the jelly doughnuts. That was okay with him. He enjoyed the company, too, especially on the days when they rode to Roseburg or Klamath Falls, trips that took several hours.

As much as Bob missed the clear crisp air of the mountains, and as much as he disliked living with Cora, Medford High offered something the wilderness didn't: girls. Bob had developed a flirty way with the opposite sex. He had thick dark hair, blue eyes, big dimples, and a lean frame. He took pride in dressing well—he usually wore a coat and tie or a sweater to school—and he was a good dancer. He was also polite and had a natural charm and a way with words. The girls took notice.

Now, across the crowded dance floor of the Dreamland Ballroom, Bob watched a girl dance, riveted on her every move. He liked her looks—5 feet 2 inches, light brown hair, blue eyes, and a great body. He asked about her and learned that her name was Barbara Koehler and that she was a junior at nearby Central Point High, five miles north of Medford. She was popular, a good student, and active in choir, plays, yearbook staff, student government, and cheerleading. The previous summer she'd been crowned Miss Southern Oregon, and he remembered seeing her picture in the newspaper.

Not shy about approaching girls, he waited for the five-piece orchestra to play a slow song and then made his move. She accepted, and beneath the large crystal ball shimmering overhead, they danced slow and close to "Stardust." She liked the way he moved, and the way he looked so stylish in his sport coat and tie and nicely shined shoes.

They danced the next dance, and all the rest of the dances that night. Bob made a point of holding Barbara extra tight during "I Don't Know Why I Love You Like I Do." When the dance was over, he walked her outside to the parking lot. She'd driven there in her father's '37 Ford with her cousin Margie. Standing next to the driver's door, he reached into his coat pocket and pulled out a small flask of gin. He took a swig, then offered one to her. He wasn't sure how she'd respond—maybe she came from a religious family and wouldn't approve.

Barbara remembered what her father had told her—that she shouldn't drink, but if she did, she should make sure to drink only bonded whiskey, the "good stuff" that had been aged at least four years. She didn't know if this was "the good stuff," but she took a big swig anyway, and then passed the flask back. Bob smiled. He couldn't wait to see her again.

Sitting across from Barbara's parents in their living room, Bob felt as if he were on trial. He'd met the Koehlers several times when he'd come to pick up Barbara for a date, but this was the first time he'd sat down to talk with them. He desperately wanted to make a good impression. Barbara was an only child; he knew that her parents doted on her, and that she would do just about anything not to disappoint them.

Like many families in the Rogue Valley, the Koehlers had been hit hard by the Depression. Barbara had spent her early years living in a two-story farmhouse in the apple and pear orchards outside Central Point. It was a rural, bucolic setting. The family had hogs, chickens, and cows, and from her upstairs bedroom window she could see Mount McLaughlin. In the summers she played on the banks of nearby Bear Creek and pushed her cousin Margie in the swing her dad had hung from the big oak tree in their front yard. But when the Depression hit, the family lost the farm and moved into a small house in town. That's when Mr. Koehler went to work for Greyhound.

Mr. Koehler asked Bob what his plans were after high school. Bob thought for a moment. He'd already worked at a number of jobs, but all of them were seasonal and none of them interested him as a career. His newest job was delivering jugs of milk in the morning for Hansen's Dairy with his friend Swede. He was now living in Swede's unheated garage, sleeping on a cot next to Swede's '31 Chevy. Anything was better than the verbal abuse from Cora.

"I'm not sure of my plans," he said.

Judging from Mr. Koehler's scowl, that wasn't the right answer. And Bob didn't dare tell him that he'd just been suspended from school for a semester and there was a chance he might not even graduate. A couple of weeks earlier he'd ducked into one of the boys' restrooms between classes to take a few quick nips from his flask of gin, only to have the principal walk in and bust him. The worst part of it wasn't getting tossed out of school, it was incurring Cora's wrath.

The idea of joining the service had occurred to him. Across the ocean, British prime minister Neville Chamberlain was ceding Czechoslovakia to Hitler and declaring that he had secured "peace in our time." A Gallup Poll showed that most Americans approved of this act of appeasement. Maybe this would be a good time to join. But Bob wasn't yet eighteen, and as much as Cora seemed to want him out of her way, she'd made it clear that she wouldn't sign the necessary release form.

"What sports do you play?" asked Mr. Koehler.

"None, sir, I have to work after school."

He had the feeling this wasn't going well. The more questions Mr. Koehler asked, the more intimidated Bob felt by his stern demeanor. Mr. Koehler had just gotten home from work and was still dressed in his Greyhound uniform, not a stitch out of place, like a commandant in the inquisition room. Even his white gloves were spotless. Mrs. Koehler, who'd recently started work as a secretary for a cousin's fruit-packing company, seemed kinder. She even seemed to like him.

The months that Bob and Barbara had been dating had been the happiest of his young life. He loved Barbara's sunny, outgoing personality—the opposite of the dark cloud he faced at home. He hadn't yet told her that he loved her, but he was sure he did. And she'd made it clear that she thought he was awfully cute. They'd already been intimate, starting with necking out on Old Stage Road, then going all the way for the first time in the backseat of her father's car late one night, parked under the oak trees across the street from the Baptist Church.

By the time they left Barbara's house, Bob had the distinct feeling that Mr. Koehler didn't think he was good enough for his daughter.

As crazy as she was for Bob, Barbara broke off their relationship a few days later. She told him it was because he wasn't around enough, always going off to Crater Lake for days at a time to help his dad on the road crew.

But Bob knew the real reason. This was 1938, and in the Rogue River valley, nice seventeen-year-old girls didn't go against their fathers' wishes.

Bob stepped off the bus into the depot in Eugene carrying his tattered valise. He set out on foot for the University of Oregon campus. It was the spring of 1939, and he'd traveled north from Medford to pay Barbara, now a freshman, a surprise visit. He was still in high school, scheduled to graduate a year behind his class because of his suspension. Bob and Barbara hadn't dated for almost a year, and both were seeing other people, but Bob hadn't given up. He'd written her a dozen letters, and although she'd responded only a couple of times, he held out hope that it was possible to rekindle the passion they'd once had.

Nearing the boardinghouse where Barbara lived, he wasn't sure if she'd even be there. He knew it was a bold move to pop in on her unannounced, but he was counting on the surprise factor—that she'd be so happy to see him that they'd have a romantic weekend together and he'd be back in the saddle. In one of her letters she'd mentioned that she felt a tinge of homesickness, so he'd brought a small box of her favorite pears.

Lately he'd been thinking a lot about all the good times they'd had together, especially the dances at the Dreamland Ballroom, where they had effortlessly glided across the floor as if they'd been practicing together for years. To him, she was prettier and more graceful than Ginger Rogers, who regularly appeared on stage at the Craterian in Medford with her group The Redheads.

At the boardinghouse, Bob sat nervously in the waiting room while someone went to find her. He worried that now that she was a college girl she wouldn't have time for a guy who was still in high school. Maybe he wasn't sophisticated enough. Maybe he wasn't as smart as the college boys she'd been seeing.

He glanced up and saw her descending the stairs. She was every bit as pretty as he remembered, even more so. She moved toward him, a quizzical look on her face. It wasn't the big smile he'd hoped for.

"What are you doing here?" she asked.

"I just thought I'd come up and see you," he answered.

Two girls entered the room, and Barbara didn't introduce him.

"This is a nice house," he said awkwardly.

"Yes, it is," she responded. He'd caught her totally off guard. Her first reaction was that she wished he wasn't there. She was in college now, taking literature and history classes, going to fraternity parties. Now that she'd met people from places such as Seattle and Portland, to her Bob seemed so unpolished. She had purposely not answered most of his letters, not wanting to encourage him. And a college girl wasn't supposed to date a high-school boy, even if he was older than she was. She was dating guys who talked about going into business or law. In Bob's last letter, he'd talked about enlisting in the service when and if he graduated.

"Bob, I have other plans," she told him.

"I don't suppose I could talk you out of them," he ventured.

She shook her head. He didn't need her to explain any further. He turned toward the door.

"I'm sorry I bothered you," he apologized.

"Maybe we can see each other this summer when I come home," she offered weakly.

"That'd be nice," he replied.

He caught the first bus back to Medford. Watching the pastoral scenery roll by, he felt a hollow pit in his stomach. By the time the bus reached Medford, he'd made up his mind: as soon as school was out, maybe sooner, he would leave town and join the Navy.

3

Tim McCoy

of Dalhart, Texas

The minute Tim McCoy walked through the front door, he knew something was wrong. He'd been playing across the street at his Aunt Bee's house, his refuge when things at home weren't right. In the past three years, he'd spent as much time at Aunt Bee's as he had at home, staying there for months at a time when his mother was in the hospital.

Maybe that was why his father, Harrell McCoy, wore a scowl. Maybe his mom needed to be sent away again for more treatment. Tim was only eight, but he'd already learned to recognize the signs: she'd mope around, not getting dressed all day, sleeping a lot, crying, barely able to take care of the house. Then Dad would bundle her into the Model T and drive the eighty-five miles from their home in Dalhart down to Amarillo, where she'd stay until she was well enough to come home. It was hard for Tim not to have his mom around and to not know for sure what was wrong with her. He'd come to rely on his dad, a salesman at Rhodes and Wilson, the local furniture store, and Aunt Bee, an ex-schoolteacher who had a great touch with kids.

Or maybe his father was just upset at him for leaving his marbles and tops on the floor. If that was the case, he'd most likely be getting the razor strap. Not that his dad was mean; he just believed in firm discipline. At 6 feet 1 inch and 225 pounds, with broad shoulders and powerful arms, Harrell McCoy was an imposing man. But Tim was a tough little guy, and rarely flinched when punished. Besides, his father was his hero—an honest, hardworking man who had a sense of humor and could build or fix just about anything.

He glanced at his dad. Normally a man with a positive outlook, on this day Harrell glared straight ahead, not saying a word, his suit jacket slung over the back of a chair. He nodded toward the window. Tim and his mother looked outside. The sky was an ominous black, thick with grit and dirt swirling off the prairie in every direction. Maybe they were in for another "black duster," a powerful windstorm that whipped up such massive clouds of fine silt and soil that you couldn't see your hand in front of your face. After a black duster, sand would be piled as high as the eaves on houses and fence posts would be buried. These storms had all but denuded the land, the worst of them blowing topsoil as far away as Washington, D.C., and onto ships in the Atlantic Ocean.

"Got the bad news today," he announced.

Tim's mom, Capitola Boatwright McCoy, known to everyone as Cappy, sighed. One of thirteen children of Irish-German ancestry raised on a farm in Comanche, Texas, she was a small woman, 5 feet 1 inch, 115 pounds, who relied heavily on her Baptist faith.

"Whatever it is," she said, "the Lord will take care of us."

Tim studied his parents. He'd heard that farmers in the area were abandoning their property, that businesses in town were failing, and that friends of his parents had been forced to stand in breadlines. But the Depression was still a vague concept. He was an outgoing kid who spent his time playing with his friends, spinning tops, and pitching washers against the side of the house. His mom's illness weighed on him sometimes, but other than that all seemed well.

"They're closing the store," his father said.

His mother asked when.

"Tomorrow. I'll be lucky if I get paid for this week. I'm out of work."

Tim peered out the window of Aunt Bee's living room, hoping to see his father's car. He hadn't seen either of his parents in weeks. His mom had been hospitalized again, and his dad had been out of town, working for $1 a day for the WPA, helping to build a farm-to-market road from Brownfield to Lubbock. Supposedly, his mom was being released, and both his parents would be home soon.

But Tim had learned that things didn't always go the way he wanted.

It was 1934 and the Depression had landed hard on Dalhart, population 4,500. For years the people in Dalhart had taken great pride in their community. Settled under the Homestead Act, which had given farmers and ranchers large tracts of marginal land that could not be irrigated, the town had experienced a long run of prosperity. But now, after years of bad agricultural practices, the farms were in trouble, worsened by the drought and the black dusters. Livestock were dead or dying and the crops withered. On the rare occasions when it rained, the runoff removed what little topsoil was left, slicing out gorges forty feet deep. Families were leaving in droves.

Dalhart was doing its best to fight back. Wealthy local rancher Uncle Dick Coon had become legendary for his generous treatment of suffering farmers and cowboys, giving them money to survive. Some of these men had formed "The Last Man Club," vowing to remain under any circumstances. Harrell McCoy, a staunch New Deal Democrat, had joined the club, but as the Depression deepened, his resolve weakened. He would go where he could find work.

Tim spotted his dad's Model T coming up the street. He raced out the door to greet it, but there was no passenger. The doctor had decreed that Tim's mom wasn't ready to come home yet.

Tim's heart sank. He didn't know that his mother had almost died while delivering him and then fallen into a deep depression from which she'd never fully recovered, her condition compounded by his father's desire to have more children. All Tim knew was that he wanted his mom home.

Dr. George W. Truitt, a visiting preacher from Dallas, stood at the pulpit, pointing a finger at the congregation of Lubbock's First Baptist Church gathered under a large tent. Tim had the feeling the preacher was pointing directly at him. He and his parents had moved to Lubbock from Dalhart after his mom was released and his father's job with the WPA ended.

"Alcohol is the force of evil!" thundered Truitt. "Do not succumb to its insidious temptation."

"Amen!" echoed the congregation.

Sitting next to his mom and dad, Tim, now nine, nodded in agreement. Neither his mom nor his dad had ever tasted a drop of alcohol, and he was certain that he never would either.

Today was the last day of the weeklong revival, the day Tim was to be baptized. And who better to do it than George W. Truitt, the most famous evangelical preacher in Texas, if not the whole South? To his followers, he had the power of the Holy Spirit, and he was an early-model Billy Graham, learned and charismatic. He preached that true greatness consisted not of great wealth, or shining social qualities, or vast amounts of study, but in using all of one's talents in unselfish ministry to others. To Tim, Truitt was more impressive than even Babe Ruth.

As with many Lubbock families of the time, the Baptist Church was at the center of the McCoy family's life, not only spiritually, but socially as well. At home, every meal began with a prayer, and every day ended with quotes from the Scriptures. Tim's mother's mental health had improved since they'd moved to Lubbock. It helped that she didn't have to stand in breadlines; Harrell had found a new job as a salesman for Great Plains Furniture, working ten hours a day, six days a week for $18 a week.

On their way home from Tim's baptism, the family passed a gathering of nonbelievers. Tim would hear nothing of their cynicism. He liked going to church and living in Lubbock. He had become active in the Boy Scouts and loved the jamborees and campouts. He'd also made a best friend, Byron Varner, whose parents owned the Main Street Café downtown and lived in an apartment above it. Tim spent a lot of time there, eating hamburgers and playing with Byron in the alley behind the café. Byron was a year older, but he admired Tim's never-back-down personality and the way he was always the first one to climb the high dive at the city pool and take the leap.

Back home, Tim's mom prepared Sunday dinner (always served at noon), and he retreated to his room to look at his new trumpet, a birthday present his parents had purchased on the installment plan—three payments of $2 each. He loved his new instrument. His goal was to get to play in the band when he reached high school. Fingering the valves of the trumpet, he heard his parents arguing. They weren't yelling, but their voices were tense.

"I can't go through it again," his mother said.

Slowly, quietly, he began to play his trumpet—nothing special, just noise to drown out the tension.

It was early September 1939 in Texas, the temperature over 100 degrees. Walking home through the Oak Cliff section of Dallas, Tim, now a sophomore in high school, had a big decision to make—to go out for the track team at Sunset High and defend his 880 state championship, or get an after-school job. Despite all the efforts of the New Deal, 10 million Americans were still unemployed. Tim made $2 a week getting up before dawn to deliver the *Dallas Morning News* on foot. He couldn't afford a bike. Tim's parents had divorced at the end of his freshman year in Lubbock; he and his mother had moved to Dallas at the urging of her three sisters and two brothers, all of whom lived there. Her brothers were both successful insurance men and promised to look out for them. His father had remarried and moved to Austin; Tim hadn't seen him since. Tim wasn't happy about the move, or the divorce. Dallas seemed big and unfriendly. None of the kids at school had divorced parents, and it embarrassed him. He didn't like leaving his friends in Lubbock, especially Byron. He didn't like living in an apartment. But most of all, he resented his dad for deserting the family.

Continuing home, he started to run despite the stifling heat. His new neighborhood, Oak Cliff, located on the south bank of the Trinity River two miles from downtown Dallas, had been intended to serve as a resort but had instead become a working-class neighborhood. Tim had heard that Bonnie and Clyde had used it as a place to lie low. (Later, Lee Harvey

Oswald would live in a rooming house in Oak Cliff.) To Tim it seemed harder-edged than Lubbock.

He often ran home from school, mainly just to burn off some of his considerable energy. At 5 feet 7 inches and a wiry 130 pounds, he was hardly an imposing presence, but was very athletic, and not one to back down from a fight. In his freshman year at Lubbock High, he'd won the regional championship in the 880, traveling all the way to Guymon, Oklahoma, to win the finals, a victory he dismissed as no big deal. This year he also wanted to go out for the wrestling team.

He got good grades, too, mostly As and Bs. But the only class he really liked was band. He liked practicing his trumpet, mostly playing compositions by John Philip Sousa or religious songs. But he understood the reality that earning money would most likely have to be a higher priority than sports and band practice. He knew his dad was supposed to send $8 a month in support but rarely did. Occasionally, his mom took in ironing, but she didn't look for a steady job, partly because her brothers didn't think women should work. To bring in money over the summer, Tim had mowed lawns, worked at a roller rink, and caddied at Glen Lakes Country Club for his Uncle Ben.

If there was anyone Tim looked up to it was Uncle Ben, the successful founder of Trinity Universal Insurance. Ben had bought stock in a little start-up beverage company in Dallas called Dr. Pepper and watched his investment grow into a fortune. Tim loved riding with him in his shiny new car to the country club and spending holidays with him at his resort house on Lake Texahoma. It made him think that someday he too could be a wealthy insurance man. That was the dream.

Breathing hard when he arrived back at the apartment, he opened the door and stepped inside. With no air conditioner, it was hotter inside than out. His mom stood near an open window, a fan positioned to blow on her. She was ironing someone else's clothes, sweat beading on her forehead. Tim studied her for a moment and knew what his decision had to be. The next day he found a job delivering the *Dallas Evening News* after school. There'd be no more track.

* * *

In the summer of 1941, not even Joe DiMaggio's fifty-six-game hitting streak could distract Americans from the threat of war. German troops had occupied Paris, and Hitler had reneged on his nonaggression pact with Russia. In secret military discussions over command and strategy, the U.S. Joint Chiefs of Staff and their British counterparts concluded that Germany was the predominant member of the Axis powers, so if America entered the war, the Atlantic and Europe would be considered the decisive theaters. Any future American military effort would be concentrated there, and operations of U.S. forces in other theaters, such as the Pacific, would be secondary. Part of this reasoning was that Germany's offensive capabilities were greater, and that its superior technology had the potential to develop a secret weapon that could destroy its enemies.

Tim wasn't as concerned about the threat of war as he was about getting an occasional date and making money on his new job selling soda pop at the Wednesday night wrestling matches. On a good night he could make as much as 75 cents, not to mention getting to see legendary wrestlers such as Silent Hubert, Strangler Lewis, Danny McShane, and Sailor Tex Watkins. He knew the matches were fixed (he'd seen the capsules of blood in the dressing room), and yet he liked watching anyway. But it was the money that was important; he liked being able to help out his mom with the rent. She was anxious by nature, always expecting the worst, and he was the opposite, constantly assuring her that things would be okay. He considered it his duty to keep her spirits up.

In the fall of 1941, soon after Tim started his senior year at Sunset High, Byron came to visit from Lubbock. Despite having lived on opposite sides of the state for three years, they were still great friends. Byron liked not just Tim's sense of humor and intrepid approach to life but also his compassion, like the way he treated Sidney Segal back in junior high. Sidney, a small, plump Jewish kid, was everyone's favorite target, and he rarely made it down the hall without getting punched in the shoulder or being called "kike" or "Jew boy." He attached himself to Tim, most likely because Tim was outgoing and friendly to everyone. Sidney soon became his shadow, following him everywhere. Tim accepted the role of Sidney's protector. He had taken to heart what he'd heard Reverend Truitt preach about a person's true calling being "to lend a helping hand." When Tim moved to Dallas, nobody was sadder to see him leave than Sidney.

Seeing Tim for the first time in a couple of years, Byron noticed a change. On the surface, Tim was still full of spunk, bragging about getting paddled in band class for acting out. But now he was less directed, more intense, a bit of a loose cannon. It was almost as if he'd grown a chip on his shoulder. Not that they talked about it. In Texas, circa 1941, best buddies didn't talk about their feelings.

Byron talked about joining the Navy. The idea appealed to Tim, too. He was tired of working four jobs, and he reasoned that in the Navy he would make better money and could send most of it home to help his mom. If there was a war, he figured he'd be safer on a ship in the middle of the ocean than in a muddy foxhole.

The only possible wrinkle was getting his mother's permission, since he was only seventeen. To his surprise, she gave it, figuring he was probably going to drop out of school anyway. The next day Tim walked across town to the recruiting depot, took his physical exam, and signed up. The day after that, he marched into the office at Sunset High and dropped out. The fact that he was still several months short of graduation didn't bother him; he could finish after he had served his time. A steady income was more important.

On November 1, 1941, still not shaving daily, Tim kissed his tearful mother good-bye and boarded a train for boot camp in San Diego, California. On that same day, halfway across the world, six of the newest and largest Japanese aircraft carriers, carrying 423 combat planes, were assembling in Tankan Bay in the Kurile Islands, ready to set sail for Pearl Harbor.

4

Gordy Cox

of Yakima, Washington

At the age of two, Gordy Cox was playing behind his house in Wayne, Alberta, with his older brother, Larry. They started chasing one of the family's new colts, and Gordy got too close. The colt kicked him, nailing him in the left eye, shattering the bone just below the eyebrow and knocking him cold. Larry ran to get their mother, Nellie, who scooped up Gordy, put him in the family's buggy, and drove ten miles to the nearest doctor. But the doctor was gone, and the closest town was Drumheller, another ten miles over rough, inhospitable terrain, too treacherous for a horse and buggy and an unconscious child.

Now frantic, Nellie found two railroad men who volunteered to help. They led her to a flat-bedded railroad platform car powered by a pump handle. With Nellie cradling Gordy in her lap, the two men pumped all the way to Drumheller, then escorted them to the doctor, who stitched the wound and applied ice to relieve the swelling. Gordy remained in a coma for the next two days.

Eventually, the injury healed. But in the months and years to come, Gordy struggled with his vision, especially close up. Reading was difficult, and he was always behind in school. He flunked the first grade.

"Gordy's a little slow," his mom would explain. "He got kicked by a horse."

* * *

Things always came tough for Gordy. Born at his grandparents' remote farmhouse on the Canadian prairie on June 13, 1923, Gordy was two months old before his parents hitched up the horse and buggy and drove into town to register his birth. They put down the wrong date.

He was still an infant when they scraped together $100 for a down payment on a plot of farmland ten miles south of Wayne. The land seemed like a good buy—there was a spring and two lakes, a barn, and an old log structure to shelter the family's dozen pigs, workhorses, cows, turkeys, and chickens during the frigid winters. The house was another matter: it had no electricity, refrigerator, or indoor plumbing. Nor were there any tractors or combines to do the farming; all the work was done with horses. And there was no market nearby. Everything was homegrown—bread, vegetables, meat. Milk came from their cows.

Gordy always tagged along behind Larry, the most daring of the four Cox brothers, the one who always rode his horse at a full gallop. His two younger brothers, Willie and Don, were talkative and adventuresome. Gordy was the only one who wasn't a daredevil. He was shy and afraid of just about everything. When visitors came to the house, he hid under the dining room table. At school, he wouldn't meet the teachers' eyes, and on the playground he walked away from confrontations.

To get to school, three miles away, Gordy rode with Larry on a family horse, holding on for dear life as Larry did his best to scare him, flying through fields at full speed. Sometimes on the way home, Larry detoured by the Two Bar Ranch, daring Gordy to try riding one of the owner's sheep. He told him that was how all the great rodeo cowboys at the Calgary Stampede had gotten started.

Eventually, Gordy asked for a horse of his own. "There's a Depression on, son," his father told him. "There's no money."

A few weeks later, a man stopped by the farm trying to sell a little white pony that was half Shetland. Gordy's father offered the man ten bushels of oats in trade, and he accepted. Gordy named the horse Weasel because he liked watching weasels on the farm sneak up behind jackrabbits and kill them. Weasel had previously been a workhorse, pulling coal cars in the mines; he had an ornery streak that made it tough on Gordy at first. Short-winded from his work in the mines, he had a bad habit of ducking sideways and sending Gordy flying whenever he got tired. After a while, Gordy figured out Weasel's tricks and they got along fine. He rode him to school almost every day, stabling him in the barn the school kept for the kids' horses. At lunch he came out and fed him half his sandwich. During the winter, he hitched him to a sleigh and rode across the snow-covered fields. In the spring, he rode him to the south slope of the hill behind the house. Weasel would graze on the grass, and Gordy would stretch out on his back in a field of crocuses and daydream, the clouds billowing across the sky.

At the age of ten, Gordy decided he had to have a violin. Never mind that he'd never played one, or that his parents had no money. As luck would have it, his mother spotted a contest in a magazine—anybody selling $10 worth of Gold Medal garden seed could win a new violin.

The odds were against him. First, he'd have to write away to get the seeds—no easy task for Gordy—and then he'd have to sell them. It was 1933, smack-dab in the middle of the Depression, and the neighbors who might be his customers were also struggling to get by. Not to mention that some of them lived twenty miles away, and the Coxes had no car. Still, his mother encouraged him to try.

Nellie Cox was the spiritual backbone of the family. Not that she was religious. Occasionally she read the Bible, but going to church was never part of the family routine. Besides, the nearest church was a dusty ten-mile ride away. Nellie preferred spending what little spare time she had reading to her four boys, often from the classics. She'd only completed the eighth grade, but everyone knew how smart she was. Whenever the teacher at the children's school was sick, she stepped in to substitute. At home, she never stopped working—she baked bread three times a week, boiled water collected in rain barrels behind the house on the wood-fired stove for washing and baths, cleaned the family's clothes on a scrub board, sewed clothes, darned socks, canned vegetables, made butter, nursed wounds. And she did it all with no electricity, refrigeration, or running water. She loved to ride her horse, Dexter, and once every six months she hitched him up to the buggy to make a trip into Wayne to buy supplies.

With his mother's help, Gordy sent away for a full order of seeds, and then he set out on Weasel to sell them. He was gone all day, traveling round-trip fifty miles. Not many people had the cash on hand to pay him. "I can come back," he offered. Two weeks later, he rode back to collect. Some had the money, others didn't. Steadily, he neared his goal.

If and when he earned his violin, he didn't aspire to play in a symphony, or even a school orchestra. He just wanted to be able to accompany his mother, who loved to sing at family gatherings. Those were always special times—aunts, uncles, and cousins singing, playing the fiddle, reading poetry, dancing. It didn't matter that Gordy had two left feet on the dance floor.

He was, however, good at getting his chores done around the farm. He and his brothers were not yet teenagers, but they were expected to shoulder their share of the workload. Gordy milked the cows morning and night, shoveled hay, carried water from the well to the house, and hauled wood.

It took three months, but he finally sold his full order of seeds and collected the money from the neighbors. He sent it all in, and a month later his shiny new violin arrived in the mail. Now all he had to do was learn to play it.

Gordy's dad, Julian, nicknamed Shorty, was a slender 5 feet 7 inches. He was a man of few words but a hardworking farmer, out in the fields from dawn to dusk, fighting a losing battle against the Depression and falling wheat prices. A drought added to the struggle, wiping out his entire crop. He replanted it, but a wicked wind lifted the soil off the seed grains and they blew away. The wind blew the dust so hard that Nellie had to light lamps in the house in the middle of the day. Dirt blew in under the doors and through the window frames. She stuffed rags in the cracks, but still the dust swirled inside. In winter snow blew into the house. Outside, snowdrifts piled so high around the barn and corral that Gordy rode Weasel right over the tops of the fences.

To provide food for his family, Julian took a job working in the Red Deer Coal Mine in Wayne, ten miles from the farm. He hoped it would be temporary, but in the meantime he moved the family into town. All six of them lived in a one-room shack with no electricity, running water, heat, or even an outhouse. Nellie hung a sheet across the room to divide the space and cooked atop a coal-fueled heating stove. It was Gordy's job to walk the railroad tracks with a bucket every day and pick up lumps of coal that had fallen off the trains.

Because so many farmers and ranchers had moved into town looking for work in the mine, Wayne had become a boomtown, its population swelling to 3,000. Located in the heart of the Alberta Badlands, an area known to hold one of the richest dinosaur fossil beds in the world, it was a forbidding landscape. Summers were scorching hot, winter temperatures were way below zero. The gathering place in town was the Rosedeer Hotel, home of the Last Chance Saloon, where miners went after work to drink and play poker. But not Gordy's father. He wasn't much of a drinker, and he'd learned long ago that he was a lousy poker player. He continued to hope that he and the family would return to the farm.

But any hope he'd had of returning was lost when the cows he'd left on the farm with a caretaker were stolen. Adding to his frustration, work at the mine slowed down and Julian was laid off. Now there was no money, no work, no cows, and no crops. Not even a garden. About to lose the farm, he sold the property, took what little profit he made, packed up the family's meager belongings, including the farm equipment and Weasel, and moved the family two hundred miles north to Colinton. Located ninety miles north of Edmonton, it is a picturesque area known as the gateway to the Great North Country. The family found a small farm to rent, with a run-down old house topped by a leaky roof. Now instead of sweeping up dirt and dust, they mopped up the puddles from the rain and battled the frigid winter, when the temperature dropped to thirty below and stayed there for months. On one occasion, it plummeted all the way to seventy-two below.

For entertainment, Gordy sometimes tried playing his violin, but being tone-deaf didn't help. Mostly he played with his brothers. The neighbors had children, but the days were short, with little time for anything besides school and chores. Gordy's main responsibility was helping his brother Larry gather and cut wood. He continued to flounder in school.

After years of struggling to make a go of farming in northern Alberta, and tired of the cold and isolation, Julian decided to move the family again, this time to Yakima, Washington. He'd heard there was work there. Before moving, he held an auction to sell off all of the farm equipment and animals, including Weasel. Gordy pleaded to keep him. His dad said no.

As Weasel was led away, Gordy ran after him, tears streaming down his face, giving him one last hug around the neck.

The next day the family boarded a train south, stopping in Calgary to visit relatives. Gordy was in the seventh grade, but it was his first time in a big city. He'd never experienced a house with a flush toilet, or bread that wasn't home-baked. Larry coaxed him to go downtown with him. A prostitute approached, beckoning them down an alley.

Gordy turned and ran home. He wondered if America would be so perplexing.

In early June 1937, Gordy Cox crossed the border into the United States in the backseat of the 1928 Pontiac his dad had bought for the trip. It was Gordy's first time in a car.

Yakima, named after the Indian tribe and located in a verdant valley in south-central Washington 145 miles southeast of Seattle, was a leading agricultural center, known for its fruit. With a population of almost 10,000, it seemed huge to Gordy. It even had an electric streetcar. But it didn't have any jobs. Soon after arriving, the whole family went to work outside the city limits picking fruit. The Depression was still on, and hundreds of families had come to the Yakima Valley, many of them farm owners and business-men displaced by the Dust Bowl in the Midwest. Most of them lived in a large transient-labor camp south of town and were treated as lower class by the Yakima townsfolk, who referred to them as Okies, including the Coxes.

Working alongside his parents and brothers, Gordy spent his first months in America picking apples, pears, strawberries, cherries, apricots, and peaches. The only fruits he'd seen in Canada were the sweet purplish black saskatoons and chokecherries that grew wild on the prairie, and it didn't take long for him to develop a dislike for the fruit he picked. At night he slept in a tent with his parents, or outside under the stars with his brothers, enduring wind, rain, and noise from the other migrant workers. Working together, the family made less than $100 a month.

In September, just as school was starting, Gordy's dad got hired as an irrigator for a farmer living in Naches Heights, twenty miles north of Yakima. The job paid $100 a month and came with an old house that had more conveniences than any place they'd lived—cold running water and electricity, a single bulb hanging in each room. To Gordy, now enrolled in the eighth grade at Marcus Whitman School, it felt like the Ritz. But at school, he felt isolated from the other students, who were better off. Sometimes they called him "Okie." He ignored them, choosing to stay mainly to himself. In time, his dad lost his job and the family moved again, this time into a house in Yakima, and Julian went back to work picking fruit with the migrant workers.

Entering high school, Gordy wore the same clothes he'd worn in the sixth grade.

Gordy looked smooth in his new skates, gliding across the ice at Yakima Ice Rink, the only person left in the arena. This was his favorite time of the evening. He loved the quiet. It was his job to lock up the rink, and most nights he would skate for a few minutes before heading home, gliding effortlessly from end to end of the rink.

He was dreading tomorrow at school. As captain of the school's hockey team, he was supposed to say a few words about the team at the school's sports assembly, but the thought of standing up and speaking before the whole student body terrified him.

Now a junior, he'd done his best to pass unnoticed through Yakima High. He still had trouble reading and was barely passing his classes. He'd taken violin lessons, but without much success, and the violin was now stored away in a closet. Mostly he kept to himself, and as for girls, he'd never had a date; even the thought of talking to the opposite sex made him nervous. His high-school calling card, if he had one, was as the right-winger for the hockey team. At 5 feet 5 inches, 130 pounds, he wasn't the best or toughest player on the squad—he did his best to avoid the contact and hitting—but he was the best skater, helped by his job at the rink. Skating gave him confidence, whereas in other sports he felt awkward and intimidated.

He finished locking up the rink, then rode his new Schwinn home. His old bicycle had been stolen, and he had had to buy a new one to make his deliveries on his morning paper route. For a year now he'd been delivering *The Oregonian* on the hilly west side of town, struggling out of bed at 5:00 a.m., an especially hard task on the mornings after he'd worked late at the skating rink. On the positive side, his two jobs provided him with the money to buy his bike, new skates, and movie tickets. A week earlier he'd splurged on a black cowboy hat, just like the one Hopalong Cassidy wore. He was able to indulge himself because his dad was now working as a road builder for the WPA, and his brother Larry, who'd dropped out of school after the move from Canada, was now sending half his paycheck home each month from his job with the CCC.

Arriving home at midnight, Gordy went to his room and pulled out his schoolbooks. As he tried to read his history assignment, his eyes grew heavy. Some days it was all he could do to keep his eyes open in class. He finished the first page, then realized he didn't remember anything he'd just read. It was this way almost every night, a struggle not only to stay awake but to make sense of the words. It bothered him that other kids came to class every morning with their homework neatly done and an understanding of the material. He knew he was trying, but he was just slow. His mom still blamed it on being kicked in the head by the horse.

He awoke the next morning, still terrified at the thought of going before the whole student body. He thought of calling in sick, but that would mean not getting to play in the game. He rolled out of bed, delivered the newspapers, then rode to school. By the time the assembly finally began, he felt the sweat rolling down his back, and his mouth had turned dry. He had not written out what he was going to say because he thought it would be even more embarrassing if he got up there and couldn't read his own words.

As the student body cheered the concluding remarks from the captain of the football team, Gordy turned to a teammate. "I can't do it," he blurted, then stood up and bolted out of the gym, leaving his surprised teammate to talk to the student body.

Later at practice, his teammates and coach didn't mention the episode. They didn't need to. Gordy had dealt himself another blow to his self-esteem, which was already in the basement.

It was late 1940, and the idea of dropping out of school and joining the Navy seemed like a good plan to Gordy. His brother Larry had joined the Army right out of the CCC, and his letters home talked about all the new friends he'd made and places he'd visited.

But there were a couple of big obstacles. One was passing the physical. Gordy had recently started wearing glasses, and that worried him. The other problem was that he was only seventeen and would need his parents' approval. He doubted he'd get it, especially from his mom, but it was worth a shot.

During the previous year, he'd gleaned a vague understanding of the growing threat of war from reading the headlines every morning as he folded the newspapers, but that all seemed remote and unconnected to his world. Besides, he'd heard his father talking about how FDR was promising that America wouldn't get involved. What was real to him was that he was flunking English class. He had a book report due on *Silas Marner*, but he hadn't been able to get past the first few pages of the book. He'd all but given up on school.

He presented his case to his parents. As he'd expected, his dad approved but his mother insisted he finish high school. Over the next couple of weeks, he continued to plead with her. Finally, convinced that he wasn't going to finish school anyway, she relented. Now all that stood in his way was passing the physical and proving his U.S. citizenship. He needed to get ahold of his birth certificate, which showed that even though he had been born in Canada, his parents were American citizens, which made him one, too. It took several weeks, but he finally got the proof. And to his surprise, he passed the Navy physical, including the eye exam.

In January 1941, Gordy Cox boarded a train in Seattle on his way to boot camp in San Diego, California. The thought of serving on a submarine had not crossed his mind.

Part Two

SUBMARINERS

5

Chuck Ver Valin
USS *Gudgeon*

Standing with his sailor buddies outside the whorehouse on Hotel Street in Honolulu, Chuck was having second thoughts. Sure, he wanted to lose his cherry—he was nineteen, and if his buddies were to be believed, he was the last of the virgins. But this didn't feel like the way to go.

It was March 1941, and Chuck was stationed on the USS *Maryland*, a battleship that had recently, along with the rest of the Pacific Fleet, shifted its base from a West Coast port to Pearl Harbor as a deterrent to Japanese expansion. Chuck hadn't really given much thought to why the fleet moved; he was just happy to be in the Navy and traveling to new and exciting places.

His three months in boot camp at Newport, Rhode Island, had been easy for him, thanks in large part to his experience in the CCC. He was used to discipline and regimentation. He loved the food and, not surprisingly, scored well on the rifle range, getting assigned as an antiaircraft machine gunner. After boot camp, his whole company was assigned to the *Maryland*, including his new best friend, Wesley Strevous, whom he'd met on the train to boot camp from Buffalo. Strevous had attended Cornell for a year, and to Chuck he seemed so much smarter than his friends back home. After boot camp, they'd traveled together to Long Beach, California, and when they arrived there, Chuck was wide-eyed at the fragrant orange groves around every other corner, the hundred-foot-high palm trees, and the abundance of long-legged southern California blondes.

It was shortly after arriving in Pearl Harbor aboard the *Maryland* that Chuck applied for submarine service. Part of the appeal was money. Submariners made $20 more a month than the sailors of the regular fleet, and would double their pay in war. He'd seen submariners on the deck of their ships, and they seemed more relaxed. Whenever the crew of the *Maryland* was topside, they had to wear dress blues and have boots, belt buckles, and buttons polished perfectly. Not so with the submariners; they wore dungarees and T-shirts. Plus, they had a reputation as elite crews. Chuck didn't think of himself as elite, but still, it was worth a shot.

The line of sailors waiting to get inside the whorehouse on Hotel Street snaked halfway down the block. Many of the men had been drinking beer and cheap rum. The bars such as Two Jacks and the Trade Wind maintained a four-drinks-per-person limit, usually serving all four drinks at once to encourage the men to guzzle and move on, a policy that made for a lot of quick drunks.

Chuck didn't stop in any of the bars. Other than a few sips of hard cider in high school and a couple of swigs of rotgut wine back in Buffalo, he didn't imbibe. And as for girls, he'd never come close to going all the way. There'd been a few kisses with Irene, the girl back home, but she'd moved out of town. She'd written several times, and even promised to wait for him, but he wasn't counting on it.

Edging closer to the front of the line, he wished now he'd never confessed that he was a virgin. His buddies had made it their mission to get him initiated, and there was no shortage of brothels on Hotel Street to provide the opportunity. Located on the edge of Honolulu's Chinatown, it was the city's vice district, where men came to get drunk, tattooed, and laid. There were fifteen brothels, run-down places with names like the Senator Hotel or Bronx Room. Chuck was headed to the Rainbow Hotel.

Prostitution in Honolulu in 1941 was big business. As it was stateside, it was illegal, but police and government officials looked the other way. Honolulu officials reasoned that with so many young servicemen full of raging testosterone, they couldn't fight nature and figured it was better that these men sought release from prostitutes than from the respectable

young women of Hawaii. It was also a way to keep venereal diseases somewhat under control. The 250 registered prostitutes were required to have
weekly checkups; they also had to pay taxes and a $1 yearly license fee
as "entertainers." Many of the prostitutes had followed the fleet from San
Diego and Long Beach and San Francisco. Some serviced as many as one
hundred men a day, and because they got to keep $2 of the $3 fee, they
could make up to $50,000 a year.

With most of the Pacific Fleet now stationed at Pearl, there were long
lines day and night on the narrow sidewalks of Hotel Street; sometimes the
wait could last three hours. It was estimated that as many as 30,000 Marines, sailors, and soldiers visited the vice district daily.

Soon Chuck was at the door, then up the stairs to the second floor,
where he was greeted at a makeshift booth by the madam, a short Chinese
woman. A sign on the side of the booth said No Coloreds. Although
Honolulu was a racially mixed city, and only 24 percent of the population
were white, most madams ran segregated brothels to avoid racial conflict.
Navy officials had advised government officials that their officers and enlisted men, almost all white, would not frequent brothels where coloreds
were served.

"That'll be three dollars," said the madam.

Chuck thought about walking away, but with several of his shipmates
in line behind him, he knew that wasn't possible. He paid, then took a
seat on a bench alongside other sailors waiting their turn. They smelled of
liquor and cigarettes.

Like all the other brothels in town, the Rainbow Hotel was set up like
an assembly line—one room where the customer was greeted and the fee
collected, another room for the men to get undressed, another room for
the event, and another room for putting clothes back on. On Hotel Street,
time was money.

The madam finally motioned for him to enter the next room. Nervously, he opened the door. The room was divided by a flimsy piece of
plywood that didn't go all the way to the ceiling or to the end of one wall.
His side of the room was bare except for a washbasin. Slowly, he undressed,

leaving his underwear on. On the other side of the plywood he could hear a prostitute and a sailor having sex. It didn't last long.

He heard a door on the other side of the plywood open. A voice summoned him to walk around the divider. "Bring your clothes with you," she said.

He walked around the partition and looked briefly at the prostitute. She was a brunette, and at first glance she seemed attractive, young, tired. She was naked. "What's your name?" she asked, barely looking at him.

"Chuck," he answered. He moved toward the end of the cot, embarrassed to let his eyes wash over her. She moved next to him and sat down, her leg against his, her hand resting on his thigh.

"So, what's it gonna be? Straight up?"

He hesitated, trying to muster the courage to make his request, furtively letting his eyes wander over her body. He decided he might as well ask; the worst that could happen was that she'd say no. But before he could speak, she leaned forward and took an alarm clock off of a stand next to the cot and started to wind it. "What's that?" he asked.

"A clock," she replied. "Ya got three minutes."

"This may sound strange to you," he stammered, "but what I'd really like is to just talk with you."

"Just talk?" she echoed. "That's it?"

"Actually, there's something else," he added. "When you see the next guy, my friend . . . would you tell him that we did it? You know . . . had sex."

She regarded him skeptically.

"I mean, I'll pay you a dollar extra," he assured her.

She studied him for a moment, then smiled. "Sure, whatever you want," she said.

Three minutes later, he emerged from the room and passed back through the waiting area, greeted by his crewmates like he'd just run back a kickoff a hundred yards. "Alright, Chuckie boy; welcome to the club."

To his surprise, Chuck was accepted into Naval Submarine School. It was located at the base in New London, Connecticut, which had been built to accommodate the buildup in the submarine force. He was apprehensive about the school's reputation for being a tough program with lots of studying, but he also felt a sense of pride about joining such an elite branch of the Navy.

As soon as he arrived on base, Chuck felt comfortable, even with the class work. He tested especially well in mechanics and enjoyed the calisthenics and marching. He met with physicians, psychologists, and senior officers who poked and probed to find out if he was physically healthy, emotionally stable, and temperamentally capable of getting along well with other men during long periods of close confinement when nobody but the skipper or lookouts would see sun or stars, or smell air untainted by fumes from diesel fuel. But to Chuck, submarine service evoked a greater sense of fraternity, as well as a higher sense of purpose, than did being part of the surface fleet.

It was early 1941 and the pro-Navy leadership in Washington, D.C.—FDR had served as undersecretary to the Navy—was providing more money to build up the fleet, including submarines. In World War I, U.S. sub forces had been next to worthless, accounting for zero sinkings of enemy ships. Zero. But since 1930 the sub fleet had grown substantially in size and prestige. In 1936, $238 million had been allocated for construction of new ships of all designs—3 aircraft carriers, 7 battleships, 11 cruisers, 108 destroyers, and 26 new subs—and these ships were now either newly commissioned or soon to be.

The new subs were attracting a younger group of officers who saw the chance for an earlier command. Prior to the construction of these new vessels, U.S. subs had always been considered a defensive weapon, assigned primarily to coastal defenses—Manila, Hawaii, and the East and West coasts. To take on a bigger, more offensive role, they needed to be capable of long-range missions, which would mean more fuel capacity. In order to keep up with the fleet's surface ships, whose top speed was 17 knots, the new ships had a new, lightweight, high-performance diesel engine developed by private enterprise. They could dive within 60 seconds, and most had eight torpedo tubes—four forward and four aft. All had 3-inch deck guns, and each had four engines turned by a generator. The commander could use two engines for cruising and two for charging batteries, or four for running at maximum speed. The new submarines also had more powerful batteries that would allow a submerged sub to run at 2 knots for forty-eight hours or at maximum submerged speed of 5 knots for one hour. At 300 feet in length they gave the crew more elbow room for long cruises. They would be the backbone of the Pacific submarine fleet by December 1941.

Chuck graduated fifth in his class of eighty at Submarine School and was assigned to the newly commissioned USS *Gudgeon* on the West Coast, a ship soon to join the Pacific Fleet at Pearl Harbor. He was happy to be going back to Hawaii; he'd liked it when he'd been there several months earlier aboard the *Maryland*.

Graduation from Sub School and assignment to the *Gudgeon* did not mean the end of his studies, however. As with all new submariners assigned to a ship, Chuck's main course of study would become the ship itself. He would be required to know every valve, pipe, gauge, switch, or hatch, as well as draw accurate diagrams of the more than thirty main systems in the sub. Not only would he have to know his own specialty—he was assigned as a diesel mechanic—but he also needed to know the duties of a torpedoman, an electrician, and all the other jobs on the ship. Only when Chuck could convince his section chief and the skipper that he knew the material would he be qualified and win his silver dolphin insignia.

He would be joining a submarine force wedded to an antiquated strategy named Plan Orange, designed after the defeat of Germany in World War I. Japan was viewed as the biggest naval threat to America, especially after the Japanese began advocating expansionism and the conquest of China. Over the years the Japanese navy had steadily grown, and as part of the treaty ending World War I, Japan had been awarded the Marianas (less Guam), Carolinas, and Marshalls. These islands, if developed as naval bases, would cut off U.S. lines to the Philippines and would enhance the power and mobility of the Japanese fleet. Plan Orange assumed an initial Japanese attack would come on the Philippines, America's most vulnerable area. To prevent this, the plan was for a small Army garrison and the Asiatic Fleet to hold them off until the Pacific Fleet could sail to the rescue from Pacific waters, including Pearl Harbor. Plan Orange dominated all U.S. naval planning and thinking.

In 1940, the U.S. naval forces in the Pacific had been divided into two fleets: the Asiatic, which guarded the Philippines, and the Pacific, based in Pearl Harbor. When Japanese troops moved into Indochina to build air bases, U.S. naval officers were convinced that war with Japan was inevitable. By October 1941, the number of submarines in the Asiatic Fleet had been increased to twenty-nine (out of a total of fifty), leaving the Pacific Fleet at Pearl Harbor seriously depleted.

Rear Admiral Thomas Withers was in charge of the Pearl Harbor fleet, and on paper he had twenty-one subs, but in November 1941, only ten were actually in the harbor. Most of the rest were at Mare Island in California for repairs. The *Gudgeon*, with Chuck now on board, was one of the ships in Hawaii.

In Japan, Prime Minister Tojo had made the decision to widen the war beyond his nation's expansion into China, with plans to invade the Philippines, Hong Kong, Singapore, and the Malay Peninsula, as well as Thailand and Java for their rich oil deposits. To accomplish this, a key strategy was the total destruction of U.S. naval forces in the Pacific. The first target would be the U.S. fleet at Pearl Harbor. If it could be destroyed in a single strike, the U.S. Navy could not recover in time to mount a counteroffensive.

It was 7:00 a.m. Sunday morning, December 7, 1941. In the waters just outside Pearl Harbor sat five U.S. submarines, including the USS *Gudgeon*. For the past two days the *Gudgeon* had been practicing firing dummy torpedoes. The Navy brass were concerned about the performance and accuracy of their new Mark XIV torpedoes. The entire Pacific Fleet was on high alert due to the growing threat of a military strike by Japan.

Wearing only his dungarees, Chuck readied himself for the day. Walking across the deck, he whistled "Elmer's Tune"—a song stuck in his head ever since he'd heard it the night before on the *Lucky Strike Hit Parade* on Armed Services Radio. He'd spent Saturday night studying the sub's electrical system so he could pass that part of his qualifying test.

At eight o'clock the ship's Sunday morning calm was disrupted by an announcement over the PA system: "Now hear this, now hear this. This is the captain speaking. Pearl Harbor is under attack. There are air raids on Pearl Harbor. This is not a drill. I repeat: This is not a drill. Prepare to dive."

Chuck wasn't sure what to think, but an attack on Pearl Harbor seemed too far-fetched to believe.

The *Gudgeon*, with the normal complement of five officers and fifty-five enlisted men on board, submerged, staying under the surface for most of the next twenty-four hours. The next morning, December 8, they were ordered to return to Pearl Harbor and arrived that afternoon. Chuck stood on the deck, unprepared for the devastation he saw—the water in the harbor coated with oil; half-sunken ships still burning; bandaged men lying everywhere. And the smell, the horrible smell: a mix of smoke, oil, and burned flesh.

On one of the burning ships he saw a man crawling out of a porthole with torn skin hanging from his arms. Everywhere there were medics and men being carried away on stretchers. Chuck scanned the skies over the valley to the east, looking for enemy planes to come sweeping down again. He glanced at battleship row, or what was left of it, looking for his old ship, the *Maryland*. Moored next to the USS *Oklahoma*, it was spared the direct torpedo hits that sunk the *Oklahoma* and killed hundreds of men.

The *Gudgeon* docked at the sub base and the crew went ashore to await orders. Word spread that FDR had declared war. "Let's go into Pearl City tonight and kill some fuckin' Japs!" someone shouted.

With everyone restricted to base, that wouldn't happen. The next day the *Gudgeon* crew began loading torpedoes and supplies. They were going to war.

On December 11, 1941, Chuck was at his station below deck as the *Gudgeon* slid past the still-smoldering ruins of battleship row and out into the open waters of the Pacific. Plan Orange had already been abandoned; the sub commanders were now under new orders to do whatever was necessary to disrupt Japanese naval forces until America's fleet could regain its strength.

Like the rest of the crew, including the officers, Chuck didn't know where they were headed. He did know, however, that the *Gudgeon* was the first U.S. warship to head off on an offensive strike against imperial Japan in this new war. Among the men there was a sense of fear, but even more than that, the mood was revenge. Almost everyone on board had lost a friend in the attack on Pearl Harbor. Four of Chuck's ex-crewmates on the *Maryland* had been killed.

A day into the voyage, thirty-eight-year-old Lieutenant Commander Joe Grenfell, a 1926 graduate of the U.S. Naval Academy, opened the ship's orders. Their destination was Bungo Suido, the southern entrance to Japan's Inland Sea. The *Gudgeon,* alone and unprotected, was going right smack at the enemy's homeland.

Chuck had mixed feelings. On the one hand, he was proud to be taking it right to the "bastards who did that to our men and ships at Pearl Harbor." He had boundless faith in Grenfell and the other officers. But he was also scared. Would they run into the Japanese fleet that had carried the planes to the raid on Pearl? Did the Japanese have secret antisub weapons that nobody knew about? What if the enemy was tracking the *Gudgeon*'s every movement? Was the *Gudgeon* mechanically capable of what might be a two-month trip? What if he wasn't psychologically strong enough to endure the journey? Adding to his level of apprehension was the fact that the ship had been ordered to adhere to strict radio silence.

With the attack on Pearl Harbor, the rules of combat had changed. The London Naval Treaty, a pact the United States had signed following World War I that authorized submarines to strike only enemy warships and merchant vessels escorted by warships, was no longer in effect. Late in the day on December 7, the Navy Department had issued the order: EXECUTE UNRESTRICTED AIR AND NAVAL WARFARE AGAINST JAPAN. That meant every ship was now a target.

Adding to the anxiety, there was a critical shortage of torpedoes available at Pearl Harbor, with no sign that production could increase fast enough to solve the problem; the order was to use no more than two torpedoes when shooting at a merchant ship.

By the third day of the voyage, Chuck and the rest of the crew had settled into a routine. He stood watch—four hours on, eight hours off—and slept in the enlisted men's crowded bunk space in the aft torpedo storage space. On watch, he tended to the diesel engines, making sure they were performing properly, the strong smell of diesel fumes a constant. Most of his free time he spent studying so he could pass his qualifying tests. What little time he had left, he joined friends in playing poker and drinking coffee in the crew's mess. Others played cribbage or acey-deucey, but he stuck to poker: five-card draw and seven-card stud. He loved the rush of gambling, even if he was at risk of losing a week's pay in one sitting.

One week passed at sea for the *Gudgeon,* then a second, the journey proceeding slowly, tediously, and, as ordered, cautiously. Grenfell was under orders to run submerged in daylight as soon as they got to within 500 miles of the Japanese coast, but he did so at 1,000 miles. At night he ran on one engine to conserve fuel.

One night while playing cards, Chuck noticed a mild pain in his side. He dismissed it as a strain he'd gotten while loading supplies onto the ship. In the morning the pain was still there, up under his ribs.

After living with the pain for several days, he went to see Doc. Each submarine had a pharmacist's mate, or Doc, as he was called by the crew, and it was his duty to keep the crew as healthy as possible. Usually, the extent of the training given these men consisted of first-aid awareness and a rudimentary understanding of commonly prescribed painkillers and antibiotics. Beyond that, they mostly winged it. Stories abounded of pharmacist's mates heroically performing emergency surgeries with knives and spoons from the mess kitchen.

After a brief examination, Chuck was ordered to his bunk and given an ice pack to keep on his side. "I'm not sure what it is," Doc said. "It could be your appendix."

Chuck knew that if the pain was caused by his appendix, he could be in serious trouble. It didn't help when he overheard the pharmacist's mate tell an officer that he'd "be a goner if that thing bursts." Chuck pressed the ice bag tight to his side. He also knew that the ship was entering Japanese waters and was likely to encounter the enemy soon. The last place he wanted to be when the action started was confined to his bunk.

Over the next twenty-four hours, the pain worsened, especially when he tried to take a deep breath. It was Christmas Day.

On January 2, 1942, twenty-one days after leaving Pearl Harbor, the *Gudgeon* arrived at Bungo Suido. They were close enough to land that they could see navigational beacons ashore and sampans with running lights. The pain in Chuck's side had disappeared as mysteriously as it had begun, and he had been told by the pharmacist's mate to have it examined by a doctor upon returning to Pearl. Now he was just scared. He was in a metal tube under the ocean, thousands of miles from his home in New York, a place he might never see again.

It didn't take long for Grenfell to spot a small coastal freighter. He closed to within 2,600 yards. As later reported, torpedoes were readied for firing and the necessary calculations were hastily taken. A new guidance system had been installed in U.S. subs: it received data from the periscope or sonar on the enemy's bearing, range, speed, and "angle on the bow," and then was supposed to automatically plot the course of the target relative to the course of the submarine, computing and setting the proper gyro angle in the torpedo to intercept it. But to obtain an accurate range estimate, the captain had to calculate the height of the target's mast, then extrapolate from the horizontal lines in the periscope's crosshairs using a slide rule. At the same time that Grenfell was sorting out this data, he had to keep sweeping around the horizon for enemy escorts and aircraft.

In peacetime, U.S. subs had trained primarily with destroyers with known masthead heights. But now the target ships would have unknown masthead heights, and in most cases these ships would be zigzagging. These

zigs and zags had to be considered. Another potential problem was the
torpedo spread—how to space the firings so as to score hits. In practice,
three torpedoes were fired—one forward of the bow, one at the middle,
and one astern; the spread compensated for errors in speed estimates or
changes in the target's speed. But because they were under orders to fire
two rather than three shots at merchant ships, the spread technique had
to be revised, requiring a higher degree of accuracy in estimating speed
and range, but also the length of the target ship; all this was being done in
the heat of battle. In addition, the captain had to be calculating his ship's
escape route immediately after firing in case an escort ship chased down
the torpedoes' bubbles. This required that the sub dive neither too steeply,
which could structurally endanger the ship, nor too shallow, which would
leave the shears (external housing and support for the ship's periscope)
exposed and make them vulnerable to counterattack.

But the biggest problem facing the *Gudgeon*, as well as all American
subs at the onset of the war, was the growing concern that these subs were
equipped with defective torpedoes; in prewar testing these Mark XIV torpedoes, the only ones the United States had produced, either had run too
deep or their Mark VI magnetic exploders had not detonated. By design,
a trigger in the Mark VI allowed the torpedo to explode at a distance beneath a ship, where it had no armor. When this explosion reached the hull,
it would cause catastrophic failure to the keel.

Following a perfect approach by the *Gudgeon*, the small coastal
freighter was dead-center in the crosshairs. "Fire torpedo one . . . fire torpedo two," ordered Grenfell. Everybody on board waited for the explosion. Nothing.

The *Gudgeon* escaped, but now the real possibility existed that they
were deep in hostile waters armed with useless torpedoes.

After almost two weeks of patrolling near Bungo Suido, the *Gudgeon* started
the trip back to Pearl Harbor, Captain Grenfell surprised that they had
gone over a week without spotting anything despite patrolling in a busy

shipping lane. But shortly after turning for home, they encountered another freighter, this one estimated at 5,000 tons. It was night, and the
Gudgeon was on the surface, recharging its batteries. Grenfell maneuvered
to within 2,500 yards, and despite orders not to fire more than two torpedoes at merchant ships, he fired three. From his place in the hull, Chuck
felt the shock of an explosion. As the *Gudgeon* fled the area, everyone on
board shared in the jubilation of believing that they had sunk their first
ship and that their torpedoes weren't ineffective after all.

Like everyone else on board, Chuck felt relieved to be returning to
Pearl Harbor. They'd been gone over six weeks—six weeks of unrelenting
tension. Rumor had it that the whole crew would be housed at the Royal
Hawaiian Hotel. What a treat after the cramped and foul-smelling quarters
of the submarine—fresh air, good food, big beds, and, who knew, maybe
even a woman.

The sense of relief was short-lived. On January 24, the *Gudgeon* received a coded message that three Japanese submarines were headed in
their direction.

The tracking of Japanese submarines by naval code breakers had been
made a high priority after December 7. As later confirmed, Japanese submariners were irresponsibly chatty, communicating almost daily to their
commanders or home base in a code that was easy for the Americans to decipher. The three subs for which the *Gudgeon* now lay in wait had brazenly
been patrolling off the California coast, firing a few shells into a refinery
near San Pedro that did no damage but caused great fear with the citizens
of Southern California. This alerted Navy intelligence, which began tracking the subs, their job simplified by the subs' frequent radio transmissions
as they proceeded on a great circular route back to their base in Kwajalein.
Perhaps emboldened by sneaking so close to the California shoreline, the
subs also fired a few shells onto Midway Island as they passed, further be-
traying their position.

At 9:00 a.m. on January 27, just as projected, one of the subs crossed
the path of the submerged *Gudgeon*. Spotting it through the periscope,

Grenfell was dumbfounded. "Look at this," he said. "They're coming along, fat, dumb, and happy. They're not even zigzagging. The men are lounging on the deck, sunbathing and smoking."

Grenfell ordered battle stations, then fired three torpedoes from the bow tubes. Eighty-one seconds later, he heard a dull explosion.

Not positive if they'd scored a direct hit, Grenfell cautiously brought his ship closer to the surface. There was no submarine in sight, no propeller sounds or sonar. It's not known for sure if the torpedoes worked; there is speculation that I-173 tried to dive but forgot to close its hatches, thus flooding the ship. In any case, the submarine disappeared from radio traffic forever, making it the first major Japanese warship sunk in World War II.

Chuck's reaction surprised him. He expected to feel a sense of revenge, and in fact he'd shouted and raised his fist in triumph when he heard the explosion, until he visualized the Japanese crew in their control room, doing the same job he did. Surely they must have heard the swishing sound of the torpedo approaching, and surely for an instant before the explosion they knew what was about to happen. Rationally, he knew they were the enemy and needed to be eliminated. Still, it bothered him.

6

Bob Palmer

USS *Tuna*

When Bob joined the Navy in September 1939 just before Germany invaded Poland, it was not for duty and country. He wanted to get away from his stepmother Cora and from the pain of the breakup with his sweetheart Barbara Koehler.

Initially, Bob thought joining the Navy was the greatest thing that had ever happened to him. At boot camp in San Diego, California, he loved everything about it: the playing of taps in the evening, the colors, saluting the flag, and even all the marching on the Grinder, which is what the recruits called the marching compound. Sometimes in the morning when they raised the flag and played reveille, he'd feel so much pride that he got tears in his eyes. For the first time in his life, he felt he belonged. He liked the simplicity and regimented routine. His life had purpose. But by the time he finished boot camp, he was beginning to have doubts, thinking the only skills he'd really learned were how to march and how to peel potatoes. When he was assigned to the USS *Wright,* an aging World War I mother ship to seaplanes, he had hopes of working as an airplane mechanic, but in the three months he'd been at Pearl Harbor, all he'd done was scrape paint from the hull of the old ship. About the only thing he felt good about was all the letters he'd written home for his crewmates. It surprised him how many of them didn't know how to write.

Then one day the ship's executive officer asked if anyone on the crew could type. Bob was the only person who raised his hand; in his junior year he'd taken a typing class, thinking it might be a good way to meet girls. The officer instructed him to step forward.

"You just volunteered," he said.

The next day, Bob reported to the USS *Tuna*, a submarine, and was assigned to be the man in charge of clerical duties, the ship's yeoman, or as crewmates often called the position, "first pussy." And that's how he became a submariner.

Bob quickly regained the sense of purpose he'd initially felt when he joined the Navy. He liked his crewmates on the *Tuna*. What struck him most about this crew as compared with that of the *Wright* was how much smarter the men seemed. They could all read and write, and they were good at mechanical and engineering problems. Plus, there was a camaraderie and togetherness that he hadn't felt before. It wasn't something the crew talked about, it was just there.

He admitted, however, to being nervous on his first training dive. It was his first time aboard a sub. The ship plunged downward at a steep angle and there was a lot of clanging and banging, the sound of rushing air, and the sight of men furiously spinning valves. It was the noises that scared him most. As the ship's yeoman, he had the sense that he was just along for the ride, a reluctant passenger on a scary ride at an amusement park. He felt the ship throb, almost like it was groaning. He held on to the desk in his little cubbyhole of an office, hoping everyone else on board was too busy to notice how scared he was. In the weeks ahead, he got progressively less frightened with each dive, but he was never completely at ease.

Bob couldn't believe his good luck. It was October 1941, and when the *Tuna* got sent to Mare Island near San Francisco for repairs, he found out that Barbara was now working as a secretary for an insurance company in San Francisco. She had dropped out of the University of Oregon after a year and was living in a cramped studio apartment on Pine Street with her cousin Margie and Aunt Fern. He wasted no time in calling her, and to his great joy she agreed to go out on a date with him.

That first date didn't go quite as he'd planned. The day before he was supposed to meet her, he forged an officer's signature on a weekend pass for a shipmate and got caught. Sentenced to a week in the brig, he couldn't call. When he finally got out and called, he apologized profusely; to his relief she quickly got over being angry and gave him another chance.

When he arrived at the apartment and Barbara opened the door, he stood there, mouth agape. She was even cuter and shapelier than he remembered.

For her part, she thought he looked pretty damn cute himself, all decked out in his sailor suit. He'd matured since she'd last seen him, his lean frame filled out a bit, his face fuller, more mature. And those eyes, sky blue and friendly, reminded her why she'd first been attracted to him back in high school, and why she'd let him sweet-talk her into the backseat of her father's car across the street from the Baptist Church.

They went out for dinner at Mona's Nite Club—veal cutlets and mashed potatoes—and a lot of close dancing. She invited him to spend the night. Because her aunt and cousin shared the small studio apartment with her, he would have to sleep on the couch. That was fine with him. He was just happy to be with her again. She was as affectionate as he remembered, and she still had that flirty way that got him excited.

For the next six weeks, he came to see her on every weekend pass he got, taking the one-hour bus ride from Mare Island into San Francisco, then a twenty-minute walk to her apartment. They even began to talk about marriage.

On December 4, 1941, her parents drove down from Medford for a visit. Barbara summoned her nerve to tell them that she and Bob were dating again, and that she was in love, and that they'd talked of getting married.

"Over my dead body," her father replied.

On Sunday morning, December 7, Bob awoke late at his brother Darrell's house in Medford. Home on a four-day pass, he'd come to tell his father and Cora that he planned to marry Barbara after he completed his stint in the Navy.

Getting dressed, he listened to the big band sounds of Tommy Dorsey on Mutual Radio. The programming was interrupted with a terse two-sentence announcement: "The Japanese have attacked U.S. Navy ships at Pearl Harbor. Enemy ships have been reported close to our shores."

He spun the radio dial, searching for more news. All servicemen on leave anywhere in America, he learned, had been ordered to return immediately to station. He wouldn't be able to see his dad and tell him about his plans with Barbara. By early afternoon, he was boarding a bus in his Navy blues to head back to California.

Settling into his window seat, he braced for the long ride, resolute in his country's purpose.

On her way to work the morning of Monday, December 8, Barbara stopped at a newsstand, paid a nickel, and bought a copy of the *San Francisco Examiner.* The headline bannered the news: U.S.–JAP WAR! Later that day, along with the whole nation, she listened to President Roosevelt's historic "a day which will live in infamy" speech.

For the people in San Francisco, the impact of the sneak attack was especially sobering. The vulnerable West Coast was now confronted not only with the reality of America being at war but also with the task of preparing for the very real possibility of an enemy invasion.

San Francisco quickly moved to a war footing, but confusion and invasion fever reigned. Within hours of the first word from Pearl Harbor, sentries recruited from the California State Guard, armed with guns and bayonets, were posted on the Bay Bridge and the San Francisco waterfront. Checkpoints were established, and cars were inspected for Japanese occupants before being allowed to pass. Any Japanese was detained for questioning. From San Jose to Marin County, a blackout was quickly put in place. The California State Automobile Association put up 3,000 signs in the area, ordering headlights dimmed. Traffic slowed to a crawl, worsened by accidents caused by cars and trucks driving with only parking lights on.

Air-raid signals blared and searchlights scanned the skies. The Army base at the Presidio was darkened. A few miles away in San Francisco Bay, however, Alcatraz was lit up like a ballpark; officials worried that darkening the prison would encourage escape attempts. Heavy-duty antiaircraft guns were installed next to the Golden Gate Bridge, and guards patrolled for possible sabotage. A three-mile-wide submarine net was stretched across the opening of the bay. Civilian defense officials designated certain buildings as public air-raid shelters, and signs indicating their locations were quickly posted. Civilian patrolmen started a training course for defense against chemical attack, and 16,900 gas masks were sent from Washington, D.C., to equip the city's protective services and civilian defense workers. Commercial fishing fleets were placed under the protection of the U.S. Coast Guard, and Japanese-American fishermen were forbidden to practice their trade. At the phone company building across from Barbara's office, sandbags were piled two stories high.

At Barbara's apartment, her aunt taped butcher paper over the windows in compliance with the blackout and filled the tub with water in case the Japanese bombed the reservoirs and contaminated the water. Her neighbors joined together and demanded that local merchants dim their store lights like everyone else. On December 11 a front-page story reported that two squadrons of Japanese bombers had flown over the Bay Area the night before. The story even carried a map detailing the route the bombers had taken, one squadron passing over Mare Island and then heading north toward Mendocino County, the other group circling over San Jose before disappearing to the southwest. The story turned out not to be true, but still, it jangled everyone's nerves even more.

Eager to do her share, Barbara volunteered with the Red Cross Emergency Team and was assigned to put gas masks into boxes for distribution throughout the city. Bob was confined to his base, and it took several days for him to get a call through to Barbara. He didn't waste words.

"Let's get married," he proposed.

"When?"

"Now. As soon as you can find a church?"

She accepted his proposal.

With so many sailors and soldiers about to ship out for the war, young couples all over America had decided to speed up their wedding plans; churches all over San Francisco were booked solid. It took Barbara several calls to find a church and minister, but she finally set up a ceremony at San Francisco's Trinity Church at nine thirty at night, December 16, 1941. Then she called her parents to break the news.

"No, no, no" were the first words out of her father's mouth.

But when she persisted, her parents reluctantly agreed to return to California for the wedding. How could they stand in the way of their daughter marrying a man about to risk his life for his country? Bob also called his dad and stepmother, and they too agreed to attend.

Barbara took care of buying the rings as well, spending $30 out of her savings for two simple gold bands. She'd also bought a new black and gray knit dress and matching pillbox hat for the occasion. She was nineteen; Bob was twenty.

With their parents in attendance, they were married as planned, although Barbara's father had made it clear he didn't approve. Not only were they too young, he thought that with Bob shipping off to war in a few days, this was no way to start a marriage. Plus, he was still having trouble letting go of the feeling that Bob wouldn't be able to provide for his daughter. But the outbreak of war and the photo images of the death and destruction at Pearl Harbor had created a national will and unity of purpose, and a respect for the men going off to defend the American way of life, especially in a branch of the service as dangerous as submarines.

Beneath all of Bob's big smiles and excitement about getting married, he also felt a sense of inadequacy—he hadn't been able to afford the rings; he didn't have enough money to pay for the reception dinner at Vanessi's in North Beach; he couldn't afford to provide his new wife a nice apartment while he was gone; he didn't earn enough so that she didn't have to work. Maybe his new father-in-law was right; maybe he wasn't good enough for Barbara. It helped that she told him otherwise, and that she loved him for his heart, and good looks, and sense of humor, and not his money. But still, Bob worried. He was also worried, of course, about going to war and dying, but he knew it was his duty, his responsibility. He took some solace in knowing that his Navy pay would double in wartime and that he'd be able to send most of it back to Barbara.

On January 9, 1942, the *Tuna* departed San Francisco on its way to Pearl Harbor. Bob was on the deck straining to catch a glimpse of Barbara as it sailed under the Golden Gate Bridge. She'd promised to be there to wave good-bye, but her boss wouldn't let her off work. She cried most of the day.

Three weeks later, Bob was on the deck again as the *Tuna* left Pearl Harbor on its first patrol. It had just enough room to slide by the stern of the battleship USS *Nevada*, aground across the channel. Bob was shocked by the devastation to the ships in Pearl Harbor, and he worried that the *Tuna* was not sufficiently ready for battle.

The crews of the submarines making up the Pacific and Asiatic fleets, including the *Gudgeon* with Chuck Ver Valin, now shared a deep mistrust for the Mark XIV torpedo and the Mark VI magnetic exploder, believing the torpedo ran deeper than designed and the magnetic exploder was defective, causing it to explode prematurely. There was little information on how to adjust or repair the device. The skippers had been instructed to set the torpedo to run deep beneath the keels of the enemy and let the exploder take care of the rest. But because of the shortage of torpedoes, no live tests had been conducted prior to sending subs out on patrol. Reports from the early patrols had substantiated the concerns. In the first three weeks of the war, American subs had fired ninety-six torpedoes, with only three hits. Several captains urged Admiral Withers, commander of the Pacific Fleet, to give orders to deactivate the exploder and fire the torpedoes for direct contact hits. Admiral Withers refused, reminding the captains that there was a critical shortage of torpedoes at Pearl Harbor and that they needed to trust their weaponry. The submarine force had no choice but to place blind faith in this order and the new weapon.

John DeTar, the captain of the *Tuna*, wasn't happy with the decision.

Like several other skippers, he toyed with the idea that once he left Pearl Harbor and reached the combat zone, he would deactivate the exploder and shoot for contact, which he hoped would improve the possibility of an explosion. If necessary, he would swear his men to secrecy and doctor the reports to justify using more than one torpedo.

For this mission, the *Tuna* was assigned to patrol off the east coast of Japan and in fact to go right into harbors. Bob tried to hide his nervousness. He'd heard the concerns about the torpedoes. He also worried about the crew's readiness for battle; they were undertrained and inexperienced. Worse, he lacked confidence in DeTar: instead of sleeping in his quarters, the captain slept on a mattress in the conning tower; he strutted around with a pistol strapped to his side; he strictly rationed the crew's use of fresh water even though he had two distillers on board; he forbade the men from taking showers and ignored their complaints; and when the hydraulic system malfunctioned, more than once, he accused someone on the crew of trying to sabotage him. Bob didn't know if it was possible, but he was already thinking about requesting a transfer after this patrol.

Every day, he sat in his yeoman's cubicle, staring at a framed photo of Barbara.

It was very dark as Barbara walked up Pine Street in her high heels; the streetlights were turned off because of the blackout. She was returning from the Red Cross office, where she'd gone after work to help pack boxes with emergency medical supplies. She'd watched teams of volunteers in a mock emergency medical drill, and the images of bandaged patients and men in helmets played on her nerves. The danger of an attack now seemed even more real, especially following numerous reports of Japanese warships off the California coast. It was February 2, 1942.

As she neared her apartment, she was looking forward to sharing her big news with Fern and Margie. She'd been to the doctor earlier in the day and gotten the word that she was pregnant. She was thrilled, and would write Bob that night to tell him he was going to be a father. She hoped he'd get the news before heading off on patrol. She would write her parents as well, not sure if they'd be happy about the news.

She also wrote her cousin June back in Medford:

Oh, it's so awful to have him gone, June. He's been gone only three weeks but I miss him terribly. I received two letters from him Saturday and another two today, which is the first I've heard from him. All of them were written while he was in Pearl Harbor and sent by clipper. I don't know where he is now though. It's awful not knowing, but guess I'll have to get used to it.

The crew of the *Tuna* was on edge: DeTar's disturbing behavior, repeated malfunctions of the hydraulic system, lack of confidence in the torpedoes, and the numbing fear of being on a mission to penetrate deep into enemy waters all took their toll. Moreover, the trip across had taken longer than scheduled, and DeTar had kept the ship submerged much of the way, including at night, despite orders to the contrary. He continued to maintain his strict rationing of drinking water.

Upon reaching the coast of Japan, DeTar guided the ship into a harbor—one suspected of being mined—close enough that he could see people ashore through the periscope. Bob heard a scraping against the port side of the boat; it was a cable from a mine.

DeTar kept the ship in the harbor for twenty-four hours, with nothing accomplished other than rattling the crew's nerves. As they headed back out to sea, DeTar spotted a freighter in the distance. He closed to within 3,500 yards and fired three times, in direct defiance of orders. All three shots missed.

As they tried to flee the area, a Japanese destroyer moved in quickly and began dropping depth charges, at least twenty of them, one explosion after another shaking the *Tuna*, knocking out the lights and twisting the hull. Bob and the rest of the crew held on in terror.

One of the blasts damaged the propeller, causing it to squeak; now if they tried to run, the destroyer overhead would hear them. DeTar's only option was to wait it out and hope the destroyer would eventually leave. But for the next twenty-three hours, the destroyer stayed, dropping more depth charges.

Barbara hurriedly opened the special-delivery letter from her mother, sure it was in response to the letter she'd sent announcing she was pregnant.

"Your father and I . . . ," it began.

That phrase was always a signal to Barbara that she was in trouble. In the letter, her mother spelled out the reasons she thought it was not the right time for Barbara to be having a child—she was too young; her husband was at war, with no guarantee of returning; a child needed two parents; money would be a problem; there would be plenty of time later to have a child.

Barbara fought back tears. It wasn't just that her parents didn't think having a baby was a good idea, it was the furious "how could you let this happen" tone of the letter.

After twenty-four hours on the ocean floor under steady depth-charge bombardment, the *Tuna* finally escaped, heading east toward deeper, safer waters. Soon the crew began pursuit of a 4,000-ton freighter.

Defying orders again, DeTar deactivated the magnetic exploder on his remaining torpedoes. Bob was no torpedo expert, but it made sense to him. The torpedoes they'd fired earlier hadn't sunk anything, so something needed to be done.

DeTar moved in for the attack. At 2,000 yards, he fired. Bob heard the explosion; this time they scored a direct hit. After a few minutes, DeTar brought the *Tuna* to the surface to observe the damage. The freighter was splitting in two.

Standing on the deck, Bob watched the freighter going down, but instead of a sense of vindication, he had a sick feeling in his stomach. In the oily, fiery ocean, men, women, children, and dogs struggled to stay afloat;

the freighter had been carrying civilian passengers. He heard screams and saw desperate, outstretched hands disappear under the water. He knew that the freighter was probably carrying supplies to be used against American troops and ships, but later that night he could still see the images of the outstretched hands.

After receiving the letter from her mother, Barbara had confided her situation to Estelle, a woman with whom she worked. Estelle was twenty-nine, and to Barbara she seemed worldly wise. Estelle told her about a clinic, reassuring her that it wasn't some back-alley place but a clean facility, with a receptionist, nurses in white uniforms, and a doctor who was known as the safest and most experienced abortionist in the city. Patients received printed instructions for follow-up care.

Although she didn't know anyone who'd had an abortion, or at least anyone who admitted it, Barbara had heard tales of "coat hanger" abortions and hospitals having "abortion wards" filled with women suffering from botched procedures. She knew it was illegal, and risky. She'd made the decision to tell people, including Bob and her parents, that she'd had a miscarriage.

Her whole life Barbara had pretty much done what her parents told her; going against their advice seemed wrong. While her mother had not directly told her to have an abortion—she would never do that—the letter made it seem that having a baby at this point in her life would be a huge mistake.

As badly as Barbara wanted a child, she saw her parents' point. A few days earlier, she'd seen a newspaper headline declaring JAPS SINK TWO MORE AMERICAN SUBS. Manila was about to fall, the Germans were sweeping through Europe, and military leaders were forecasting a long and bloody war. As much as she didn't like to think about it, there was a good chance that Bob could get killed. She didn't know any single mothers.

She was also persuaded by her mother's point about the financial difficulty she would have in raising a child, especially if Bob didn't return.

She would have to quit her job to raise the child, and that would mean she would have to move back home with her parents in Central Point. She definitely didn't want to do that.

But what if Bob wanted her to have the baby? She'd written and told him she was pregnant, but she wasn't sure if he'd even gotten the letter. They'd talked about having children, but it was something they figured would happen later, after the war, after their lives were more settled.

As she wrestled with her options, half a world away Bob's submarine sailed through the debris and bodies from the sinking Japanese freighter.

7

Tim "Skeeter" McCoy
USS *Trout*

Stripped to the waist, seventeen-year-old Tim wiped the sweat off his freckled shoulders, his lean frame glistening in the tropical sunshine. Along with the rest of his new crewmates on the submarine USS *Trout* in Pearl Harbor, he was helping to load 3,517 rounds of artillery shells on board for a special mission. The fact that most of the ship's torpedoes had been unloaded signified something was up. Why would a submarine about to head off toward enemy waters be without a full load of torpedoes? They were due to leave tomorrow, January 12, 1942.

Tim had been a submariner for only two days. After only five weeks of basic training in San Diego, his entire company of new recruits had been rushed off to Pearl Harbor just days after December 7.

Tim had arrived in San Diego by train from Dallas, and for him, boot camp seemed easy enough, mostly just marching and learning Navy terminology. He liked getting to sleep in a hammock and living in a big barracks with other recruits. His company had taken a bus to the harbor once and boarded an anchored training ship for an orientation session. But that was the extent of his training before shipping out.

He had no regrets about dropping out of high school at the start of his senior year to enlist. It was time for him to get out on his own, and the guarantee of three square meals a day and a regular paycheck made sense. His decision had nothing to do with what Hitler was doing in Europe—it was all about getting out from under his mom's feet and earning enough to help her out. It seemed unlikely that his father was ever going to provide his mom with any financial help.

When he first arrived in Hawaii, he felt like he'd reached the edge of his world. But this wasn't Hawaii the tropical paradise; there would be no hula girls, grass huts, or splashing in the surf. The Hawaiian Islands were now under martial law. Barbed-wire fences lined the beach at Waikiki. Tim and the men in his company would be restricted to base. After docking, they rode a bus straight to the submarine base at Pearl Harbor, the whole company assigned to the submarine tender USS *Pelius*, a huge floating repair shop for subs.

Two days after being assigned to the *Pelius*, Tim answered a call for volunteers for the USS *Trout*, one of twelve new fleet submarines commissioned in 1940 in the hasty prewar Navy buildup. Its skipper, Lieutenant Commander Frank Fenno, had been asked how fast he could get the ship ready for sea. It was urgently required to deliver much-needed antiaircraft ammunition to Corregidor, the small island fortress in Manila Bay nicknamed "the Rock." Fenno said he needed only a couple of replacements for his crew and could be ready to go in a couple of days. That's when Tim volunteered and became a submariner.

Tim figured a submarine would be safer than a surface vessel because it could see the enemy while the enemy couldn't see it. But more than that, there was something daring and adventurous about being a submariner that appealed to his cocky nature. He was assigned as a mess cook, which meant a lot of peeling potatoes and cleaning dishes. There was really nothing else on board he was qualified to do, except help load tons of artillery shells for the "secret mission" the ship was leaving on in the morning.

The Japanese knew the Philippine Islands were essential to controlling the western Pacific and providing a lifeline to Indonesia and its many resources, as well as to Australia. By the time the *Trout* left Pearl Harbor, Japanese forces had created a hopeless situation for the 100,000 U.S. and Philippine troops on the Bataan Peninsula. Manila had been evacuated and General MacArthur had moved his headquarters to Corregidor, now the final U.S. foothold against the invading forces.

On Corregidor, the main defensive feature was the man-made rock tunnel near the middle of the tadpole-shaped island. It had become an underground storehouse for the Philippine and U.S. forces, as well as for a large portion of the Philippine treasury's gold and silver. The Japanese were bombarding the island by air and with artillery fire from Cavite on the mainland, pounding it relentlessly day and night, making life on Corregidor unbearable; even the tunnel trembled. It was the *Trout*'s destination.

The antiaircraft gunners on Corregidor urgently needed more long-range, mechanically fused, high-altitude projectiles, the ammunition Tim had worked up a sweat to get onto the *Trout*. For Tim, it had all happened so fast—boot camp, coming to Pearl Harbor, volunteering for submarine duty—that he didn't have time to sit around and develop a case of war nerves.

As the *Trout* sailed for Corregidor, every inch of its interior space was crammed with the cargo of ammunition, a priority so great that the spare torpedoes had been removed, leaving only eight torpedoes on board. Commander Fenno was under orders not to engage the enemy unless his own safety was in peril. Having seen the destruction at Pearl Harbor and eager to sink Japanese ships, he was unhappy about the assignment, so he engineered a compromise with his commanding officers. After dropping off his load of artillery shells, he would pick up a load of torpedoes and fuel at Corregidor, then patrol the Formosa Strait and the lower reaches of the East China Sea on the way home.

To Tim, everything was new and exciting. He'd been a submariner for less than three days and he was already headed into combat. When the ship made its first dive beneath the surface shortly after leaving Pearl Harbor, he loved it: there was no claustrophobia, no fear of being under the water. In fact, he liked being submerged better than riding on top. "It's as smooth as glass," he said, describing the underwater ride.

It was also a cultural awakening. Other than one trip to Oklahoma, he'd spent his whole life in Texas. That was his identity, his culture, his accent. Now he was surrounded by guys from New Jersey, Minnesota, California. They all had their different ways of expressing themselves. Not everyone appreciated his cocky manner. Fortunately, there were two other Texans on board, and he immediately gravitated to them, quickly picking up the nickname "Skeeter." He wasn't exactly sure why they called him that. Maybe it had to do with him always buzzing around like a pesky mosquito.

The *Trout* reached the entrance to Manila Bay on the afternoon of February 3. But the water around Corregidor was heavily mined, and it would be too risky to proceed to port. With tons of high explosives on board, the sub was a gigantic fireball waiting to happen.

After waiting until nightfall, Captain Fenno, a class of '25 graduate of the Naval Academy, took off on a zigzag course through the heavily mined harbor. He was following a motorboat guided by a torpedo boat squadron commander, Lieutenant John Bulkeley. As Fenno maneuvered the 307-foot-long, fleet-type submarine in the wake of a fast-moving torpedo boat in the pitch-black night, it was as quiet as a church on board. Halfway to their destination, Tim heard a mine scraping down the port side of the sub.

For forty-five nerve-racking minutes, Tim and the rest of the crew held their breath. Finally, the ship pulled alongside the south dock and darkened its lights. The crew immediately went to work, passing cases of artillery up through the rear hatch and unloading them on the dock. Tim cast a glance toward Cavite across the bay, from where Japanese artillery emplacements could easily blow them to smithereens. In the distance, the sound of artillery fire rumbled through the hills of Bataan. Tim saw explosions; the night sky lit up like someone had waved a giant sparkler through it. Despite his being in great shape, his muscles quickly wearied.

While the ammunition was being unloaded aft, the *Trout* took on ten torpedoes through her forward hatch. Each torpedo weighed 3,000 pounds, and with no crane or hoist to help, the crew, aided by Filipino stevedores, grew even more exhausted. On the port side, the ship took on 27,000 gallons of fuel.

As he continued to work, Tim looked down the dock and spotted dozens of carloads of locals arriving. Because of the constant bombardment that Corregidor had been under, supplies had dwindled and food was scarce; the civilians had come in hopes of a handout. Seeing their desperate and pleading faces, Fenno ordered all possible supplies to be brought to the dock—cigarettes, medical supplies, and food. Tim helped carry up food supplies. When the job was finished, all that was left on board for the rest of the mission was the ingredients for spaghetti—breakfast, lunch, and dinner.

Nearing midnight and the end of the unloading of the ammo, Fenno inquired what type of ballast was available to replace the twenty-five tons of shells that had just been removed. Without sufficient ballast, the ship would have trouble diving and be dangerously top-heavy when on the surface. He said he'd take anything—crushed rocks, stone, sandbags. But every sandbag on the island had already been used for protection against the constant bombardment. A new plan was hatched: the ballast would come from the gold bars and silver coins from the Philippine treasury hidden in the tunnel. The amount was staggering for the time: $38 million in U.S. Treasury checks, $31 million in American and Philippine currency, $9 million in silver Philippine pesos, and over six tons of gold worth $9 million. After a call to MacArthur, it was agreed that a portion of the treasure—$20 million—would be transferred to the *Trout*.

Soon tons of gold, securities, and silver were being loaded onto five-ton flatbed Army trucks for the trip to the dock. With the help of locals, Tim and the crew began loading 319 bars of gold, passing them by hand down the hatches into the sub. Each bar weighed forty pounds, a total of almost six and a half tons. It took only minutes to load them. Next came the 630 bags of silver, each bag containing a thousand pesos. Tim wasn't sure how much each bag weighed, but by now they each felt like a ton. By the time the money was loaded, every available inch of space on the inside deck of the *Trout* was stacked with the bars of gold and the bags of silver.

As Fenno readied the ship for departure, Tim saw one of his crewmates, Doug Graham, furtively untie one of the bags of silver coins, reach inside, pull out a handful of coins, and stick them in his pocket. Tim had heard Captain Fenno talk about the integrity of delivering their cargo, and stealing ran contrary to Tim's Baptist upbringing. He debated whether to blow the whistle on Graham but decided to sleep on it for a few days.

With the final transfer of funds completed, the *Trout* turned and headed toward the open sea. On board was the richest ballast any ship had ever carried. Fenno's instructions were to transport the money directly back to Pearl Harbor for transfer to the American treasury and not engage the enemy. But Fenno was itching to sink a Japanese ship. He set course for the East China Sea.

Two weeks after leaving Corregidor, Fenno got his wish. The *Trout* sank a 2,700-ton cargo ship off the northern coast of Formosa using three torpedoes. Tim was still wrestling whether to say anything about Graham's taking the coins. It upset his sense of right and wrong, especially after he heard Graham talking about being a deacon in his church back home in Sacramento, but he finally decided not to make an issue of it. He was the youngest and the lowest-ranking man on the ship, and this was not a good time to alienate anyone. He would, however, turn Graham in after the war, he told himself.

The next week was uneventful except for the foul winter weather: gale winds and mountainous seas. It gave Tim a chance to continue his naval education. So far, he'd studied how to operate the bilge system, how to fire a torpedo, how to go into the engine room and start the big Fairbanks-Morse engine from scratch, and how to put power to the screws (propellers). Sometimes he felt like he was back in school again, constantly reading manuals, looking at drawings and blueprints, listening to the officers' instruction. But this wasn't like school back in Dallas, where he was rarely interested in the assignments. He liked studying about the submarine. It was important to him to move up in rank.

Not satisfied with just one sinking, Fenno scored another kill, this time an enemy gunboat passing through the Bonin Islands south of Japan near Iwo Jima. Fenno wanted more, but soon a message arrived from Pearl Harbor ordering him to return to base. Word had come from Washington—a sub loaded with gold and silver was too valuable to risk chasing after enemy gunboats and freighters.

On the afternoon of March 3, 1942, after fifty days on mission, Tim was topside as the *Trout* moored port side to the USS *Detroit* at Fleet Air Base in Pearl Harbor. Its precious cargo was quickly transferred to the *Detroit* to be taken to America. For the mission, Commander Fenno was awarded the Distinguished Service Cross for "extraordinary heroism." Tim and the rest of the crew all received a prestigious Silver Star Medal. And for his part in guiding the *Trout* through the minefields of Manila Bay, as well as his heroic efforts in the climactic final hours of the Philippine defense, including the personal evacuation of General MacArthur and his family from Corregidor, Lieutenant Commander John Bulkeley was presented the Congressional Medal of Honor by President Roosevelt.

At a time when there was almost no good news to report from the war, the *Trout*'s mission made headlines across the country and helped lift the nation's beleaguered spirits. Seventeen-year-old Tim McCoy felt proud to have been part of such a heroic effort.

Tim sat in his hotel room, staring out the window, trying to figure out something to do to pass the time. He and the rest of the crew of the *Trout* were staying at the posh Royal Hawaiian. The Navy had taken over the three fanciest hotels on the island—the Royal Hawaiian, Moana, and Halekulani—to house and feed the sailors between combat patrols; enlisted men stayed for free, officers paid $1 for a suite. Before the war, these were the hotels for movie stars and rich tourists, off-limits to servicemen.

Tim was bored, unimpressed with Hawaii, or at least Honolulu and Waikiki. Sailors had taken to calling Oahu "the Rock," comparing it to Alcatraz: isolated, overcrowded with military personnel, a departure point for the horrors of combat and possibly death. For many of these young men, the tension was relieved only by alcohol. For the first time in his life, Tim had awakened with the curse of a hangover.

Out his window, he saw men standing in line to catch a bus. He'd always been an impatient, fidgety kind of kid, and to him, Hawaii was a place where he was always waiting—waiting to wash his Skivvies, waiting for chow, waiting to be sent off to battle again. It also felt like a lot of the locals didn't like servicemen. With the arrival of so many sailors and Marines, the population on the island had ballooned dramatically. Services were strained. In addition to the flood of service personnel, thousands of others had come to the island seeking the promise of important war work. At first these new arrivals, or malihinis as the natives called them, were greeted warmly, but soon this swarm of new people were viewed with a wary eye: they drank and cussed too much, made too much noise, and started too many fights.

To Tim, like most Navy men, Honolulu was a dirty town inhabited by Japs, Chinks, and dark-skinned people running around unwashed and barely able to speak English. Racial slurs and epithets were part of normal conversation. Men who'd never interacted with people of color or different ethnicity now found themselves in the minority. Tim didn't feel comfortable walking the streets. The atmosphere felt tense, especially with so many of the men wandering the streets drunk, most of them not good at handling their liquor.

Another thing Tim didn't like about the island was the lack of women. Most of the white women on the island had returned to the mainland after December 7. Tim heard an estimate that the ratio of men to women in Honolulu was 500 to 1. With such scarcity, sailors looked at every woman they saw as if she were a Betty Grable or a Hedy Lamarr. The Navy and the USO staged dances, but as with everything else on the island, the men had to stand in line to wait their turn to dance. Tim had been to one dance at the Navy Rec Center in Waikiki, but with over a thousand men attending and only about thirty women, he left early.

He wasn't interested in the brothels, either. Honolulu brothels were now servicing up to 30,000 men a day, and for many of these servicemen it would be their only encounter with a woman before they died. There was also the chance of catching a venereal disease. (More men in World War II would get VD than be wounded in action.) To a huge number of young servicemen, it was worth the risk. Not to Tim.

"I have no desire to be the hundredth guy some whore does it with in a day," he said. "Or, for that matter, the first. I can't even imagine."

Tim quickly glanced at his cards, then glared at Petty Officer Joe Boyle sitting across the table. For some unknown reason, Boyle had made it his assignment to ride Tim. Along with four crewmates, they were playing poker in Boyle's room at the Royal Hawaiian. One of the other players was Doug Graham, whom Tim had seen steal the coins on the *Trout*. Between Boyle, Graham, and the ten beers he'd downed, Tim was feeling irritable.

"Where's your ante?" asked Boyle.

"I forgot," replied Tim, tossing a matchstick into the pot. He took another swig of his beer.

"Is everybody from Texas as stupid as you?" needled Boyle.

Tim set his cards down.

"Kiss my ass," he muttered.

"What did you say?"

"You heard me, asshole."

Boyle slowly stood.

Common sense should have told Tim that fighting with an officer was a sure way to get washed out of the submarine service, sent to the brig, or court-martialed, or all three. But at that moment, none of that occurred to him. He unloaded from somewhere south of the lobby, his right fist nailing Boyle squarely on the jaw. Down he went, out cold.

Tim turned and headed out the door. He didn't know anything about maritime law, but he was pretty sure he was in big trouble.

8

Gordy Cox
USS *Sculpin*

The physical part of boot camp was easy for seventeen-year-old Gordy. He'd always been wiry and full of energy. All of the hockey and skating, as well as riding his bike up and down hills in Yakima to deliver newspapers, had prepared him well for the calisthenics and marching. Plus, he had a good attitude, happy to be on his own, proud to be in the Navy. Unlike many of the inductees, he didn't grouse about sweeping the Grinder or spending endless hours learning to tie knots. He'd even been able to send part of his weekly $21 boot-camp pay home.

Gordy was good about writing to his mother about life in the Navy. He always used U.S. Navy stationery and often signed with his whole name—Gordy Cox—but never added an "I Love You" or any other sign of affection.

February 1, 1941
The Navy gave me $100 worth of clothes and I have to learn a different fold for each article. . . . I've never seen so many crack-pots in one bunch as in this company. . . . We start marching Monday with a gun as big as a cannon. . . . The sun is plenty hot here and my neck is getting burned and my feet are sore.

February 26, 1941
I had my first liberty last weekend. I think San Diego is the prettiest town

I was ever in, especially Balboa Park. . . . While I'm thinking of it you
had better write me an invitation to come home on leave. They won't let
us go if we don't have a written invitation from home. . . . I am going to
take a test in a few weeks and maybe I'll qualify for the Communication
and Clerical School, the radio division of it, but I doubt I'll make it. . . .
I have never heard so much profane language in my life, but haven't
heard any new words.

March 22, 1941
Boy we sure live in a swell barracks now. There is linoleum on the floor
which isn't half bad to swab. . . . I still only make $21 a month. I got
paid yesterday so I thought I'd send you a little money. You need it and
I don't, and if you don't need it now you can stick it away. If I keep it I'd
just waste it.

Gordy set down his test paper. He'd answered only half the questions, and
he had no doubt he'd flunked. For most of his life he'd been told he was
slow, so there was no reason for him to believe he'd do any better on a test
now that he was in the Navy.

The test was one given to the thousand recruits who'd just finished the
seven weeks of boot camp. Those who scored in the top 20 percent would
go on for special training. The rest would be assigned to a ship and go to
sea. That was fine with Gordy.

When the results of the test were finally announced, Gordy was one
of the 20 percent who'd passed. They assigned him to Communications
School.

"I can't imagine how dumb those guys who failed must be," he said.

March 30, 1941
I'm trying to listen to Jack Benny and write at the same time. . . . Well,
we got started to school yesterday. I have to learn to type. It doesn't seem
so hard. They also gave us some dot and dash we have to learn. . . . I'm
flat broke.

April 10, 1941
There's a bunch of guys came in from Newport Training Station. Most of them are from New York. They sound as bad as the Texans. . . . Thanks for the card and the dollar but I really didn't need it.

April 16, 1941
There's a few guys here who keep getting me mad, but don't think I'll have any trouble. . . . Just think, in one month and a week I'll start drawing $36 per month and an automatic promotion to second class seaman.

May 12, 1941
I saw Martha Raye yesterday and a glimpse of Edgar Bergan [sic], but old Charlie and Snerd were in their suitcase. There are quite a few movie stars that come down here. Lew [sic] Costello the comedian was here. I got to talk to Budd [sic] Abbott for a little while. Well, so much for famous people. After all, they're the same as everyone.

June 10, 1941
Saw Bob Hope the other day. You probably heard the program over the air. . . . There are lots of Texans down here that are better than us. Just ask them.

August 17, 1941
Well, I'm still here and they haven't shipped me out yet. I haven't done any work lately except scrub a little paint. . . . I never saw so many dopes, most of them never do anything sensible. . . . Most of the guys are disgusted now but I think it will be better after we get out to sea.

Gordy graduated from Quartermaster Signalman's Radio School in Communications School and was waiting at the base in San Diego for assignment when there was a call for volunteers for submarine service. He'd never thought about being a submariner and had no intention of signing up, but while standing in line, a friend gave him a shove in the back and he was a volunteer. He could've easily stepped back into line, but not wanting to draw attention to himself, he agreed to go. The next day he signed the papers, and a week later he was on a ship heading to the sub base at Pearl Harbor.

September 12, 1941
I've been ashore out here and it is a dump. There isn't anything here. The town of Honolulu is like Front St. in Yakima, all of the people here are Japs or something that looks like almost Japs. If a person sees a real Hawaiian he's lucky. . . . I'm making $46 a month now and would like to save some of it. . . . A person has to have a lot of money out here to have a good time. I can't figure out where they get all that stuff about romantic Honolulu. It's the dirtiest and shackiest [sic] town I've ever been in.

October 2, 1941
Suppose everyone has gone back to school by now. I kind of wish I were going back with them. I guess I didn't realize that I was doing alright then or else I thought the Navy was too much of a good thing. It wouldn't be so bad if a person could see some white people when he went ashore instead of a bunch of Japs, Chinks, and Hanakies. The Hanakies look like Philippinos [sic] only blacker. The only people that will talk to you are someone trying to get your money or a drunk sailor. Speaking of dumb sailors reminds me about the other night. Elmer, a friend of mine, talked me into drinking two or three beers and if it hadn't been time to come back to the ship then I probably would have been a drunken sailor. It's sure a job to keep from going out and getting drunk or something. There's nothing else to do. . . . I haven't gotten a letter from you since I came back off leave. Have you forgot that you have a sailor son or did you disown me?

October 20, 1941
Looking forward to June 13, 1944. That's when I get out. I wish I could finish high school now. Somehow I don't regret joining the Navy

*but I wish I were out. I learned considerable since I joined although it
wouldn't help me in getting a job. . . . I don't know whether I'll be back
home for Christmas. I doubt whether Roosevelt himself knows, although
there are rumors about being back on the 1st of the year. . . . Hula
dancers—Phooey. The only hula dancers over here are in photo shops
where you pay 50 cents to get your picture taken with them, and half of
the time they're not real Hawaiians.*

It was November 8, 1941, a month before the attack on Pearl Harbor,
and Gordy was aboard the USS *Sculpin* as it sailed into Manila Bay. The
Sculpin, named after a small, grotesque fish with a large shining head and
short tapered body, was one of twelve submarines being transferred from
the Pacific Fleet at Pearl Harbor to the Asiatic Fleet based in Manila. For
Gordy, a guy with no mechanical background or training, the submarine
was still one big mechanical puzzle. Because he hadn't been to Sub School
like a lot of guys on the crew, he was scared he wasn't smart enough to
learn what he needed to become qualified or perform under pressure. It
helped that he was assigned as a mess cook.

He was happy to be coming to Manila. Anything, he figured, had to
be better than Honolulu and the unfriendly locals. From what he'd heard,
Manila was a city where the locals treated servicemen well, even if it was
only to get them to spend their money. Plus, the Philippine women were
supposedly very friendly. And as far as the threat of war, if the top brass were
concerned that it was about to start, the news hadn't drifted down to Gordy.

Admiral Thomas Hart had been put in command of the Asiatic Fleet,
and he believed that a major weakness of the war plan was the inadequacy
of that fleet. He also believed that a Japanese attack on the Philippines was
imminent, so he took over with an iron fist, requesting reinforcements. In
response to his plea, top Navy brass sent him the submarine tender *Holland*
and an escort of twelve submarines, including the *Sculpin,* swelling the
Asiatic submarine force to twenty-nine. Fearing that the surface ships stationed in Manila Bay would be vulnerable to an attack, Hart ordered them
withdrawn to the south. All the subs remained in Manila Bay.

Gordy knew nothing of these strategic decisions. He was just eager to get liberty in Manila so he could go ashore and find out if Filipino women were as friendly as advertised. Before heading ashore, however, he and the crew had to listen to a lecture from an officer warning about the danger of venereal diseases. "It's worse here in the Philippines than anywhere," the officer said, showing the men photos of genitals grossly deformed by syphilis and gonorrhea. "But I'm sure some of you guys won't heed the warning. And you'll be sorry."

December 8 and dawn was breaking over Manila Bay. Gordy was in his bunk. Several days earlier, he and his buddy Otis Taylor had gone to a cabaret in Manila, and while a couple of other crewmates danced away the evening with some of the Filipino girls, he and Otis had pounded down a half dozen Canadian Club and 7-Ups. They hadn't danced because neither knew how.

To Gordy, Manila was as seedy as Honolulu, only dirtier. What struck him most were the ramshackle houses and the poverty, orphans wandering the streets, begging for handouts, sleeping in alleys. He had yet to meet any Filipino women.

Stirring in his bunk, Gordy vaguely heard someone ordering him to get up. It seemed too early. As he drifted back to sleep, someone else shook him. "The Japs have bombed Pearl Harbor!" a voice shouted.

Within minutes everybody on board was at his station, getting the *Sculpin* ready to leave the harbor. The skipper, Lucius Henry Chappell, had already received a message from Commander Hart, alerting all submarines and Navy aircraft to immediately begin waging unrestricted warfare. It was assumed that it would be only a matter of hours, maybe minutes, before the Japanese began attacking the Philippines. With all the submarines lined up together, they were sitting ducks.

The Japanese plan was for roughly simultaneous attacks on Malaya, Thailand, American-held Guam and Wake, Hong Kong, Singapore, the Philippines, and Pearl Harbor. The raid on Pearl Harbor was meant to destroy the U.S. Pacific Fleet in its home port. The other attacks were meant to serve as preludes to full-scale invasion and occupation, as well as to secure resources the U.S. embargo was preventing from reaching Japan.

The Philippine Islands, some 7,000 in number, form a natural barrier between Japan and the rich resources of Southeast Asia. Under American control since the Spanish-American War, in 1941 the Philippines formed the westernmost U.S. outpost—5,000 miles from Pearl Harbor and over 8,000 miles from Gordy's home in Yakima. By contrast, Manila was only 1,800 miles from Tokyo. By 1941, Japan controlled much of the surrounding territory, including Formosa, a strategic air base only 600 miles to the north. Although the United States had maintained military forces in the Philippines, including a substantial number of indigenous units, the islands were largely unprepared for hostilities with Japan. A key to the Japanese strategy was to strike and destroy MacArthur's air force there. If American airpower were destroyed, Japanese troops would be able to invade and capture the Philippines, then push south to capture Borneo, Sumatra, Java, Timor, and New Guinea. The Japanese fully expected that MacArthur would have the planes ready to fight.

For reasons never fully explained, MacArthur did not have his planes ready and his ground troops were spread too thin, even though the Japanese intent to attack was clear. American radar had picked up enemy aircraft heading toward the Philippines and Clark Field from Formosa the morning of the eighth. They struck at noon, and by the end of the raid forty minutes later, one-half of America's total airpower in the South Pacific had been destroyed. In all, fifty-five men were killed and over a hundred wounded. The disaster at Clark Field would give air control to the Japanese, and, coupled with inadequate ground forces and a disabled Navy, the fate of the Philippines seemed hopeless.

With the American Navy's Asiatic surface fleet having been sent to the south, the weight of the naval defense of the Philippines now fell to the submarine force. Sunshine Murray, the designated operations officer for Asiatic submarines, hastily addressed the skippers of the twenty-nine subs moored in Manila Bay: "Don't try to go out there and win a Congressional

Medal of Honor in one day. The submarines are all we have left. Your crews are more valuable than anything else. Bring them back."

Gordy joined his crewmates as the *Sculpin* waited its turn with the other submarines to refuel and load stores and torpedoes. With all the subs gathered in the bay like targets on a firing range, there was great urgency to get these ships out to sea before more Japanese planes came swooping down out of the sky.

Late in the afternoon of the eighth, the *Sculpin* sailed out of Manila Harbor, one of five subs assigned to patrol the eastern side of the island. After leaving the other ships, it sailed east through the San Bernardino Strait at the southern tip of Luzon, the biggest Philippine island, then headed north, up the east coast to patrol off Lamon Bay, a possible landing sight for a Japanese invasion from the east. En route, the ship stayed submerged during the day and surfaced only after dark. Each evening, Gordy looked forward to coming up for air.

Shortly after the ship left Manila, its air-conditioning had quit. Efforts by the auxiliary men to fix it failed, and with the engines running hot, the heat was dispersed through the sub. The temperature inside the ship hovered between 100 and 105 degrees. Like the rest of the crew, Gordy stripped down to just his shorts. All the men were sweating profusely, dripping onto the deck, making walking through the boat a slippery proposition. Sleeping was also difficult. With not enough bunks to go around, the men slept in shifts, grabbing any available bunk. The mattresses soon became completely sodden. Gordy tried placing a towel atop the mattress, but it quickly got soaked too, and when he hung it up, the humidity inside the ship prevented it from drying. Adding to the discomfort was the fact that the ship had been in such a rush to leave Manila that there was a shortage of distilled water. Drinking water was rationed. Showers weren't allowed.

Gordy soon developed a severe rash, particularly bad in his armpits and crotch. At first he worried that it might be a symptom of one of the venereal diseases the crew had been warned about, but he knew he had not had sex in the Philippines. He soon learned it was a heat rash.

The pharmacist's mate tried several treatments, but none worked. With each day, the conditions on the ship worsened—a dwindling supply of drinking water, no showers, slippery deck, wet mattresses, high temperatures and humidity, and a growing stench. The only relief was at night when the ship surfaced and the men could go topside for air, but outside it was 80 degrees and humid, offering little respite. The meal schedule was changed so that dinner was served while the ship was on the surface in order to keep down the heat from cooking.

This was no way to start a war, thought Gordy.

After a few days, a treatment was discovered to combat the rash—torpedo fuel. It was not the fuel's only alternative use. On most World War II subs, the pure grain alcohol used for the fuel in torpedo motors was also used to produce a short, powerful high with little in the way of a hangover, which was ideal for men in a stressful environment who wanted a bit of relief but didn't want to be fuzzy on duty. Conventional alcohol was prohibited on board; the Navy believed that life at sea was uncompromising enough, especially during wartime, and any abuse of alcohol would be totally unacceptable. But that didn't stop the *Sculpin*'s crew from hiding a mini-still in the machinist's room. The torpedo-fuel cocktails they concocted were known as "Pink Ladies," so named because the Navy added a pink coloring to the torpedo fuel to indicate it was not meant for drinking. The crew sneaked slices of bread out of the kitchen that they used to filter the fuel. Usually, they mixed the fuel with coffee. Gordy had tried a sip from a coffee cup only once but hated it, figuring it must be an acquired taste. Instead, he spent most of his spare time studying. From his perspective, the information about the operation of the submarine he was trying to digest was hard enough to grasp while sober, so why make it even harder by ingesting 180-proof Pink Lady? He did, however, apply the torpedo fuel to his rash. It stung like hell, but it did diminish his rash and cool him down.

Gordy retrieved the Pall Mall tucked behind his ear, then struck a match. It didn't light. He tried again, but still no luck. The humidity inside the ship made it tough to light a match. He tucked the cigarette back behind his ear and continued to read his manual on the ship's hydraulics.

Gordy had taken up smoking shortly after coming aboard the *Sculpin*. Everybody, it seemed, smoked: FDR, Clark Gable, Joe DiMaggio. By Gordy's count, there were only a couple of guys on the ship who didn't. Cigarette smoke permeated the ship, adding more carbon monoxide to the air, and another smell to deal with. For Gordy, smoking had become a way to deal with the tension. There was now a heightened sense of urgency and alarm to everything happening on board. They were in enemy waters, and their base back in Manila Bay had been destroyed.

Moving north, the *Sculpin* found itself running right into the throat of a fierce December storm that relentlessly pounded the ship, making the search for the enemy even more difficult. The constant bobbing up and down and pitching to and fro was unnerving. At times it felt as if the ship was totally helpless against the raging sea and squalling sheets of rain. The bouncing was also making Gordy seasick.

Despite its being a goal of every new submariner to become qualified, Gordy didn't feel driven to pass the test. He studied because he'd been told to. But down deep he had doubts that he'd ever be able to qualify. Sometimes he would read the same sentence in his manual over and over and still not understand it. But he persisted, spending his spare time studying rather than joining crewmates for poker or acey-deucey at the mess tables.

Gordy donned his rain gear and climbed the ladder to take his position as the port-side lookout. They were on the surface to recharge the batteries. Standing on the platform, he leaned against the waist-high ring; there was no hook or chain to secure him. Swells crashed over the bow and against the superstructure, banging him around in his little cage. No stars. No lights. Just darkness and the storm.

This was the third day of the storm. Standing lookout, he was soaked to the bone, cold, wet, and miserable. Raindrops coated the lens of his binoculars. The visibility was abysmal. The ship rode a swell, then dove down the other side, driving the bow straight into the next swell, kicking the screws out of the water as she went over the top and down again—

movements endlessly repeated, hour after hour, pounding the ship's machinery and wearing on Gordy's nerves. He threw up again and again.

After several days of their being buffeted by the storm, a shipmate on lookout spotted two Japanese battleships in the distance. Getting a bearing was difficult. The vessels could be seen only when the *Sculpin* crested atop a swell. At first Captain Chappell, a soft-spoken, easygoing southerner, chose not to fire on the two ships. Part of the cautious breed of captains in charge at the start of the war, he was respected and well liked by his crew. But despite Chappell's caution and the difficulty in getting an accurate reading, he couldn't resist the temptation to fire his first shots of the war. He launched two torpedoes. They both exploded halfway to the target.

The Asiatic sub force was off to a miserable start. None of the twenty-nine subs assigned to protect the Philippines had sunk an enemy ship. Several had had close-range opportunities, but their torpedoes had malfunctioned. Facilitated by the pitiful failure of the U.S. Navy's submarine force and its flawed torpedoes, the Japanese had successfully invaded the Philippines.

Critics, including Clay Blair Jr., a leading submarine historian, were quick to point out the mistakes that had been made in the planning and execution of the submarines' defense of the Philippines. For starters, the sailors' training had been inadequate. This limited preparation had neglected such basic factors as the psychological effects of long-term patrols or even how much food to take on board. Poor maintenance of the ships was another issue. Almost without exception, the Asiatic Fleet's subs suffered continuous engine breakdowns because of outdated or poorly repaired equipment. Another mistake was basing the subs in Manila, which had been good for liberty and recreation but unwise as a base for operations. When MacArthur's airpower was destroyed, the fleet was left unprotected. Once the combat began, the plan of defense was weak. Captains were told to patrol briefly and cautiously, and to place survival ahead of inflicting damage on the enemy. But with the submarines cast as the main naval offense, critics believed a bold call for action was needed, not caution. And perhaps the Navy's most dangerous mistake was its failure to adequately test the Mark XIV torpedo. Even the simplest of tests would have revealed the weapons' flaws, and measures could have been taken to repair them so that the ships would not have had to go into battle effectively unarmed.

Within the submarine force there was a feeling of frustration for failing to stop the Japanese advances. By the end of December, the Asiatic Fleet had mounted forty-five separate attacks, firing ninety-six torpedoes. Postwar Japanese records confirmed only three ships sunk. In terms of the overall impact on the war, the loss of Manila and Luzon was a greater military setback to the United States than the loss of its battleships at Pearl Harbor. It let the Japanese overrun the Philippines and launch their invasions to the south. Admiral Ernest King, Chief of Naval Operations, later called it "a magnificent display of bad strategy."

With the American fleet forced to flee its base at Manila, the *Sculpin* and the rest of the subs no longer had a safe harbor. The *Sculpin* was ordered to proceed to Balikpapan, on the east coast of Borneo, to refuel, its crew already exhausted, the war less than a month old. Gordy was happy for the respite, even if it would only be for a few hours. A few days earlier he had been given a certificate acknowledging his graduation from polliwog (a sailor who had not crossed south of the equator) to the status of shellback (one who had). It was a Navy tradition, and it had given him a measure of pride at a time when he was feeling overwhelmed by all he still needed to learn about the ship. He placed the certificate in the scrapbook he carried in his belongings.

Despite the bad start to the war, the crew had the feeling that the problems were just temporary. America was on the right side of the conflict, God was on their side, and their power would soon prevail.

After forty-five long, grueling days on its first patrol, the *Sculpin* arrived for supplies and repairs in the harbor at Surabaya, Java. The second-largest city in Indonesia after Jakarta, Surabaya was an important commercial center for Southeast Asia. Java was a Dutch colony, and a key target of Japanese expansion.

For Gordy, the stop couldn't come soon enough. What was supposed to have been a three-week patrol had lasted twice as long. But now, much to his relief, they were scheduled for a leave of five days.

Located on the north side of Java in the Bali Sea, the harbor at Surabaya was crowded with American ships fleeing south from the advancing Japanese. Many of these ships had been damaged, either by storms or in battle. There was a shortage of everything—spare parts, torpedoes, food. The work to repair vital machinery, especially engines, was being rushed to hurry the ships out of the harbor before the expected Japanese attack. Their previous port, Balikpapan, had already been invaded, and it was only a matter of time before Surabaya was hit.

To get away and relax, the crew traveled by train to a large Dutch army base at Malang, a city in the mountains two hours from Surabaya. Gordy marveled at the beauty of Java, an island he'd never heard of two weeks earlier. It dawned on him that the slogan "Join the Navy and See the World" was true. Nine months ago his entire world had consisted of Yakima, Washington, and already he had been to San Diego, Hawaii, the Philippines, Borneo, and Java.

When the crew returned to Surabaya after a couple of days in Malang, Gordy was overwhelmed by the stench that greeted him upon reboarding the ship, a foul brew of sweat, diesel oil, and cooking fumes. He'd become adjusted to it while on patrol, but returning to the ship after the fresh air of the mountains had been a shock. Javanese laborers had been brought in to scrub the whole boat, and the mattresses had been sent out for cleaning, but the odor remained. Gordy dreaded the prospect of going out on patrol again.

With the war less than two months old, news was still sketchy and often inaccurate. Rumors ran wild. Most of the news that filtered down to Gordy was discouraging. Guam, Wake Island, and Manila had fallen. Singapore was under attack. So was Indonesia. A couple of days after the *Sculpin* left Java,

Japanese planes heavily bombed Surabaya and Malang. It was assumed that Japanese forces would soon steamroll their way right into Australia.

When Gordy had first signed up for the submarine service, he'd been told of the closeness and camaraderie of the crew, a band-of-brothers sort of togetherness. But so far, even though he'd just completed a war patrol, he didn't share that feeling. He didn't even know the names of half the men on the ship. He might see them at meals, or in their bunks, but he really didn't have any interaction with them.

On February 17, a convoy was spotted. As Chappelle prepared the ship for a surface attack, they were spotted. "Prepare to dive!" he ordered.

As the *Sculpin* passed 225 feet, Gordy heard a depth charge detonate, then another and another, each one getting closer. The ship shook violently. To keep from getting tossed to the deck, he held on to a pipe. There were two more depth charges, each of them rocking the ship. Lightbulbs burst. Pipes sprung leaks.

In the maneuvering room, depth control was lost, and the *Sculpin* plunged to 275 feet, then 325. Her maximum red-line depth was 250; anything below that could cause the pressure to pop the hull and create massive, unstoppable leaks. The captain struggled to get the ship under control. The rudder and stern planes froze.

At 345 feet, the captain brought the ship to an up angle and cut to two-thirds speed on the screws, bringing a halt to the ship's plunge. Everyone on board breathed a momentary sigh of relief. But while they had been fighting for depth control, a fire had broken out in the control room; salt water had leaked in and shorted electrical wiring. Black smoke filled the control room. Quickly, an extinguisher was used to put out the fire, but the smoke made breathing difficult.

Soon the leakage was stopped and the *Sculpin* was eased back up to 250 feet. The rudder and planes began working again. But from other parts of the ship, reports of broken gauges, grounded motors, and electrical shorts reached the control room. They were having trouble slowing down the propellers. At this speed, the Japanese would surely pick them up on their sound gear.

The chief electrician climbed into the electrical cubicle and removed a nut that had come loose and fallen off, jamming the controller. That slowed the screws, cutting down the noise and reducing the risk of being detected. Soon the depth charges stopped, and the convoy moved south.

A few days later, the *Sculpin* spotted a merchant ship, but missed with two torpedoes, then a few days after that they fired at a large destroyer, missing once again. The destroyer turned and came after them, dropping five depth charges, the first two coming very close, shaking the ship so badly that the starboard shaft began to squeal and give away their location.

Suddenly, Gordy heard a noise coming from the aft part of the ship— a loud, metallic banging against the hull. Bam. Bam. Bam. The noise was sure to give away their position, if it hadn't already.

He heard loud voices. "Somebody grab him! Quick!" Then there was the sound of a struggle.

In the aft torpedo room, one of the crew had been overcome with panic and the crushing fear of dying at the bottom of the ocean 8,000 miles from home. The man had picked up a wrench and begun wildly banging on the side of the hull, getting in several clean hits before the men around him tackled him and pinned him to the deck. To keep him under control, they dragged him to the mess area and bound and gagged him.

The depth charging stopped, and the *Sculpin* escaped to calmer waters and received a message to move southeast of Timor and head for Australia for desperately needed repairs to men and equipment damaged by the depth charging.

Later, Captain Chappelle would write in his report about the repeated failure of the torpedoes: "If the truth be told, the Commanding Officer was so demoralized and disheartened from repeated misses he had little stomach for further action until an analysis could be made and a finger put on the deficiency or deficiencies responsible and corrective action taken."

For Gordy, his first two war patrols had been worse than anything he could've imagined. He wished he'd never volunteered.

Part Three

ASSIGNMENT: *GRENADIER*

9

Chuck Ver Valin
USS *Grenadier*

Chuck was eager to end this patrol aboard the *Gudgeon*. It was the sub's fifty-third day at sea. The previous three patrols had been fifty, fifty-two, and twenty days in duration, and to this point in the war—August 1942—no other American submarine had spent as much time on patrol, or survived so many depth charges. The *Gudgeon*'s previous patrol had been at Midway Island in early June, one of twelve subs assigned to protect the island from an expected Japanese invasion that had been detected by American code breakers. The battle turned out to be the first decisive American victory in the war, with four Japanese carriers sunk and over 300 planes lost.

Chuck stood on the deck as the ship eased into the harbor in Fremantle, a small town located fifteen miles south of Perth on the west coast of Australia. This last patrol had been a harrowing one. With ten other subs, the *Gudgeon* had been patrolling the waters west of Truk, an island to the north of New Guinea. After a failed attack on two large transports, they were counterattacked by two destroyers that dropped a total of sixty depth charges, many of them rattling the ship. A severe storm was the only thing that saved them. Leaks occurred throughout the ship, and in the words of the executive officer, Dusty Dornin, "the crew was shaken up considerably." It would be Chuck's last patrol aboard the *Gudgeon*.

In early 1942, the people of Australia faced the danger of invasion from Japanese forces rapidly pushing south. These fears intensified with the fall

of Britain's supposedly impregnable fortress of Singapore and the capture of 15,000 Australian troops. Then, on February 19, Japanese planes
bombed Darwin, on the northern coast, an attack seen as a prelude to a
full-scale invasion.

With most of their military already stationed overseas, Australians
knew they were vulnerable to a war fought on their home soil. Word spread
of the Japanese atrocities in China and Korea, with millions slaughtered.
The country had unprotected coastlines and no hope for protection from
its motherland, Britain, which was fighting for its own survival; nor could
they count on the Dutch, who had already lost their homeland to the
Germans and were seeing their resistance crumbling in the Dutch East
Indies. To protect against an invasion, citizens of Perth and Fremantle did
what they could in setting up a defense, erecting barbed-wire entangle-
ments on the beaches, digging slit trenches, blackening streetlights, and
installing air-raid alarms.

Australia now looked to America as the "keystone" of the effort to stop
the Japanese advance. But the Americans were battle scarred and in retreat
as well, having been run out of the Philippines and forced to depend heavily on a submarine fleet armed with inexperienced leadership, exhausted
crews, and defective torpedoes.

The arrival on March 3, 1942, of the submarine tender *Holland,* followed by Gordy Cox's ship, the *Sculpin,* inaugurated Fremantle as the U.S.
Navy's primary submarine base for the rest of the war, a place for the Navy
to repair damage, assess losses, heal wounds, and find temporary relief
from the stress of war. In addition to a good harbor and sufficient piers,
Fremantle had the advantage of being outside the range of land-based
Japanese aircraft.

The American sailors were universally welcomed in Perth and Fremantle, greeted with huge relief, gratitude, and an almost starry-eyed ecstasy.
The citizens took pleasure in seeing American uniforms on the street. As
more and more submariners arrived, hotels, taxis, and cabarets all thrived.
To house the sailors on leave, the Navy rented out entire hotels. Organiza-

tions fell all over themselves to treat the Americans well. A giant Fourth of July celebration was held at the Perth Zoo.

Within a few short months, the Americans had become a pervasive presence. About the only place this wasn't recognized was in the newspapers; because of security issues, the government was censoring coverage of the American arrival, and most of the time the press pretended the Americans hadn't arrived. But an article in the *Fremantle Sentinel* titled "The Anglo-Saxon Race—America and Australia Unite" defied the censorship:

> *The Americans are well-liked here, and on all sides favorable comments can be heard. The recent arrivals are a fine type of men, particularly well set up, and also smartly uniformed. The absence of heavy drinking, and also the fact that they have friendly manners, these things are winning for them much appreciation. These men are certainly a good type, well paid and mostly skilled men.*

The Australian press made every attempt to paint the notion of Anglo-Saxon superiority, repeatedly warning about the "Yellow Peril" and the savagery of the "myopic, slant-eyed Asians." Nobody was more impressed with the superiority of these newly arrived men than Australian women; it was widely known that each new ship was greeted by a welcoming chorus of admiring females.

With so many Australian boyfriends, husbands, and lovers gone to war, the women had been deprived of local male company, and the newcomers personified the Hollywood dream: they were described as handsome and worldly, a mixture of vulnerability and brashness, usually somewhat courtly in their manners, somehow less crude than the Australian men they were used to. Plus, the Americans had money to burn. The wartime pay of submariners was three or four times the pay of local men, and the sailors didn't hesitate to spend it, treating the women to fancy presents and expensive entertainment. The ultimate dream for many of these women was to hook one of these men and eventually move to America.

Relationships quickly developed, ranging from the intensely romantic to the coldly commercial. There were six brothels on Rose Street in Perth, but unlike in Hawaii, attractive local women were available and eager. Most of the men visiting the brothels were older sailors, the guys Chuck liked to say "didn't want to waste time going out with nice girls to sip tea."

Sexual liaisons became common knowledge, and it didn't take long for conventional morality to crack under the American presence. Married women, their husbands off to war, also seemed eager to participate in this new social order. Perth/Fremantle was described as a living lab for demonstrating that during wartime, inhibitions break down.

Some of the Americans exhibited a self-confidence that bordered on arrogance, but the Australians were willing to tolerate the occasional bad behavior and bravado. Of course, not all of the servicemen were just about sex and romance. Most of the men were homesick and lonely and sometimes scared, looking for nothing more than the warmth of human contact; many were invited to private homes for a meal or an evening of talk. Chuck met a pretty blond girl from South Perth who invited him to her parents' house. He appreciated the home-cooked meal, but he also felt a little guilty because he was really only interested in the girl for, as he put it, "shacking up."

For Chuck, the two-week leave in Perth had been a wild time. Most of the *Gudgeon*'s crew had stayed at the Wentworth Hotel downtown, and he spent his nights drinking and chasing women, amazed at how many attractive and available women he'd been able to meet. During the day, he usually went to the beach or to the racetrack (he still harbored hopes of getting involved in harness racing after the war). Another daytime diversion for the sailors was going out in the countryside to hunt kangaroo. Chuck tried it once, but he never even got close enough to a kangaroo to fire his Navy rifle. But he still fared better than one of his crewmates, who opened fire on something moving behind a thicket, only to discover he'd just killed a local farmer's prize horse.

*   *   *

By October 1942, Chuck had been in Australia for two happy months. He'd transferred off the *Gudgeon* to the *Pelius*, a submarine tender. He was serving on a relief crew responsible for repairing the subs that came into port, readying them to go back into battle while their crews went on leave. Being on a relief crew was a common rotation for men who'd been under the stress of patrol, giving them a break before sending them back into combat. Chuck's job was helping to overhaul the diesel engines. He was enjoying the respite, but he was also getting anxious to go back out on patrol, back to a higher sense of contribution to the war effort.

But on this day, he wasn't thinking about torpedoes or evading depth charges. He was fixated on spending the evening with nineteen-year-old Gwen Haughey, a wavy- and dark-haired, brown-eyed beauty he'd met a few days earlier when he and a shipmate were strolling through an arcade in Perth. A private in the Royal Australian Women's Army who served as a messenger and secretary to the base commander, Gwen had been walking with a friend, and even though she was wearing her unflattering green wool Army uniform, Chuck thought she was just about the prettiest thing he'd ever seen. He got her number, and when he called to ask her out to a movie, she accepted, requesting that he pick her up at her house so that her family could meet him.

Gwen was the middle child of three sisters. Her mother was from England and, to help the family get through the tough times, often took in laundry and ironing. Gwen had warned Chuck about her father, a strict Irish Catholic and an ex-rugby player who'd owned racehorses before the Depression but who went broke because, according to him, the Filipino jockeys he'd hired had lost all his money by throwing races. Now he traveled the countryside shearing sheep. He had always closely monitored Gwen's dating, regularly taking her to the neighborhood priest for lectures on morality and proper behavior, and once, when he spotted her laughing and having a good time with a boy from the neighborhood, he gave her a whipping—with a whip. Chuck was prepared to be on his best behavior.

Like most Australian girls her age, Gwen was fairly ignorant about America. Most of what she knew had come from Hollywood films, which portrayed a mostly rich, glamorous lifestyle, with no images of the grinding poverty that Chuck and many of the other sailors roaming the streets of Perth had lived through. Her first impression of Chuck fit the image—handsome and well mannered, nicely paid, a young man willing to risk his life to save her country from the Japanese. She'd heard stories about the atrocities at Nanking and that the Japanese were cannibals, celebrating their conquests by ceremonially eating some of the vanquished. For her, these brave American men, risking their lives, were heroes.

Chuck approached the front door of Gwen's house in Victoria Park, a working-class section of Perth. He checked to make sure his uniform was just right, desperately wanting to make a good impression on Gwen's parents.

Entering the house, Chuck introduced himself to her family. From his fellow sailors, he'd learned the advantage of showing up with gifts to sweeten the first impression. Perhaps as much as anything, the Americans' long-term impact in Australia would be measured in what they introduced into Australian culture—Coca-Cola, hamburgers, peanut butter, spaghetti and meatballs, and American-brand cigarettes. To Gwen's sisters, Chuck gave chewing gum; to her father he presented a cigar and a 5-cent pack of Lucky Strikes; to her mother he gave candy.

As Gwen went to get a sweater, her mother followed her into a back bedroom. A moment later they both emerged wearing sweaters, both of them moving toward the door. Chuck looked puzzled. He held the door open for them, quickly getting the picture—Gwen's mother would be joining them on their first date.

They went to see Cary Grant in *Penny Serenade*. Chuck ushered Gwen to their seats; her mother took a seat two rows behind them. Along with everybody else in the theater at the start of the movie, they stood for the singing of "God Save the Queen." He could feel her mother's eyes boring into him from behind.

After the movie, they headed straight home. On the front porch, Gwen's mother stood right next to her. Chuck politely thanked them for a nice evening, then watched as they retreated inside. Clearly, this wasn't the first date he'd imagined. Still, he was totally smitten, and determined to see Gwen again.

It had been three months since that first date, and he was still head over heels. Being in love was a new experience for Chuck. He'd been infatuated with Irene back in high school, but that was kid stuff compared with this. At night he went to sleep thinking about Gwen, and when he opened his eyes in the morning, she was the first thing on his mind. Their time apart always dragged. They didn't get to see each other for fifty-one days at the start of 1943; he was in the Java Sea on his first patrol aboard the *Grenadier*, the sub he'd been assigned to after serving on the sub tender *Pelius* for a month. He would lie in his bunk thinking about places they'd been together, especially Leighton Beach and its idyllic, long white beach and gentle, warm surf, where they'd gone several times. Sometimes when he thought about her, he actually felt a chemical rush. And this wasn't just lust. They'd finally shared their first kiss, but Gwen had made it very clear that she would remain a virgin until her wedding night. That was fine with Chuck. He'd even talked with Gwen's commanding officer, who'd requested to see him to ask him his intentions with Gwen. He assured the lieutenant that his motives were honorable. He'd told his friends that she was the "marrying kind," and besides, on some of the nights he wasn't with her—she didn't get much time off—he had other opportunities to satisfy his physical needs. On a couple of occasions, he even had dates with two women the same night, getting off a streetcar with one to meet another on the corner. He rationalized this behavior the same way many of his fellow servicemen did—he could die tomorrow, so why hold back? After all, he and Gwen weren't officially engaged or anything. In fact, the subject of marriage hadn't been brought up yet. Nor had he actually uttered those three little words.

Chuck was glad to be assigned to the *Grenadier*. When he enlisted he'd said he'd consider staying in the Navy if he made second class petty officer by the end of his six-year hitch. He liked the work and the challenge of learning the intricacies of the submarine. He felt a sense of purpose, and a bond of brotherhood with the other men in the crew; he felt part of an elite fraternity that regular citizens couldn't understand. How could others possibly know the helpless quivering in your gut while lying several hundred feet beneath the ocean's surface with explosions shaking every rivet of your ship and driving your heart right past your throat into your mouth? They couldn't.

Upon first being transferred off the *Gudgeon,* Chuck missed the buddies who'd been with him on that first patrol when they were the first American warship to sail out of Pearl Harbor. In comparison, his new crewmates on the *Grenadier* seemed inexperienced, many of them on their first patrol. But he had confidence in its hard-nosed skipper, Captain John Fitzgerald. Fitzgerald wasn't a leader who demanded respect; he earned it, and he was friendly and accessible to his men. He was only 5 feet 7 inches, but as a collegiate boxing champ he had gained a "hard as nails" reputation; one of the officers on the ship, Lieutenant Al Toulon, called him "a little bantam with a tough face." On that first patrol up into the Java Sea there was a calm professionalism about Fitzgerald that Chuck appreciated, a leader not likely to buckle under the pressure, yet maybe a little more approachable than the other skippers he'd served under. Once while walking with Gwen in Perth, he'd run into Fitzgerald, and when he introduced Gwen, he was struck by how friendly and polite the captain had been.

Chuck slowly untied the bow of the little package Gwen had just given him. It was March 19, 1943, and Chuck knew that sometime within the next forty-eight hours he would be shipping out on his second patrol aboard the *Grenadier.* The crew never knew precisely when they would sail—departure times were kept secret during wartime—but they usually knew within a couple of days. He had traded with a crewmate to get this time off, and Gwen's commanding officer had generously granted her request for the evening off to be with Chuck. It seemed that Chuck had made a favorable impression on his visit.

Chuck opened the small gift box and removed a Saint Christopher's medal, a symbol of devotion to the patron saint of travelers, including sailors.

He slipped the chain over his neck. "It's weird," he said. "For the last few days I've had a feeling that something is going to happen on this patrol."

"Like what?"

"I don't know. It's just a feeling that won't go away."

"Why do you think that is?"

He took her by the hand. "Probably because for the first time in my life I have somebody I really care about."

It was the closest he'd come to saying he loved her.

She put her finger to his lips. "You're going to be all right," she said. "And I'll be waiting for you when you get back."

He rubbed the medal. "I'll never take this off," he promised.

10

Bob Palmer

USS *Grenadier*

Waiting on the pier at Hunter's Point in San Francisco Bay, Barbara Palmer could barely contain herself. It was April 29, 1942, and the submarine tender USS *Pelius*, with her husband Bob on board, was due in from Pearl Harbor within minutes. He was scheduled to be home on leave for three weeks, and they planned to cram as much living as possible into their time together. She'd even rented a studio apartment for the two of them in the same building on Pine Street where she'd been living with her Aunt Fern and cousin Margie. A month earlier she'd written and told him that she'd had a miscarriage. Maybe when the war was over she'd confess to the abortion, but not now. The procedure had taken place without any complications, and in fact she walked the two miles from the clinic back to her apartment afterward—in high heels.

Bob was proud to be part of the war effort, and especially proud to be part of the crew of the USS *Tuna*, as good a group of men as he ever hoped to serve with, but when he learned that the *Pelius* was returning from Pearl Harbor to Mare Island for repairs, he saw a chance to get back home to see Barbara. He'd thought about her constantly, especially after getting her letter about the miscarriage. He wasn't trying to escape combat, but he'd finished the first patrol on the *Tuna* with an earache that needed medical treatment. That was the excuse he needed.

On a building behind the pier where Barbara waited, two large signs offered evidence of the nation's war footing and fear of saboteurs: LOOSE

LIPS SINK SHIPS and KEEP YOUR TRAP SHUT. In San Francisco, an almost palpable paranoia had spread regarding enemy saboteurs, with constant warnings to be on the alert and to report any suspicious behavior to the FBI. One sign warned: THERE IS NOTHING TOO VILE FOR AXIS SABOTEURS TO STOOP TO TO ACHIEVE THEIR EVIL PURPOSES.

Eleven days prior to Bob's homecoming, sixteen B-25 bombers under the command of Major James Doolittle had taken off from the USS *Hornet* and conducted a daring raid on Tokyo. After dropping their bombs, the planes flew to China, where they all ran low on fuel and the crews either crash-landed or bailed out. Doolittle received the Congressional Medal of Honor.

In the weeks leading up to Bob's return, Barbara had seen signs of the war everywhere on the home front. "Remember Pearl Harbor" had become the great rallying cry and could be seen in almost every facet of propaganda—posters, pennants, napkins, patches, matchbook covers. The "V for Victory" sign had also become ubiquitous; people flashed it from cars, shops, sidewalks, recruiting rallies, and homes. Patriots hung banners in windows declaring that theirs was a Victory Home. Mothers put it on baby carriages. Donald Duck and Mickey Mouse flashed it in promoting war bonds. Little Orphan Annie encouraged kids to distribute V for Victory leaflets. Joe Palooka enlisted.

Everywhere Barbara went in the first few months of the war, she saw anti-Japanese publications and drawings with depictions of bucktoothed Japanese. The anti-Asian racism that had been fermenting on the West Coast boiled over following Pearl Harbor, especially in California. Seventy-five percent (94,000) of Japanese-Americans lived in California, and despite whatever loyalty they had to America, they were automatically considered guilty of sedition. In the aftermath of December 7, 1941, they were harassed, assaulted, evicted, and denied basic needs such as food, clothing, medical care, and shelter. They suffered property damage to their homes and businesses and faced constant threats of mob violence and lynching.

Although Barbara didn't actively participate in any of the overt discrimination, like most Americans she had no sympathy for the Japanese. Why would she? Her husband was in constant peril of being blown to smithereens by one of their torpedoes or depth charges.

On February 19, 1942, FDR had signed Executive Order #9066 prescribing the confinement of Japanese-American citizens in internment camps erected east of the Sierras. The roundup of these Japanese-Americans began in late March, with thousands hastily rousted from their homes, businesses, and farms and carted off to assembly centers at Santa Anita and Bay Meadows racetracks before being shipped to permanent internment camps.

A few pacifists objected to this treatment, but Lieutenant General James DeWitt, the commander of the West Coast evacuation, countered: "A Jap is a Jap. It makes no difference whether he's an American or not." Many of these Japanese-Americans held to a belief that complying with their government's orders would confirm their loyalty to America, but it made no difference, even though no Japanese-American was ever brought to trial on charges of espionage or sabotage. They were forced to adapt to primitive conditions in the internment camps, with overcrowding, barbed-wire fences, and dirt and dust a way of life. Armed guards stood watch over them. They lived with rumors and threats—that they would all be sterilized, that they would all be shipped to Japan after the war. They started each dreary day with the Pledge of Allegiance.

But none of that mattered to Barbara as she watched the USS *Pelius* ease its way to the dock. Bob had been gone for only three and a half months, but it seemed like an eternity. She was ready to bring him home to the privacy of her new studio apartment.

Bob's leave in San Francisco flew by. He and Barbara crammed as much living and loving into three weeks as possible, including a trip home to Oregon. Although Cora didn't buy Barbara's story that she had suffered a miscarriage after an adverse reaction to a shot at the dentist, Bob did, or at least he didn't push for more details. He scored a few points with Barbara's dad when he helped him fix the carburetor on his car. "At least that boy will always be able to get a job as a mechanic," said Mr. Koehler. At the end of the leave, Bob and Barbara both agreed that his departure this time was even more gut-wrenching than when he'd left right after they'd been married. On their last night together, she couldn't stop crying.

Bob rode the *Pelius* back to Fremantle, where he worked on relief crews for two months before being assigned as the yeoman for the *Grenadier*. He was an enlisted man, just like the mechanics, torpedomen, and all the other guys who got their hands a lot dirtier on the job than he did, but he identified with the officers. His little office kept him in close proximity to the officers' quarters, and he talked to them frequently, taking great pride in the service he provided. His logs were always grammatically perfect, thorough, and precise, with great attention to detail.

As the recorder of the *Grenadier*'s log, Bob had meticulously familiarized himself with the ship's design and history, taking pride in memorizing details and facts, such as that she was commissioned on May 1, 1941, and was 307 feet in overall length and 27 feet abeam and had a surface speed of 21 knots. She had ten torpedo tubes—six forward and four aft—and carried one 3-inch antiaircraft deck gun and two antiaircraft machine guns. After the initial shakedown exercises in the Atlantic, she sailed for the Pacific, and on February 4, 1942, she left Pearl Harbor on her first war patrol, commanded by Captain Allen Joyce, going closer to Japan than any Allied vessel since the beginning of the war, sneaking within one mile of the beach just north of Inubo-saki Lighthouse. On her second patrol she sank a large merchant vessel of 14,900 tons, then underwent a scary twenty-three-hour depth charging, surviving a total of seventy blasts that damaged the propeller shaft, knocked out lights, caused leaks, and twisted the superstructure. After repairs back in Fremantle, the ship's third patrol was spent primarily on station around Truk and Tol Island, and resulted in the sinking of a 15,000-ton tanker. Again, she survived a depth charging that severely shook the ship, returning to port on September 18, 1942. Bob joined the crew shortly after that.

The primary object of the *Grenadier*'s fourth war patrol, captained by Lieutenant Commander Bruce Carr, had been to lay a field of thirty-two mines in the approaches to the harbor in Haiphong, Indochina. The plant, one of the first submarine minefields of the war, was successfully executed at night as the *Grenadier* dodged junks and islands in water as shallow as twenty-six feet. Returning to base, the ship was forced to dive during another depth charging, the force of the blow as they hit bottom ruining the sound gear and causing chlorine gas to accumulate, which caused considerable suffering and breathing difficulties among the crew, but no permanent casualties. Upon reaching Fremantle, Lieutenant Commander Carr was relieved by Captain John Fitzgerald.

As the *Grenadier* prepared to pull away from the pier at Fremantle to start its sixth patrol, Bob frantically looked through the drawers in his office. He couldn't find his wallet.

It was March 20, 1943, and the *Grenadier* was headed for the Andaman Sea, from the Gulf of Martaban down through the Mergui Archipelago to the Strait of Malacca. Her assignment was to investigate and destroy enemy shipping. The *Grenadier* was the first American submarine assigned to the area.

Bob checked his pants pocket, then his footlocker. He closed his eyes, trying to remember where he'd last had it. It didn't take long to figure it out. He'd left it at Leslie Phillips's house, on the nightstand where he'd emptied his pockets before tumbling into bed.

He'd met Leslie a couple of nights earlier. He and Len Clark, his new best friend on the *Grenadier*, had been hitting the pubs in Perth and living it up like sailors about to go back into enemy waters. They ran into Leslie and her friend Hazel at the Prince Edward Hotel. Bob and Leslie hit it off right away, and when Leslie invited him to come for dinner the next night, Bob didn't see the harm. He told her about Barbara, and she told him about her husband, who was fighting in North Africa. Her offer of a home-cooked meal was just too good to pass up.

Bob put his hand to his neck and frowned, realizing that not only had he left his wallet at Leslie's, he'd left his ID and dog tags there, too. Not that he'd need any of that stuff on this patrol, but it was just irritating. He'd told Leslie he'd see her when he returned to port, so he'd pick up the items then.

11

Gordy Cox
USS *Grenadier*

It took Gordy over a year from the time his hot and stinky patrol aboard the *Sculpin* landed in Fremantle until he was assigned to the *Grenadier*. During that time he mostly worked on sub tenders, helping ready ships to go back into combat. He had time to write a lot of letters home.

> *April 3, 1942*
> *I'm getting along okay I guess. One day I'm cussing the Navy and everything else and the next I feel almost happy. But I know one thing for sure and that is that I'll never make good in the Navy. I just don't fit here. . . . I guess you'll have to wait until I see you to find out where I've been and what I'm doing. . . . Have you got any of that money that I sent? I've taken some pictures but they won't pass the censors so I can't send them. . . . I've only received one letter since the war started.*

> *April 27, 1942*
> *Everything is still okay on this end so you have nothing to worry about. It's very quiet here now. It's hard to believe there's a war going on. . . . I made seaman first the other day which I should have done long ago.*

Gordy liked Fremantle. Rear Admiral Charles Lockwood, a popular, can-do type of officer, was put in charge of sub operations there. He had been associated with subs his whole career, and one of his first commands, despite contrary advice from naval brass in Washington, was to lease four hotels—the Prince Edward, Wentworth, Ocean Beach, and Majestic—in the Fremantle/Perth area for the returning crews. He had made improving morale a high priority. The area had excellent recreational facilities, and there was no shortage of women.

Gordy had been transferred to the tender *Holland*. He figured he'd been selected because he hadn't qualified yet. During the previous three months while on patrol, he'd tried to study, but with his duties on the ship, his difficulties with reading, and the constant stress of combat, he doubted whether he'd ever be able to qualify.

On the *Holland* he was assigned as a mess cook again, an assignment he wasn't happy about. He also spent four hours every night on watch. Even though Fremantle was beyond the range of land-based Japanese planes, the fear was that an attack could be launched from aircraft carriers.

He continued to write home.

May 5, 1942
I hope you have stopped worrying about me. There's really not much reason to. You said yourself that when a person's time comes it don't make much difference where they are. . . . There sure isn't much to do over here. I've been trying to find a good pastime but as yet I haven't. I've met a couple nice girls and their families, but liberty isn't very good and there isn't much to do when you do get over. . . . All of the music over here was out before I left home.

The Navy decided to move part of its fleet stationed at Fremantle, including the *Holland*, even farther south to Albany. Should a Japanese attack sink the tender *Holland*, the fleet would have no way to repair damaged subs.

Gordy rode the *Holland* into Albany. From the deck, he could see a small town surrounded by barren hills. The town, population 300, was only a couple of blocks long. The crew of the *Holland* numbered close to 600, and with an additional 150 men from two subs that had accompanied it south, plus a destroyer tender and its crew, the resources of Albany were overwhelmed. But its people were eager to be hospitable, believing the survival of their country depended on these American servicemen.

With the ship moored in Princess Royal Harbour in King George Sound, the crew received liberty every fourth day. Almost daily Gordy listened to crewmates venting about the bad torpedoes. But it wasn't just the crews who were upset. Admiral Lockwood also listened to his frustrated skippers' complaints about watching helplessly as faulty torpedoes either ran deep, fired prematurely, or were duds. Lockwood tried to get the Bureau of Ordnance to conduct torpedo performance tests, but they refused, blaming the skippers for not preparing and firing the torpedoes improperly. So Admiral Lockwood ordered his own tests, which showed conclusively that the torpedoes didn't work. But the Bureau of Ordnance still rejected the results and told Lockwood to halt his testing. He didn't, and the further testing eventually caught the attention of Admiral Ernest J. King, commander in chief of the U.S. fleet, who intervened. Finally, eight months after the war started, the Bureau of Ordnance admitted that the Mark XIV ran deep. The solution included installing new firing pins machined from a light, high-strength aluminum alloy, using metal that reportedly came from the propellers of Japanese fighters shot down during the Pearl Harbor raid. Immediately, the number of sinkings increased dramatically. But the early course of the war had already been seriously compromised and the lives of thousands of submariners unnecessarily jeopardized, a mistake and scandal later described by naval historian Clay Blair Jr. as "the worst in the history of any kind of warfare."

Gordy continued to write home regularly.

June 14, 1942
I have a very nice girl friend over here. Her name is Linley Austin, Lin
for short. She is a pretty blond. I go up and have supper with her and her
parents almost every liberty and then go to the show or the dance. That's
about all I do.

July 9, 1942
I'd like to let you know where I am but that would be impossible. . . .
I'm still going with Linley Austin. We are going to a high school ball on
Friday. I can't dance very good, but nobody knows the difference. . . .
I'm sending some more money for you to stick in the bank. If you need
any of it go ahead and take it. . . . I've been to a few pictures lately, but
they are ones I've seen before. A person has to do something to keep from
getting any battier. I haven't been drunk yet but it's a wonder. I've done
almost everything else. . . . I've written to almost all of my old friends but
never received any answers. I guess everyone has forgotten me. . . . If you
remember please send me Readers Digest and an algebra book.

July 13, 1942
I still haven't heard from anyone back there. You can't realize how much
I would like to get home right now. Guess there's a lot of fellows feel the
same way.

Gordy celebrated his nineteenth birthday in Albany. In August, American forces invaded Guadalcanal, and after a ferocious battle, they secured the island in the first major land victory of the war. Word of the triumph slowly reached the submariners in Western Australia, but Gordy was more focused on his own situation. He wanted off the *Holland* and out of Albany, and if that meant getting reassigned to a submarine and going out on patrol again, that was fine by him. He soon got the transfer he wanted, not to a submarine but to another tender, the *Pelius* back in Fremantle. As it was with so many American sailors in Australia, he said good-bye to his girlfriend, Linley, both of them promising to stay in touch and keep the fire burning.

On the *Pelius,* he was assigned to polishing brass. Each day he would sit on the forward deck and polish away for a couple of hours, then go hide and nap or write letters.

October 20, 1942
[to his brother Willie after their brother Larry had married]
I hope you can keep a couple good looking babes from getting married back there. I'd hate to have to steal somebody's wife when I get back. . . . Keep the old town in one piece and I'll help you tear it up when I get back.

October 24, 1942
I have a friend who can sneak my letters past the censor so I can talk to you about the war. I'm now stationed in Fremantle, Australia. I was in Manila when the war started. . . . I'm completely out of danger now. I'm hoping to get transferred again, but I don't know where I'll go after that. . . . We were in Albany. That's where Lin lives. . . . I've only heard from Lin once and it's been almost two months since we left there so I have practically forgotten her. . . . I have figured out a way to tell you where I am and will use it in the future. In the p.s., take the capital letter at the beginning of each sentence and it will spell my location. The p.s. will have no meaning. . . . Do you realize I have half my enlistment completed? I hope the war is over when my time is up.

November 20, 1942
Well, I don't seem to be getting anywhere in the Navy. My enlistment is half over and I'm still seaman. All the fellows I joined with are third or second-class petty officers. Well, maybe if I hang around here long enough they'll realize I'm here and give me a rate. It hasn't done any good to study. . . . Tell Donald as to joining the Marines that it is entirely up to him but if it were me I would try to stay out of the service and get a job in defense work.

One morning just before he was to go on duty chipping paint, Gordy was sitting on a five-gallon can of paint thinner nursing a hangover and feeling sorry for himself. With his head in his hands, he heard a voice speaking in an Australian accent. "What's the matter, mate?" He could see a pair of brown shoes and coveralls, and quickly learned that it was a lieutenant J.G. (junior grade) in the repair crew.

Figuring he might as well tell the truth, Gordy unloaded his complaints. After listening to him, the officer issued a stern rebuke. Sensing he had nothing to lose, Gordy asked to see the commander.

The next morning he got his wish, and after stating his case again, he was surprised by the commander's response. "You'll be at sea tomorrow," he said, and assigned him to the *Grenadier*, which needed several men for her next patrol.

A few days before heading out on patrol with the *Grenadier*, Gordy wrote his mom again:

March 17, 1943
I'm not the good little boy that left home as you have probably gathered. I've been having a good time the last couple weeks but it's about over. I won't be able to write for a while, but don't let that stop you from writing.

12

Tim "Skeeter" McCoy
USS *Grenadier*

Tim got lucky. Punching an officer in a beer-fueled poker game was a remarkably dumb thing to do, but the fact that it was wartime and every hand was needed kept him from being severely punished. Instead, he was transferred off the *Trout* and assigned to the sub tender *Pelius*, which left Hawaii the next day bound for Fremantle, Australia. For the next several months Tim worked on relief crews getting subs ready to go back out into battle and trying to stay out of trouble.

It had been several months since the first American ships had arrived on the west coast of Australia, and there were mounting complaints from the locals about the American presence. The initial goodwill and tolerance were starting to wear thin. The sight of drunken sailors staggering down the street, some of them with young Australian girls on their arms, was getting old. In the first few months of the Americans' arrival, people had accepted the sexual flings and the loosening of morals, deeming it okay for local girls to have a frolic on the beach after the sun went down with a guy about to leave for war. For the most part, the warnings about the unrealistic hopes of falling in love and then galloping off to America went unheeded and now the reality of fickle lovers, unwanted pregnancies, venereal diseases, broken hearts, and tear-jerking separations was beginning to take hold.

Eventually, Tim got reassigned to the *Grenadier,* and he was on board as the ship headed out of Fremantle on its sixth patrol. Like his new crewmates Chuck Ver Valin, Bob Palmer, and Gordy Cox, he had mixed emotions about this patrol. On the one hand, he was eager to get back in battle and feel he was contributing to the war effort. He had taken his work on the relief crew seriously, but he liked the danger and the rush of combat. He hated the Japanese. It wasn't because of anything that had happened to him growing up in Texas; he'd never even seen one. This was a hatred born out of the destruction he'd seen at Pearl Harbor. To him, they were everything the propaganda had portrayed: "little bucktoothed, slant-eyed savages."

But while stationed in Fremantle, he, like Chuck, had found the love of his life, Valma Gray, a beautiful blue-eyed redhead who had recently been crowned Miss Perth. They'd met at a dance, and he'd wasted no time in letting her know how he felt, telling her he wanted to marry her after the war and take her back to Texas with him. For her part, Valma was enchanted by Tim's courtly manners and enthusiasm. She also found his Texas accent endearing. From that night on, he'd spent every possible minute of leave with her. The night before leaving on this patrol, he'd proposed and given her an engagement ring. She'd accepted and promised she'd wait for him.

The *Grenadier* left Fremantle on its sixth patrol on March 20, 1943. For the first seventeen days there were no sightings of enemy ships. Then, on the night of April 6, a small freighter of about 2,000 tons was sighted off Phuket Island. A surface torpedo was fired and there appeared to be an explosion, followed by the wounded freighter firing at the *Grenadier*, its shells zinging over the sub or landing in its wake. The *Grenadier* returned fire from its deck, but when the freighter moved into shallow waters near the beach, Captain Fitzgerald ordered the ship to submerge and move to the safety of deeper water.

The next sixteen days were again uneventful, with no sign of shipping in the area. Anxious to inflict damage on the enemy, Captain Fitzgerald sent a request to move to a more fruitful area. Then, on the moonlit evening of April 22, 1943, before the request to move was granted, the lookout spotted a worthy target: two large enemy freighters. Upon closer look, he saw they were unescorted. Relatively easy prey.

Tim felt the rush of adrenaline when Captain Fitzgerald ordered the men "to man battle stations." Fitzgerald was Tim's kind of captain—tough, straightforward, a look-you-in-the-eyes kind of man. His decision to aggressively pursue the freighters was not second-guessed. If the tide of the war in the Pacific was going to turn in America's favor, as it slowly had been since the battle of Midway, then the mentality of the new breed of submarine skippers was that they needed to spearhead the attack, to be aggressive.

Fitzgerald had gained even more respect from his crew earlier in the patrol when he confronted Thomas Trigg, a muscular mess cook from Texas and the only black on the crew. He was easily the most disliked man on board; the crew thought he was sullen and disrespectful. At the time, America was still a Jim Crow, segregated country, and most of the men on board had never been around blacks. The Navy was still segregated, and on submarines a black could only be assigned as a mess cook, helping to serve the men and wait on the officers. It was not uncommon for someone to wake Trigg in his bunk and order him to bring coffee to the skipper. Most blacks in the Navy were compliant, but not Trigg. Built like a linebacker, he'd arrived on board with a chip on his broad shoulders (or at least that's how the crew described it), a chip nobody on board was eager to try to dislodge. Earlier in the patrol, when someone allegedly witnessed him spitting into the officers' soup, a livid Fitzgerald ordered him up to the bridge and challenged him to a fistfight, an invitation Trigg declined. Fitzgerald put him on notice that he had filled out court-martial papers and would file them when they returned to port. The incident had elevated Fitzgerald's standing with the crew even higher.

Dawn had broken over the Strait of Malacca on April 23, 1943, when the *Grenadier* surfaced. The bright sunlight gave the promise of a warm, tropical day. Hours earlier, after encountering the two freighters, Fitzgerald decided to do an end-around on the surface to intercept them. But after getting into position and submerging, all he could see through the periscope was the plume of smoke of the two ships zigzagging away. He gave the orders to surface. Never mind that standard submarine procedure was to always stay submerged while in enemy waters, or that he was disregarding the fact that the enemy knew a submarine was in the area.

Shortly after the sub surfaced, the lookout on duty, George Stauber of New York, spotted a Japanese dive-bomber coming in their direction. "It's coming in low out of the northwest," he informed the skipper.

Fitzgerald hesitated briefly, waiting to confirm the sighting. As soon as he saw the plane, he gave the order to dive. "All ahead emergency!" he commanded.

The bow plunged underwater, heading down at a steep angle. At 120 feet, the executive officer turned to Fitzgerald. "We should be safe at this depth," he said.

In the engine room, Tim heard a turbulent swishing noise. A second later he heard a metallic click: the sickening sound of a firing mechanism activating. Then came the explosion, deafening, like "two trains colliding head-on at full speed." It was an aerial torpedo, a weapon weighing 1,900 pounds with a warhead of 500 pounds of TNT. Dropped from a low-flying torpedo plane and capable of hitting a submarine up to 300 feet beneath the surface, it was a hallmark of Japanese tactical effectiveness.

The *Grenadier* shook violently, listing hard to port, slamming Tim against the bulkhead and knocking other crew members off their feet. In an instant, the ship was going down, stern first, plunging toward the bottom of the ocean.

The lights flickered and then went out. So did all electricity and power for propulsion.

They were in total darkness, out of control, and plunging toward the ocean floor. Behind Tim, two men were sprawled on the deck, unconscious. Others struggled to their feet, groping for something to hang on to. Ceiling cork fell to the deck, lightbulbs shattered, locker doors flew open. Men were cut and bleeding. Groans echoed through the compartments.

At 300 feet, the ship slammed into the ocean floor, quickly settling into the silt at a 20-degree angle, bow up. A quick assessment by the crew revealed massive damage.

The propeller shafts were seized in a vise-like grip, pressed against a bulkhead. And with no propeller, the ship was dead.

In the engine room, close to where the blast had occurred, tubes were bent, pipes ruptured, gauges and valves broken. In the radio room, somebody had forgotten to securely fasten the ship's radio transmitter, and the explosion had sent it flying against a bulkhead, smashing it beyond repair and leaving them with no way to radio for help.

But the biggest problem was the salt water pouring through the loading hatch and other openings. To Tim it sounded like Niagara Falls. If these hatches couldn't hold under the pressure, he was about to die a horrible death. He thought about Valma.

Surprisingly, nobody was seriously injured from the initial explosion and despite the massive damage the ship and outer hull were still in one piece. Working frantically, the electricians quickly activated the emergency lighting, casting everything in an eerie red glow.

"Fire in the maneuvering room!" a voice cried out.

The smell of smoke rapidly permeated the ship. An electrical fire spread swiftly, sparks and short circuits popping everywhere. Tim knew that if the maneuvering room was lost, getting back to the surface would be impossible.

"Stay calm," encouraged Fitzgerald.

Stay calm? They were in a submarine that was on fire on the ocean floor, with salt water spraying into the engine room.

"All available hands man the bucket brigade," Fitzgerald ordered.

Tim found comfort in Fitzgerald's voice, trusting his leadership. The plan was to move the excess water from the engine room to the forward torpedo room, which would hopefully balance the boat, the first step in getting back to the surface.

The heat from the fire was intense, a temperature gauge now showing

120 degrees. Tim stripped to his shorts and stood in the bucket line between the motor room and forward torpedo room, passing along the buckets. There was urgency to the crew's efforts: if the water level reached the main propulsion motors, there was no chance of ever restarting the engines, and no chance of escape. Adding to the peril was that the ship had come to rest on a shelf, dangerously close to deeper water, with a strong current pushing it in that direction. If they went over the shelf, the pressure would tear the ship apart.

Men began to pass out from the heat and exhaustion. The ship's interior grew even hotter; the thermometer read 124 degrees.

An hour passed. Then another. Fighting against time, the crew continued its efforts to control the fire and balance the water level. They worked nonstop through the morning and into late afternoon. Men continued to drop from exhaustion, choking and gagging from the smoke. Still, they remained calm, everyone too busy to panic, and everyone still trusting the skipper. But the situation grew grimmer: renewed efforts to free the propeller failed and the available oxygen supply continued to diminish.

"If you're not working on the line, just sit still and conserve oxygen," ordered Fitzgerald.

After fifteen hours on the ocean floor, and with all efforts to restart the engine and free the propeller unsuccessful, the captain devised a new plan to raise the boat back to the surface. His strategy was to blow the water from the main ballast tanks, which could make the ship buoyant enough to rise to the surface, where it would be easier to restore full power and fix the propeller.

The necessary calculations were figured and refigured, but there were uncertainties. Maybe the ship was too embedded in the silt on the ocean floor to shake loose. Or maybe the crew had not bucketed enough water forward to balance the boat and allow it to rise on an even keel.

Captain Fitzgerald waited until 2100 to give the order to blow the ballast tanks; if they did make it back up, it would be under the cover of darkness. Finally, his voice boomed over the intercom. "Stand by to surface. Close all vents. Open all flood doors. Blow all ballast tanks."

Tim knew that if this plan didn't work, they were doomed. And even if it did work, they could still be doomed. Most likely the Japanese were waiting on the surface, ready to finish the job and send them back down to a watery grave.

As the ballast water was blown out, Tim felt the *Grenadier* shudder and then ever so slightly begin to lift. There was a momentary pause—she was either going to fall back to the ocean floor or rise to the top. The ship sank back to the floor.

Fitzgerald wasted no time in repeating the procedure, but once again the ship failed to rise.

With the air compressor failing, they were down to their last chance. Again, the ship shuddered, but this time it broke loose and started to rise, slowly, floating toward the top like a cork. The crew cheered.

Captain Fitzgerald was at the number one periscope as the *Grenadier* neared the surface. A quick 360-degree revealed no enemy warships, just a few sampans in the distance. The ship broke on top. "Permission granted for all hands to come topside," he announced.

Tim stepped onto the deck, the warm tropical night air filling his lungs. He glanced at his crewmates. Standing nearby were Chuck Ver Valin, Bob Palmer, and Gordy Cox, three young men he barely knew, all shirtless, all sucking in the fresh air. None of them knew anything about the others' love life or home life or religion. But now, in the middle of a moonlit sea thousands of miles from home, they were together, more scared than they'd ever been. Their ship was dead in the water, deep in Japanese territory, and they all knew that with daylight would come the enemy.

Part Four

CAPTURED

13

Chuck Ver Valin
USS *Grenadier*

The *Grenadier* lay dead on the ocean surface; only the slightest breeze blew across the Strait of Malacca. Standing on the deck, Mechanic's First Mate Chuck Ver Valin and the rest of the crew were drenched in sweat from the fifteen-hour ordeal in submarine hell at the bottom of the ocean. The coast of Malaysia lay a dozen miles to the east, but it might as well have been a thousand miles away.

By Captain Fitzgerald's calculations, they had eight hours of darkness to try to restore power to the ship and escape to safer waters. Luckily, there had been no destroyer or escort ship assigned to the merchant ships, but most likely other enemy ships would be in the area, or planes patrolling from a nearby base. In the morning, the *Grenadier* would be a sitting duck. Fitzgerald ordered the crew to gather around him.

"Men, it looks like I've got us in a hell of a mess," he said.

Indeed, he had made two crucial errors: he had not retreated to safer waters after they'd been spotted and he had surfaced in daylight. But nobody on the crew was blaming him.

The first order of business was clearing the ship of smoke by opening all the vents and using the engines to help suction it out. The second task was readying the ship for a possible battle. The ship's biggest deck armament, a 3-inch gun, had been knocked out of commission by the initial blast, but the 20mm gun was still operative. Below deck there were approximately twenty rifles, plus several handguns.

"Bring up all the guns," Fitzgerald ordered. "We'll need all the help we can get."

Chuck brought up a Browning automatic rifle. He'd been a great shot growing up and scored high in marksmanship at Submarine School, but this rifle was nothing like the one he'd used to hunt squirrel for the family's dinner back in New York.

On deck, Fitzgerald watched the sub's slow drift and its wide, phosphorescent wake. He heard the sound of the diesels, barely rumbling, echoing forward in the calm night. And he heard the soft silence of the bow wave, telling him what he already knew: his ship had little chance of regaining power.

Efforts continued to fix the ship's radio; without a working radio, there was no way to send out an SOS. Its transmitter had been severely damaged in the initial blast from the torpedo. The subsequent electrical fires had shorted out the receiver. Still, hope persisted that the radio could be repaired.

All the frames from the engine room through to the aft torpedo room were badly bent inward. The torpedo hatches were damaged, the gaskets so badly cut that Fitzgerald could slip his hand all the way between the knife edge and the hatch cover. All the hydraulic lines to the tubes, vents, and steering mechanism were ruptured. One of the mechanic's mates, Bernie Witzke, a rangy nineteen-year-old from Saint Paul, Minnesota, looked like he'd slept in a vat of axle grease.

In the mess hall the shock of the explosion had knocked dishes and phonograph records to the deck, shattering most of them. Chuck knelt down and sifted through the pieces, shaking his head to discover that all of his favorites—Armstrong, Ellington, Crosby, Goodman—were broken. He found a Victrola submerged in the sink. He sat on a bench, the sweat rolling, drips trickling from his nose, a pool of perspiration collecting in his shoes.

The cook had made sandwiches and coffee for the crew, but few of the men were eating, too consumed with repair tasks to think about food. Chuck hadn't been thinking about eating either, but when he walked by the table and saw a big can of peaches, he grabbed a soupspoon and dove in, the sweet thick syrup soothing his parched throat. Most of the smoke had been purged from the sub, but the intensity of the heat and toxic air had taken its toll, many of the men going about their business in a semi-dazed state, many still coughing.

If all efforts failed to get the engines started again and the screws turning, Fitzgerald's Plan B was to cobble together a set of sails and rig them to the periscope shears. They would hope to catch a trade wind and ride it to nearby Pilgrim Island or to the Malaysian shore. Once there he could disembark the crew and blow up the ship. Even though Japanese forces had captured Malaysia, it was possible that the crew could find sympathetic Malaysians to provide them refuge until a rescue could be organized. Or, if they couldn't make it to land, maybe they could sail to one of the sampans in the distance and commandeer it to shuttle the men to land.

Efforts to repair the radio failed. Whatever was going to happen to them, nobody would know.

Fitzgerald remained on the bridge for several hours, awake through the changing watches. At 2:30 a.m. he toured the boat, stopping in the engine room to offer encouragement. Returning to the deck, he cast a lonely figure, his granite jaw set, his slate gray eyes relentlessly studying the sea.

Chuck knew that if the ship was to escape, the engines needed to be able to turn the shafts. Normally, it took only 450 amps to get it done. Finally, after several hours of hot, sweaty labor, they got one shaft to turn, but only barely, and it took 2,750 amps to accomplish that. The shafts had been bent too badly.

At 0400, the bone-weary engineering officers and electricians reported to Fitzgerald on the bridge. "Everything possible has been done to reestablish propulsion," reported Lieutenant Al Toulon. "I believe there's nothing further we can do."

"Pass the word for all hands on watch to start rigging a sail," replied Fitzgerald. "On the double."

14

Bob Palmer

USS *Grenadier*

Bob sat in the forward torpedo room; he had a gash on his forehead and dried blood smeared his face. He'd helped gather canvas from all parts of the ship—mattress covers, tarpaulin from spare parts, torpedo covers, seat covering—and now he was part of the team assigned to cut and fit these pieces into a sail. Half the men snipped, the others sewed. Bob was on the sewing team; he had learned to handle a needle and thread as a boy, mending holes in his socks and britches.

"Skipper's ready to try rigging a sail," someone yelled.

"This could work," Bob said, holding the makeshift sail aloft.

As he helped carry the sail up to the deck, he coughed, still trying to clear his lungs. Dawn was breaking. The air was motionless, the sea like molten glass. Bob licked his finger and held it skyward into the gray-black morning, feeling nothing more than the slight chill of the waning night. When the sun came up, he hoped, so too would a breeze.

Captain Fitzgerald was on the bridge, perched on a jump seat behind the conning tower, staring down over the bow at the work party of sailors stringing up the sail along the lower guy wires to the antenna trunk. The patchwork sail was unlike anything he had seen when he was sailing in Chesapeake Bay as captain of the Naval Academy's sailing team.

But there was no wind and the sail hung limp. For the next two hours, as the sun came up, the sail would catch an occasional puff of wind, then go slack again. By 0800, all hopes of riding the wind to shore were abandoned.

Fitzgerald began to consider the unthinkable, the last choice any captain wants to make—to abandon ship. His thoughts were interrupted by one of his lookouts: "Enemy ship approaching from the northwest. Looks like a destroyer or a light cruiser."

Captain Fitzgerald quickly gathered the entire crew on the forward deck and pointed toward the approaching ship, now about five miles to the northwest. He began to choke back tears. "I'm sorry for this mess," he said. "I just hope I can get us out of it."

The men were silent.

By Bob's figuring, the captain had two options. The first was to take the *Grenadier* back down again, with the crew on board. If he did that, it was highly unlikely he could get it back up.

The second option was to abandon ship. If they did that, the ship would fall into enemy hands; it would be the first American submarine ever captured. Neither Bob nor anyone else on the crew had received any training on what to do if forced to abandon ship—or if captured by the enemy.

"I want all important documents and papers destroyed, including all Australian money," said Fitzgerald. "We can't let the Japs know where our home port is. Destroy any equipment that could help them."

Bob hurried down the hatch, opening his footlocker and duffel bag, making sure to remove all his money, which wasn't much. A couple of officers weren't so lucky. A few nights earlier, Lieutenant George Whiting had won $800 in a poker game, but he had to stuff it in a bag to go overboard. It was the same fate for the $400 hidden inside a flashlight that Lieutenant Toulon, an Annapolis grad, had won in a cribbage game.

Bob fought the temptation to stuff his pockets with mementos. He picked up a framed photo of Barbara, gave it a kiss, and set it on top of the bunk.

Bob turned, distracted by what was going on behind him. Several of the men were passing a flask. Bob assumed it was Pink Lady. It dawned on him that these men passing the flask back and forth would most likely be drunk when they had to abandon ship.

Chuck picked up the pillow on his cot and gently placed his watch under it in the middle, then set a picture of his parents to the left of it, a photo of Gwen to the right. Then he covered his little shrine back up with the pillow, giving it a pat as he turned and headed back up on deck.

Bob entered his yeoman's cubicle and began frantically stuffing paper into a duffel bag: the ship's logs and records of the ship's patrols, targets, torpedoes fired, fuel intake, mechanical repairs—all data the enemy would definitely want. As the ship's yeoman, Bob had compiled this data. Now it was his job to destroy it.

Lieutenant Kevin Hardy was also stuffing the ship's documents into a mailbag. To help it sink, he jammed rocks into the bag. The rocks were originally brought on board to weigh down bags of garbage thrown overboard during the patrol so the sub wouldn't leave traces of where they'd been. Bob put rocks in his bag too, and he and Hardy both cut air holes in the bags to help them sink.

With all hands on deck, Captain Fitzgerald stayed below, cradling a submachine gun. Making sure nobody was still down, he opened fire on vital equipment—radar, coding machine, cryptograph machine—anything he thought could give the enemy useful information. Bullets and shredded parts flew in every direction. When he was satisfied enough damage had been done, he headed up to the deck.

15

Tim "Skeeter" McCoy
USS *Grenadier*

Tim picked up a framed photo of his new fiancée, the red-haired Miss Perth, and put the photo on a bunk. Then he headed to the deck.

With everybody and everything cleared out from below, Fitzgerald surveyed the situation on deck. The bags of data, money, and everything else that could betray their origin had been thrown overboard, destined for the ocean floor. To the northwest, the Japanese ship was still bearing down on them, although lookouts now recognized that it was not a destroyer or light cruiser, as they had first thought, but some sort of merchant ship.

To the starboard side, Tim noticed one of the bags with the ship's documents just bobbing like a cork in the water. It had floated too far from the ship to reach from the deck.

"Somebody's got to go out there and bring it back," said Fitzgerald.

"What about sharks?" someone asked.

Tim stepped forward. "I'll do it."

That Tim was the first to volunteer didn't surprise anyone. In his short time on the *Grenadier*, he had already gained a reputation as the first to run his mouth and the last to back down. He dove into the water and started swimming. Neither he nor anyone else on board had seen the sea snakes swimming nearby. Poisonous sea snakes.

It took him a minute to reach the bag. From his spot in the water, he could still see the sub, but not the enemy ship in the distance. Pushing the bag in front of him, he turned and headed back toward the sub.

Halfway there he glanced to his left and spotted one of the snakes, five feet long and swimming behind him. He grabbed the bag, trying to shield himself. The snake moved closer.

Tim didn't know that sea snakes are air breathers and that although they can swim under the surface, they must come to the top for air. Mostly, they inhabit tropical waters and feed primarily on fish. Although not normally aggressive toward swimmers, they will attack if provoked, their hinged mouths able to open as wide as a man's thigh. Unless treated with antivenom, their bites can often be deadly. Frantically, Tim continued swimming toward the ship, the bag still with him.

The men on deck watched helplessly, one eye on their crewmate, the other on the Japanese ship. Several of the men held rifles brought up from below deck; two had machine guns, but no one wanted to risk a shot with Tim and the snake swimming too close together. Then, without saying a word, Second Mate George Stauber, the lookout who had first spotted the dive-bomber and yelled out the warning to the captain, stepped toward the edge of the ship, a pistol holstered at his side. Raised in Ohio, he had scored high marks at the shooting range.

He drew his six-shooter from his holster, extended his arm, and without seeming to aim, fired at the sea snake. It was a perfect shot, hitting the snake right in the head, blowing it to pieces. A few seconds later, Tim scrambled out of the water and back onto the ship, tossing the mailbag onto the deck. More weight and more holes were added and it was thrown back into the water, where it sank immediately.

"Jap plane coming out of the northwest!" yelled Bernie Witzke.

Everyone turned to look, and there, about a mile away, another Japanese dive-bomber was coming right at them. Tim spotted the two 100-kilogram bombs tucked under its wings. The *Grenadier* was a sitting duck.

Tim scrambled for cover behind the conning tower while the gunners took their position at the 20mm. The men with rifles and machine guns crouched into position. "Hold your fire until he's closer," ordered Captain Fitzgerald.

The single-engine plane swooped in, taking a run up the port side. When it was a quarter mile away and at 65 degrees elevation, Fitzgerald thundered the word for the two 20mm and two .30-caliber machine guns to open fire. A solid wall of fire erupted from the sub's deck, tracers streaking across the bright morning sky. The plane fired back. Tim heard the sound of bullets ricocheting off the deck and the clinking of bullets hitting the plane.

Chuck swung his rifle into position. He'd shot a lot of rabbits and squirrels as a kid, so he knew he needed to aim in front of the plane. He fired, the gun's report echoing a foot from Bernie Witzke's head. "Hit the goddamn Jap, not me," yelled Bernie.

Chuck fired again. The plane was low and close enough that he could see the pilot's face. With so much fire bursting from the deck, he couldn't be sure if his shots scored a hit. He glanced up toward the conning tower, where Captain Fitzpatrick was firing away with his pistol like a gunslinger.

The plane suddenly pulled its nose up sharply and changed course to the left, going around the stern to get into position for a run on the *Grenadier*'s port side. The gunners all held their fire until the plane was close enough again, then let loose with another fusillade, the machine guns wildly blasting away.

"He's dropping his bombs," Tim shouted.

Standing nearby, Lieutenant Toulon quickly surveyed the trajectory. "They're going to miss, they're going to miss," he yelled.

The bombs drifted over the ship and exploded 200 yards off the *Grenadier*'s starboard side. The plane wobbled momentarily, then veered to the left, heading toward land. Fitzgerald ordered the men to cease firing.

Tim took a deep breath. The Japanese ship was still bearing down on them.

Fitzgerald ordered the men below deck one more time, instructing them to bring up as many mattresses as possible and toss them over the side. Tim wondered why, but did as instructed. Grabbing one end of a mattress, he glanced over and saw Bob Palmer furtively pull a bottle of pills out of his duffel bag and stick it in his pocket. Maybe it was for some kind of allergy, thought Tim.

With the mattresses in the water, Fitzgerald gathered the men around him again. He glanced at the approaching ship, then at the faces of his men, many of them, including Tim, still not old enough to vote.

"Prepare to abandon ship," Fitzgerald instructed, voice cracking.

The last order of business was to pass out the life preservers—belts that fit around the waist and inflated when the cord was pulled. With not enough to go around, the stronger swimmers were instructed to go without. Tim didn't take one. The rifles that had been brought up on deck and used to fire at the plane were thrown into the water.

As Tim and the rest of the crew prepared to jump overboard, Fitzgerald ordered Chief of Boat Withrow below deck to open the vents. Down below, Whiting first hurried into the officers' quarters and found a Victrola and a stack of records that had not been damaged. He hustled to the ship's PA system and pulled a record out of one of the sleeves, then set it on the turntable.

Upstairs, as the men readied themselves to go overboard, they heard the music—Glenn Miller's theme song, "Moonlight Serenade."

Tim remembered he and Valma had listened to that song the first night that they met in Perth, and the exhilarating rush he felt at having just met someone so beautiful.

He crouched, ready to jump overboard.

16

Gordy Cox
USS *Grenadier*

On his last trip below deck, Gordy pulled two pearl-handled knives from his footlocker. He'd bought them in Borneo when the *Sculpin* stopped to refuel after fleeing the Philippines. He also pulled out a ring his mother had given him for good luck when he left home in Yakima. Reluctantly, he tossed the ring and knives back into the footlocker and climbed up to the deck.

With the sound of Glenn Miller wafting through the tropical air, he jumped into the water, surprised at how warm it was. He wasn't wearing a life belt. A rubber life raft, loaded with cigarettes and sandwiches, was lowered into the water behind him.

Finally, with all the men off the ship and into the water, Fitzgerald gave the word to Whiting to open all vents.

Treading water twenty yards away, Gordy heard a whooshing sound, then watched Whiting and Fitzgerald jump off the ship and swim away.

It took just seconds for the *Grenadier* to begin capsizing. First the stern went under, then the shears and conning tower, and finally the bow, all in stunning silence.

Gordy felt sick. In the short time he'd been part of the *Grenadier* crew, he felt closer to these men than to the men on the *Sculpin*. Now their home was on its way to the ocean floor.

Turning, he saw the Japanese ship, now less than a mile away.

"They're going to shoot us," someone yelled.

The men swam in different directions, figuring they'd be harder targets if they spread out. Wearing just his dungarees and a T-shirt, Gordy swam toward the rubber raft; Trigg, the black mess cook, whose court-martial papers had gone down with the ship, was the only man in it. Trigg waved him away. "There's not enough room," he yelled.

Bob Palmer also approached the raft, and he too was shooed away.

"God damn nigger!" Bob yelled, dog-paddling away.

Within ten minutes of the *Grenadier* going under, the crew and its officers were spread out over a square mile, half clinging to mattresses, the rest floating with their life belts. Nobody seemed in peril of drowning, and no sharks had appeared, at least not yet. The sea snakes were keeping their distance.

On a mattress nearby, Lieutenant Hardy, an Annapolis grad and liked by everyone on the crew, clung to the side with one hand; in the other he held a water-soaked copy of *Reader's Digest* that he'd stuffed in his pocket before jumping overboard. He opened the pages and began reading the jokes from "Humor in Uniform" to the four other men clinging to the mattress. At first they looked at him as if he was nuts, and then they started laughing.

A shot fired from a deck gun startled Gordy. He waited for more shots, but none came. Then the ship turned and heaved closer. It was a merchant ship that had been converted into a corvette, a highly maneuverable armed escort, lighter than a destroyer. Its flag with the rising sun of the empire was clearly visible.

The ship completed another turn, and then the engine stopped. Gordy was one of the men closest to the ship, and he looked up and saw a rope ladder swing down over the side. On the deck, two Japanese seamen standing behind mounted machine guns signaled him and the others to start climbing up the ladder.

Gordy waited for an order from Fitzgerald, but unable to spot him, he swam to the ship, followed by several other men, and more swimming in that direction. He reached up and grabbed the bottom rung, then started his climb up, his arms weary from his two hours in the water.

As Gordy reached the top of the ladder, a Japanese seaman grabbed his arm and jerked him over the ship's rail and onto the deck. He scrambled to his feet, now face-to-face with a seaman and his rifle and bayonet. As he glanced around at the other Japanese, his first thought was how short they all were.

The Japanese seaman moved toward him, jabbing the air with his bayonet, barking orders in Japanese. Gordy stood frozen, not understanding the instructions. The man continued yelling, then swung his rifle, the butt smashing Gordy in the shoulder, knocking him to the deck, the bayonet now an inch from his nose.

The seaman motioned him to stand up and take off his clothes. Gordy removed his T-shirt and dungarees. The guard signaled him to keep going. Gordy took off his Skivvies. Totally naked, he glanced at his crewmates, who were also being ordered to strip as soon as they climbed aboard. They did as instructed, heaping their clothes into a big pile. The guards stood around them, bayonets pointed at the men.

They were ordered to sit in rows, officers and crew together, knees to their chests, arms on knees, heads down. The sun was now full in the cloudless sky, and it was hot, very hot.

Gordy thought about his mother. How long would it be, he wondered, before she found out that he'd been captured? Would the Navy inform her, or would she figure it out when his letters stopped coming? But mostly he wondered what the Japs were going to do with them. By his count, there were six guards, with rifles and fixed bayonets and two mounted .50-caliber machine guns, all aimed at the crew. Maybe the Japs would decide their prisoners were too much trouble and were going to shoot them and throw their bodies overboard. But that seemed unlikely. No American submarine crew had ever been captured, so this would probably be a big deal for the

Japs, not only a great propaganda tool but also a chance to gain information about the strategy and technology of American submarines.

Soon the ship headed full steam toward Malaysia (then called Malaya). Sitting in the middle of the crew, Captain Fitzgerald watched the guards, and when they turned their backs, he spoke in a hushed voice. "Don't give them any information," he instructed. "Just name, rank, and serial number. If they ask the name of our ship and where we're stationed, tell them it's the USS *Goldfish* and that we're stationed in San Francisco, and we're on a photoreconnaissance mission."

They'd been on board for an hour, maybe more. The deck of the main hatch they sat on was blistering hot, and they were starting to get sunburned. Gordy was beginning to get the idea that this ragtag crew of Japanese seamen didn't know what to do with them. Captain Fitzgerald stood up and identified himself as the ship's commander. He was taken at gunpoint down below.

Within minutes, Gordy and the rest of the crew heard him scream in pain.

The ship continued its course. For Gordy and others, it had been more than twenty-four hours since they'd eaten. In the early afternoon, a tin of cigarettes was passed around, each man getting one cigarette, lighting it off the nearest man. When they were finished, a guard collected and counted the butts, making sure nobody had stashed one away.

After several hours, they each received one cup of water and another cigarette, as well as a hardtack biscuit. Most devoured the biscuit quickly, but Gordy saved his, figuring he'd need it later. After a while, a guard brought up a five-gallon bucket to use as a toilet.

Late in the afternoon a guard motioned for the men to put their clothes back on. Rummaging through the messy pile, Gordy knew he'd have no chance of finding his own 30-inch-waist pants. He settled on a pair with a 34-inch waist, cinching a belt tight, its excess length hanging halfway to his knees.

As the sun disappeared below the horizon, a guard ordered the men to lie down on the deck. Gordy hadn't slept in thirty hours. Exhausted, he quickly fell asleep, awakening just before dawn as the motion of the rolling ship stopped and the engines went into reverse. The ship shuddered; it had pulled into a harbor.

Still lying down, Gordy heard voices coming from a dock. He rose to his knees to look, but a guard shoved him back to the canvas hatch cover. Other guards, more emboldened, moved between the rows of men, randomly selecting men to slap across the face or hit in the back with their gun butts.

A guard yanked Gordy to his feet and shoved him toward the starboard side of the ship. It was still dark, but Gordy could see soldiers on the dock. A guard tied his hands behind his back and blindfolded him, then did the same to everyone else in the crew.

Following the men in front of him, Gordy stumbled down the gangway and along a rutted road toward a waiting convoy truck. Unable to see, he felt a hand on his back, someone pushing him up into the back of the truck.

Half the crew was loaded onto one truck, the other half onto another, all of them still blindfolded with hands tied. Squeezed in between Chuck Ver Valin and Bob Palmer, Gordy felt the truck begin to roll down the rutted road.

Part Five

THE CONVENT ON LIGHT STREET

17

Chuck Ver Valin

POW

Jammed in tight with his crewmates, Chuck Ver Valin bounced along the bumpy road in the back of a convoy truck, blindfolded, hands tied behind him. He heard a whisper that they had landed on Penang, an island of Malaya. Another convoy truck with the other prisoners followed.

Known as the "pearl of the Orient," in 1941 Penang was a tropical island paradise filled with lush vegetation and exotic beaches, a popular destination for Asian travelers drawn by its sparkling sea and powdery white sand. It had been under British rule until the Japanese invaded in 1942. The balmy air held a sweet fragrance, reminding Chuck of the orchids he'd smelled walking down Hotel Street in Honolulu.

After a short ride, the truck abruptly stopped. A Japanese soldier opened the back flaps and ordered the men out. Other soldiers untied their hands and removed their blindfolds. The morning sunlight filtered through a grove of coconut palms. Chuck eyed a complex of beautiful white buildings that looked like a school or convent.

Brandishing rifles with fixed bayonets, soldiers hustled the crew through a large, solid wooden gate that opened onto an open grass courtyard, a setting that was serene, almost spiritual. Chuck's knees shook.

Before the Japanese commandeered it during their invasion, the Convent on Light Street was a prestigious Catholic school for girls, noted for a devotion to the arts and its botanical gardens. Located on several acres of land close to the harbor, it was named after Captain Francis Light, who first claimed the island for the British in 1786. Scrubbed white buildings with sturdy columns and arched corridors bordered a grass courtyard filled with coconut, mango, palm, fig, and breadfruit trees. Wild orchids scented the air, and the sound of waves drifted in on a gentle sea breeze.

Chuck felt a gnawing in his stomach. During the Depression, many nights he went to bed hungry, but that hunger was different. Back home he knew the next day would somehow provide something to eat. This was a different kind of hunger. All he'd had to eat since the ship had been torpedoed forty-eight hours earlier was a bowl of cling peaches and a hardtack biscuit. Word quickly spread that they'd be served breakfast soon.

Inside the grounds, the crew was separated; the officers, who'd stepped forward to identify themselves, were led to a room upstairs, and the rest of the men were divided into two groups and placed in adjoining rooms that had been used as classrooms before the invasion. The rooms were empty now, with barren white walls and concrete floors. Shuttered windows faced the open courtyard.

Four guards, armed with rifles and bayonets, ordered the men in Chuck's room to form two lines and stand at attention, shoulder to shoulder. These guards wore different uniforms than the guards on the ship. Chuck figured that they were part of the Japanese army, and from the stories he'd heard, an army that could be brutal.

Slowly, one of the guards walked down Chuck's line, glaring at each man. Next to Chuck, Gordy shifted his feet to get comfortable. The guard spotted the movement and moved in front of him. Without warning he swung his rifle butt and caught Gordy on the jaw; he crumpled to the floor. The guard kicked him in the ribs, then motioned for him to get back on his feet. Chuck reached down to help his crewmate up. Bad mistake. The guard rifle-butted him across the back, buckling his knees and bringing tears to his eyes.

For the next four hours, Chuck and everyone else in the room stood at attention, staring straight ahead. Every time someone moved or looked anywhere but straight ahead, they got a rifle butt in the back or to the stomach.

Chuck struggled to stand straight, his whole body aching from the strain. Another hour passed, and new guards entered, bringing with them a renewed sense of arrogance and brutality. One of them stood directly in front of Chuck and glared. Chuck stared straight ahead. The guard screamed, then smashed him in the face with his fist. Chuck staggered but didn't go down, quickly retaking his place in line, standing at attention, not daring to wipe the blood streaming from his nose.

Dusk came, the light in the room was turned on, and the men still stood at attention. There was still no food or water.

One of the men passed out, falling to the floor in a heap. A guard ordered the men next to him to pull him back up to his feet and support him in an upright position. These orders were given in Japanese, and although nobody on the crew spoke the language, they could decipher the meaning from the gestures and the situation. Other men passed out as well, and they too were propped back up by their crewmates.

Through the night they stood, the guards taking turns walking up and down the lines, randomly stopping to punch someone, sometimes in the face, sometimes in the stomach. By dawn, everyone had been knocked to the floor at least once, each collapse greeted by laughter from the other guards.

Daylight brought the hot tropical sun, draining the strength of the men even more. Still, no one brought them food.

It was Chuck's turn to go to the head. This had been the men's only respite, a trip made three at a time: out the door and down the corridor to the left, accompanied by a guard. The head was a small windowless room, containing only a toilet. Chuck and the other two men squeezed inside, shutting the door; the guard stood outside. While the other men urinated, Chuck quietly lifted the tank lid. Using both hands, he scooped out a handful of tank water and poured it into his mouth, swallowing slowly, savoring each drop. The other men did the same.

The second day passed and the men had still not been allowed to sleep or eat. Like almost everyone else, Chuck had a black eye and a swollen lip.

On the third day, the shutters on the window were opened and he looked out onto the courtyard. Two guards appeared, holding a stumbling man in khakis between them. His face and arms were a mass of bruises, his eyes swollen shut; he had been beaten almost to the point of being unrecognizable. It was Captain Fitzgerald.

Dragging him across the grass, the guards stopped next to a long wooden bench. Two other guards stood alongside, holding clubs the size of baseball bats. Fitzgerald was placed on the bench, then, on signal, the guards started raining down blows on his arms, legs, and chest like they were driving a circus tent stake. It was a contest to see who could hit the hardest and make the captain scream the loudest. Five . . . ten . . . thirty blows. They took a breather and started again.

Chuck felt like throwing up.

The beating lasted ten minutes, then a guard took two leather straps and tied Fitzgerald to the bench, his head dangling over the edge. He was barely conscious. Another guard raised one end of the bench, elevating Fitzgerald's feet above his head at a 30-degree angle. A guard carrying a teakettle approached.

With one guard holding a hand over Fitzgerald's mouth, another slowly poured the water out of the teakettle up his nose. He coughed and choked, flailing his arms, desperately gasping for air. Each time he moved, a guard hit him. Then another poured more water up his nose.

When the kettle was empty, they refilled it and poured it again up his nose. And again. And again.

Finally, Fitzgerald passed out.

Dragging the captain slowly back across the courtyard, the guards smirked, knowing they were being watched. They pulled him up the stairs and out of sight.

18

Bob Palmer

POW

The crew nicknamed the meanest guard Goldtooth Maizie (pronounced May-zee) because of the gold cap on one of his front teeth. When the light hit it just right, it sparkled, and he liked to flash it when he glared at the crew.

On this morning, he'd chosen Bob Palmer to pull out of line. Slowly, he ran his bayonet down Bob's forehead, pressing just hard enough to break the skin and leave a trickle of blood. Bob felt the cold steel continue down the midline of his face, between his eyes and down his nose, stopping on his upper lip. Goldtooth Maizie held it there for several seconds, grinning, flashing his gold tooth. Then, with a quick upward flick, the sharp edge of the bayonet ripped into the bottom of his nose, blood squirting everywhere.

Goldtooth Maizie shoved him back in line.

For three days Bob had been a captive, and for three days he had not eaten or slept or even sat down except on the ship.

But his suffering was not nearly as bad as that of his crewmate Charles Taylor, who'd gotten a bad case of gonorrhea in Fremantle; he had been trying to treat it with sulfur pills while on patrol, without much success. It had gotten much worse since being captured; his testicles had swollen to several times their normal size. To help relieve the pressure, he'd torn a hole in the crotch of his pants. His testicles had turned a grotesque purplish blue, extending like an eggplant out of the hole in his pants. He could only move if he reached down and cradled them in his hands to relieve the pressure. At times the pain was excruciating, and he would moan and double over. Crewmates pleaded to the guards to get him treatment; instead they made him stand at attention or crawl around like a dog, sometimes poking at his testicles with their gun butts.

Just prior to the scuttling of the ship, Bob had hustled back down below deck and fetched a bottle of sulfur pills. Several other men on the crew had seen him do this, including Chuck, and when someone questioned him about it, Bob claimed he did it for Taylor. Chuck didn't buy it, believing Bob had gotten the pills for himself.

As hellish as the physical torture was, the uncertainty was worse. What was coming next? Bob wondered. Would they be lined up against a wall and shot? Would they be starved to death? Would the torture and beatings get worse? Did the Navy know they were there or that their ship was missing? Would his resolve to survive weaken?

Sometimes it was hard to think about anything other than his immediate situation and surviving the next five minutes, or the bayonet being pricked under his nose. He tried to think about Barbara. He closed his eyes and saw her standing next to him at the church in San Francisco on their wedding night; how beautiful she looked. He remembered lying in bed next to her, his arms around her; how good she felt. He created a dinner menu in his head: big slices of honey baked ham, with mashed potatoes and glazed carrots. It was the glazed carrots he savored, the sweet taste filling his senses.

In whispers the crew pondered strategies for survival. They knew that they were at the mercy of their captors, but they all shared the same goal—to get home—and everything they now did would be to achieve that result.

Specific strategies were slowly beginning to emerge. It was clear that Tim McCoy was determined to stand up to the guards and be as big a pain in the ass as he could. Gordy Cox was going to make himself as invisible as possible and do whatever he could to avoid being noticed. Chuck Ver Valin thought he'd be best served by never showing them pain, never looking weak.

Bob's plan was to go inside his head and escape to a world where he was with Barbara again. She would be the light at the end of the tunnel, his reason to keep going. A part of him wondered if he had the strength and courage to keep going. Maybe under the pain of torture, he'd cave in and tell the Japanese whatever they wanted to know. As the ship's yeoman, he knew more than anyone except the officers about the ship's recent history and patrols. If surviving to see Barbara again meant revealing what he knew about any of that, then he couldn't be sure he wouldn't crack, no matter how much he loved his country and the men in the crew. Still, he was determined not to give the enemy anything they could use.

Bob heard the thump outside the window, the now-familiar sound of a coconut hitting the ground in the courtyard. On his way to the toilet, he'd seen them lying there, tantalizing. The last food he'd had was the hardtack biscuit on the Japanese ship four days earlier.

As a boy growing up during the Depression in southern Oregon, with its rich farmland, he had not suffered as much as others that he knew from a lack of food. The twisting, churning hunger pain in his stomach was a new experience.

He ran his hand over his face, feeling the stubble of his beard. It had been almost a week since his last shave and shower. The layer of soot and grime collected during the 125-degree ordeal at the bottom of the ocean in the *Grenadier* had been washed away in the ocean, but the days in captivity had given him a patina of sweat and dust, tinted with dried blood. More fastidious than anyone else on the crew, he always paid attention to his appearance, whether he was in civilian clothes or his Navy blues. He placed a shower just below sleep and a full plate of food on his wish list.

Bob was beginning to see a pattern in the guards' selection of targets. The bigger guys were singled out, the smaller Japanese guards taking pleasure in inflicting pain and humiliation on a larger man. At 5 feet 9 inches and 160 pounds, Bob presented a smaller physical presence than many of the crew. Now he wished he was even smaller.

Everyone looked out the window, watching Goldtooth Maizie and another guard drag Captain Fitzgerald across the courtyard toward the bench again. He was wearing only his Skivvies. Two other guards, armed with machine guns, stood nearby. The crew could see that Fitzgerald's entire body was black and blue.

Goldtooth Maizie strapped him to the bench, just as they'd done before, but this time, instead of pounding him with clubs, they doused him with water and began beating him with thick leather straps. The sound of the straps snapping against the captain's body echoed across the courtyard. Bob turned his head, unable to watch.

Just as before, Goldtooth Maizie lifted a teakettle and poured water up Fitzgerald's nose while another guard held his hand over the captain's mouth. After the fifth teakettle of water, Goldtooth pulled a chair next to the bench and climbed on top. Looking down at Fitzgerald, he readied himself, like a bully at the pool getting set to execute a giant cannonball. Then he jumped, butt-first, landing directly on Fitzgerald's stomach. Fitzgerald convulsed, the force of the landing shooting water up and out his nose and mouth. Then the other guard climbed atop the chair and did the same thing.

After ten jumps apiece, the guards removed the straps from Fitzgerald and dragged him back across the courtyard and up the stairs.

Like everyone else on the crew, Bob had never questioned why America had gone to war. Seeing firsthand the destruction at Pearl Harbor had only intensified his belief in America's commitment to fight an evil enemy. But now that he'd seen the enemy up close, it was even more evident to him that the Japanese were not human.

19

Tim "Skeeter" McCoy
POW

It was Tim McCoy's turn to be pulled from the line by Snake. That's the name the crew had given the guard who slithered in and out of the lines. Snake always carried a stick like a policeman's billy club, and his specialty was the Devil Dance.

Using his club, he spread Tim's feet two feet apart, then ordered him to go into a half knee-bend up on the balls of his feet, arms raised straight over his head, palms together. Slowly, Snake circled, tapping him with his club on the calves, then the thighs, making sure Tim maintained the Devil Dance stance.

Tim had won the state 880 as a freshman back in Lubbock and had always thought of himself as having strong legs, but after several minutes, his legs wobbled and his heels touched the floor. Snake smacked his butt with his club, hard.

After a couple more minutes, the exhausted nerves in Tim's calves, thighs, and arms began to twitch, his whole body vibrating as he struggled to maintain the position. Snake grinned, summoning Goldtooth Maizie to join him watching Tim suffer.

Finally, unable to hold the stance, Tim straightened his legs. Four sharp whacks to the back of his legs, harder than anything his father ever administered back in Texas, sent him sprawling to the floor.

"Fuck you," he muttered.

* * *

Dragon had once lived in Hawaii and spoke limited English. "You kill our pilot," he spewed at the crew. "Now you pay."

It was true. The return fire from the deck of the *Grenadier* had hit the pilot of the dive-bomber that had tried to sink it. He'd managed to fly his plane back to land, but he died soon after landing.

Dragon stepped in front of Tim.

He swung his club, hitting Tim square in the shoulder. Tim braced himself, determined not to flinch. Dragon swung again, hitting him in the elbow, then the hip, knees, and shins. As Tim absorbed each blow, barely moving, Dragon got madder with each hit.

Tim had no doubt he could survive this. He was resolved to be not just tough but the toughest of all the crew, even if it put others in danger, even if it cost him his life. He had no doubt that if all things were equal, he could kick any of these guards' butt. He would have the same attitude he'd had as a teenager: he'd put a chip on his shoulder and dare anyone to knock it off. The guards would never be able to get anything from him. He would live to marry Valma and to show his father he was more of a man than he.

Dragon turned and handed his club to another guard, then whirled around, unloading a right cross to Tim's jaw. Still, Tim didn't flinch or go down, standing stoically, staring straight ahead.

"You think you tough," yelled Dragon. "You will break."

After a few hours Dragon came back. He told the crew that they were not prisoners of war but captured enemy, and the only reason that they were still alive was because of the humane treatment they were receiving. "We feed you now and let you rest."

Dragon ordered them to sit down. Easing his body to the concrete floor, Tim felt a huge relief. This was the first time the crew had been allowed to sit in the four days since they had been brought to the Convent on Light Street. His legs trembled.

Another guard entered, carrying an armload of straw mats. He dumped them in the middle of the floor and motioned for the men to each take one and roll it out. To Tim and the other men the two-foot by five-foot, half-inch-thick mat felt like a mattress.

Maybe, Tim hoped, things would improve. There was still a guard with a rifle and bayonet stationed at the door full-time, but the other guards in the room now carried wooden clubs instead of guns, and with the exception of Goldtooth Maizie and Dragon, they seemed less inclined to hit the prisoners. One of the guards even hinted that he'd try to find sulfur pills to help relieve Taylor's suffering.

A couple of hours after the mats had been delivered, Dragon entered. "You will eat now," he announced.

Two soldiers entered carrying two buckets, one filled with a watery porridge, the other with bowls. Tim joined the other men in a line and received a bowl and a ladleful of the gruel, but no spoon. Returning to his mat, he studied the contents of the bowl, uncertain of what it was. It was opaque, with some sort of grassy substance floating in it; he would later learn it was millet. Cautiously, he put the bowl to his mouth and began to sip. He finished everything in the bowl, but it did nothing to stop the gnawing in his stomach.

Another soldier entered carrying a bucket of water with a ladle and set it near the door. Swatting away a mosquito, Tim waited his turn in line, then scooped out a ladleful and gulped it down. When everyone was finished, the soldier threw each prisoner a Japanese cigarette, lighting one man's smoke, having the rest light theirs off a lit cigarette. Tim inhaled deeply, savoring his smoke, smoking it down to his fingers. The guard walked down the line, collecting the butts.

Tim returned to his mat, and when the guards gave no additional orders, he curled up and fell instantly asleep for the first time in five days.

Fifteen minutes into his sleep, Tim and the others were awakened and ordered to do push-ups. A push-up contest was becoming part of the routine, the guards taking delight in kicking the fallen men.

Tim's arms quivered. It was hard to concentrate, not just because he was so weak but because he was distracted by Charles Taylor's moaning.

The venereal infection had worsened, and his testicles were even more swollen. Pleas by the men for medical attention for Taylor had gone unheeded.

Tim finally fell. A guard stared down at him and kicked him in the side. Tim didn't flinch.

The guard ordered the men to line up and stand at attention. At the end of the front line, Taylor tried to stand erect but the pain was too much; he doubled over at the waist. The guard with the rifle and bayonet approached, prodding him with his blade to stand up. Taylor slowly, agonizingly, straightened, the pressure in his testicles unbearable.

The guard poked toward Taylor's midsection with his bayonet, the blade coming within inches of his testicles.

"Get away from him," warned Tim, lined up next to Taylor.

The guard ignored Tim, pressing the blade even closer.

With a flick of his wrists, the guard jabbed the tip of the steel blade into Taylor's testicles, releasing the pressure and the infection. Taylor gave a horrific scream. Blood and pus exploded, splattering the guard's uniform and face. Shocked, he stumbled backward, dropping his rifle. Taylor, writhing, fell to the floor.

Impulsively, Tim charged out of the line.

The guard didn't have time to pick up his rifle. Tim plowed into him like a linebacker, knocking him straight over backwards. Before Tim could regain his balance, the guard scrambled to his feet and bolted out the door, leaving his rifle on the floor.

As his crewmates moved to attend to Taylor, Tim picked up the rifle and flung it out the door into the courtyard.

20

Gordy Cox
POW

Feeling a pounding on the bottom of his feet, Gordy Cox awakened to see Goldtooth Maizie hovering over him. He'd been asleep only twenty minutes. Goldtooth and the other guards were rousing everybody, ordering them to line up at attention.

A Japanese corporal entered. Short, fat, and bucktoothed, he was dressed in leather high-top shoes, knee-high socks, matching beige knickers and shirt, brown belt, pith helmet, and riding crop; he looked like a caricature Gordy had seen on a Victory poster after Pearl Harbor. In broken English the officer ordered the men to form a single line and file out the door, warning that they'd be shot if they didn't stay in order.

In the courtyard, the crew from the other room joined them, the first time since arriving at the Convent on Light Street that the enlisted men had all been together. Gordy could see that the men from the other room were just as battered, bruised, and bedraggled as he and his companions. Three other Japanese officers, each with a machine gun, joined the corporal and flanked the men.

The corporal announced that they'd be questioned soon, and if they lied and didn't tell the "Christian truth," they'd be killed.

The Christian truth? Gordy had not gone to church much as a kid, but he was thoroughly convinced that these people knew nothing about God and the Christian truth.

The men were ordered back to their rooms and to stand at attention.

The corporal entered Gordy's room and walked around it very slowly, stopping to glare at each man. He turned and pointed at an electrician's mate and motioned for him to follow him out the door. Gordy watched them exit, figuring this was the start of the questioning. But where were they going? How bad would it be?

The crew had received no training on how to respond if captured and interrogated. All they knew was what the captain had told them when they were on the deck of the merchant ship: that they were from the USS *Goldfish*, based in San Francisco, and had been dispatched on a search and photographic mission of the area.

Gordy's strategy for survival was simple: Keep a low profile. Don't try to overanalyze or overthink anything; just put your head down and get it done. His philosophy would be I'm alive today, and that's what matters.

Ten minutes passed, then thirty, and an hour, and there was still no indication of what was happening to the electrician's mate. Gordy hadn't heard any gunshots, so at least his crewmate hadn't been shot.

After an hour and a half, the corporal appeared again, alone. Once again, he walked around the room, staring at each man. He motioned to Bernie Witzke, one of the tallest men in the crew. Gordy wished he'd picked him. If he was going to die, might as well get it over with.

The guards had taught the crew to count off in Japanese, each man given a number to shout out at roll call twice a day. Any man forgetting or mispronouncing his number got hit. They learned other words, too.

"Benjo?" asked Gordy, motioning toward the toilet.

Snake pulled him and Robert York from line and led them to the head, tapping his stick as they walked. Gordy glanced to his right, noticing an open gate across the courtyard. He looked at York, who'd also spotted the opening, and they both knew what the other was thinking: if they took off running, they could be out the gate in seconds. Snake didn't have a gun.

It took only a second for them to abandon their escape plan. They didn't know what was on the other side of the gate; they were on an island controlled by the Japanese; they were exhausted; and they had been repeatedly warned that if anyone tried to escape, ten crewmates would be killed.

Inside the darkened head, Gordy spotted something scrawled on the wall. He edged closer, straining to make out the words.

York leaned over to look, and read: "Keep your peckers up, men."

It had been written in blood by Captain Fitzgerald.

Gordy had lost track of the days. How long had they been captives? A week? Ten days? Since the interrogation of the crew had started, the hours seemed to pass even more slowly. None of the men who'd already been questioned, including Tim McCoy, had been seen since they were led away.

No one had seen Captain Fitzgerald since he'd been taken away after the last round of torture. What had they done with him? Was he still alive?

One by one, the men left the room for "questioning" and didn't return. For the ones remaining this was torture; not rifle-butt-to-the-jaw cruelty, but a mind game even more brutal. Each time another shipmate didn't return, it seemed more and more likely that the guards had extracted whatever information they could and then killed them.

Gordy wondered whether he really knew anything that would be of value to the Japanese. Surely they already knew about submarine engines and what the Americans were running. And as far as war strategies, or naval planning, or secret codes, he didn't know anything about that. He was just a first mate, an enlisted sailor, doing what he was told.

Since the start of the questioning, the harsh nature of the torture to the men still in the classroom had lessened, but only slightly. They were given food daily—a hardtack biscuit in the morning and a bowl of watery rice soup for dinner. Sometimes the guards seemed bored, so to amuse themselves they took delight in finding new forms of torment, such as making the men do push-ups with a guard's foot pressing down on their back.

Goldtooth Maizie entered the room and ordered everyone to pair off in twos and stand face-to-face. Gordy stood with York, noticing how drawn his crewmate's face looked, welted from mosquito bites. Two weeks with almost no food was taking its toll, evidenced in the men's lack of energy, hollow eyes, and prominent rib cages.

"You slap other man," ordered Goldtooth Maizie.

At first the men didn't understand the order. Goldtooth Maizie stepped between Gordy and York and demonstrated, slapping Gordy hard across the cheek.

"Now you do it!" Goldtooth Maizie screamed.

Gordy slapped York on the cheek.

"That not right!" yelled Goldtooth Maizie. "Hit hard . . . like this." He slapped York and the crack of hand against face echoed around the room. "Now you do right."

Gordy slapped his friend, much harder this time.

It wasn't hard enough for Goldtooth Maizie. He struck Gordy across his back with his club.

This time Gordy swung hard, the blow knocking York off balance.

As the guards watched and laughed, the sound of slapping filled the room, the guards stepping in to demonstrate when someone didn't slap his partner hard enough. When they tired of that game, they upped the ante, making the men hit each other with closed fists, only accepting blows that drew blood or dropped the other man to the floor. When York's first blow completely missed Gordy, Goldtooth Maizie stepped between them and sent Gordy crashing to the floor with a shot to the jaw.

21

Chuck Ver Valin
POW

Half the men had been taken away for questioning when the corporal entered and pointed at Chuck. He followed the corporal into the bright sunlight, then across the courtyard to a two-story building on the left. His legs wobbled. A door opened and the corporal shoved him inside.

The dimly lit room was bare except for a long table at one end and a lone chair in the middle of the floor. Two officers sat rigidly behind the table, flanked on one side by two soldiers with guns and bayonets, and two soldiers on the other side with clubs. One of the officers studied a stack of papers in front of him. Next to him sat a man in civilian clothes, the interpreter.

Chuck stood in front of the table, hands at his side. The corporal whirled around and slapped him hard on his cheek. "You bow," commanded the interpreter.

Chuck did as instructed, a slight nod of the head. The corporal slapped him again. "Not right," said the interpreter. "Full bow." This time Chuck bowed from the waist.

He was ordered to sit down in the chair, eyes straight ahead. He glanced to the guard standing beside him. Another slap. "Do as instructed. You want trouble?"

He shook his head. Unlike Tim, Chuck's brand of toughness was not going to include defiance. It was like when he was playing for the town baseball team growing up and tore off a piece of skin about the size of

Delaware sliding into second on the rock-hard infield dirt. The blood from the raw wound kept sticking to the inside of his uniform pants; every time he moved, it ripped off another little chunk of flesh, but he never let on, he never complained. In Submarine School he'd gotten through by learning to just focus on what was directly in front of him rather than allowing himself to be intimidated by what difficulties lay ahead until he reached his goal—graduation. Now that he'd finally found a young woman he loved and wanted to spend the rest of his life with, he wasn't going to let these Jap bastards keep him from her.

The guard slapped him again. "Speak when spoken to. What is your name?"

He replied with his name, rank, and serial number.

"What name of your ship?"

Chuck hesitated. "The *Goldfish.*"

"You lie. We know name of your ship. Tell one more lie, you suffer."

"Where submarine come from?"

"San Francisco."

"I tell you not to lie. Now you suffer."

The guard reached into his pocket and pulled out a bamboo sliver a little bigger than a toothpick. He stuck it up Chuck's nose and then flicked it, sending a sharp pain shooting through his nose and eyes.

"Lying get you killed."

The guard flicked the little bamboo stick again.

"Now you tell truth. You been on other sub?"

One of the guards with a rifle moved toward him and waved the bayonet in his face, then dragged it down his chest, pushing just hard enough that Chuck could feel the blade against his sternum. He remembered that one of the officers, Dick Sherry, had been with him on the *Gudgeon.* Maybe they already knew.

"Yes," he answered.

"What name of sub?"

"USS *Gudgeon.*"

"You sink any our ships?"

Chuck felt the bayonet pressing against his chest. "Yes," he answered.

"What name of that ship?"

"I don't know."

"You pick up survivors?"

"There wasn't anybody to pick up."

Without warning, the corporal threw a vicious punch, knocking Chuck straight over backwards in the chair.

Chuck felt blood streaming from his nose and lip. The corporal kicked him hard in the ribs. "Get up!"

Chuck struggled to rise, but the corporal kicked him again. A soldier straddled him and poured a pitcher of cold water on his head. "Up!"

Chuck got to his feet and slumped back onto the chair. The corporal slapped him.

"Where you going in your submarine?"

"I don't know," he replied.

The corporal grabbed Chuck by the hair and pulled him toward the table where the officers sat. He slapped his hand down on the table and intertwined two pencils between Chuck's fingers. Then he placed a cloth around his hand, knotted it, stuck another pencil into the knot, and started to turn it, drawing the fingers together. With each turn, Chuck's fingers twisted and separated between the second joint and knuckle; it felt like they were breaking. He screamed. The corporal twisted another turn.

"Now tell me where submarine going."

"I swear I don't know."

The corporal slugged him in the face again.

When Chuck came to, he was being dragged back across the courtyard and into a large classroom. Through his fog he saw the crewmates who'd been questioned before him. Like him, all the men in the room had been beaten and tortured.

22

Bob Palmer
POW

The guards competed against one another to invent new ways to harass and humiliate the men. They made four men carry another man around the room on a tabletop, their arms raised above their heads until the men's arms wearied and they dropped the tabletop, sending the man crashing to the floor, where the guards kicked him. They also enjoyed making the men imitate farm animals. Bob was forced down on all fours and told to moo like a cow. Gordy neighed like a horse, and pretty soon the whole room turned into a barnyard symphony of barking, mooing, clucking, and screeching. It would've been funny except Goldtooth Maizie wandered around the room, randomly kicking men in the ribs. The shot to Bob's side sent him tumbling to the concrete, gasping for air.

Goldtooth Maizie ordered the men to sing and dance around the room. Reluctantly, they twirled and spun, some humming, some singing, all trying to remember the songs they'd last heard on leave in Perth . . . "As Time Goes By" . . . "Dancing in the Dark" . . . "By the Light of the Silvery Moon" . . . "It Had to Be You" . . . "I Don't Want to Set the World on Fire."

Suddenly, one baritone voice rose above the rest. From where he danced, Bob couldn't tell who it was, but he recognized the song—"The Old Rugged Cross." He hadn't gone to church much as a kid, but he started humming along, and so did everyone else, singing or humming, the sound echoing across the room.

On a hill far away stood an old rugged cross,
The emblem of suffering and shame . . .

There'd always been a sentimental side to Bob. As he listened to the hymn, tears streamed down his face.

Dragon entered and ordered them to stop singing, then had them line up and count off in Japanese. He walked down the lines, sneering at each man, telling them that their way of life was no good and that they were cowards.

He stopped in front of Bob. "Why you no die with ship? Not honorable to be captured. Real warrior never give up. That why you lose war. Japanese warrior braver, never surrender. In whole history, we never lose war."

Bob stood erect, saying nothing.

"You no prisoner of war. You criminal. Red Cross no come for you."

Bob was no expert on international politics, but he knew that the Japanese had not signed the Geneva conventions and believed that they were not obligated to abide by the agreements' rules for the humane treatment of captured enemy combatants.

The only positive thing to have happened was with Charles Taylor. It had been a couple of weeks since the guard punctured his swollen testicles. Taylor was recovering, and the guards had even taken to bringing him what they claimed were sulfur pills. Bob believed it was just aspirin, figuring the guards felt guilty about what had happened. No extra punishment had been given to Tim for knocking over the guard.

Despite Taylor's improved condition, health problems for the crew were mounting. Some of the men had contracted crabs when they were on leave in Fremantle and now everyone had them—in their hair, beards, and eyebrows. Several men had fevers and flu-like illnesses. Tom Courtney had bone-shaking chills and a raging fever, and after a couple of days, he became delirious and then unconscious. Pleas to the guards for medical attention went unanswered. The pharmacist's mate suspected dengue fever, spread by the bite of infected mosquitoes. There was no treatment other than rest and lots of liquids. The fever usually could last nine or ten days, sometimes, but not often, turning fatal.

When Bob woke up in the middle of the night, shivering and shaking, he knew something was wrong. The chills quickly turned into a fever, and he was drenched in sweat. His head pounded. He moaned, calling out Barbara's name.

23

Tim "Skeeter" McCoy

POW

A second round of questioning had started, and judging from the tortured screams heard from the interrogation room across the courtyard, the methods used to get information from the men this time were even more brutal. Tim waited to be called.

Despite his cocky, I'm-not-backing-down bravado, Tim shared the same hardships as his buddies—isolation, hunger, anger, despair—but fear was the most powerful emotion. Fear of death, pain, or humiliation. Fear of Japan winning the war and ruling the world. Fear of never seeing Valma again. Or his mother.

It had been several weeks since anyone had seen Captain Fitzgerald. This really depressed Tim. To keep his morale up, he found comfort in the Scriptures he'd learned in the Baptist Church. Since joining the Navy and dabbling in the ways of alcohol and women, he'd strayed from the church, but he hadn't forgotten passages from the Bible, and he sometimes recited them to himself.

He thought about his mom back in Dallas. He remembered his uncle and the times he'd caddied for him at the country club or rode with him in his big car out to the lake. He imagined himself being rich like that. But mostly he thought about Valma back in Australia, and how lucky he was that she'd promised to wait for him. He imagined taking her home to

Texas, and how everyone would see how gorgeous she was and he'd be so proud. He wondered if she knew he'd been captured.

But prayer and imagination were temporary escapes, always interrupted by the reality of his imprisonment. Sleep was the only real escape from their situation, and the guards knew it, rarely letting a night pass without waking the men.

Just as Tim was drifting off to sleep, he heard hobnail boots clicking on the walkway outside. Tim had learned to recognize Goldtooth Maizie's walk, different from the other guards' footfalls, and the angry clattering of the wooden window louvers as Goldtooth ran his rifle butt across them. He did it every time, and every time it pissed off Tim. The door flew open, and Goldtooth Maizie marched in, grinning, his gold tooth shining.

Tim braced himself. Maybe he'd spit on Goldtooth Maizie this time, or punch him. No, that wouldn't be a good idea. Not because he was afraid of what Goldtooth Maizie might do to him, but because the guards knew that the best way to deal with a hotheaded prisoner was to retaliate against one of his crewmates.

Goldtooth Maizie pointed toward Bob Palmer, motioning him toward the interrogation room. Tim watched Bob, who had been ill for several days and was barely able to lift his head, shuffle out of the room, Goldtooth Maizie pushing him in the back.

By Tim's calculations, it was now late July and they'd been held here for three months. He figured he'd lost fifty pounds and he hadn't had a bowel movement in twenty days. The worst time was when he, like so many others, including Bob and Chuck, had come down with dengue fever—chills, fever, aching, sweating, drifting in and out of consciousness. It took all his energy just to lift his head. Some nights he'd shiver and shake and moan so badly that it seemed dying would be easier. But after ten days, the fever broke and he regained a measure of strength. And he was one of the lucky ones who hadn't been called for a second round of interrogation. He guessed it was because he was one of the lowest-ranking men on the ship and the Japanese concluded he didn't have any information that would be useful to them.

The crew was now housed in rooms down the corridor and around the corner from the larger rooms in which they had first been imprisoned; there were three or four men to a room. Except for the thin mats on the wooden plank floor, Tim's room was bare. About the size of a toolshed, the room was so small that when he lay down with his head at one end, his feet brushed the opposite wall. Before the Japanese takeover, the nuns had used this room and others like it for prayer and meditation. The only light the men had was what filtered through the shuttered small window in the door.

Tim figured they'd been transferred either because their captors were bringing in more prisoners and needed the bigger rooms or because they were trying to further break the men's spirit by isolating them. It had been ten days since he'd seen anyone in the crew other than the two men in his room. At least when he'd been in the big classroom, he had had thirty-five other men sharing the pain and humiliation. Now he didn't even know if his crewmates were still alive.

24

Gordy Cox
POW

On his trips to the *benjo*, Gordy had eyed the breadfruit and coconuts that had fallen from the nearby trees, but with the guards always watching, they might as well have been a mile away. He'd eaten coconut when he was stationed in Manila, and liked it, but he'd never tasted bread-fruit, a lime green oblong fruit that weighed up to ten pounds and grew on fifty-foot-tall trees. To feed the constant gnawing in his stomach, he'd even picked and eaten flowers growing next to the walkway leading to the head. Others in the crew had done the same thing, and now all the plants had been picked clean.

On this night, Gordy hatched a plan, particularly daring for someone so dedicated to being invisible. He was going to retrieve one of the fallen coconuts. With no guard in sight, he slowly opened the door of his small room, checking in both directions. The coconut lay on the ground, a hun-dred feet away. The courtyard was dimly lit, with little moonlight on this night. The guard station was at the far end. The best way, he decided, was just to make a dash for it.

Crouching low, Gordy shot across the walkway and onto the courtyard. Keeping his eyes on the coconut, he swooped low and gathered it up on the run like a defensive back picking up a fumble. Cradling it in his arm, he sprinted back across the courtyard, making it back inside the room undetected. He was able to pry up a plank from the floor and use it to crack open the coconut, sharing the unexpected feast with his roommates.

The men hid the coconut meat under the floor, enjoying it over several days.

Gordy heard noises outside his room and peeked through the shutters. Across the courtyard he saw two guards setting up a .30-caliber machine gun and aiming it toward the row of rooms housing the crew. Maybe this was how it was going to end—to be lined up outside the rooms and then just mowed down. But would that be worse than a slow death by starvation and beating? As the day wore on, he watched more and more movement by the guards.

The next morning, August 5, 1943—103 days after they had been captured—the door to his cell flew open and two armed guards herded him and his two roommates out of the room onto the grassy courtyard. Soon the rest of the enlisted men joined them, forming two lines. Since being isolated, it was the first time he'd seen his crewmates, including Bob Palmer, who'd survived his bout with dengue fever and the second interrogation.

Goldtooth Maizie ordered the men to march toward the big wooden gate they'd passed through when they first arrived at the Convent on Light Street. Shuffling in that direction, they were a pitiful lot: gaunt, dirty, dispirited.

Outside the gate, convoy trucks waited. With bayonets pointed at them, the crew struggled to climb aboard, and then the canvas flaps were closed. This time there were no blindfolds or tied hands. They were too weak to attempt an escape.

The men sat silently as the trucks rumbled down Light Street, heading toward the pier. Nobody knew where they were headed. Gordy thought nothing could be as torturous as what they'd survived the last 103 days. Surely he could endure whatever came next.

The ride was over quickly. The flaps opened, and Gordy saw that they were at the same dock where they'd landed. A small freighter, the *Hir Maru*, similar in size to the one on which they had arrived, was waiting. Hurriedly, the men formed two lines and marched up the gangway toward the forward hold.

A guard ordered them to stand at attention. The ship's commanding officer approached the men, a long, silver sword at his side.

Part Six

FROM BAD TO WORSE

25

Chuck Ver Valin

POW

After being reminded by the ship's commander that they were cowards for surrendering and that the Japanese way of life would prevail, Chuck and the rest of the crew were placed in the hold of the ship. The men were crammed together with barely enough room to lie down. The air in the hold was stale and humid; the men sweated onto the wooden planks of the deck, making it slippery. Chuck and several others were bruised from a rifle beating they'd received upon boarding the ship, but Chuck would not let his captors see his pain.

For five days the *Hir Maru* rolled and pitched on the open sea, destination unknown. The men had been given two 5-gallon buckets to serve as toilets, but with the heavy sea and meals of bad rice, the buckets overflowed, the situation made even worse when the majority of the crew came down with diarrhea. In the cramped quarters, there was no privacy and no way to escape the growing mess and the stench.

Soon the entire deck of the hold was soaked in waste. There were no mops; Chuck used his shirt to try to clean some space on the floor, but it was futile. He was able to remain standing, but other men were too weak and dehydrated. Some passed out, and others simply lay down on the filthy deck.

Chuck felt the engines reverse, then stop. The men were ordered out of the hold and up on deck, then led down a gangplank and loaded onto trucks; the flaps were quickly closed to block their view. They did not know it, but they had landed in Singapore. It was August 10, 1943, and all of the men were still together. Nobody knew the whereabouts or condition of Fitzgerald or two other officers who were missing.

Singapore had been heralded as an "impregnable fortress" and considered the strongest of all British bastions. But in February 1942 it had fallen to the Japanese after only seven days of battle, the largest surrender in British history; over 50,000 British and Australian troops were captured, as well as most of the European citizens living there.

After a twenty-minute ride, the trucks stopped and the crew climbed down and surveyed their new surroundings, a large fenced internment area encircled by barbed wire. Inside the fence stood thatched huts built on stilts; a short ladder allowed entry. The men were marched into the yard, then separated, seven or eight assigned to each hut.

For the next forty-six days, the camp would be their home. Each day they were loaded onto trucks and driven to an abandoned horse-racing track. Chuck imagined it in better times, filled with elegantly dressed patrons, magnificent thoroughbreds, and jockeys in beautiful silk colors.

The men picked weeds on their hands and knees for ten hours under the brutally hot sun, with no water or food. Chuck's back ached relentlessly and his knuckles were scraped raw. Some days the guards ordered the crew to go back to where they'd started picking and do a better job. Each day on the other side of the track he could see Japanese troops training, the sergeants screaming and slapping the trainees with the same ferocity that the guards at the Convent at Light Street had treated the American prisoners. It was more proof, not that he needed any, that these people were savages. He took consolation in the fact that compared with the treatment the crew had received in Penang, this camp was more humane. The rice portions at night were a little bigger, the harassment and beatings from the guards not as frequent, and they weren't constantly awakened in the middle of the night. They received cigarettes, and were allowed to shave and bathe. For the first time in months Chuck felt clean. He could survive this, he believed.

He even joined a discussion about an escape plan. The details of the plan were vague, but the idea was to tunnel under the fence, then hollow out logs and use them as canoes to paddle to one of the many small islands bordering Singapore. The whole crew would have to be included; as they had in Penang, the guards made it clear that if anyone tried to escape, anyone left behind would be severely punished or killed.

To Chuck, it seemed impossible that such a plan could succeed. Still, if men he considered smarter and wiser than he thought it was worth risking, who was he not to go along? Besides, an escape plan gave him hope, and if there was one thing he and his crewmates needed, it was hope. In time, however, the plan was abandoned when it was concluded that even if they got away safely, they would have no place to go. "What are we gonna do . . . paddle to America?" said Chuck.

At night in their huts, the men shared stories of the different types of interrogation and torture they'd suffered in Penang. Everyone had a story. Bob Palmer told how a bamboo sliver had been jammed under his fingernail and set on fire, and his other fingernails had been pulled off with a pair of pliers. Chuck described how a guard had held his head while another burned off his eyebrows and lashes with the flame of a candle.

The rumor spread that the crew was to be transferred to another prison camp; maybe to China, or to Japan. On September 24, 1943, they were loaded back on trucks, taken to the dock, and marched at gunpoint onto the *Asama Maru*; it was much larger than the ship that had brought them to Singapore. Chuck had a bad feeling about what lay ahead.

26

Bob Palmer
POW

In 1943, Americans back home knew nothing about Japanese Hell Ships. These unmarked vessels, usually freighters, were used to transport American POWs to Japan, China, Manchuria, or Korea to be used as slave labor. Because the ships were unmarked, the U.S. Navy had no way of knowing POWs were crammed into their holds; thousands of captured American soldiers and sailors, men who had already endured months of torture, malnutrition, and disease in prison camps, had already been killed by American torpedoes and bombs. Built in 1925 as a passenger ship, the *Asama Maru*, part of a convoy of Japanese ships in the South China Sea sailing north from Singapore, was such a ship.

It was hard for Bob Palmer to look at his crewmates, now so emaciated and dressed in rags. Along with other prisoners, Bob showed signs of beriberi. A disease caused by a deficiency of vitamin B_1, it was rarely seen in America, but it was common in countries where white rice was a staple food. It could be easily cured by a change in diet or by vitamin supplements, neither of which would be forthcoming from their captors. Bob also had a tingling, burning pain in his legs, then a feeling of stiffness and heaviness, symptoms due to lack of exercise, as well as all the bending and squatting he'd been forced to do while pulling weeds on the track in Singapore.

The ship had been on the seas for eight days when a loud explosion jarred Bob from his sleep in the middle of the night. He recognized the sound of an exploding torpedo; it sounded as if it had hit one of the nearby ships in the convoy.

In response there was a series of smaller explosions—depth charges being dropped on an American sub below. Bob knew the terror those submariners were feeling; he wondered if he'd ever been out drinking beers back in Perth with any of the guys on that sub.

The attack lasted for about an hour, and when the guards returned they were noticeably surlier. Bob figured that one of the ships in the convoy must have been sunk, and the *Grenadier* crew was now going to pay the price.

A sense of doom swept through the crew. Maybe they weren't going to get off the ship alive. Maybe they'd be beaten to death, or torpedoed, or taken up on the deck and pushed overboard. Who would ever know? Bob closed his eyes and thought about Barbara. He imagined the two of them holding hands and sitting on a big boulder next to the rushing waters of the Rogue River, a picnic lunch, including an apple pie, spread out next to them.

After a couple of more days at sea, Bob felt the ship's engines reverse and its forward motion stop; the engines shut down. They had arrived at a port, but where?

Bob heard a commotion and looked up to see a dozen screaming Japanese charging down the stairs, carrying rifles with bayonets fixed. They were drunk. Bob saw that they were Imperial Marines, much larger and more solidly built than the crew of the *Asama Maru*. The biggest marine, a broad-shouldered guy over 6 feet tall and 200 pounds, walked over to the foot of the stairs and yanked out one of the oak handrails. It was eight feet long and five inches around.

The crew was herded out of the compartment onto the landing hatch. A guard signaled Bob to step out of the line and stand on the hatch cover, hands over his head. He did as instructed. Holding the handrail like a baseball bat, the biggest marine stepped behind him and took a vicious swing, connecting to the lower part of Bob's back. The force of the blow lifted him off his feet and drove him across the hatch cover. He slammed headfirst into the bulkhead five feet away, slithering to the deck, all feeling in his lower limbs gone.

Another marine kicked Bob in the side, then dragged him off to the side and deposited him in a heap.

The next man was directed to the hatch cover, and the big marine took another swing, this one even more vicious. Then the next man was ordered forward, and the next, until every man had been clubbed.

With each swing, the big marine tried to outdo himself. Some men lost consciousness. Others urinated in their pants. When the men collapsed against the bulkhead, temporarily paralyzed, they were kicked and poked, then dragged off to the side. If the first blow didn't drive them into the bulkhead or knock them off their feet, the marine struck again.

Bob watched as Tim stepped onto the hatch cover and looked defiantly at the big marine. Putting his hands over his head, Tim took the blow across his butt, but he didn't flinch.

The marine swung again, even harder, this blow landing on his lower back. Tim stood firm.

Infuriated, the big marine wound up again; the blow struck Tim in the small of the back. And again he didn't go down. Finally, the marine's fourth blow sent Tim staggering forward, his head banging against the bulkhead, his legs crumbling under him. He curled up into a ball. Standing over him, the marine kicked him in the back.

After the last man was hit, the crew staggered to their compartment, many having to crawl. The men who had lost control of their bladders were not able to clean themselves.

Bob didn't know how long he'd been drifting in and out of consciousness when he heard the guards screaming and yelling. He was jerked to his feet and pushed toward the hatch, and then up the stairway toward the deck. The ship had landed in Japan.

27

Tim "Skeeter" McCoy
POW

Tim was one of the last to climb out of the hold onto the ship's deck, greeted by the early morning sunlight and fifty Japanese Imperial Marines yelling and prodding him with bayonets and clubs.

Wobbling down the gangplank to the pier, he staggered through the gauntlet of marines. One connected with a rifle butt, another with a fist. He struggled to stay upright. If he fell, he'd be pummeled. His legs, bruised and stiff from ankle to hip, ached. Ahead of him, Gordy stumbled and was immediately jumped by three marines. Tim could only watch as Gordy tried to crawl forward, unable to get back up. Of all his crewmates, Gordy was the one he wanted to help the most. He seemed so vulnerable.

It was October 9, 1943. The *Asama Maru* had landed at Shimonoseki, population 105,000, a port city on the Sea of Japan. Located on the southwestern corner of Honshu, Japan's largest island, and narrowly separated from the smaller inland of Kyushu, Shimonoseki was an important railroad and industrial center, with shipyards and chemical plants, as well as a primary training location for the Imperial Marines.

Tim and the other captured submariners shuffled away from the pier, heading into town. As they slowly moved through the streets, civilians poured out of their homes and shops to view the emaciated and foot-sore prisoners. For most, it was their first glimpse of an American. Some shouted and shook their fists; others hurled rocks. A small woman stepped toward Tim and spit, hitting him in the neck.

Of all the degradation he'd suffered so far, this was the most humiliating, because he was now on the enemy's soil. It took all of his self-control not to attack the woman.

The crew was imprisoned in a single-story barracks at an old marine training base. Straw mats carpeted the concrete floor and the windows were nailed shut. Each prisoner was issued a rough woolen blanket and a crude bar of soap.

The camp commander entered, informing the crew that each morning and night they must bow toward the emperor.

Tim wanted to laugh. Back in Penang he'd been slapped and punched for not bowing correctly. Since then, he'd bowed every morning and evening as instructed, but he told himself that he was really bowing to FDR. He used the same inner strategy when bowing to or saluting a guard: in his head, he was saluting Captain Fitzgerald.

Tim was having trouble shaking the image of Fitzgerald being dragged out of the courtyard unconscious, his whole body one continuous bruise. Back in Singapore, the men had discussed Fitzgerald's decision to pursue the ships in search of a kill. Had he been too aggressive and too concerned with building his own reputation? Would they have escaped if he'd given the order to dive more quickly instead of questioning the lookout's word that he'd spotted the dive-bomber? And every submariner knew that a captain was not supposed to keep his sub on the surface in daylight, especially not so close to land and when the enemy knew you were in the vicinity. But not once did anyone blame the captain; the crew's respect and admiration for his toughness, courage, and strategy were unassailable.

On the morning of October 12, three days after their arrival, the crew was mustered together just outside the door of their barracks and ordered to stand at attention.

Ten minutes passed, then twenty. For Tim, his body weakened and his legs in pain and swollen from beatings, standing at attention was one of the hardest forms of torture. To distract himself, he thought about Valma back in Perth and how positively beautiful she'd looked when he proposed to her.

He wondered if his divorced parents knew that he'd been captured and was a POW. If they knew, were they talking to each other or dealing with it separately? Was his Uncle Ben, the successful insurance man, supporting Tim's mom? Tim had been sending part of his pay home each month. Certainly his mom would have noticed by now that the checks had stopped. Or maybe the Navy was still sending her money?

He assumed his mom had turned to the church for support. She'd often said that it was her faith in God and the Baptist Church that helped her get through those long periods in the institution. Tim thought back to the days in Lubbock when he and his mom and dad had listened to Reverend Truitt preach the gospel and expound about the wages against sin and the certainty of a God and his promise of eternity. He'd carried a Bible with him onto the *Grenadier*, and it bothered him that he'd abandoned the ship without it. Since falling into the hands of the Japanese, he'd often tried to let the Scriptures flow through him as one way to survive this crucible. In Matthew, Jesus taught that he should "turn the other cheek," but the truth was that the injunction from Exodus about seeking justice in "an eye for an eye" was more to Tim's liking.

According to Tim's interpretation of the Bible and Jesus' teachings, he believed that there was no true authority except God, and that it was a believer's responsibility to work and pray to change a wrong. He had no doubt that Japan was a godless and backward nation, and the guards who carried out its rules were godless too. So Tim would, as the Bible instructed him, give unto Caesar only that which was owed him: he could obey his captors with his words and actions in order to survive, but never with his heart, which would remain loyal only to his country and to God.

Standing in front of the barracks, the men remained at attention. Finally the camp commander stepped forward and started calling out names of crew members to step forward. Tim waited for his name to be called. It wasn't. Neither was Chuck's or Gordy's.

But Bob Palmer's was. Tim watched as Palmer and twenty-eight other submariners stepped forward and then were marched away, around the corner and out of sight.

A few days later, Tim and the remaining members of the crew were marched to a nearby train yard and shoved aboard a small coach car. After a slow, uncomfortable two-day trip, the train finally stopped in front of a large steel mill. The men could see Japanese workers coming and going in the morning mist.

Assembled next to the train, the men were marched away from the mill, through a residential district and past shacks of corrugated metal. People hurried out of their houses and lined the street as they straggled by, and once again the men were yelled at, spit upon, and pelted with rocks.

Finally the prisoners reached the bottom of a steep hill. At the top, shrouded in the mist, sat a large concrete four-story building with metal-framed windows, ominous and cold.

They trudged up the hill and into the building—quickly dubbed "the Castle" by the crew—and were escorted down a long corridor, passing several rooms with large metal doors. At the end of the corridor, they were divided into two groups of twenty-two, half of the men going into one room, the other half into another; Tim, Chuck, and Gordy were in the same group. Each room had two rows of bunks with thin straw mats. Before the men had a chance to relax, they were ordered back out into the hall. There they were informed that they had joined the hundreds of other prisoners assigned to Prisoner of War Camp #3, in the Fukuoka district.

The new interpreter explained that they would all be working in a steel mill three miles away and be paid 10 sen (the equivalent of less than 2 cents) a day. They could use the money to buy cigarettes or candy from a camp store. For meals, they would receive morning rice, a *bento* (box lunch) to take to work, and rice in the evening. Everyone would be required to work except those with a serious illness, as determined by the Japanese camp doctor. Each man would be issued a thin, light green burlap jacket and pants, and a wool overcoat (taken during the Russo-Japanese

War of 1904–1905 when the Russians surrendered to the Japanese). They would also receive one pair of split-toe socks, a pair of flat-soled shoes with a V-shaped thong, and a G-string—a thin piece of cloth attached to string tied around the waist—that would serve as underwear. This was fine with Tim; he was glad to be out of the Navy-issued T-shirt and dungarees that he'd been wearing since the *Grenadier* had been torpedoed.

The POWs would also receive a razor with one blade, a toothbrush, and a bar of soap. They would be permitted to bathe after work each night, but because there was only one tub for hundreds of prisoners, those getting to bathe first would be rotated by room. The camp doctor had set aside one room for those seriously ill. Colds or the flu would not be considered an illness.

And finally, if the camp commander eventually deemed they were worthy, they would be allowed to write their families and to receive mail and Red Cross packages, and they would not be beaten. Tim, now prisoner #526, didn't believe it. Not for a second.

28

Gordy Cox

Fukuoka #3

Gordy Cox, prisoner #528 at Fukuoka Camp #3, closed his eyes, trying not to think about how hungry he was.

"Hey, 528, get back to work," ordered Dave Megeson. The engineer had been taken prisoner when the Japanese invaded Wake Island.

Gordy opened his eyes and ignored Megeson. They were standing in the pipe shop at the Yawata steel mill, where Gordy and a dozen others from the *Grenadier*, including Tim McCoy and Chuck Ver Valin, had been assigned to work. Gordy despised Megeson.

In 1901 the Japanese government had built a steel mill at Yawata, convenient to Japan's largest coalfield and iron ore from China. By World War II the Imperial Iron and Steel Works at Yawata had become the largest such complex in Japan. Yawata was known as the Pittsburgh of Japan. Gordy considered his assignment to the pipe shop in the steel mill a stroke of luck, even if he arrived at the job each day before sunrise and left after sunset. Others in the crew had been assigned outside jobs, and with winter fast approaching, the conditions were wet and miserable. Still other men had been assigned to the coal-hauling detail, where they had to breathe coal dust every day and deal with the soot and grime. The pipe shop was inside a large galvanized metal building, open on one end but sheltered from the rain and wind. Two small furnaces were usually going, which provided some heat, although keeping warm was often a struggle. Gordy's job was to help put in the ends of the pipes before they were bent. Although it hadn't been discussed, Gordy believed the pipes would be used on Japanese ships. POWs were not trusted to make the bend, except for Megeson.

Behind Megeson stood two army guards, as well as a "pusher." The pushers, or managers, were usually ex-soldiers who'd fought in China and had been discharged because either they'd gotten wounded or they were too old. Most had lost some of the fire of patriotism and were not as hard on the prisoners as the guards were. Normally, there were always a couple of pushers on duty, with one guard patrolling the shop.

Gordy glanced at Megeson, resisting the urge to tell him to get screwed. He considered Megeson a turncoat of sorts, a snitch. A large, broad-shouldered man from California, Megeson had somehow wrangled his way into a favored position with the guards and pushers. A benefit of this elevated status was that he received extra food, which meant he hadn't lost a lot of weight; in fact, he probably outweighed Gordy by a hundred pounds.

Gordy wasn't alone in his contempt for Megeson; none of the prisoners liked him. On several occasions, Tim had told others in the crew that he wanted to give him "an old-fashioned Texas whipping." But Gordy had no intention of fighting him, or anyone else. Stay invisible, he reminded himself. At the Castle, he never argued or showed disrespect to the guards, and at work, he always did as he was told. He made a point of going to the bathroom with at least one other prisoner so that the guards would never catch him alone.

Megeson moved closer to Gordy. "Are you just going to stand there?" he asked.

Gordy glanced up. Megeson was hovering over him. "Get away from me," he muttered.

Megeson took one step back and sucker-punched him right between the eyes.

Gordy crumpled to the floor, blood gushing from his nose. Dazed, he looked up and saw Megeson straddling him, motioning for him to get up and fight. The two pushers stood right behind him, grinning. Gordy considered the situation.

He didn't try to fight back.

* * *

Back in Yakima, Nellie Cox, Gordy's mother, did not know yet that her son's ship had been sunk and the crew captured. She continued to write:

> *March 11, 1943*
>
> *Everybody is out in the garden now getting ready to plant. The government wants everyone to raise all their own food they can this year. We are starting food rationing now. . . . You would find everything very much different at home now, Gordon. . . . So many of the girls have gone soldier and sailor crazy and write to everyone they can get names of. Do you remember that redhead that lived in the little house up the street north of us? She is getting married to a sailor. She will be 16 this month. Just to get the guy's money is all it is. It's terrible such goings on. . . . I hope you don't change too much and pray God will bring you safely home to us.*

Slowly, painfully, Gordy trudged back up the hill in the rain to the Castle. Several days had passed since Megeson had knocked him down and broken his nose and blackened his eyes. The good news was Megeson hadn't bothered him since.

Gordy dreaded that walk every evening after work. It was steep, and it took most of what little stamina he had just to trudge up the incline. He hated the Castle, with its concrete floors, long corridors, and cold rooms. He hated the guards. They seemed more vindictive than the previous guards they'd encountered, if that was possible. He guessed it was because they were bitter that they'd been assigned to guard POWs rather than to fight on the front line and earn glory for the empire.

In front of the Castle, he passed the guardhouse, a five-foot by five-foot hut with small windows. He heard moaning and the sound of someone being beaten. It was the same sound he heard almost every night when he and the other men returned from work. He was convinced that these nightly beatings were a way to remind the prisoners of Japanese superiority rather than for anything the prisoner might have done wrong. On this evening, the guards had the prisoner kneeling, a stick between his knees as they beat him. It was Al Rupp, the youngest member of the crew. Rupp had gotten himself assigned to an easy work detail—carrying crates of buns to be served to the Japanese workers—after he'd purposely broken his own arm with a hammer and then faked falling off a ladder in order to get out of more-strenuous work. Faking illness had become common, though the POWs in sick bay got less food than the men working. The strategy backfired on Rupp, however, when the guards caught him stealing buns. Gordy and the rest of the crew were finding it hard to be sympathetic to his plight.

That night Gordy had to sit through yet another indoctrination lecture. Every commander and interpreter Gordy had heard had bragged about how Japan had never been defeated, going all the way back to the thirteenth century when Kublai Khan first tried to invade Japan but was stopped by a giant typhoon that smashed Kublai's armada, a divine wind the Japanese called *kamikaze*, which gave proof that their gods had protected them, and always would.

Leaving for work the next morning, Gordy passed the guardhouse, where Rupp remained on display, still moaning in pain.

Meanwhile, Gordy's mother continued to write:

May 6, 1943
Well, what are you doing most of the time to keep out of mischief? Or do you? . . . Sunday is Mother's Day. There will be a lot of lonesome mothers this year. I think such days bring only more heartache to the mothers who aren't remembered.

When Gordy looked at the other prisoners, it was hard not to feel despair. They were all weak and emaciated, their ribs and hip bones protruding, their cheeks sunken and hollow.

In the weeks since the crew had arrived at the Castle, several of the prisoners from other countries had died. For Gordy, their deaths were hard to accept; he believed that with a little more food they might have lived. He also believed that it was possible to tell which of the prisoners was about to die. It was something intangible, a sense that they were no longer willing to fight for survival. It wasn't just the vacant look in their eyes and the blank expression on their faces; it was in their voices and in the slump of their shoulders. For the first time, he'd seen the look of death in a couple of his crewmates. But Gordy refused to give in. Every night he told himself, "I made it through another day. That's as good as I can hope for."

It was hard to deal with the knowledge that the Japanese didn't care if the prisoners died. Repeated requests for more food were ignored. It didn't make sense to Gordy: if they fed the POWs more, they would be more productive. But the Japanese believed that Australia would be captured soon, and they'd have all the slave labor they needed.

There was a rumor going around the camp that the Red Cross had sent parcels, enough so that all 1,200 prisoners being held in Fukuoka Camp #3 would get one. Gordy was skeptical. Like everyone else on the crew, he knew very little about the Geneva conventions. The Geneva convention signed on July 27, 1929, laid out guidelines for the treatment of prisoners of war as proposed by the International Committee of the Red Cross. It stated that POWs had a right to be treated with honor and respect, and forbade the use of torture to extract information. Captives were required to provide only their true name and rank. Opposing countries, referred to as belligerents, were mutually bound to notify each other of the capture of prisoners within the shortest period of time possible, and the conditions in the POW camps were to be similar to those in the base camps used by the country's own soldiers; further, the POW camps could not be located near the war zone. Also, belligerents were to, "so far as possible, avoid assembling in a single camp prisoners of different races or nationalities." By Gordy's count, there were at least a dozen nationalities at Fukuoka #3.

Other mandates of the 1929 convention required food to be of a similar quality and quantity to that of a belligerent's own soldiers, and POWs could not be denied food as a punishment. Adequate clothing had to be provided, and the sanitary conditions had to be sufficient to prevent disease. Medical services had to be provided, and provisions had to be made for religious, intellectual, and recreational pursuits. The labor of prisoners of war was to be safe and not war related. Prisoners were to be allowed to correspond with their family within a week of capture, and they were to be allowed to receive letters, parcels, books, food, and clothing. And if any escaped prisoners of war were retaken, they were to be liable only to disciplinary punishment.

In the eight months since their capture, none of the treatment that Gordy and his shipmates had experienced conformed to the Geneva convention of 1929. While he hoped the rumors of the Red Cross parcels were true, another week passed with still no sign of the packages.

After two weeks, Gordy walked past the area where the guards in the pipe shop ate their lunches. Seated at a table, two guards were passing a white box between them. Gordy did a double take. On the outside of the box, clearly marked, was the Red Cross insignia. Food wrappers lay scattered across the table. A guard reached inside the box, pulled out a Camel cigarette, and lit it, blowing the smoke in Gordy's direction.

Back home, his mother wrote again:

May 21, 1943
How are you and what have you been doing with yourself? I hope to hear
from you soon. It is about time now again.

29

Chuck Ver Valin

Fukuoka #3

It was late morning, December 15, 1943, and the snow was falling in Fukuoka. Lined up outside the Castle, the crew of the *Grenadier* shivered, trying to figure out why they hadn't been marched off to work this morning.

Chuck felt the cold penetrate to his bones. He'd seen his share of snow and cold as a boy growing up in upstate New York, but back then he could put on his long johns, or huddle around the furnace with his brothers and sisters, or be inside a warm schoolroom. Now he just had his thin prison uniform and wool coat, and in his deteriorating state, it was hard to keep from shivering.

"What are they doing with us?" he whispered to the man standing next to him.

Nobody knew.

Maybe the guards were going to blindfold them and take them to wherever it was that the twenty-nine other crewmen had been taken. Or maybe those guys had been executed. Getting shot was never far from a POW's mind.

The cold air wasn't helping Chuck's toothache. His jaw was swollen, and the pain shot all the way up to his ear. He'd heard horror stories about the camp hospital—men having legs amputated without anesthetic, or men being given injections and dying a few minutes later. In the three months since they'd arrived in Japan, many of the crew had been to the hospital, mostly for treatment of dysentery, but some as a way to get out of going to work. Not Chuck. He was one of the few who hadn't missed a day of work so far, although on many of those days he'd felt horrible. Part of it had to do with his natural stamina; he'd never missed work at any of his summer jobs or when he worked for the CCC at Watkins Glen. The other reason was that he didn't want to go anywhere near that hospital. He'd take his chances at work.

Rubbing his jaw, trying to get relief from his toothache, he glanced down the hill that led up from the steel plant. A small unit of guards was marching toward them, bayonets fixed.

The Japanese victories in the early stages of the war in the Pacific had created a problem for the Imperial Japanese Army: what to do with the unexpected large number of POWs. In early 1942, only one POW camp in Japan proper existed. Almost all of the 140,000 Allied troops captured in the first year of the war were held in the territories where they'd been taken prisoner.

The Japanese Army Ministry in Tokyo established a POW Information Bureau to deal with the problem. Different solutions were discussed, including killing all the prisoners. But in April 1942 the government decided to begin transporting most of the Allied POWs to Japan to supplement the Japanese workforce, which was already running short on manpower. By February 1943, the Japanese had opened dozens of POW camps in Japan. To provide labor, most of the camps were located close to mines or industrial areas.

Chuck surveyed his new surroundings. The guards had marched the crew, along with all of the hundreds of other prisoners being held at the Castle, to a new prison site—but still called Fukuoka #3—ten miles to the east, located on the flat terrain just outside Tobata, about 300 yards from the bay and just west of the larger city of Kokura.

The new camp had been specifically built to house POWs. The Japanese army wanted to relocate them away from the steel mill, which they worried might eventually come under aerial attack by American planes. It wasn't that they were concerned about the safety of the men; they wanted to protect their substantial labor force.

Chuck noticed that 500 yards from the new camp was an enormous power plant, with six giant smokestacks, each about a hundred feet high. He assumed that these smokestacks would become targets for American bombs, and with the camp so close, they wouldn't be any safer than they had been back at the Castle. In fact, they might be less safe: whereas the Castle was concrete, the new camp structures were made mostly of wood. But he'd learned by now not to try to understand Japanese logic.

A tall wooden fence, topped with barbed concertina wire, surrounded the camp. Inside the compound stood ten barracks of very light frame construction, each building with a capacity of 150 men. There were two rows of two-tier bunks running the length of the building, the lower bunk six inches off the ground, the top tier reached by ladder. Each bunk contained a thin mat, and at the head of each bay was a small shelf where the prisoners could place their meager belongings and the pack of ten Japanese cigarettes they received each week. The floor was concrete, the roof a type of Japanese tile. There was no source of heat except for a small, charcoal-burning stove set in the middle of the room; it was to be lit only from 5:00 to 8:00 p.m. Light came from a single overhead bulb. Small windows provided light during the day, with special blackout curtains for air raids. The *Grenadier* crew would be sharing their quarters mostly with Marines and civilians who'd been captured by the Japanese on Wake Island in the fall of 1942.

To the rear of the barracks in a separate room there was a cement urinal and four sinks with cold water. The latrines were in another small room; there were six wooden stalls, each enclosing a hole to squat over. The waste was gathered in a large tank underneath the room, which had to be cleaned by the prisoners. For bathing there were two large cement tanks outside, each ten feet square and three feet deep. The galley was located in a wooden building containing large steam-operated pots for making rice and tea. The prisoners were in charge of cooking the meals under the supervision of a Japanese mess sergeant. Each barracks appointed men to bring food from the galley to the barracks in buckets.

Compared with the Castle, this new camp seemed like a resort on Seneca Lake to Chuck.

On his lunch break at the pipe shop, Chuck could barely stand the throbbing pain of his toothache; the pressure from the infection swelled the side of his face. Still, the last thing he wanted to do was ask a guard if he could have medical attention. He was more concerned about his crewmate and friend Charles Doyle, who'd been sent to work despite having pneumonia. Since arriving at work in the morning, Doyle had just sat hunched in a corner; his eyes were sunken, his breathing labored, and his legs covered with infected boils. He stared off into space with the look all too familiar in the camp.

Chuck eased his way next to Doyle in the corner and gave him a nudge. Doyle didn't respond.

A deathwatch had become part of the camp routine. The question "How many died today?" was asked every evening when the men returned to camp from work. Usually the answer was three or four, the numbers increasing with the onset of winter and the increase in cases of pneumonia. The guards and Japanese doctors were usually not sympathetic to the pneumonia cases, sending them to work anyway, although today the guards were not bothering Doyle.

Doyle, who was from Weymouth, Massachusetts, was one of Chuck's best buddies on the crew. Chuck often teased him about his thick New England accent. In the evenings they liked to talk, sometimes about baseball. Doyle was a big Red Sox fan and argued that the Sox's young phenom, Ted Williams, was a better hitter than the Yankees' Joe DiMaggio. They talked about going to a game together if they survived.

Doyle slumped over. Chuck urged him to get up, but Doyle didn't respond.

*　*　*

Chuck squeezed the arms of the dentist's chair. He'd finally caved in and asked a guard if he could see a dentist and they'd taken him to a clinic in nearby Tobata. The tooth was abscessed and infected, and the dentist had just informed him that he was going to have to pull it, without Novocain or any painkiller.

The guard had also let him know that as soon as the tooth was pulled, he had to go straight back to work. That was okay with Chuck. The routine of working in the pipe shop helped him keep his sanity.

Since being transferred to the new camp, Chuck and the prisoners had continued working at the steel mill, their routine the same every day: Get up at 5:30 a.m., form lines and count off, and eat a bowl of millet. Walk several hundred yards to a railroad switching station and climb onto an open flatbed car, then ride thirty minutes to the steel mill for their jobs as stevedores, mechanics, machinists, and pipe fitters. Chuck worked in the pipe shop alongside Gordy and Tim. Prisoners too sick to work either stayed in camp and were assigned jobs in the barracks, or were in the hospital. Workers at the steel plant usually received larger rations than those who stayed back, and that was one of the reasons that there wasn't much protest over sick men such as Doyle being sent to work—not that protesting would've done any good. At the lunch break—which was usually thirty minutes, sometimes shorter—prisoners received another bowl of millet. Dinner was usually another small bowl of millet or daikon (a Japanese radish) soup.

Originally, the prisoners at Fukuoka #3 received approximately two cups of food per day, but it had recently been reduced to one cup. There was some debate among the prisoners why their rations had been cut. One camp argued that it was to have them suffer a slow death by starvation. Another argument was that all of Japan was suffering from a food shortage, and it wasn't just the prisoners who were getting less to eat. A third theory involved an incident that had happened a couple of months earlier. Several of the American Marines had boasted to the guards that they could beat them in a footrace. The guards accepted the challenge, and each side picked their three fastest men. The three Marines finished one-two-three.

After the race, the guards concluded that the prisoners were too strong, so their rations were cut by a third. From his point of view, Chuck believed that the cut in rations was to starve them to death, yet keep them alive long enough that they could be productive laborers.

Using what looked to Chuck like an ordinary pair of pliers, the dentist climbed into position and yanked out the infected tooth. Chuck let out a fierce scream, doing everything possible to fight back the tears.

Twenty minutes later, his mouth filled with gauze, he was back on the job in the pipe shop.

Exhausted and cold, Chuck sat on the edge of his lower bunk in the barracks, waiting for another day to end. He was also waiting for the nightly poker game to end and his bunkmate, Johnny Johnson, the son of a coal miner from Cartonsville, Illinois, to come join him. To help protect themselves from the freezing cold, the two men had taken to sleeping in the same bunk together, using each other's body heat and an extra blanket for warmth. Raised in a world where words such as "queer" and "faggot" were an accepted insult, neither man had given a second thought to spooning through the night; here survival trumped social stigma. Besides, others in the crew were doing the same thing.

The infection had finally subsided from Chuck's pulled tooth. He had not received any instructions from the dentist on post-removal care, and he had kept the gauze in his mouth for three days. He took it out only after Johnny had complained about how much it stank.

Chuck was especially tired on this evening. He couldn't explain why some nights after work he still had energy, while on others it was all he could do to climb into bed. Usually, when he felt better, he passed the evening playing poker after dinner. Gambling and poker had become his favorite recreation since joining the Navy. Back in Australia he'd been to the horse races several times, and on the sub he'd been a regular in the five-card-draw and seven-card-stud poker games. On one patrol on the *Gudgeon*, he'd won a couple of hundred dollars, which he sent home to his mother. In prison camp, he and the other gamblers had fashioned a deck of cards out of the discarded Japanese cigarette packs and used twigs gathered from the prison compound for chips. The men played for cigarettes, or sen, or in some cases food. Winners often bartered, maybe trading three cigarettes for half a bowl of millet. Or when somebody had been brazen enough to steal commodities such as beans or peanut oil from the galley, those items would be introduced into the economy. Chuck's advantage was that he had quit smoking since being captured, and the cigarettes he received every week were valuable barter.

Stealing had become a way of life at Fukuoka #3, prisoners risking severe consequences to steal a handful of rice, a pack of cigarettes, or anything they thought might improve their situation, even if it was a stick found along the road leading to the camp. Most of the prisoners sent to the guardhouse who were severely beaten and put on display were there for stealing or for being suspected of stealing. This thievery included stealing from fellow prisoners, an offense that ran the risk of incurring even harsher vigilante justice from the other prisoners than the guards might inflict. The Marines were sometimes the target of the thieves because they seemed to have more-valuable items. After they'd been captured on Wake Island, they were allowed to bring clothes and other personal belongings to prison camp with them. Also, they had been assigned to work in truck and auto repair and had access to better stuff there.

On this night, Chuck was too exhausted for poker, content to let his mind drift to thoughts of Gwen and Leighton Beach. By his calculations, the patrol should have returned to Fremantle seven months ago; he assumed that by now she knew that something had happened. But did she know that the crew had been captured, or that they were now in a prison camp in Japan?

Chuck thought back to when he was in school, regretting that he was such a troublemaker and that he hadn't tried harder in his studies. He wished he'd had the discipline and maturity he had in Submarine School back in high school. Now, sitting on the edge of his bunk in Fukuoka #3, he wondered why he'd been so hard on his teachers. They didn't deserve all his pranks and back talk. If this POW nightmare ever ended, he promised himself, he would go back to the old school and apologize to the teachers.

Although he'd been raised a Catholic, religion was not a big part of Chuck's life. More than once when he'd heard other prisoners praying for God to watch over them, he questioned how a benevolent God with all powers of good and kindness would allow such a barbaric situation to happen in the first place. There were occasional services on Sunday evenings conducted in another barracks by a priest who'd been captured in the Philippines, but the only time Chuck went was on Christmas. To him, the Saint Christopher's medal Gwen had given him had become his vessel of faith and hope.

Still waiting for Johnny Johnson, Chuck heard a commotion near the front opening of the barracks. He looked up and saw three Marines push a battered and bloodied Thomas Trigg into the barracks. Trigg looked like he'd just gone ten rounds with Joe Louis.

"Let that be a lesson to you, nigger," barked one of the Marines. "Don't even think about stealing from us again."

Trigg stumbled across the concrete floor, collapsing into his bunk. None of the *Grenadier* crew moved to help him. Although Chuck, like the rest of the men, disliked Trigg, there was a part of him that felt sorry for him. He was the only black man on the crew, and surely he had to feel alone and discriminated against. But when Chuck tried to put himself in Trigg's shoes, he wondered why Trigg would have ever signed up for submarine service. But of course neither Chuck nor anyone else on the crew had ever sat down to talk to him about how he felt about the situation.

Finally, Johnny returned to the bunk, and he and Chuck lay down close together, holding on to each other, struggling to get warm.

Chuck shot straight up in bed, awakened by a screaming guard pointing a bayonet at his face. Everybody in the barracks was ordered to get up and stand at attention at the foot of his bed, "encouraged" by a dozen guards prodding them with bayonets. Like most of the other prisoners, Chuck had worn his prison uniform to bed to keep warm.

Being awakened in the middle of the night was nothing new to the crew, but this was the first time it had happened since they had been transferred to the new camp. It was late February 1944, and snow was still on the ground.

In the previous three weeks the crew had begun to face the reality that they might not all survive. On February 4, the first of the *Grenadier* crew passed away. Justiniano Guico, a Filipino of Chinese ancestry who'd been raised by an aunt in Los Angeles, had been a mess cook and the only other minority on the ship besides Trigg. A good-natured guy, he'd been treated especially badly by the guards, many of whom either had fought against the Chinese or hated anyone they suspected of being Chinese. Two weeks later, Charles Linder, a quiet married man from upper Michigan, died. Pneumonia was most likely the cause of death for both men, but Chuck believed they had just given up, losing the will or the strength to struggle. Their deaths had just strengthened his resolve to stay alive. Charles Doyle, despite his dire condition, was still alive, but just barely.

The guards ordered everyone to strip naked. As most of the guards began furiously pillaging through everything in the barracks, obviously searching for something, the other guards marched the prisoners outside into the snow and ordered them to stand at attention. Chuck guessed the temperature was below freezing.

While the search inside continued, the men struggled to keep at attention. Chuck shivered and shriveled, the biting cold numbing every part of him. He heard the guards rampaging through their stuff, turning over bunks and ripping apart clothes. It was anybody's guess what they were looking for; maybe stolen food that someone had stashed somewhere in the barracks.

An hour passed, and then another; now a freezing rain was falling. Chuck wondered if the men who were the sickest, especially Doyle, would survive this ordeal.

Of all the humiliation and degradation he'd suffered since his capture, this pissed him off more than anything else.

When the prisoners were finally allowed back into the barracks, it was a complete shambles, but evidently the guards hadn't found what they were looking for. Chuck was furious, but not surprised, by this action. He knew that the Japanese had no respect for anyone who surrendered rather than fought to the death: that was Bushido, the national code by which all Japanese warriors lived and fought. But to him this incident felt more personal, more invasive. The guards had violated his personal property and home, even if that home was a POW barracks.

It wasn't just the guards who had him pissed. He was angry that the prisoner responsible for the stolen goods—whether it was a crewmate or one of the men from Wake Island—didn't have the balls to step forward, admit his guilt, and take his punishment so that everyone else didn't have to suffer. But that kind of cowardice didn't surprise him anymore; ten months as a POW had taught him that captivity and the constant threat of death had a way of making many men think more about their own self-preservation and survival than what was best for everyone.

Of course, there was also the possibility that nothing had really been stolen, and the search was just another form of psychological torture.

Later that day, Johnny Johnson told Chuck that Charles Doyle was dead.

Chuck struggled to stay composed. First Guico, then Linder, and now his buddy Doyle, the Red Sox fan. He and Doyle would never have a chance to go to a game together.

He volunteered to help dispose of the body. He lifted his friend onto a pushcart and, accompanied by a guard, wheeled Doyle out of the camp toward the town of Tobata, two miles away. The journey was slow, the road slippery and full of holes.

Chuck had never been philosophical or spiritual. But pushing Doyle's body along the bumpy road gave him pause. Being a submariner had allowed him to maintain a distance from the violence. You fire a torpedo or a deck gun and you don't see the eyes of the enemy. You don't have your buddy blown to bits next to you in a foxhole or while landing on a beach. And even though other prisoners had been dying every day since they'd arrived in Japan, he didn't know those men. This was different.

Pushing the cart, he glanced down at his dead friend. Doyle did not look comfortable even in death, his once sturdy body wasted away to skin and bones, his hollow eyes still wide open, his stare the same in death as it had been at the end of his life.

In Tobata, a large outdoor furnace awaited; the disposal of all the dead POWs was the same. Chuck wheeled the cart to its opening, then pulled Doyle's stiff body off it and with a mighty heave threw him into the fire.

Stepping back, he pulled Gwen's medal from his pocket and clutched it tight, tears flowing. Later, a small wooden box with Doyle's ashes would be returned to the barracks wrapped in a purple handkerchief, to be placed on a shelf with a row of other small purple-wrapped boxes.

30

Bob Palmer

Ofuna

ob took a deep breath, inhaling the fresh air. It was October 19, 1943, seven days after he and the other twenty-eight men, including the offi-cers, had been blindfolded and separated from the rest of the crew. They'd been taken on a two-day train ride that ended at Ofuna, a railroad junction town on the eastern side of central Honshu, fifteen miles southwest of Yo-kohama and three and a half miles inland from Tokyo Bay. This was only the third time they'd been let out of solitary confinement.

Bob eased next to a crewmate and whispered a greeting. A guard standing nearby rifle-butted him in the back, knocking the wind out of him and sending him to his knees.

The prison camp at Ofuna was created as a "transit camp" where the *kempeitai,* the Japanese counterpart of the German Gestapo, interrogated prisoners, usually with the use of torture. Located on the site of a former school about a mile south through a tunnel from the railway station, the camp was on the opposite side of the road from a large temple and sur-rounded by hills. It had opened on April 7, 1942. Unlike all the other prison camps in Japan, which were controlled by the Japanese army and POW Information Bureau, the Ofuna camp was under the control of the Japanese navy. All the prisoners were captured Allied seamen or pilots, in-cluding many officers. Japanese officials had chosen the twenty-nine *Grena-dier* crew members to come to Ofuna based on their rank or job on the ship as determined during the earlier interrogations. They believed each had special information and needed more-thorough and forceful interrogation. As the ship's yeoman and record keeper, Bob had made the list.

The prison compound contained barracks of unpainted wood, with a tar-paper roof and wood-planked floors, built around a large, open area, surrounded by an eight-foot wooden fence with barbed wire on top. The prison barracks were connected, and each one was divided into small cells, six feet wide and nine feet long. There were ninety cells, each one housing one prisoner. Each cell had a thin bamboo mat for sleeping and a blanket that had to be kept folded during the day. There were no mattresses or pillows. The walls were thin and the floorboards were so widely spaced that the ground below could be seen; spiders and flies were regular visitors. The door into the cell had a peephole, and a small window facing out to the parade ground was at the top of one wall. The window in Bob's cell was too high to see anything out of other than sky.

Bob was struck by the utter stillness of the camp. He'd been a chatty sort of guy growing up in Oregon, and the hardest part of Ofuna so far was being locked in solitary confinement. He and the other prisoners were supposed to be let out once a day in the morning for a brief period of forced exercise, usually about half an hour of running around the inside perimeter of the compound. Sometimes they weren't let out at all. During this exercise time, guards closely monitored the prisoners, and anyone caught talking or passing a note was beaten. Whether it was being in solitary confinement twenty-three hours a day, or the enforced silence, Bob felt more threatened by the guards. They'd all been given nicknames—Swivel Neck, The Termite, Smiling Jack, The Butcher, Liver Lips, and Big Stoop—names whispered during the exercise period.

As he and the other prisoners started running around the perimeter of the camp, he glanced to his left and spotted a familiar face. He could barely contain himself: it was Captain Fitzgerald. The last time he'd seen him was at the Convent on Light Street when Fitzgerald was being dragged away unconscious after being waterboarded.

* * *

Tim McCoy, just before he got kicked off the *Trout*.

Bob Palmer—those eyes, sky blue and friendly, reminded Barbara of why she'd first let him sweet-talk her into the backseat of her father's car.

"Growing up, I went to bed hungry lots of nights," Chuck Ver Valin said. "Joining the Navy gave me three square meals and a regular paycheck."

When Gordy Cox's mom realized he wasn't going to graduate from Yakima High, she gave him permission to join the Navy. He was seventeen.

Barbara Palmer on her wedding day in 1941.

"Our wedding night is a trauma I don't think I ever got over," Gwen Ver Valin said.

Gordy and Weasel.

Gordy watched the *Grenadier* (pictured here on its inaugural cruise), his home, the place where he ate and slept, vanish beneath the ocean surface in stunning silence.

"The Convent on Light Street was such a beautiful place," Chuck Ver Valin said. "It's hard to fathom that so much evil took place there."

The POWs who were too sick to trudge off to labor at the steel mill stayed behind in their barracks at Fukuoka prison camp.

Tim knew that when he got out of that bunker, he would find the sonuvabitch who snitched on him and beat the hell out of him.

I.D. photo taken of Gordy when entering the POW camp in Japan, October 1943.

"In the fifties I bought a little boat to take my son sailing," Bob Palmer recalled. "He was my life."

"My men called me the Big V," Chuck Ver Valin said. "But not to my face."

When Bob saw Barbara again after almost thirty years, the first thing he said was, "Oh my God, you're as beautiful as ever."

Bob had trouble buying his son Marty's claim of PTSD. "That's a convenient scapegoat. Strange, there were none from World War II and Korea . . . only Vietnam."

"You never really get over losing a child," Chuck Ver Valin said.

A sign greets visitors to Gordy's house in Central Oregon: "Two people live here—one nice person and one old grouch."

"For a long time, I felt like I lived in his shadow," Tim McCoy, Jr., said about his father. "Now I feel like I stand in his light. He's been one hell of a mentor."

Bob turned his back to the door of his cell, shielding his hands from view in case a guard was watching him through the peephole. It was Captain Fitzgerald's birthday, and Bob was preparing a present for him, a ball of rice that he was crafting out of portions he'd set aside from his own servings over the last few days. If he was caught, surely he'd get another beating.

Still black and blue from the last beating administered for talking during an exercise period, Bob gently squeezed the rice ball, molding it into shape. To Bob's surprise, the gummy rice was holding together well. He knew his biggest problem would be smuggling it out of his cell past the guards and sneaking it to Captain Fitzgerald during exercise, but it was worth the risk; Bob would do anything for his captain.

Bob Palmer's hero wasn't Joe DiMaggio, or FDR, or his father: it was Captain John Fitzgerald. He admired everything about the man: the fact that he'd been a boxing champ at the Naval Academy, the aggressive way he pursued the enemy, the considerate way he'd peek his head into the yeoman's office and ask Bob how he was doing, the remarkable courage he'd demonstrated under torture. For Bob, who had been convinced that the Japanese had killed Fitzgerald, arriving at Ofuna and discovering that his revered captain was still alive lifted his spirits like nothing had since being captured.

By the rules of the Geneva convention of 1929, officers were not supposed to be beaten or made to perform labor. But of course the Japanese had not agreed to these rules, and had been even harsher in their treatment of Fitzgerald. In Penang, he and Lieutenant Whiting and Lieutenant Hardy were the only men who'd received the water torture, and Fitzgerald had been subjected to far worse. After one episode of his water torture he'd been beaten so badly that he couldn't even move when he woke up. On the morning he was taken out of camp, he was told to take a bath, but his right arm was paralyzed and his body was so sore that Whiting had to bathe him.

Bob slowly paced his small cell, contemplating the best way to smuggle out the rice ball. Maybe he could hide it in his armpit. If he hid it in his crotch it might make him limp, though that wouldn't necessarily raise suspicion.

Bob's physical condition had deteriorated since his arrival at Ofuna. He hadn't had a bowel movement in over two months; there were boils on his legs and he weighed less than 120 pounds. He had bruises all over his body. On his first night in camp, four guards entered his cell and beat and stomped him over and over while he curled into the fetal position, covering his head with his arms, just hoping to survive.

The routine at Ofuna, Bob quickly learned, was tightly regimented. Each morning at five minutes before reveille, a guard marched down the corridors yelling at the prisoners to get up. After folding their blankets and placing them in a corner of their cells, they were marched outside and forced to run around the compound, usually for a distance of three or four miles or until a prisoner fell. Guards armed with baseball-bat-sized clubs were positioned at four different places round the perimeter. Anyone lagging behind was beaten across the back and legs. Almost all of the prisoners were either malnourished or suffering from beriberi, so few made the run without being beaten or collapsing, including Bob. Twice in his first month he was caught trying to whisper to other prisoners and the guards made everyone stand at attention for ten straight hours. But their favorite trick to punish Bob was something he called the Ofuna Crouch—bent at the knees, back straight, arms overhead, and up on the balls of his feet. As soon as he wavered or fell, which he always did, a guard beat him with a club and forced him to resume the position. Each day, after exercise period was over, he and the other prisoners were marched back to their rooms and fed one teacup of rice and a cup of thin soup, precisely measured.

Fitzgerald had been taken to the interrogation center and questioned almost daily by officers he'd named the QKs, or Quiz Kids. One focus of their questioning was where the *Grenadier* and other American submarines were based. (Someone on the crew—and nobody knew for sure who it was—had coughed up the real name of the sub.) Fitzgerald was determined to provide them with no useful information, no matter the consequences. From their questions, he determined that they believed American subs were stationed in Sydney on the east coast of Australia, so he played along, telling them the *Grenadier* had arrived there directly from Pearl Harbor by traveling east of the Marshals and past the Fiji Islands. They also wanted to know how many American subs had been sunk or damaged. Again he lied, telling them fifty subs had failed to return and over forty were seriously damaged. On questions about the design and specifics of the *Grenadier,* he provided them only with information that was readily available in *Jane's Fighting Ships,* a book he knew they had in their possession. When they intercepted a radio broadcast from Australia that mentioned American subs refueling at Exmouth on the northwestern Australian coast, he maintained he knew nothing about that, even though the *Grenadier* had taken on fuel there on its fateful last patrol. To make sure that Lieutenant Hardy and the other crew members told the same story, he left short, cryptic messages in the *benjo* after each interrogation or whispered to them as they exercised. Bob had been questioned several times and he had repeated the same story.

Still holding the rice ball, Bob paced the four steps across his cell and then back the other way. By his calculations he still had a couple of minutes before the guard opened his door.

Pacing his cell was what he did every day, pacing and thinking. Usually his thoughts went to Barbara. He relived their wedding night—the late-night ceremony at the church on Dolores Street in San Francisco, dinner at Vanessi's, making love in the apartment on Pine Street. He pictured what it would be like if he survived all this: She would greet him as he got off the ship and walked down the gangplank. She would be wearing the new charcoal-colored dress and pillbox hat she'd bought for their wedding. She'd be so beautiful, so happy to see him. It would be the happiest day of his life. He'd been unfaithful on leave in Australia, but in his mind, that had nothing to do with how much he loved Barbara. Getting home to her was what mattered. Maybe he'd stay in the Navy; before he left he'd talked to Barbara about maybe trying to become an officer. That had impressed her. Or maybe they'd move back to Oregon. In his head he designed the house they'd live in on the Rogue River. He would be able to fish right

from the porch. Barbara would cook the trout and serve it with sweet potatoes and huckleberry ice cream. And then they'd make love. And there
would be kids. Maybe three, maybe four.

In his darkest hours, he worried that Barbara had given him up for
dead and had already met someone else.

Hearing the guard's footsteps approach his cell, he stuffed the rice
ball under his arm and waited. The door opened; it was Big Stoop.

Walking toward the door, Bob felt the rice ball start to slip and pressed
his elbow closer to his side, pinning it more firmly in place. He wasn't worried about being beaten; he didn't want the rice ball to be taken away before he could give it to Captain Fitzgerald.

Moving briskly down the long corridor, he made it outside and stashed
the rice ball under a bench, then turned to look for Fitzgerald; there was
no sign of him.

"Speedo, speedo," Big Scoop gave the command to start running.

Forty-five minutes later, exhausted and sore from being clubbed several times, Bob finally wobbled to a stop; there was still no sign of Fitzgerald. Shoved along by Big Stoop, he headed back toward his cell, the rice
ball still hidden under the bench.

Sitting at the bar in the Sir Francis Drake Hotel, Barbara Palmer eyed her
watch. It was January 1944, nine months after Bob had been captured.
She'd come to the hotel with friends, a married couple who had arranged
to have a male friend come and join them for a drink. The guy was already
ten minutes late.

In May 1943, a month after the ship had gone down, she had been at
home early one evening when there was a knock at the door. It was Western Union with a telegram from the Department of the Navy, informing
her that the *Grenadier* had been lost on patrol and the whereabouts of the
crew were unknown. She cried herself to sleep that night. For a week she
stayed home from her filing job with Southern Pacific on Montgomery
Street, alternately crying and checking with the Red Cross and the Navy

to see if there was any news on the crew. She heard nothing. She took a bus home to Medford to spend a few days with her parents and Martin and Cora, Bob's father and stepmother. Her father was surprisingly supportive. He and Bob had gotten along better on Bob's last trip home, Bob winning points by talking with her father about the workings of the submarine. Barbara's mom, although sympathetic, was quick to remind her what she'd said about the hardships Barbara would encounter raising a baby if anything happened to Bob. For his part, Bob's father refused to accept the possibility that his son was dead, diverting the conversation to talk about what a lousy job FDR was doing and how his policies were responsible for Bob's being missing. Barbara was not political, but she wondered why Martin disliked FDR so much, considering that it was a WPA project building the roads and lodge at Crater Lake that had employed him during the Depression. But questioning her elders wasn't part of her personality.

Still seated at the bar, Barbara checked her watch again. Her "date" was now twenty minutes late.

Coming to the Sir Francis Drake had become one of her favorite things to do in the last couple of months. She loved the hotel's elegance and high style, with its classic crystal chandeliers, gilded ceilings, curved marble staircase, and a lounge that overlooked Union Square and the Powell Street cable cars. Plus, it was a favorite spot of naval officers, and she took every opportunity to ask them if they'd heard anything about the *Grenadier*. None had, of course, but they usually bought her a drink. She appreciated their company.

Since returning from visiting her parents in Oregon, Barbara had done her best to keep busy. With friends, she went to several USO events. It made her feel better to dance with the servicemen and feel like she was helping the war effort. She went to Grace Cathedral, where volunteers gathered to help sort supplies to be sent to servicemen. And not a week went by that she didn't check with the Red Cross and Navy for any possible news about the *Grenadier*. In November 1943 on a trip to the Red Cross, seven months after the sinking, she saw a new listing:

U.S.S. Grenadier (SS210)

Prisoners of War

The following men reported missing on the U.S.S. Grenadier are carried as Prisoners-of-War on the records of the Casualties and Allotments Section, Bureau of Naval Personnel, Navy Department, Washington, D.C.

The names were listed in alphabetical order, from Ralph Adkins to Peter Zucco. Her eyes went straight to the P's: Piaka, Pierce, Poss, Price . . . but no Palmer. She read it again, over and over, and could not find Bob's name. She counted the names: forty-one. She didn't know the exact number of men on the ship, but thought it to be around sixty. She looked for Captain Fitzgerald's name. It was not there either. Did some of the men survive and not others? Had Bob drowned? Was he shot trying to escape? She went to the Navy offices on Treasure Island and she called back to the Red Cross almost daily, and always got the same answer: "I'm sorry, we have no further information at this time." She cried every night, every morning.

In early December 1943 a small package arrived at her apartment on Pine Street with an Australian postmark. She hesitated to open it; she didn't think she could take any more bad news. Finally, she unwrapped it, and her knees nearly buckled. It contained Bob's Navy dog tags and wallet and a short note from a woman named Leslie Phillips, informing her that Bob had left these at her house before his last patrol, and she figured Barbara would want them back. There was no explanation of why Bob had been at her house. Barbara assumed the worst.

The more she thought about it, the angrier and more hurt she got. Instead of continuing to cry herself to sleep every night, she resolved to start going out again. "I guess if he could go out, so can I," she told her cousin Margie.

A naval officer in his dress whites sat down next to her at the Sir Francis Drake bar. He signaled the bartender for a cocktail. She noticed he wore the dolphin insignia, the symbol of the submarine service.

As she usually did when she met Navy men, she told him that her husband had been on the *Grenadier* and was reported lost at sea. The officer expressed his regrets, then introduced himself. His name was Robert Kunhardt, and his submarine, the *Sawfish,* had just returned to San Francisco for a major overhaul after suffering damage from depth charges on its last patrol. He would be in town for three weeks.

The bartender brought his drink. He was, by Barbara's initial estimate, well mannered and nice looking, 5 feet 7 inches, with broad shoulders and blue eyes.

Three hours and several drinks later, they said good-bye, making a date for the next night. Her original date never showed. Returning to her apartment, Barbara shared her excitement with her roommate. "He's a graduate of Annapolis and an officer," she enthused. "I can't wait to see him again."

Through the thin walls of his cell, Bob heard a guard's footsteps coming down the corridor. He quickly finished urinating and moved the floor plank back into position. Normally prisoners were supposed to summon a guard when they had to go to the toilet, but sometimes the guards didn't respond, and prisoners had learned to remove one of their floor planks and relieve themselves on the ground below, a practice that ran the risk of a beating if detected.

Bob spotted a fly and quickly took off his T-shirt and swatted it out of the air. He picked it up and put it into a pencil box he'd been given to store his dead flies. Flies were everywhere in Ofuna, and the camp commander had set up a system in which prisoners were rewarded with an extra cigarette for each box of flies they collected. Bob had become an expert fly killer.

His cell door opened, and Liver Lips stood in the doorway, motioning for him to follow. The guard always carried a thick bamboo stick that he used to hit prisoners; usually, being summoned by Liver Lips meant a trip to the interrogation room or a beating. Bob took a deep breath and followed Liver Lips down the corridor.

Bob told himself that whenever the intensity of the beatings increased, it was a sign of an Allied victory somewhere, and the POWs were paying the price. Getting accurate details on the war's progress, of course, was not easy. Guards had told him that San Francisco had fallen and Tojo was in Washington, D.C. The most reliable source on war news came from the newest prisoners to arrive in camp, but because the prisoners weren't permitted to speak with one another, this wasn't always possible. Still, Bob had been able to whisper to Captain Fitzgerald about the rice ball under the bench, and Captain Fitzgerald had been able to let Bob know that he'd found it and eaten it with great appreciation.

Arriving at the medical office, Liver Lips pushed Bob inside. Bob stiffened. The medical facilities at Ofuna were woefully bad, with no doctor and only a minimum of supplies. There was a "medical technician" on site by the name of Kitamura Congochyo, a man the prisoners had nicknamed "The Quack" and considered to be one of the most sadistic men on staff. Since arriving at Ofuna, Bob had seen men with a wide array of medical problems—from scurvy and beriberi to intestinal parasites and pneumonia—denied treatment. When the men were allowed to go to the medical office, nobody seemed to come back improved. Some never came back at all. There was no shortage of horror stories: amputations performed with no anesthetic, bamboo strips used for acupuncture to the eyes. If the Red Cross was sending medical supplies, they weren't being used on prisoners.

Upon entering the office, Bob spotted a familiar face across the room, Greg "Pappy" Boyington. Standing next to him was The Quack. Liver Lips pushed Bob in their direction. With the possible exception of Captain Fitzgerald, Bob admired Boyington as much as anyone in camp.

Boyington, an ace Marine fighter pilot from Idaho, had recently arrived in camp after being shot down in a dogfight over the island of New Britain. A notorious bad boy with a proclivity for fistfights and drinking, he had formed a flying unit of misfits called the Black Sheep Squadron. His nickname was Pappy because he was ten years older than everyone else in the squadron. The Black Sheep quickly became a lethal force, credited with ninety-four downed Japanese planes. Nineteen of those were by Boyington, five of those in one day. After being shot down, he was pronounced missing in action and presumed dead. (In March 1944 he was awarded the Navy Cross and the Congressional Medal of Honor, to be held in Washington, D.C., "until such time as he could receive it.") Brought to Ofuna after his capture, he arrived in camp with an infected thigh wound he'd sustained when he was shot down. Since being in camp, he'd been beaten endlessly, his request for medical attention to his wound ignored until now.

The Quack ordered Boyington to lie down on a table, then signaled Bob to stand next to him. Bob glanced down at Boyington's gaping wound, almost gagging at the look and smell of the infected leg. He quickly figured out why he'd been summoned: he was there to hold Boyington down by his shoulders.

Using a knife that looked like it had been borrowed from the kitchen, The Quack sliced open Boyington's thigh. Keeping his hold on Boyington, Bob turned his head. If he'd had anything to eat, he was sure he would've thrown it up. Boyington gritted his teeth, but didn't flinch or yell out.

After probing the wound, The Quack removed a bullet fragment, then wrapped the leg in gauze and ordered Bob to help Boyington back to his cell. Boyington declined the help and hobbled back on his own. Bob was positive he'd just spent time with the toughest guy on earth. He felt reenergized and even more determined to be strong.

31

Tim "Skeeter" McCoy

Fukuoka #3

Working in the pipe shop at the steel mill, Tim waited until there were no guards or civilian pushers hovering nearby. Now was the time to make his move. "Whistle if you see somebody coming," he said to Gordy Cox.

Gordy nodded, although he wasn't sure he even had the strength to whistle. In the last couple of weeks, the malnutrition and dysentery had taken their toll. It was all he could do every morning to get up for roll call and climb on the flatbed car for the thirty-minute ride to the steel mill. Still, he was one of many who thought that going to work was better than taking their chances at the camp hospital.

A Japanese worker had recently changed the blade on one of the nearby band saws. Tim eased his way toward the saw, sliding past other prisoners and Japanese workers. Nobody paid him any attention. Of all the *Grenadier* prisoners, he was the one always moving around, leaving his position, testing the limits. He was committed to doing whatever he could to make things tougher for his captors, and nothing had diminished his resolve—not standing naked in the snow or watching the dead bodies being wheeled out of camp to the crematorium.

Reaching the band saw, he glanced around. It wasn't just the guards he was worried about. He was also leery of the civilian workers, the pushers. For them to catch a POW stealing was not only a victory for the empire but also a way to earn personal praise or, better yet, be rewarded with extra food; their rations had also been reduced.

Confident that nobody was looking, he grabbed the blade and pulled, bending it in the middle. It didn't break. He pulled harder, this time snapping it in two. He quickly took half the blade and stuffed it into his pocket, and then turned and headed back to his station.

Now his task was to file it down into a knife blade, and then smuggle it out of the pipe shop and sneak it past the guards and into camp.

Tim waited in line to board the flatbed car for the ten-mile train ride back to Fukuoka #3, watched by two armed guards.

He climbed up onto the flatbed car and sat down on his small, three-legged wooden stool. The POWs had talked the factory administrators into letting them make these stools in the carpentry shop so that they wouldn't have to sit on the wet, dirty floor for the thirty-minute ride. What the Japanese didn't know was that most of these stools had been crafted with a false bottom, and the POWs used them to smuggle things in and out of camp. The most frequently smuggled items were cigarettes and food.

Tim had successfully filed down the saw blade and slipped it into the false bottom of his stool; his plan was to deliver it to Dr. Herbert Markowitz, a Navy doctor who had been captured on Wake Island. Exactly what the doctor would use it for Tim wasn't sure, maybe to lance the boils the prisoners had developed from malnutrition. The reason didn't matter to Tim; all that mattered was that Dr. Markowitz had said he needed it. Like all the prisoners, Tim had great respect for Dr. Markowitz, although he knew that the doctor was limited in what he could do because of the lack of supplies and the fact that the Japanese controlled everything that went on in the hospital.

As the train slowly pulled away, Tim nervously surveyed the guards. Since the stools with the false bottoms had been built, contraband had been smuggled in and out on a semiregular basis, and nobody had yet been caught. The train entered the mile-long tunnel. A few weeks earlier there had been a discussion among a group of POWs about jumping the guards in the dark of the tunnel and stealing their guns. That idea was quickly dismissed, the prisoners concluding that their chances of survival if they escaped would be zero.

Inside the tunnel, Tim closed his eyes and tried to relax. When the train reached the camp, he would calmly climb down and walk past the guards stationed at the main gate, just like he did every day, carrying his stool in his hand, just like all the other prisoners.

As he often did, he let his thoughts drift to Valma back in Perth. Did she know he was alive? Was she still wearing the engagement ring he had given her? He and Chuck had talked about how they'd both fallen in love during their last leave, and how fast the time had flown by in those exhilarating days. For Tim, Valma was his first real love. Back in high school in Dallas, he'd been too busy to have a steady girl, always working after school to help support his mother. The few girls he'd met since joining the Navy had been a challenge to his Texas Baptist morals—that and the copious amounts of beer he'd become fond of imbibing. But Valma was different: beautiful and smart and devoted. He'd heard a rumor before the last patrol that there was going to be some kind of legislation enacted back in America that would allow war brides to be given special consideration in moving to America. Tim and Valma had discussed taking advantage if something like that was available. She had seen photos of California and movies that made America seem beautiful and glamorous, and once they were engaged she had made it clear she was willing to follow Tim back home. In his last letter home he'd told his mother about Valma and included her address, encouraging his mom to write her. He wondered if she had.

As was usually the case, when he thought about his mother, he also thought about his father. Even as a POW, he had not been able to let go of his anger toward his father for abandoning him and his mom. It had been a long time since he'd seen his father, and he wasn't sure he ever wanted to again; it was hard not to remember the image of his mother ironing other people's clothes in their scorching hot Dallas apartment. But he did wonder if his dad knew what had happened to him.

The train slowed to a stop, and Tim grabbed his stool and closed ranks with the other prisoners, his heart pounding. He knew that if he was caught, he'd probably be beaten and thrown in the little cement box next to the entrance so everyone could look at him as they marched in and out of camp. It was too small to even stand up in; surely he'd go crazy in there.

A guard eyed him as he approached the prison entrance. Tim looked straight ahead, not changing his stride. In a few more strides, he was safely past the entrance and walking down the camp's main passageway toward his barracks.

Later that evening, he delivered the blade to Dr. Markowitz. His bravado was renewed.

Tim pointed to his shoes. "Shoes," he said.

A young Japanese boy standing next to him in the welding shop nodded and repeated the word. Tim smiled.

It was part of his daily language lesson. When he and his crewmates were first captured, they had absorbed a lot of face slaps and rifle butts to the shoulder because they didn't understand the guards' orders. A few of the prisoners had made no effort to learn any Japanese other than their prisoner number, which they needed to know during roll call. Their attitude was: "Let those little Nips learn to speak English, because they're going to need to when they figure out they ain't going to rule the world." But Tim was doing his best to learn as many Japanese words as possible and to teach his captors English. Being able to converse with the guards and civilians, he believed, might give him some small advantage. Anything to beat the system and help him survive.

A month earlier, he had been transferred from the pipe shop to the welding shop. He missed not working side by side with his buddies Chuck and Gordy anymore, but he was really happy with his transfer; he thought he had just about the best job of anybody on the crew, even if he'd had to lie to get it. Because of a shortage of Japanese welders, the factory administrators had put out a call to the prisoners for experienced welders. Tim had never welded anything in his life, but a fellow prisoner named Ripper

Collins, who'd been a first-class welder on the USS *Houston* before it was sunk and its crew captured, told him he'd put in a good word for him to get the job. "It's a great place to work," Collins said. "There are no guards and they have a bunch of Jap kids to work for you." When Tim said he didn't know how to weld, Collins assured him, "I'll just tell the Japs you're rusty. They'll never know. I guarantee I can teach you how to be a great welder in just two weeks."

Within a week, Tim was welding flanges like he'd been doing it for years. He had also made friends with some of the Japanese boys assigned to help him. They were in their early teens, not quite ready for military service yet required to report to the factory every morning at 6:00 a.m. and work until 3:00 p.m. and then go to school until 9:00 p.m. Tim would work on his vocabulary with several of the boys who were interested in learning English, especially with one he'd nicknamed Babe because the boy liked baseball.

"*Kenchi?*" he asked, offering Babe a cigarette during lunch break.

Babe smiled and accepted.

The boys liked to think they were "big guys," so Tim offered them one or two Japanese cigarettes a day from the pack he'd get each week. He wasn't much of a smoker himself, so he'd trade his smokes to them in exchange for their *bento*, which was usually some rice wrapped in a cornhusklike leaf with a tiny slice of either fish or pickled white radish to go with it. To make his supply of cigarettes last longer and to get more food in return, he cut the cigarettes in half. In the two months he'd been working as a welder, he'd put on several pounds and gained back some of his strength. He'd even developed a taste for the pickled white radishes. He was, however, cautious in these cigarettes-for-food trades, aware that the guards would punish him if they found out. But so far he hadn't been caught.

After finishing Babe's *bento*, Tim relaxed, waiting for the factory whistle to end the lunch period. Instead, the quiet was interrupted by the loud, shrill wailing of an air-raid siren. With everyone else, he hurried to a reinforced area of the plant.

Tim listened for the drone of airplane engines overhead. In the last two months, air-raid drills had become an almost daily part of the routine at the steel factory. Although there had been no actual bombings as yet, some of the men who'd been captured most recently were saying that American B-29s would soon start bombing Japan. Allegedly, these planes would be taking off from airfields being built on the recently captured Marshall and Solomon islands. Tim had mixed feelings about these rumors. On the one hand, he wanted to see Japan leveled by American bombs. But he knew that the Yawata steel mill and the surrounding industrial complex would most likely be a primary target. He did not want to die from his own country's bombs.

Soon, the all-clear siren rang out and he breathed a little easier.

Sneaking into the storeroom next to the food galley, Tim looked back over his shoulder to make sure there were no guards in sight. A stack of fifty-pound burlap bags filled with soybeans sat straight ahead.

Of all of his limit-testing capers, he knew this one was the most daring and the one most likely to land him in the dreaded guardhouse. When he'd first spotted the unguarded stack of soybeans, he'd become fixated on pulling off this heist. He knew he couldn't steal a whole bag, but he thought he could drain out three or four pounds and cover his tracks so that they would never be missed. He planned to sneak them back to his barracks, and each day he could take a couple of pocketfuls to work and bake them with his welding torch.

Quickly, he moved to the stack of soybeans and pulled out a two-foot piece of bamboo he'd hidden inside his shirt. He had cased the job the previous day and knew that the bags were stapled at the top and could not be opened without cutting the bag, so he'd sliced off one end of his bamboo stick at a sharp 45-degree angle.

With a quick jab, he punctured the side of a bag, and then pulled out a pair of borrowed dungarees that he'd knotted at the cuffs. With the hollowed-out bamboo serving as a drain spout, he placed a leg of the dungarees at the end of the drain and watched as the beans flowed smoothly out of the bag, filling a part of one leg, then the other.

Satisfied, he withdrew the bamboo from the bag and watched as the slit closed behind it, resealing the bag good as new. Although he'd taken more beans than he'd initially planned, it was only a hundred yards back to the barracks, where he planned to stash the beans under his bunk.

With the dungarees slung around his neck like an Ivy Leaguer's sweater, he slipped back out of the storeroom and headed for the barracks, trying to stay calm. But standing directly between him and his barracks was a guard, and the guard was staring directly at him.

Tim continued walking, eyes straight ahead, arms folded across his chest in hopes of camouflaging his contraband.

It didn't work. The guard stepped in front of him and signaled him to stop. For an instant, Tim thought about running. But he knew that would be useless.

The next morning, he lay curled up in the guardhouse, barely able to move, as the other prisoners filed past him on their way to catch the train to work. Standing next to his cage, a guard angrily pointed at him: *"Daszu dotabo!"* he shouted. ("Bean thief!") *"Daszu dotabo!"*

32

Bob Palmer
Ofuna

A guard summoned Bob to join a work party in unloading a newly arrived truck. It held seventy-two cases, each containing eight cartons of Canadian Red Cross food. Bob wondered how many boxes the Japs would steal. He hoped Captain Fitzgerald, the ranking officer in the camp, would demand all of it go to the prisoners.

Bob now had another reason to admire Captain Fitzgerald: the captain had started secretly keeping a journal in case an accurate account of their treatment would be needed after the war. Fitzgerald scribbled his thoughts in a small notebook he'd stolen from the hospital and kept it hidden under a plank in his cell. In case it was discovered, he was careful about his language.

Jan 6, 1944. Questioned again. They have been at me every day since my capture off Penang. This time mostly political and history of naval officers in U.S.N. Back in cell took a lot of will power to take the last part of starch from my rice bowl in order to stick a snapshot of my wife to a piece of plywood.

Jan 24, 1944. 21 men left camp today for another camp. Was questioned again yesterday, general topic, why was the U.S. submarine force morale so high. The tobacco situation is becoming very acute—looks like we might all become non-smokers in a cou-

ple days. I believe they are short of this commodity and no ships
to provide same, ok by me!

Jan 25, 1944. Q.K. again morale of submarine [force] and what
makes it high in U.S. Wonder what the Japs are driving at? It
snowed, first I'd seen since Nov. '41 in Portsmouth, N.H. Physically am much colder here—no heat whatsoever, and barracks are
well ventilated.

Feb 2, 1944. Peg's birthday. Hope to be present for the next one.
Coffee and cigarette particularly good today. Exceed my chocolate ration for the occasion.

Feb 3, 1944. Are we prisoners? Unarmed enemies! Have been
told many times that we're not POW's and names not sent in—a
helluva note!

Mar 3, 1944. Had my first piece of steak since capture, was about
$\frac{3}{16}$ inch thick and about 2½ inches in diameter, was very small but
enjoyed very much.

Mar 5, 1944. Sleet, rain and snow, high wind and cold as hell—
the most miserable day this winter; while taking the bi-weekly
bath, snow was blowing into the bathroom—slightly chilly!

Mar 14, 1944. 20 men left today. I've missed five transfers out of
here so far, maybe the next time, I hope.

After his entry of March 14, Fitzgerald talked briefly with Bob during the exercise period, letting him know he'd requested that all of the
men from the *Grenadier* be transferred to another camp, but obviously it
hadn't helped. One of the reasons Bob had hoped to be transferred was

that at a new camp the prisoners might be allowed to get mail. Nobody at Ofuna had received anything.

Robert Kunhardt stood in the doorway of Barbara's apartment on Pine Street, fumbling for the right words. In a couple of days, the *Sawfish* would be sailing for Pearl Harbor to rejoin the war. The overhaul had taken longer than expected, and Kunhardt had been in San Francisco for two months. He and Barbara had seen each other every possible chance during his leave. Sometimes she'd walk straight from her job as a file clerk at Southern Pacific and meet him for dinner; other nights they'd go dancing or out for drinks. He was usually in his dress whites, and other patrons often bought them drinks, a way of contributing to the war effort.

There was so much Barbara liked about Robert Kunhardt, including the fact that he was an officer and a graduate of Annapolis, where he'd been captain of the sailing team. He talked of one day becoming an admiral. Clearly he had ambition, and her parents had repeatedly told her that she should find somebody who would be able to provide for her, and not just on a sailor's salary. Kunhardt had grown up in affluence in Greenwich, Connecticut; his family owned a successful import-export business and was able to send him to fancy prep schools during the Depression. He talked about taking her back east after the war to meet his family, and spoke fondly of his mom and dad. He wanted to own his own yacht and told her he'd take her to fancy lawn parties on Long Island's North Shore like something out of *The Great Gatsby*, a book he loved. She couldn't remember Bob ever reading a book.

Lieutenant Kunhardt seemed mature and sophisticated. Barbara had never been anywhere outside of Oregon and California, and his stories of New York and Washington, D.C., sounded so worldly. She also liked to listen to him talk about the submarine and his duties as an officer. It all sounded so brave, yet at the same time frightening. She'd already lost Bob, and the thought of losing another man seemed unbearable.

But for all the attraction and all the promise of an entrée into a world

of privilege and class, she wasn't yet ready to completely give up hope for
Bob; it seemed almost unpatriotic. After all, they were still married. What
if he was still alive? What if one day he came home and learned that she'd
run off with another man? It had been only ten months since he was reported lost. What kind of wife wouldn't wait twice as long, or ten times as
long? Her dilemma wasn't helped by the fact that she didn't know any of
the wives or family of the other men on the *Grenadier*; there was no one to
share her grief with or seek comfort with. There was also the simple fact
that he was, after all, her first true love, and down deep, she still loved
him. Of all the guys she'd dated, he was the most passionate and romantic and daring. Kunhardt, for all his intelligence and bright future, was a
by-the-book guy. The first time she'd brought him back to her apartment
(her roommate was in the hospital), she had been the one to initiate making love. "You're still married," he hedged. "I don't know if this is right."
She assured him it was. On another occasion, he invited her to a party at
the officers' club at Hunter's Point but asked her not to tell any of the
officers that she was married or that her husband was missing in action.
She did as he asked, infatuated with being part of the elite world of commissioned officers, something that was never going to happen with Bob.
The only possible red flag she saw with Kunhardt was that he'd imbibed a
little too much on a couple of occasions and had been rude to waiters. But
she liked to drink, too, so it wasn't something she worried about.

Standing in the doorway of her apartment, she and Kunhardt fidg-
eted, both having trouble saying good-bye. During the two months they'd
been together, he had repeatedly talked about recent American victories in
the Pacific—the Marines taking Bougainville, U.S. troops invading Tarawa
in the Gilbert Islands and New Britain in the Solomons, and most recently
the capture of Kwajalein in the Marshall Islands. These were places she'd
never heard of, but when he talked of the inevitability of a Japanese surrender, there was strength in his voice and believability in his conviction.

After their final good-bye kiss, he asked if she'd wait for him to return.
"Of course I will," she promised.

* * *

Back in the prison camp at Ofuna, Captain Fitzgerald wrote in his journal:

Apr 16, 1944. During the past week the rice ration has taken another 25% drop. By actual test the quantity we now receive can and has been fitted into a tea cup. It's said that rice is now short but if so how about the truck which backed up to the kitchen last night and hauled several bags of it away.

Apr 17, 1944. Rations throughout Japan cut, ours to 213 gms/meal. So it looks like tightening the belt and forget it! For two years this camp has had a full bowl, now only a ½ bowl or less, don't suppose we'll starve but the midsection is somewhat lean and this launches a bit of complaint.

May 29, 1944. They must realize that Japan cannot win the war and are beginning to think what the reactions will be upon return home, if this rather harsh treatment continues, some days it's fairly good, but when it's bad it's a bit of hell around here.

June 8, 1944. Questioned by naval j.g. He stated that if Japan were to be destroyed, so would prisoners, therefore, we should hope for Japan's victory. My reaction and statement to that was to the effect that if this government chose to put a bullet into me there would be nothing I could do to prevent it and doubted that it would help the Japanese war effort.

June 22, 1944. Rumor has it that more men to be transferred soon.

33

Tim "Skeeter" McCoy

Fukuoka #3

Scrunched up in his little four-foot by four-foot cement cage after he was caught stealing beans, Tim heard bombs exploding in the distance, then the sound of planes high overhead. He could see Japanese guards running for cover. He knew that the main target for the bombs was the steel mill, where all of his crewmates were at work.

It was June 15, 1944, and for the first time in the two years since Doolittle's raid on Tokyo in April 1942, American planes were attacking the Japanese homeland. In a plan implemented at the direction of President Roosevelt called Operation Matterhorn, American's newest weapon, the B-29, had been rushed into combat, its mission to destroy Japan's ability and heart to wage war. Nicknamed the Superfortress, it was one of the most advanced bombers of its time, featuring a pressurized cabin, central fire-control system, and remote-controlled machine-gun turrets. Manufactured by Boeing and assembled in factories in Washington State, Kansas, Georgia, and Nebraska, the four-engine plane was designed for use primarily as a high-altitude daytime bomber, with a range of nearly 4,000 miles and a capability to fly at speeds up to 350 mph and at altitudes up to 40,000 feet, which was higher than the Japanese fighters could fly and out of range of almost all antiaircraft fire. The long-range plan was to have these planes attack Japan from bases in the Marianas, but American forces had not yet completed construction of the necessary airfields there, so President Roosevelt secured support from India and China to use bases in those countries for the attacks. This first attack was launched from Chengdu, China, with forty-seven B-29s all loaded with tons of bombs. Their target was the Imperial Iron and Steel Works at Yawata.

For what seemed like forever, Tim lay curled in his box, helpless, listening to the explosions, worrying that his buddies were being blown to smithereens.

A month had passed since the bombing. Surprisingly, little damage had been inflicted on the steel mill, and although the B-29s had been heard passing overhead again, there'd been no more attacks targeting Yawata. After five excruciating days in the cement tomb, Tim had finally been released, although he was back three weeks later. This time it was because the guards had found four cans of pork hidden under his bunk, a stash he was convinced Trigg had planted.

During his second stay in the tomb, Tim received only one small rice ball per day. The rice had been laced with rock salt, which made him thirsty, a thirst that the spoonful of water he got each day didn't quench. The guards beat him repeatedly, and every day that he was caged, he vowed that when he was released he'd find the "gutless sonuvabitch" responsible for doing this to him.

Neither Tim nor Trigg had made any effort to hide their dislike for each other. Tim figured that Trigg just didn't like any white people, which seemed like a tough cross to bear given that the Navy was practically all white. Tim had been raised to believe that it was best if the two races stayed apart. His dad had preached that, and so had his church. He'd never really known any blacks. Maybe if Trigg didn't have such a chip on his shoulder (whether he had good cause to or not), then maybe Tim wouldn't think he was such a prick. On more than one occasion, Tim had called him "a dumb nigger." But so had everyone else on the crew, including Captain Fitzgerald.

Tim was clearly not alone in his dislike of Trigg, and the animosity had gotten worse since they'd been captured. Everyone believed that Trigg had been getting special treatment from the guards. Nobody could remember him getting interrogated in Penang. He hadn't been beaten as much, and he always seemed to be served more food. Plus, he often played sick to get out of work at the steel mill, and somehow got himself assigned to the galley, where he had access to the food supply. More than the other prisoners, he had maintained his weight, and was still an imposing figure. But Tim wasn't intimidated.

He pushed himself off his bunk and stormed in Trigg's direction. "Get out of that bed!" he screamed.

Trigg didn't budge. "What's your problem?" he said.

"You planted those fuckin' beans," yelled Tim.

"No I didn't," Trigg replied.

Tim reached down and grabbed him by the shirt, jerking him to his feet. "God damn liar!"

Trigg lunged at Tim, grabbing the wooden dog tag that hung by a chain from his neck. He pulled him toward him, their faces now a foot apart.

"Let go!" warned Tim.

Trigg twisted harder, Tim's face turning red. With a strong upward sweep of his forearm, Tim knocked Trigg's hand loose from its grip. Before Trigg could react, Tim took a quick step back and kicked him as hard as he could right square in the balls. Trigg crumpled to the floor, writhing in pain. Tim turned and returned to his bunk, congratulated by his crewmates.

34

Gordy Cox

Fukuoka #3

Nursing two black eyes and a broken nose, Gordy sat on the edge of his bunk, wondering if this hell was ever going to end. It was July 1944. The previous day, Water Snake, an eighteen-year-old civilian pusher at the mill, had beaten him senseless for no reason. Gordy's face was so swollen he was hard to recognize.

"Are you going to take a bath?" asked Tim.

Gordy shook his head, an emphatic no. The prison compound included a bathhouse with two separate rooms, one for the Japanese guards, the other for prisoners, each room with a large concrete tub big enough to hold fifty to sixty men at a time. For the prisoners, the order of bathing was rotated by barracks number between the twelve barracks and 1,200 men. By the time the second barracks had finished bathing, the water was always filthy, and like most of the crew, Gordy skipped bathing most evenings. Some evenings the layer of scum on top of the water looked thick enough to walk on. Gordy never bathed when the two barracks with the Indian prisoners went ahead of him. Most of the Indians worked all day loading coal, and by the time they returned to camp they were caked with black soot, and sometimes they washed their clothes in the tub, which was supposedly forbidden. It was Gordy's impression that the Japanese still believed that they could convert the Indians to their side, so they let them do things other prisoners couldn't.

He watched as some of his crewmates headed down to the bathhouse.

This evening, he was passing the time picking bedbugs; it had become almost a sport for him to see how many he could kill. Of the many aggravations and hardships of prison camp, perhaps the most irritating were the bedbugs and lice. Gordy wasn't always certain which bug was which; he just knew that most days they drove him nuts. The mat he slept on was always crawling with them, and sometimes when the person on the top bunk lay down, it unleashed a downpour of bugs. The bugs had crept their way into just about everything—clothes, food, hair, ears. But at least it was better than the infestation of crabs that some of the men had brought with them when they were first captured and taken to Penang. By now, most of the men, including Gordy, had shaved their heads in an effort to help relieve the discomfort. Many mornings his prison clothes would be filled with bugs. Prisoners were allowed to wash their clothes once a month, and within a day the lice and bedbugs were back. Still, Gordy considered himself lucky: a pusher at the pipe shop sometimes let him boil his clothes in a big pot next to the furnace.

Gordy watched a guard slowly make his way through the barracks, checking to make sure nobody was lying down yet. The rule was that prisoners weren't allowed to lie on their bunk until lights out, which meant no naps or resting in a prone position, not even after a twelve-hour workday.

The guard eyed Gordy picking at the bugs. It struck Gordy that the guards and workers in the plant, who were infested with the lice and bedbugs just as badly as the prisoners, were not bothered by them. Maybe they'd just gotten used to it, he thought, or maybe the Japs were truly different, and were as oblivious to the bugs around them as they were to all the pain and suffering.

Gordy reached up and plucked a louse from his eyebrow.

Resting on his shovel, Gordy glanced to the sky, first spotting the vapor trail, then the sun glistening off the plane. He didn't know what kind of plane it was, only that it was American and that almost every day it flew overhead, too high for Japanese antiaircraft. Initially, the Japanese had tried shooting it down, but the shells exploded halfway to their target.

They'd tried to scramble fighter planes up to get it, but they couldn't get close enough. Gordy had never seen the plane drop any bombs; it just flew in the same direction at about the same time every afternoon. To Gordy, it was a magnificent sight.

As a guard stationed nearby edged toward him, Gordy looked back down and resumed shoveling in the sandy dirt. A few days earlier he'd learned his lesson the hard way when a guard caught him staring at the plane. He'd absorbed a few raps alongside the head for that little mistake. It almost made him laugh; it was as if these guards believed that the plane would disappear if the prisoners didn't watch it. Clearly, it was making them jittery.

Gordy continued shoveling. For over a week he had been too sick to go to work at the pipe shop but not sick enough to be confined to the hospital. The ambulatory sick like Gordy were assigned jobs around the camp. Gordy was part of a crew digging a bomb shelter behind the camp. To him this was just another case of how dumb his captors were; digging was a lot more strenuous than his work at the pipe shop. But he'd learned early on in his captivity that logic didn't always apply here.

The prisoners had taken to calling the plane Photo Joe, speculating it was taking reconnaissance pictures, gathering information for an impending invasion. The guards had threatened that if indeed there was an invasion, all the prisoners would be marched down to Moji Bay, lined up at the shoreline, and gunned down, letting the tide carry their bodies out to sea. Gordy wondered again if it would be better to take a bullet between the eyes rather than die an ugly death of starvation. Plus, it would mean that the Japs were about to get slaughtered in their own backyard.

With Photo Joe out of sight, he turned his attention to the sand fleas. It wasn't the exhaustion of shoveling the dirt that wore on him as much as it was the sand fleas. Each new turn of earth unleashed more of these biting, hopping little crustaceans, which could jump ten inches, making the pale ankles of the prisoners the perfect target. Gordy's ankles were covered with welts and lesions, and it was hard to keep from scratching.

He paused, remembering the bugs he'd encountered when he and his brothers and parents slept on the ground when they were picking fruit back in the Yakima Valley during the Depression. He was twelve then. He thought about how hungry he'd get working those long days in the fields, and how some of his classmates called him an Okie. Eight years later, as he reached down to knock away the sand fleas, those seemed like good times.

After a week of missing work, Gordy convinced the Japanese doctor at the hospital that he was well enough to return to his job at the pipe shop. He wanted to work not so much because he was feeling better but because prisoners received more food at the steel mill. There were also more guards around the barracks, most of them with nothing better to do than make life miserable for the prisoners, showing off to each other about how sadistic they could be. In the pipe shop, Gordy could usually breathe a little easier, except when Water Snake (so named because of the way he slithered and snuck around) was on duty. Water Snake seemed to take special pride in picking on Gordy, maybe because Gordy was one of the smaller POWs.

Gordy was looking forward to lunch. Rumor had it that all the POWs at the pipe shop would be receiving a Red Cross food box on this day. So far, no Red Cross supplies had reached the prisoners at Fukuoka #3.

He took a seat at a lunch table across from Tim. Unlike Tim, Gordy hadn't gotten involved in any stealing and bartering on a regular basis. There was one time when he and another prisoner mustered up enough courage to steel some peanut oil and to trade it with some Javanese prisoners for rice. They smuggled it past the guards in a canteen, but Gordy was so nervous that he said that was the last time he'd try something like that. He'd been the same way as a young boy. When the other boys dared him to steal a candy bar, he wouldn't, not because of some higher moral code but because he didn't want to get caught.

Waiting at the lunch table with Tim, Chuck, and Robert York, Gordy spotted a guard heading their way. He was carrying one Red Cross box.

For several months Red Cross packages had been arriving in camp, but the Japanese were using them for themselves. The prisoners knew this and had repeatedly complained, but to no avail. Sometimes the guards would eat from one of the packages right in front of the prisoners, just to taunt them. Attempts to sneak into the warehouse where the boxes were stored and steal some of them had become a regular, if not always successful, occurrence. When an attempt to steal boxes was successful, the contents were like gold. Sometimes the thief devoured the food himself. Other times he'd use it in trade; nothing on the black market commanded as much in return. But when the Japanese suspected someone had stolen one of the boxes, everyone paid the price, guards trashing the barracks trying to find the stolen goods. And if they couldn't find the contraband, then they marched everyone outside and made them stand at attention all night.

The guard stopped at their table and set down the box, indicating that its contents were to be divided among the four men. Gordy opened the box and looked inside. It contained a three-ounce can of sardines, a biscuit, four prunes, and a chocolate bar. As meager as the contents were, it looked like Christmas dinner to Gordy and the others. They divided the sardines, biscuit, and chocolate bar into four equal portions; each man got a prune.

As Gordy put his piece of chocolate into his pocket to save for later, he looked up and saw Water Snake coming toward him, hand extended, demanding the prune.

Three days later Gordy sat in the barracks, listening to the exploding bombs in the distance and hoping that his crewmates at the mill weren't dead. He hadn't gone to work on this day, August 20, 1944, because his left eye was swollen shut. Water Snake had celebrated his last day before heading off to the army by taking a welding arc and torching his left eye, just because he could. Dr. Markowitz told Gordy he was lucky that he didn't lose the eye.

The bombing had started around noon. Even though the camp was several miles from the factory and separated by a hill, Gordy could clearly see the bombers.

Shortly after the first wave of B-29s had appeared, flying much lower than Photo Joe, ack-ack fire peppered the sky, and over a hundred Japanese fighters went up after them. From his vantage point, Gordy saw one of the fighters fly directly into a B-29's wing, both planes exploding, the debris hitting another B-29 and bringing it down as well. He saw another Jap fighter shoot down a B-29, and when the pilot and crew bailed out, the fighter opened machine-gun fire on them as they floated down in their parachutes. One of the men's chutes didn't open and Gordy saw him fall to his death. He watched as another fighter blew the tail off of another B-29 and the plane spiraled to the ground like a leaf in a strong wind.

With the war now going badly for the Japanese, the B-29 raids launched from the China-Burma-India theater were beginning to strike terror into the hearts of the Japanese public. Because of the long-distance fuel problems the B-29s were experiencing, they had been forced to reduce weight by carrying smaller bomb loads. They were not flying in formation, and were at a lower, more dangerous altitude, 27,000 feet, to take advantage of the jet stream. At this level, they were vulnerable to Japanese planes and antiaircraft fire. As ill-equipped to defend the home islands as it was, the Japanese Army Air Force, with the help of recently improved radar, had thrown itself fully into the task of stopping the B-29s. When earlier attempts to repel the higher-flying B-29s through conventional means had been unsuccessful, Japanese pilots had formed specialist-ramming flights, and this was the first time the strategy had been put to use. From Gordy's viewpoint, it appeared to be having success.

Finally, seven hours after the attack had begun, the last of the B-29s turned and headed back toward China. The prisoners from the steel mill straggled back into camp. Gordy met them as they entered the barracks. To his surprise, there had been no casualties among the prisoners; they had spent the duration of the raid in one of the recently built bomb shelters. The bombs had fallen all around the steel mill, but somehow had missed the target.

"A few sand-flea bites," said Tim. "That's it."

35

Chuck Ver Valin

Fukuoka #3

Chuck could hear the screams of one of the downed B-29 pilots, reminding him of the agonizing cries he'd heard from Captain Fitzgerald back in Penang. He hadn't seen any of the downed pilots yet, but everyone in camp knew they were there. If the men of the *Grenadier* had been the Japanese's most prized prisoners, the B-29 pilots had now replaced them.

Like most of the prisoners, except for those who'd grown up on the West Coast, where most Japanese-Americans lived, Chuck had not known any Japanese growing up. In the year and a half of captivity, he'd learned to hate them with every fiber in his body. To him they were Japs, Nips, slant-eyes, yellow-bellied cockroaches, bucktoothed yellow monkeys. He went to sleep every night hating them, and woke up every morning hating them even more.

During the buildup to the war, Chuck had thought the war in the Pacific was about halting Japan's expansionism. After the attack on Pearl Harbor, for him revenge was a motivating factor. But now that he had experienced how much the Japanese people hated whites, it was about race, a primal conflict of good versus evil. He'd listened to the guards and interpreters harangue the men about their almighty warrior code of Bushido and how in their eyes the men—white, Chinese, Korean—who'd allowed themselves to be captured did not deserve respect, mercy, or restraint, and were despicable and deserved to die. Maybe the Japanese weren't putting people in gas chambers like the Germans, but they were driving them to

their deaths by the tens of thousands just the same, by starvation, malnour-
ishment, dysentery, malaria, pneumonia, and beriberi. They beat them for
no reason, then told them that the only reason that they were being allowed to live was that the emperor had graciously spared their lives. To
Chuck, the Japanese were alien, grotesque, sadistic, brutal, and inhuman,
and it scared him to think that at the time of his capture they ruled millions of square miles of the world—China, the Philippines, Southeast Asia,
and a large part of the Pacific.

With so many POWs dying, Chuck had sat in on more than one conversation about survival. What allowed some men to keep going, whereas
others gave up? No simple answer emerged. Some men said it was religion that kept them going. Some said it was focusing on home and loved
ones, while others contended that it was easier for single guys because they
didn't have a wife or children to worry about. Some thought it was easier
for married guys because they had somebody waiting for them at home,
and they could escape to thoughts of being together again. Chuck didn't
think marital status had anything to do with it.

Chuck concluded that whatever it was, he had to believe that life was
still worth living and that he needed something to focus on, even if it was
hatred of his captors, even if it was staying alive just to see these Jap bastards have to pay for their savage ways.

But he couldn't say for sure why he was alive, and others, such as his
good friend Charles Doyle, died. Maybe it was easier for men like him, who
had never had much in the way of luxury and didn't expect too much out
of life, who knew more about hard work and grit and getting up before
sunrise.

Chuck took comfort in a sense of brotherhood, the shared POW experience, though with 1,200 men in the camp it wasn't one big united tribe.
There were eight nationalities in the camp—American, British, Australian,
Indian, Javanese, Dutch, Chinese, Portuguese—and everyone pretty much
stuck close to his fellow countrymen; there was little fraternization among
nationalities. Half the prisoners were Americans, and although they shared a
natural patriotic bond, Army, Marine, and Navy personnel stayed primarily

with others of the same service. Chuck noticed a special closeness within the Marines, maybe even tighter than the togetherness that he and his fellow submariners shared. He had developed a friendship with one of the Marines, Eugene Lutz, and they had even talked about getting together back home.

As far as Chuck was concerned, the guys who caused trouble, like Tim, were taking too big a risk. Survival was a lot easier, he calculated, if you did everything possible to stay invisible, like he and Gordy. But maybe in the end, none of it made any difference. Survival was a mystery. Sometimes strong men died and weak ones lived. It was like his poker games, he concluded, it just came down to the luck of the draw. The will to live was a gift.

Maybe it was an exercise in futility, but Chuck was writing a letter to Gwen back in Australia. Nothing gave him hope like his thoughts of Gwen and those glorious weeks they'd spent together in Perth and Fremantle. But he knew there was no guarantee the letter would be sent.

For the prisoners, the chance to send a letter was given randomly, often months apart; it was another form of torture. Their words were tightly scripted, allowed only on a preworded card with no chance for real communication: *I am interned at _____. My health is good/fair/poor. I work in a _____. I am treated well/exceptional. Please say hi to _____. I look forward to _____.*

Chuck knew that circling the more positive choice about his treatment did not improve the chances that the card would be sent. Recently, a batch of cards written two months before had been found in a bag in a storage room, a discovery that sucked the wind out of the prisoners, including Chuck.

Some of the men had received a letter from home, but Chuck had not. For the men who'd gotten letters, they were a lifeline. Some shared their letters, others hoarded them, a treasure more nourishing than food. They read them over and over and carried them everywhere, kissing them, pressing them against their hearts.

He closed his message to Gwen the same stilted way he had with his other letters to her: *I look forward to seeing you again after the war.* He hoped she could read between the lines—if she ever got it.

Lying in bed, Chuck debated whether to chance going to the bathroom. Getting up in the middle of the night and walking through the darkened barracks was not easy.

For one thing, there was the matter of the latrines. As disgusting as the bathing situation was in the camp, going to the toilet was even worse. The supply of toilet paper was always low, and the paper had the texture of 50-grit sandpaper. The stench from the latrines was constant, especially at night when the air was calmer. The tank was supposed to be emptied regularly, but it rarely was, and often overflowed. The job of cleaning it fell to the men in sick bay; they dipped the waste out with buckets and carried it to a small garden between the barracks where they poured it out as fertilizer. Oftentimes, guards would push them, spilling the contents of their buckets onto their legs.

Chuck continued his mental debate about a latrine run. Despite the exhaustion from a twelve-hour workday, sleep did not always come easily. As a child he'd shared a bedroom with as many as six siblings, but here a hundred men were crammed into one barracks. At least back home he had had a pillow and blankets and clean sheets and a mattress, things he knew he'd never take for granted if he survived.

The night was punctuated by men tossing and turning and snoring. Many of the prisoners had nightmares; they yelled out in their sleep, sometimes waking everyone close by. There were also men with "happy feet," a painful condition caused by vitamin deficiency that affected the nerve endings in the feet, causing men to moan and groan through the night, or get up and shuffle back and forth through the barracks, hoping for relief. But those men were few compared with the number of prisoners with dysentery who had to take endless trips to the *benjo*.

Deciding he couldn't hold out until morning, Chuck rolled out of his bunk and tiptoed across the wooden planks of the barracks toward the latrine. Tonight, the stench was especially bad. At the end of the barracks he saw a shadowy figure and he paused, debating whether to return to his bunk. Too many times he'd heard men make their way to the latrine in the middle of the night only to be intercepted by a bored guard assigned to the night watch, with nothing better to do than administer a random beating.

Before Chuck could turn around, the figure moved toward him. He braced himself.

"There's no toilet paper," the man whispered.

Chuck recognized his buddy Eugene Lutz.

Chuck resumed his course. He hoped someone had left a Japanese newspaper or some scraps of paper on the floor. As a boy his family had often had to make do without toilet paper, sometimes using pages from a Sears catalog, which by his analysis were softer than the toilet paper the Japanese supplied. In any case, he wasn't going to use the Dutch method. Like most of the other American prisoners, Chuck shared a lack of respect for the Dutch, partly because of what he perceived as their grumpy demeanor, and partly because of their propensity for not using toilet paper, a habit that even in the squalor of the prison camp Chuck found disgusting.

Able to scrape together enough pieces of paper, he finished his business, as flies buzzed around his head and fleas clung to his legs. He stumbled back through the darkness to his bunk. Not wanting to disturb Johnny Johnson sleeping next to him, he lay motionless, feeling the bedbugs crawling over his legs and biting his legs so hard it felt as if they were taking a blood-bank donation.

Hearing the grumbling and seeing the angry glares, Chuck slammed down his serving ladle and clenched his fist, ready to fight.

It was dinnertime and Chuck had recently been put in charge of dishing up the rice. In a world where every grain of rice and sip of soup mattered, the man serving the food was God, only more closely scrutinized. At every meal, prisoners examined their portions like lab scientists, comparing it with others'. If they thought they got less, they shouted or whined, and tempers often flared.

The position of server was coveted, and of all the jobs in camp, it was the most political in nature. In Chuck's case, the ranking officer in his barracks had appointed him because he thought that Chuck could be fair and magnanimous, and that he was tough enough to fend off the criticisms and threats he would surely get.

Chuck and the other servers went to the galley before every meal and filled up large pots with rice and the watery gruel the men called "Tojo Soup." After carrying the pots back to the barracks, the server dished out equal portions to all the men. No matter who was serving, the others accused him of favoritism, or of taking a hefty portion for himself before even leaving the galley.

Every prisoner's biggest concern was food—or lack of it—and obtaining it was every man's obsession; almost all the deaths in camp were a result, directly or indirectly, of malnutrition. For Chuck, it was excruciating to watch once healthy men turn into skeletons or see once proud men rummaging through garbage cans, hoping to find a guard's discarded orange peel.

Chuck didn't think anyone back home could possibly understand the extent to which hunger controlled his every waking hour. He compared it to his sex drive when he was a teenager. But now, if he could choose between a plate of meat and potatoes and a naked movie star, the plate of meat and potatoes would win.

When Chuck looked around the camp, he feared that most of the men wouldn't survive another winter, including Gordy, who was deteriorating daily. Pneumonia would most likely reach out and take them. But as much as he wanted to serve a larger portion to the most desperate, too many others were studying his every move.

Chuck didn't understand why some of the men faked illness in order to get out of work. He called them "babies." Chuck still hadn't missed a day of work, and figured he'd have to be on his deathbed before he would. It was well known that the Japanese, as a way to encourage productivity, served larger lunch portions to those who worked. There were others, however, who calculated that a hard day's labor would use far more energy than a few extra grains of rice could ever replenish, and so a camp doctrine of malingering was firmly in place.

Chuck also couldn't understand why some guys willingly traded rice for cigarettes. That was suicidal in his book, although on more than one occasion he had paid off a poker loss with a serving of rice. There were a few among the crew who believed he did it by skimming off a little rice from the serving pots.

Everyone in camp knew that to the Japanese, rice was life itself. One interpreter told Chuck that the Japanese had captured all the rice on earth, and without it, the rest of world was doomed. But the rice served in camp tasted like mushy, goopy grits, only without any flavor. Half the time there were flies in it, and sometimes maggots. According to the Geneva conventions, prisoners were supposed to be fed food from their national and cultural background, but everyone in Fukuoka #3 knew better than to expect that. Of all the food cravings Chuck had, that for sugar was the worst. He would've gladly traded five bowls of rice for one more can of sweet cling peaches like the ones he'd had just before he dove off the submarine. Like everyone else, he hoped that more Red Cross parcels would arrive soon, and each prisoner would be given his fair share. Then maybe the guys would stop accusing him of cheating them out of food.

Chuck had just finished his lunch in the pipe shop when he noticed Babe, one of the young pushers, coming toward him wearing a big grin; he was holding something behind his back.

Chuck retreated a step, not sure what to think. Of all the pushers, he trusted Babe the most, but experience had taught Chuck not to trust any Japanese completely. A couple of days earlier a piece of pipe had needed to be bent, and when nobody else was able to get the job done, Chuck took a big sledgehammer and, wielding it like a baseball bat, shaped the pipe.

Babe pulled his hand from behind his back and thrust it toward Chuck. In it he had two baseball gloves and a ball. He extended a glove toward Chuck, clearly an invitation to play catch. Chuck nodded, following him outside to a paved area.

Without speaking they began tossing the ball back and forth. Chuck smiled, enjoying the moment. He loved baseball, and this brought back memories of all the games he'd played as a kid, and the endless summer hours he'd spent at the ball field, using bats held together by electrical tape and balls coming apart at the stitches, pretending he was Babe Ruth or Lou Gehrig.

Earlier in the summer, one of the interpreters had said that Ted Williams of the Red Sox and Bob Feller of the Indians had both been killed in action. Chuck doubted that it was true, but he knew that FDR had declared that major leaguers were not exempt from serving. Williams had enlisted as a Marine pilot and Feller had joined the Navy.

Usually news arrived in camp by way of recently captured prisoners, but it was always hard to tell fact from fiction. Rumors were a constant. In the past few months, Chuck had heard plenty of them: Every POW was going to get a brand-new Ford when he arrived home. The *Queen Mary* had been sunk. Bob Hope had died in a plane crash. Malnutrition caused sterility.

He and Babe continued their game of catch, each putting a little more zing on their throws. Chuck's arm felt surprisingly good. When he was in high school and played on the town team, some of the older players liked to play burnout with him: a game of hardball chicken where two players stood fifty feet apart and threw progressively harder until they were firing as hard as they could and someone either cried uncle or got hit. He wondered if Babe knew the game. A few POWs and about a half dozen guards and pushers had gathered to watch them play.

The news the POWs most wanted to hear, of course, was about the progress of the war. By the end of the summer of 1944, a lot of positive news had reached camp, giving cause for hope: The Allies had invaded France at Normandy and the Germans were on the run; the Marines had invaded Saipan and Guam in the Marianas, and were building airstrips that would make it much easier to launch air raids on Japan. There was also word that American subs were wreaking havoc on Japanese shipping and cutting off their supply lines. The most recent rumor was that MacArthur was getting ready to retake the Philippines. There was no way to confirm any of these rumors, but Chuck wanted to believe.

Soon, he and Babe were throwing hard. Some of Babe's throws were starting to sting his hand; the flimsy glove offered little padding. Babe smiled. He was handling Chuck's throws with little effort.

Chuck knew he could advance their friendly game of catch to a full-scale game of burnout, confident he had a better arm than Babe. It would be a nice little victory, a statement of American superiority. But what if he lost? Then again, if he won, Babe and the guards might be pissed and take it out on him and the other POWs, like the three Marines who had won a race against the guards.

Deciding he was in a no-win situation, he eased up on his throws, and the lunch period ended with him and Babe back to where they started, a nice game of soft-toss catch, both of them smiling.

36

Bob Palmer

Ashio

Exhausted, Bob stood in front of the smelter at the Ashio copper mine, about to start the three-mile trudge back down the hill to the prison camp. It was March 1944. Bob and eleven of his *Grenadier* crewmates had recently been transferred from the interrogation camp at Ofuna to the prison camp at Ashio, a small mountainous town of 2,000 located about a hundred miles northwest of Tokyo. He and the others had suffered through six brutal months at Ofuna before the Japanese decided that they couldn't beat any more useful information out of them and that they would be more valuable as slave laborers at the copper mine. Captain Fitzgerald and his top officers were still at Ofuna.

Ashio was the site of the largest copper mine in Japan, producing 26 percent of the country's total output and playing a significant role in the development of Japan's economy. In the buildup to the war, the Ashio mine, by meeting increased demand needed for both foreign exchange and military purposes, was part of the foundation upon which Japan's imperialism was being built. But even within the country, it had become hugely controversial and the site of riots and environmental challenges. In its two centuries of existence, the mine's zealous pursuit of full production had eroded the surrounding hills, poisoned the farmland, and turned hundreds of square miles into an absolute wasteland. The once healthy forest that surrounded the refinery had been completely denuded. The sulfurous anhydrite from the smoke produced by the mining and smelting machinery had caused intractable pollution problems. Over the years, raging floods had carried poisonous waste from the mines, devastating the area's rich agricultural ecosystem, depositing monstrous slag piles, and causing massive fish kills in the nearby Watarase River.

But it was not ecological issues that Bob thought about as he continued slogging down the hill toward the camp; it was the angry citizens lining the road ahead, almost rabid in their hatred of America, every day a chance to spew their venom at the dirty, disheveled white men filing through their little town.

A gob of spit hit Bob on his cheek. He slowed, glancing to his left, eyeing a woman a few feet away, his instinct to grab her by the neck. He kept walking.

Sitting in her small apartment on Pine Street in San Francisco, Barbara read the certified letter from the Navy Department dated May 29, 1944, two months after she had said a tearful good-bye to Robert Kunhardt.

> *Dear Mrs. Palmer:*
>
> *You have previously been informed by this Bureau that your husband, Robert Wiley Palmer, Yeoman first class, United States Navy, was being carried on the records of the Navy Department in the status of missing. He was on board the USS GRENADIER when that submarine was reported overdue and presumed lost from a mission against enemy shipping in the South Pacific area.*
>
> *Pursuant to the provisions of Public Law 490, as amended, the Secretary of the Navy has given careful consideration to the circumstances surrounding the disappearance of your husband. In view of the fact that the list of prisoners made available by the Japanese through the medium of the International Red Cross have included the names of some of the personnel of the GRENADIER and because the possibility that your husband may be an unreported prisoner of war, the Secretary of the Navy has directed that he be continued in a missing status until information*

is received or other circumstances occur which would indicate that he
should no longer be continued in this status.

By operation of law your husband's pay will be credited to his ac-
count and any allotment registered in behalf of his dependents or for the
payment of insurance premiums will be continued so long as he is carried
in a missing status.

The Navy Department is aware of the anxiety experienced by the
relatives of those men whose fate remains undetermined. You are assured
that you will be promptly informed upon receipt of further information
concerning your husband.

Sincerely yours,
A.S. Jacobs
Commander, USNR
Head of Casualties and Allotments

Barbara reread the letter. On the one hand, she was thrilled to learn
that Bob had not been declared dead. But what if he was alive? She was
now in love with another man, a man she was convinced could provide a
better future, a man to whom she'd made love and written love letters.

Bob had beriberi. By his estimate, half of the 275 prisoners at Ashio had it,
the ones who had it the worst paralyzed from the waist down. Those men
were housed in the sickroom, or as the other prisoners called it, the Death
Hut. Bob wasn't ready to check himself into the Death Hut, not yet anyway,
but he knew his condition was deteriorating. On this morning, instead of
going to work at the smelter, he headed for the Death Hut in search of
some sort of treatment.

It wasn't his first visit. Like all the prison camps in Japan, the medical
facilities and treatment at Ashio were severely lacking. Red Cross medical
parcels had been received, but the supplies were limited. On a couple of
occasions, Bob had received a vitamin B_1 shot, and although the shots had
not eliminated the beriberi, they had at least provided him with enough

relief that he could go back to work. He appreciated that, because no work meant less food.

The word "beriberi" derives from a Sinhalese phrase meaning "I cannot, I cannot," which seemed fitting to him. Because of his impaired sensory perception, weakness and pain in his limbs, irregular heartbeat, and swelling in his legs, the long walk to the smelter felt like climbing Mount Fuji. Some days he just couldn't do it. Another symptom was a weakening of his emotional state. For most of his life, even back in high school when his stepmother Cora was treating him badly or Barbara's father had forbidden her to date him any longer, he'd somehow kept his spirits up. But lately, especially since being transferred from Ofuna, he felt a gathering sense of hopelessness and doom.

Approaching the sickroom, he hoped Dr. Dullin would be there. He wasn't sure how Dr. Dullin had been captured, but he knew the doctor had little to work with in terms of supplies. If Dullin wasn't there he would have to see Katoku, one of the guards, or Kato as the prisoners called him. To them, he was a bit of a comical figure, often strutting officiously around camp carrying a riding crop that he liked to beat against his shiny black riding britches. He also served as a medical practitioner and liked to experiment on prisoners with what some of the men referred to as his "voodoo medicine." He'd treated Bob several times by shredding some sort of herbal root and rolling it into a ball, and then placing it on Bob's leg, arm, or stomach and lighting it with a firecracker-like punk. It would smoke and stink and burn and, as far as Bob could tell, accomplish nothing except to leave a blister on his skin. Kato's treatments seemed more humorous than anything else, especially the time Bob watched him treat a prisoner for hemorrhoids by placing one of the balls on the man's head. After it was lit, the prisoner looked like he had smoke pouring out of his ears; he got no relief from the hemorrhoids.

Bob's heart sank as he entered the sickroom. Kato was right there to greet him, telling him that he wasn't going to use the burning herb treatment; today he was going to try acupuncture. Bob had never heard of it. When Kato pulled out a very long needle, Bob winced, guessing it was two feet long. Already leery of Japanese medical treatment, he knew that Japanese doctors were using Americans for medical experiments, and he didn't want to be part of it, but he also knew he had no choice. He recalled the time he'd held down Pappy Boyington while The Quack operated on him without any anesthesia. Certainly this couldn't be that bad.

Kato stuck the pin in his swollen abdomen, then removed it and made two more punctures in the form of a triangle. The pin went in easily; there was no fat in the way. It wasn't painful. Kato repeated the process in Bob's knees and elbows; that didn't hurt either. In fact, to Bob the procedure didn't seem to be doing anything except annoy him.

Kato had Bob sit on the edge of a table while he stuck the needle into the back of his neck and began angling it down his spine, deeper and deeper until it was almost all the way to his tailbone. Then slowly he removed it.

Kato then felt Bob's face. "Very swollen," he said. "This help."

He pressed the needle into Bob's temple, breaking the skin and then wiggling it back and forth, pushing it deeper. Bob held his breath.

Dozens of Chinese prisoners were working in the mines at Ashio, and Bob suspected that they had taught acupuncture to Kato. However he had learned it, Bob's condition hadn't improved. At least the procedure had no ill effects, other than rattling his nerves.

Even though he sometimes had difficulty telling the Chinese from the Japanese, he was sympathetic to the Chinese prisoners' fate. In some ways it seemed as if they had it even worse than the Americans. Indeed, the Japanese had adopted a practice known as "laborer hunting," abducting Chinese from their North China farm fields at bayonet point and bringing them to Japan as slave labor. A high percentage of these laborers died in transit to the Ashio work site. Many arrived physically weak, and even though they were starving, they still had to work.

Japanese prison camp officials gave detailed instructions covering all aspects of camp life for Chinese prisoners throughout Japan. The specific directives given to control the Chinese prisoners at Ashio included the following: "(1) Be overpowering as method of control. (2) When you capture runaways, do not let them return to the camp and work again (if they are allowed to return, other workers will be relieved to see that runaways are not killed, causing others to flee). (3) Make their living quarters as shabby as possible. (4) Make the food as poor as possible and consider it to be fodder. . . . They should be given mostly bran, corn, or leeks, not rice or wheat. . . . Feed them according to the diligence of their work."

It was November 1944, and the snow was already falling in Ashio. Given his steadily declining physical condition and the woefully inadequate clothing for the cold, Bob worried that he wouldn't be able to survive the winter. At night, the temperature in his barracks fell below freezing. Still, he continued to work. To determine if a POW was still fit to work, they were required to stand naked in front of a guard and do a knee-bend. Those that could, worked.

Bob's jobs at the smelter varied. Some days he loaded the furnace; on others, he helped push the ore cars up to the blast furnace. And on the days the furnace wasn't working properly, he helped repair it. Because of the fumes, he had to wear a respirator.

One evening Bob sat down next to Ed Keller, one of the twenty surviving men from the crew of the *Sculpin*. Keller knew why Bob was there: to drool over his latest creation. Since arriving in camp, Keller had kept a diary filled with recipes for pies, cakes, and other desserts. He called it "The POW Cookbook." The recipes were detailed masterpieces listing every ingredient and step of the procedures. Like other prisoners, Bob liked to read the recipes; he imagined sitting down at a table with Barbara and slowly savoring every delicious, mouthwatering bite. Every week he anxiously awaited Keller's newest pie recipe, each one providing another escape for him: almond; chocolate custard; peach; pumpkin; raisin nut; rhubarb meringue; peanut butter; eggnog; strawberry chiffon; strawberry mousse.

"What'ya got today?" asked Bob.

It was a cheese pie, explained Keller, handing Bob the recipe.

Fill pie shell with mixture of ½ lb cottage cheese, ½ lb Phila cream cheese, 1 cup sugar, 2 Tbsp melted butter, 8 egg yolks, 6 egg whites, ½ cup cream, ½ tsp vanilla, ½ tsp baking powder, and ½ cup of pineapple. Beat mixture until fluffy with rotary beater. Chill unprepared pie in icebox, then bake in 400 degree oven to glaze pastry, then reduce heat to 275 for about 20 minutes.

Bob finished reading the recipe. "I'll take two," he said.

Bob sat on the edge of his bunk, trying to finish the scripted postcard to Barbara. Since arriving at Ashio, he and the other crew members had been registered as prisoners of war. On a couple of occasions, they'd been allowed to share a Red Cross parcel; they were also allowed to send a card home once a month. Bob had written faithfully, but he had no idea if the cards had been sent. A few of the men had received letters from home, but he'd received nothing from Barbara.

Today he was having trouble focusing. Maybe it was the cold. The previous day the guards had made him and the other prisoners stand out in the snow, naked, for seven hours, making him wonder if the guards weren't sexually perverted. Or maybe he was depressed, finally going over to the dark side. For the past couple of months, he'd felt his mind slipping almost as much as his body. Every morning he woke up and wanted to just play dead, no thoughts, no anything. The idea of working another day in the smelter was almost too much to bear. His beriberi had gotten worse, and his legs were so swollen that every step felt like all the capillaries in his body would explode. Life had become an endless crawl through a fog. He'd thought about going to the Death Hut and just letting himself die with as much dignity as possible. But then he thought about Barbara, and he willed himself to survive the day, and the next one, and the one after that.

But on this day, he was too weak to finish his letter or even think about another slice of cheese pie.

Part Seven

SAVED BY THE BOMBS

37

Tim "Skeeter" McCoy

Fukuoka #3

Jarred out of sleep in the middle of the night by the air-raid siren, Tim McCoy rolled out of his bunk to join the other hundred men lining up by the front opening of the barracks. It was mid-March 1945. These middle-of-the-night air-raid alerts had become an almost nightly feature of life at Fukuoka #3, and they were increasingly irritating for Tim and everyone else. It was the same drill every night—spend two or three hours huddled and shivering in the shelter, return to the barracks, and then get up in a couple of hours and trudge off to work in the steel mill, exhausted and sleep deprived.

Part of what made the air raids wearisome was that nothing ever happened. Rumor had it that a lot of other parts of Japan were getting bombed, but so far not Fukuoka or Yawata. Surprisingly, at least to the POWs, the Americans hadn't bombed the nearby power plant, which seemed to be such an inviting target with its six huge smokestacks. Not that the men were complaining. They all knew that a bombing raid on the power plant most certainly would spell doom for them.

With the American invasion and capture of Saipan, Guam, and Tinian in the Marianas, America's bombing strategy had changed. The first attack launched from the Marianas targeted the Nakajima Aircraft Company's Musashi engine plant just outside Tokyo on November 24, 1944. A total of 111 B-29s took off, but engine problems, cloud cover, and a jet stream with winds as high as 200 mph at precisely the high altitudes the planes were flying made accurate bombing impossible. Only 24 of the planes dropped their bombs anywhere close to the intended target; damage was minimal. In December and January, the bombing raids across Japan continued, but in addition to the other problems faced by the American planes, Japanese defenses were becoming more effective; the Americans suffered considerable losses and many of the captured downed airmen were beheaded. In late January 1945, General Curtis LeMay was transferred to run the B-29 campaign from the Marianas and improve the success ratio.

LeMay temporarily suspended the raids on Japan, diverting the B-29s to capture Iwo Jima, considered vital to the air campaign because it could be used to base fighters capable of escorting the B-29s to Japan, as well as provide an emergency field midway between the Marianas and the Japanese targets. On February 19, 1945, LeMay decided to destroy industrial feeder businesses and disrupt the production of weapons vital to Japan. Instead of using the high-explosive bombs that had been previously employed, he would switch to incendiary bombs, which he hoped would cause general conflagrations in the large cities. The high-altitude, daylight attacks would be replaced by low-altitude, high-intensity incendiary raids at night. To increase bomb loads, the B-29s were reconfigured, reducing their structural weight. The new strategy was to drop the bombs from altitudes of only 5,000 to 6,000 feet. By flying lower, the planes would no longer have to struggle against the jet stream and could fly below most cloud covers. This would save wear and tear on the engines and preserve fuel. LeMay was confident that the Japanese night fighter forces were weak, although he admitted that flak losses could be substantial.

Another new strategy had been added to American bombing. At the beginning of the war, FDR directed that only military targets be bombed. This differed from the British approach, which targeted cities following the German bombing of Rotterdam in May 1940. But with the American bombing of Berlin in March 1944, the rules had changed. Cities and civilians were now targets, including those in Japan.

* * *

In the dark, the guards hustled the men out of the barracks, assembling them next to a fence behind the kitchen building, not far from the power plant. On the other side of the fence was a small hill. A guard opened a gate in the fence, and the men passed to the other side, ducking and crawling into a deep, dark hole—the bomb shelter. The only illumination was the guard's flashlight,

The roof and sides of the shelter were corrugated metal propped up with tree trunks and branches. To Tim, it seemed like even the slightest shock wave would bring tons of earth crashing down, burying the POWs inside.

Once everyone had crammed together on their haunches, the guards backed away, closing and locking the door behind them, leaving the men no escape.

In silence, the men waited. They had been through this many times before, and each time there was no attack, only the discomfort and dirt of being penned together inside the shelter. Tim felt the sand fleas crawling up his ankles.

Adding to their tension was the knowledge that the Japanese had lined the edge of the shelter with dozens of sticks of dynamite, with a fuse running back inside the camp. Should the guards choose, they could light the fuse and bury the POWs, leaving little trace that they were ever there.

An hour in the shelter stretched to two, then three. The men became more claustrophobic, everyone fidgeting, trying to stay calm, but nervously waiting for the all clear.

Finally, the siren sounded and the guards opened the door. Tim was one of the first to crawl out. He couldn't help but wonder if getting bombed would be easier.

Near the end of the lunch break at the mill, a small crowd gathered in the open pavement area. On one side were a dozen prisoners, and on the other were guards and civilian workers. In the middle were Rooster Boy and Tim, about to face off in a wrestling match.

Tim hated Rooster Boy. A young man in his early twenties, he was the most athletically built of all the guards. Rooster Boy had singled out Tim as the primary target for his cruelty and sadistic treatment. On several occasions, Rooster Boy pulled Tim out of the roll-call line and hit him for no particular reason other than to humiliate him. When Tim had been locked in the guardhouse after he was caught stealing soybeans, it was Rooster Boy who wrote *Daszu dotabo* ("Bean thief") on a sign and posted it next to the cage. He'd also been the one to hose Tim with freezing water while he was locked inside.

But nothing that Rooster Boy had done angered Tim as much as an incident the previous week. Tim and one of the pushers in the welding shop had been trying to teach each other vocabulary when Rooster Boy approached and signaled Tim to get back to work. When Tim didn't move fast enough, Rooster Boy picked up a brick with a pair of tongs and heated it up in a nearby furnace until it was white hot, and then launched it at Tim from close range. Somehow, Tim managed to duck, and the brick missed the side of his face by inches.

Now crouched in a wrestling position, he eyed Rooster Boy, who crouched a few feet away. This showdown had been Tim's idea, and it surprised him that Rooster Boy had accepted. Tim figured it must be a matter of personal, if not national, pride.

Tim had said that there'd be no judo, but he didn't trust Rooster Boy to abide by any rules. Although Tim had not wrestled in high school, he had been to a lot of professional wrestling matches in Dallas as a vendor selling soft drinks and candy. He had no illusions of lifting his opponent over his head and body-slamming him to the pavement like Gorgeous George might do, though thanks to his ability to steal food and the extra portions of *bento* that he finessed out of the young boys he worked with, he was in better shape than most of the other POWs. He still weighed only about 120 pounds, but that was about 10 pounds more than most of the men. Speed and agility, not strength and endurance, would be his weapons.

Tim's strategy was going to go in low, take Rooster Boy's feet out from under him, and then use his wiry quickness to get on top and pin him.

Cautiously, the two men circled each other, looking for an opening. Behind them, Tim's fellow prisoners watched nervously.

To a man, the other prisoners had tried to dissuade Tim from challenging Rooster Boy. If he won, he could expect to get punished, or, even worse, a defeated Rooster Boy could choose to take out a loss on everyone. As far as Tim was concerned, one small victory against the Japanese, even if he had to pay dearly for it later, would be worth the risk.

Rooster Boy faked a judo chop, and Tim, spotting an opening, lunged at his legs, catching him off guard. With both arms wrapped around Rooster Boy's knees, he lifted him slightly and drove him backward, forcing him to the pavement. Seizing the moment, he quickly kneeled on Rooster Boy's chest and, using the heels of his hands, pinned his shoulders to the pavement.

"*Ichi . . . ni . . . san*," he counted, and then jumped off of Rooster Boy's chest, thrusting his skinny arms into the air in victory.

It was April 13, 1945, two weeks after Tim's wrestling victory. Returning from another twelve hours at the welding shop, he saw a large crowd of prisoners congregated near the cage. He figured some poor guy was getting the crap beat out of him and the guards were making sure other prisoners watched. He knew the feeling.

To his surprise, Rooster Boy had done nothing to punish him or any of the other prisoners following the match. It was as if he'd lost so much face in front of the other guards that he'd decided to back off. As pleased as Tim's buddies were about his victory, they had all advised him to lie low. And that's what he'd been doing, except today. Inside the false bottom of his stool he'd stashed some extra rice that he'd scrounged from the boys in the welding shop. He planned to give it to Gordy.

Tim was worried about his crewmate. Gordy had not been to work in over a week, his health continuing on a steady downhill slide. His stomach was swollen from beriberi. During the day his feet and legs would swell, and sometimes when he woke up in the morning, one side of his face would be all puffy and make him look lopsided. Because he couldn't work, his portion of rice had been cut, and each day he grew weaker.

Other than an occasional nod hello while they were on the *Grenadier*'s final patrol, Gordy and Tim barely knew each other prior to getting captured. And although they had different temperaments—Gordy quiet and reserved, Tim brash and Texas cocky—their individual brands of toughness connected them. On the train ride back from the steel mill, they often sat together.

The winter of 1944–1945 had taken its toll on the camp, with three or four men dying each day. Only four men from the *Grenadier* had died, but there were now a dozen in dire shape. Recently, several survivors of the Bataan Death March arrived in camp, as well as a group of Javanese prisoners; these men looked even worse than the men in Fukuoka's sick bay. For Tim, watching the dead being hauled out of camp to the crematorium was a daily reminder that he wanted to survive no matter what it would take. His second anniversary as a POW was a week away.

Tim thought about what his life might be like if he made it home alive. The first thing he would do was take a long hot bath. Then, of course, he would gorge himself on good ol' American food, with plenty of ice cream and pie. He would drink beer and dance and live life to the hilt. He'd worry later about the moral issues that had been instilled in him by the Baptist Church. After he'd lived it up a little, he'd send a one-way ticket to Valma or maybe he'd go straight to Australia after his release and bring her back to America with him. Of course, it had crossed his mind that maybe she thought he was dead or that maybe she'd met somebody else, but he never allowed those thoughts to linger.

What helped him to stay positive were the reports on the progress of the war now filtering into camp. He'd heard that the American bombing raids had started to seriously hinder the Japanese's ability to supply their troops, including food, and that U.S. troops had retaken Manila and Corregidor. He wondered if any of the Filipinos who'd bravely come down to the dock at the start of the war and helped load the gold and silver onto the *Trout* had survived. Or had they been part of the Bataan Death March and died like so many others?

Holding tightly to his stool, he arrived at the edge of the crowd gathered near the guardhouse. "What's going on?" he inquired.

"The Japs posted a sign claiming FDR died."

At first, Tim didn't believe it; this wasn't the first time that story had gone around. But judging from the reaction of the other men, today it seemed more credible. For the most part, Tim was apolitical, but he worried that if the rumor was true, some of the POWs would lose hope. For the moment, however, his bigger concern was getting past the guard standing near his barracks. It was Rooster Boy.

Walking toward the guard, Tim kept his eyes straight ahead. This wasn't the time to get too cocky or shoot Rooster Boy a defiant glare. He could feel Rooster Boy's eyes boring a hole right through him. He continued on his path, and when he was a few feet away, he switched the stool to his left hand and issued a salute with his right, just like all the prisoners did when approaching a guard. He made sure it was snappy and by the book.

Rooster Boy didn't respond, letting Tim pass. No smile, no snarl, no salute back. Tim and his stool entered the barracks. He looked around for Gordy, but there was no sign of him.

38

Gordy Cox

Fukuoka #3

Some guys let each bite of rice linger in their mouths, trying to suck the nutrients out of each grain. Others wolfed it down like dogs. Gordy's approach was somewhere in between. On this evening, however, he was devouring the large serving of rice Skeeter had brought him, trying to polish it off before a guard spotted him with the extra serving. He'd been in the *benjo* when Tim first returned.

Outside the barracks, he heard several guards jabbering in excited voices. He didn't know exactly what they were saying, but he could decipher enough to know it was about FDR's death.

Gordy felt the tears start to well up. Spotting Skeeter, he motioned him closer. He wanted to thank him for his generosity. Skeeter had put his own safety on the line for Gordy's health, not to mention that he was giving away food he could just have easily taken for himself. If the guards had caught him, they would surely have thrown Skeeter back into the bunker. Gordy reached out and grabbed Skeeter's hand, but the words wouldn't come; the lump in his throat was too big. Finally, he whispered, "I'll make it up to you."

"Just stay alive," said Skeeter. "That's all you need to do."

June 10, 1945. Gordy watched his crewmate Tom Courtney, a thoughtful guy from Michigan, making another entry into the little journal he had stolen from a supply room and kept hidden under his bunk. Back at the

Convent on Light Street, Courtney had been one of the sickest men, but he had rebounded. Now his occasional jottings were the only written documentation by any of the crew at Fukuoka #3. Gordy asked if he could read it. Courtney hesitated, then handed him the journal.

- *3/4/45   Dope coming in about big raids on Tokyo and other big cities. Pray we live thru own bombs.*
- *4/1/45   Alarms daily and nightly now. Hitting close. Saw my first B-29.*
- *4/28/45   Dope Germany fell again. One of these times will be true.*
- *5/8/45   Alarms still go every day. But nothing happens. I pray that I won't be in the factory when Sam does hit it.*
- *5/27/45   Uncle Sam comes every other night. Dope coming in all the time about big raids and battles. Our fleet said to be out here in mass. I miss home and Alyce more than ever. Received Red + cheese. Slopes treating us better now. They see the end now. I expect to go through another HELL before this is over.*
- *5/30/45   All kinds of scuttlebutt coming in about the war and how it will end. But it's all bullshit to me.*
- *6/3/45   Something is up. Received a chocolate bar per man today. Boy you can tell this is drawing to a close. No more beatings. (Well, not many.) Chow is better, clothes, too. If we were treated same two years ago, a lot of my friends would still be here. These hounds of hell have a hell of a lot to answer for.*
- *6/10/45   God, how I pray this will end. This time of year makes me homesick more than ever. The way things look this will last forever.*

Dawn was breaking and a guard ran through the barracks, screaming for everyone to get up. Gordy struggled out of his bunk. He wasn't sure if it was from the extra rice Tim had been giving him, but he felt well enough to go to work at the steel mill even though he was still moving slowly.

Exiting the barracks, Gordy tried to quicken his pace, but it was not fast enough for the guard, who ran at him from behind, slamming his rifle butt hard into Gordy's back. The force of the blow knocked him off his feet, driving him face-first into the baked dirt.

As he struggled to get up, the guard kicked him, his boot drilling

Gordy square in the ribs, knocking the wind out of him. The guard raised his rifle butt over his head and swung it hard at Gordy again. Gordy rolled to his left, the blow glancing off his arm. Quickly, he scrambled to his feet and fell into line with the other men nearby, escaping further injury. Now he probably had a cracked rib.

From Gordy's point of view, the punishment from the guards had escalated again in June. He was sure it had to do with the relentless pounding Japan was taking from the almost daily B-29 bombings. The more extensive the destruction by the bombers, the more the guards took it out on the POWs.

On March 9 and 10, 302 B-29s had taken off from Guam and hit Tokyo with their incendiary bombs, igniting a firestorm that killed 84,000 civilians and torched 16 square miles. Only 14 B-29s were lost. The next week, the cities of Nagoya, Osaka, and Kobe were hit, killing 120,000, with 20 planes lost. In April, the Japanese aircraft factories in Nakajima and Nagoya were destroyed.

LeMay's new strategy of incendiary bombing was having a devastating effect. In April and May, Tokyo was hit again, with an estimated 200,000 killed, and although 43 B-29s were lost, over 50 percent of the city was completely destroyed. And then on May 29, 454 B-29s, escorted by P-51 Mustangs flying from Iwo Jima, targeted Yokohama. Although 4 B-29s and 3 P-51s were lost, 26 Japanese Zeros went down, and a large portion of Yokohama was laid to waste. A week later, Kobe was hit so hard again that it was no longer listed as a target. By mid-June, most of the large Japanese cities were so thoroughly gutted that LeMay switched targets, ordering the incendiary raids on 58 smaller Japanese cities.

By the end of June, the Japanese civilian population was in full panic. For the first time, the Imperial Cabinet considered negotiating an end to the war, but the Japanese military rejected the idea, determined to fight to the bitter end.

- *6/16/45 Uncle came again last night. Comes almost every night. Even Slopes tell us that it will end soon. By all scuttle Uncle is pretty close. Red +*

tobacco and medicine came in yesterday. This Red + is a big shameful joke. Uncle sends it and the Slopes take it. If we get it we are lucky.

- *6/22/45   Sirens went six times in last 24 hours. God, when will this end.*
- *6/24/45   Sirens went all night. No sleep now.*
- *6/29/45   Dope on invasion soon. Bullshit! Also country around here leveled.*
- *7/3/45   Raids every night. Close enough to hear—but still not here.*
- *7/8/45   Boy this is really getting me down. It's got to end someday. Lots of action tonight. I hope Sam comes. The dirty sons-of-bitches. Really beat up some of the boys for contraband. They will soon pay for it.*

Gordy waited in the sick-call line to see the Japanese doctor. He was desperate. In mid-July he had come down with dysentery, draining what little energy he had left. He was afraid he would develop pneumonia, from which very few POWs in camp had recovered. When a POW died of pneumonia, the Japanese listed them as having "died from natural causes." Twice, Gordy had been to see the Japanese doctor, and each time the doctor just shushed him and ordered him to go back to work.

Now Gordy could barely walk. He had a fever, intestinal cramps, and blood in his stool.

It wasn't just Gordy's physical condition that was slipping fast. Each new bombing raid and every new rumor raised his hopes that the end was in sight. The air raids would keep the men in the shelter all night, but in the morning there would be no visible damage around the camp or the steel mill. All that would happen was that four or five more men would die. And Gordy would get more depressed.

He hated the Japanese doctor.

Gordy was determined to get the doctor to take him seriously. This morning, he deposited his bloody stool into an old rag and brought it with him to see the doctor, holding it behind his back. Slowly, he moved forward in line, until finally it was his turn. Standing in front of the doctor, he laid the cloth down on the desk and unfolded it. Caught off guard, the doctor sprang out of his chair and yelled. Two guards appeared immediately on either side of Gordy, bayonets pointed. Maybe this wasn't such a good idea after all, he thought.

Sitting nearby, Dr. Markowitz heard the commotion and came running to intervene. He quickly examined the contents of the rag and had a conversation with the Japanese doctor. A few minutes later, Dr. Markowitz checked Gordy into the camp hospital.

"Doc, you saved my life," said Gordy.

Gordy knew that the hospital was usually considered the last stop in camp before the crematorium, although in the last couple of weeks several of the crew had spent time there and still made it back into the workforce.

Dr. Markowitz diagnosed him with amoebic dysentery, and also confirmed he had a cracked rib. "But you may be in luck," he said. The most recent Red Cross packages included medicine for the treatment of amoebic dysentery. For the next three days, Gordy took two white pills twice daily, and by the end of the week he was well enough to be released from the hospital and return to work duty in the camp.

He continued reading Courtney's journal.

- *7/10/45   Uncle came last night and blew hell out of area, very close. One shot down.*
- *7/14/45   Chow went down today. Going down daily. Back to starvation rations. The end must be near. Four men died in four days.*
- *7/22/45   The chow is low and getting cut all the time. Scuttle coming in all the time about invasion. If this thing doesn't end soon these sons-of-bitches will starve us to death. They are all hungry now, too. Too bad.*
- *8/1/45   Uncle Sam has been raising hell. Every day B-29s and Dive Bombers, still we are spared. Everyone says very soon we will be with our loved ones. There are beans on the job. For a few butts a hat full. Really been eating lately.*
- *8/7/45   Uncle dropped pamphlets saying we are next. Dope coming in that it should be over damn soon.*

On the morning of August 8, the air-raid sirens blared again. Gordy had heard rumors in camp that the area around Yawata and the steel mill would be next, but he wasn't sure how nervous to be; twenty-eight months as a POW had taught him not to believe anything until it happened. He was worried, however, that if it was true, Skeeter, Chuck, and a lot of the crew would be sitting ducks at the mill.

The prisoners in camp were hustled out the gate into the shelter. Pretty soon Gordy heard the ack-ack fire and the sound of planes overhead, but strangely, he heard no bombs exploding. He wondered what was happening.

It didn't take long to find out. Bombs started to fall, big bombs, and far more than ever before. From the sound of it, they were hitting the steel mill.

39

Bob Palmer
Ashio

I
n early August 1945, Bob Palmer checked himself into the little wooden shack the prisoners at Ashio called the Death Hut, the place where the sickest of the sick went to die. His weight, which had been 160 pounds at the start of the war, was now down to 80. Despite several vitamin B_1 shots, as well as experimental treatments with acupuncture and burning herbs, his beriberi had worsened. He could not continue with the backbreaking work or endure the noxious fumes at the smelter. His legs were too swollen for him to walk; he could only crawl.

The relentless bombing that the B-29s had inflicted on Japan had spared the small mountain town of Ashio from any direct hits, but it had knocked out its main railroad supply line, effectively cutting off the flow of rice into town for the townspeople as well as the prisoners. The guards routinely stole the Red Cross parcels meant for the POWs. On one occasion, in a desperate attempt to add some substance to their soup, a horse bone that a POW found walking back from the smelter was added, but it only resulted in several prisoners choking and gagging on splintered bone. On another occasion, small bits of baby shark were mixed into the soup, but the smell of ammonia was so strong that Bob couldn't eat it.

One of Bob's last jobs before entering the Death Hut was helping to scrounge around the camp for edible plants and bulbs to add to the prisoners' small ration of soup. It was an exercise in futility: decades of poor mining practices had poisoned the area's soil and robbed it of any agricultural value. Bob managed to bring back only a handful of weeds. He got diarrhea from the soup made with his gleanings; the camp doctor treated it by having him eat charcoal.

Of all the prisoners at Ashio, it was the Javanese Dutch who suffered the most. The Javanese had been imprisoned the longest, and in the spring and summer of 1945, they were, as Kevin Hardy, one of the *Grenadier*'s officers at Ashio, put it, "dying like flies." Perhaps none of the deaths had impacted the camp as much as the passing of a Javanese man who had been an opera singer before the war. According to the other prisoners, he died in the Death Hut just after singing a beautiful aria, his voice soaring above the camp, lifting everyone's spirits. They had no idea what language he was singing in, or what the words meant, only that the music seemed to come from heaven. Bob had no memory of it.

Bob knew his mental condition was almost as bad as his physical health. During the first two years of his imprisonment, he had kept his mind active with a variety of mental escapes: taking fishing trips in the Cascades; eating delicious desserts from recipes concocted by a fellow prisoner; rebuilding a '36 Ford from the ground up; building a house in which to live with Barbara. Now, as death closed in, he couldn't focus, mired in depression and hopelessness. Even thoughts about Barbara could no longer lift his spirits. All he could do was stare out the window of the Death Hut and mindlessly watch the prisoners and guards walk past.

40

Chuck Ver Valin

Fukuoka #3

On the cloudless morning of August 8, 1945, Chuck Ver Valin trudged from the train to his job in the pipe shop. This morning shaped up to be like all the others, a struggle to get through the day.

Soon after the prisoners arrived at the shop, the morning calm was shattered by the warning blast of an air-raid siren. Nobody paid it much attention, including the pushers and guards. Despite the constant sounds of planes passing overhead and the rumbling of bombs exploding in the distance, there hadn't been a daylight bombing raid over Yawata in more than a year.

Reaching his workstation, Chuck was startled by a second siren, the one the POWs called "Burping Betsy." This was unusual.

Almost immediately, he heard a racket on the roof, like it was being hit by a million BBs. He looked through the large entrance to the building and saw hundreds of smoking white sticks falling from the sky and peppering a nearby building where many of his friends worked.

To the west he saw the most incredible sight: row after row of glistening four-engine B-29s coming in low and silently over the rim of the mountains and gliding down into the valley. They were so close that he could see their bomb-bay doors open and large black canisters the size of train cars fall from their bellies. The canisters quickly burst apart, scattering thousands of small firebombs in every direction, each stick leaving a trail of white smoke behind it.

All around him frightened men—POWs, guards, civilians, pushers—ran for cover from death pouring from the sky. For all the POWs' talk and worry about being killed by American bombs one day, that day was now here.

Incendiary bombs fell in every corner of the factory and all over the city of Yawata to the south.

Antiaircraft fire erupted from a mountaintop to the north of the mill, but before the ack-ack could find its target, three P-51s swooped down like hawks and wiped out the emplacement. Chuck sprinted toward a shelter, but it was quickly filling to capacity. He returned to the pipe shop and took cover under a large stack of pipes piled against a wall.

Trying to catch his breath, he felt something move next to his legs. Looking down, he did a double take. Crouching next to him was a guard, a man he'd seen around the steel mill many times but whose name he didn't know. The guard was shaking hard. It occurred to Chuck that there was really no difference between them at this moment; they were just two human beings petrified that they were about to die.

It seemed like everywhere and everything was on fire—the factory, machines, supplies, nearby houses—flames leaping across roads and railroad tracks. The sound was overpowering, like a strong wind, crackling and snapping everything in its path, great billows of black smoke rolling through the valley, choking the air, turning the sky from a beautiful blue to a dark haze.

Chuck wondered about Gordy back in camp. He knew that those wooden barracks would go up in flames like bone-dry kindling if the incendiaries hit there.

Nothing near the steel mill escaped the devastation—trees, buildings, and animals all on fire. At the water's edge, small boats, docks, and a fishing village erupted in an inferno, impossible to extinguish. Ashes fell like snowflakes. The sun disappeared.

The ground shook as a second wave of planes unleashed more destruction, in the form of huge 500-pound bombs. Relentlessly they came, whistling to the ground like freight trains, tearing gaping craters.

After twenty-eight months in captivity, Chuck was overjoyed that these evil bastards were finally getting what they deserved—a fiery, excruciating pounding. But fear had a bigger hold on him. Cowering under the stack of pipes, pressed up against his enemy, he had never been so scared.

It was late in the afternoon when the all clear finally sounded. The prisoners were rounded up and told to head for the train to take them back to the camp. Chuck didn't know what to expect. The guard who'd been next to him had disappeared. Maybe there would be another raid. Or maybe the soldiers, or even the civilians, would turn into an angry mob and attack them.

In the semidarkness there was an eerie stillness. Other than a couple of guards herding them to the train, the whole area was deserted. None of the Japanese pushers, workers, or civilians were in sight; they had likely fled to their homes to see if anything was left. In every direction that Chuck looked, the earth was scorched. Huge pieces of metal lay scattered on the ground. Where earlier in the day buildings had stood, now there were only piles of glowing embers. Entire sides of factories had disappeared, the equipment inside smashed to bits. Black, billowing smoke still swirled around the smoldering ruins.

Accounts of the devastation quickly spread. The death toll in Yawata was over 60,000. Entire neighborhoods had been wiped out, the tightly packed houses made of straw, bamboo, rice paper, or cheap wood shooting up in flames. Miraculously, only one POW was killed; he had taken a direct hit on the back of his head from a firebomb. Another prisoner lost an arm. But nobody from the *Grenadier* was seriously injured.

Back at camp, which had escaped damage from the attack, Chuck and the other men spent the night huddled together in the shelter. Nobody slept. For Chuck, it was a better option than sleeping in the barracks, where a new infestation of bedbugs now covered everything.

The morning of August 9 dawned bright and sunny, but soon a northeasterly wind started blowing the thick layer of smoke that had drifted out to sea overnight back toward land, spreading a blanket of haze from Yawata to Kokura. At the same time, a B-29 named *Bock's Car* was winging across the Pacific toward Japan, its designated target Kokura, less than three miles from the camp. In its belly it carried an atomic bomb.

The remaining 670 prisoners at Fukuoka #3 did not know that three days earlier the *Enola Gay* had dropped an atomic bomb on Hiroshima, fifty miles to the north. An estimated 45,000 people out of a population of 250,000 perished in the initial blast, and another 20,000 died within four months. Kokura, because of its stockpile of military arms and equipment, had been designated as the target for the second bomb.

Before taking off from Tinian in the Mariana Islands, the crew of *Bock's Car* discovered a malfunctioning fuel pump on an auxiliary fuel tank. The pilot, Major Charles Sweeney, decided the extra fuel would not be essential and disconnected the auxiliary fuel tank. The plane took off, and upon reaching Yakushima, an island off the south coast of Kyushu, it was supposed to rendezvous with an instrument plane, as well as a photographic plane. But the photo plane was late, so after circling for almost an hour and using up considerable fuel, Major Sweeney proceeded toward Kokura without the photo plane. An advance weather report forecast clear skies over the target area.

Bock's Car was under specific orders to drop the bomb, named Fat Boy, only if the arsenal storage facility could be visually spotted, but upon reaching Kokura, Sweeney found that the target was hidden under the thick layer of smoke from the previous day's bombing raid. The plane circled, looking for an opening, then circled again, taking a third pass over the target; still the view was obscured. With the fuel running low because they had disconnected the auxiliary fuel tank, Sweeney decided to abort the Kokura mission and change course for the secondary target of Nagasaki.

Tom Courtney continued to write in his journal:

- *8/8/45   Uncle came today! Blew hell out of factory. Incendiary bombs all over, thousands of them. The hand of God was over us. He will see us through.*

- *8/9/45   Stayed in camp today. Sirens went five times this morning. Uncle hasn't come back though. He better be here tonight or we go back tomorrow. God be with us in that factory. Everyone optimistic now. Think it will end soon. <u>Please God, end it soon</u>!*
- *8/12/45   Shelter again. Still no work. Heard factory hit again. Also heard Russia at war and well in Manchuria. Also Red + coming now. This war about over. It is so hard to imagine what it will be like to be free again, to America that is HOT DOGS, HAMBURGERS and BALL GAMES—FREEDOM AND HOME the sweetest words in the world.*
- *8/13/45   Uncle again. Dive bombers. Shelter almost all day. Some jobs went back to factory. God I hope I never see it again. They want to kill us for sure. Keep praying.*
- *8/15/45   23-years-old today. No work today. Also no more work in factory. The scuttle really strong and spirits up. Maybe war is about over. All parties come in from factory at noon. Everything points to the end. (God in Heaven make it so. You have been with us through it all Father and have answered my prayers.)*

On the morning of August 16 a Japanese soldier entered the barracks and ordered everyone to assemble outside in the quadrangle near the guards' barracks, the largest open space in the camp. There was something ominous in his tone. Chuck noticed several men close to him offer a quick prayer.

Chuck wasn't relying on prayer or God in Heaven for his strength. Since the bombing of the factory, and with the end of the war and of their captivity possibly near, he was doing his best to keep his mind focused on the same thing he had for the past two years and four months: that honor would come in his survival and in seeing the Japanese defeated. That, and making sure he got enough to eat.

More than at any time since the crew's capture, the rumors were flying: the American invasion was set to begin; a big bomb had wiped out an entire city; there would be mackerel for dinner tonight; there were only enough rations to last one more week. The rumor Chuck worried about the most, of course, was the one that had been circulating the longest: that an Allied invasion was imminent, and as soon as it started, the POWs would all be lined up and gunned down. Certainly the Japanese had done their part in spreading this fear, including every day since the factory was bombed.

He took a spot at the rear of the quadrangle. Every prisoner in camp who could walk was there, the crowd spilling out of the quadrangle and down the main street. None of the men had slept more than a few hours in over a week. A stepladder was placed at the front of the crowd. Behind it stood the guards, all of them armed with rifles and bayonets.

Maybe this is where they finally kill us, thought Chuck.

A Japanese colonel climbed the stepladder, which was steadied by a sergeant major. The colonel looked out over the prisoners, his glare slowly shifting from one side of the silent crowd to the other. Finally, in almost perfect English, he spoke.

"The war is over," he said. "Japan has lost the war."

He paused, waiting for a reaction from the POWs. There was no shouting, no rejoicing, no slaps on the back.

Chuck wasn't sure how to react or what to think. For too long he'd gotten his hopes up that this nightmare would end, and the one thing he'd come to know for sure was not to believe anything until it happened.

Was this just another cruel hoax? Given the destruction and devastation the Japanese had suffered recently, it certainly seemed logical that they would surrender. But Chuck remembered the countless times he'd heard his captors talking about the code of Bushido, and how true warriors never give up, only cowards surrender, and that a Japanese soldier would never put down his arms.

The colonel continued: "His Imperial Majesty, in an effort to put an end to the death and bloodshed, has agreed to an unconditional surrender and cessation of war. All hostilities have been terminated. His Majesty and your General MacArthur will sign the terms of surrender on September 2, 1945. I have been ordered to inform you that as of this moment you are no longer prisoners of war. You are free. I have also been instructed to ask that

you all remain here until your authorities come for you after the surrender
has been signed.

"Please do not think harshly of those who were in charge of you, your
guards. Have compassion for them. Many have lost their entire family and
homes. Food is scarce. I would suggest that Red Cross food parcels in the
warehouse be given to them, that they might have food to eat, while they
too readjust. They were only doing their duty, as you would yours."

He stepped down off the stepladder and returned to the office, followed shortly by the guards, leaving the prisoners still staring in stunned
silence. It was hard for Chuck to fathom. Was he really free? If he wasn't,
then the colonel had done an amazing job of acting. And what was he
to think about the colonel's request for the POWs to be forgiving of the
guards? Could that Jap possibly be serious to think that all these prisoners
who'd been surviving on a cup of rice a day for more than two years were
going to give what little rations were left to the same men who had treated
them worse than dogs? Was there no end to these people's audacity?

That night the 670 former POWs dragged their blankets out of the barracks and set them on the hard dirt of the street. They would all sleep out
under the stars, leaving the barracks to the bedbugs. As midnight came
and went, most stayed awake talking, their first night of freedom spent in
dazed and elated conversation.

The next morning, Chuck awoke to one of the men running down
the main street of the camp yelling at the top of his voice. "The Japs are
gone . . . the Japs are gone!"

Sure enough, in the dark of night, the camp commandant and all
the guards had snuck away unnoticed, leaving the prisoners on their own.
Many of the POWs went scrounging for food, but found little.

Later that morning, the top-ranked officer in the camp, Army major
W. O. Dorris, addressed the prisoners, cautioning them to sit tight until
American forces arrived. "I'm not sure how long it'll take them to get here,
a week, maybe two," he said. "But I can assure you that anyone caught leaving camp early will be court-martialed."

He nodded toward the perimeter of the quadrangle, where six American Marines, armed with sabers the guards had left behind, stood guard.

Chuck glanced at Tim McCoy, who was sitting next to him, perplexed. Many times they had talked about what they would do when and if they were ever free again. Nowhere on either man's list, however, was anything about hanging around the prison camp after the war was over.

"I don't know who's coming to get us," said Chuck, "but they better get here soon, or I'm leaving anyway. They wouldn't dare court-martial us."

41

Bob Palmer

Ashio

It was August 15, 1945, six days after the atomic bomb was dropped on Nagasaki. Lying on his straw mat in the Death Hut and floating in and out of sleep, Bob was awakened by his friend and crewmate Len Clark.

Using Clark as a crutch, Bob shuffled across the wooden floor to the door, his swollen legs throbbing. In the middle of the dusty compound, all the guards stood at attention in a circle around the camp commander. They all carried rifles and they were all wearing white gloves. On the ground next to them, a voice blared from a radio: Emperor Hirohito was addressing the nation.

Every few sentences, the guards bowed toward Tokyo, their expressions as solemn as those seen in a funeral procession as Hirohito's words sunk in:

> . . . *Indeed, we declared war on America and Britain out of our sincere desire to insure Japan's self-preservation and the stabilization of East Asia, it being far from our thought either to infringe upon the sovereignty of other nations or to embark on territorial aggrandizement.*
>
> *By now the war has lasted for nearly four years. Despite the best that has been done by everyone—the gallant fighting of our military and naval forces, the diligence and assiduity of our servants of the State and the devoted service of our 10,000,000 people—the war situation has developed not necessarily to Japan's advantage, while the general trends of the world have all turned against her interest.*

Moreover, the enemy has begun to employ a new and most cruel bomb,
the power of which to do damage is, indeed, incalculable, taking the toll of
many innocent lives. Should we continue to fight, it would not only result
in an ultimate collapse and obliteration of the Japanese nation, but also it
would lead to the total extinction of human civilization.

After several more minutes, the emperor's voice stopped and the guards closed their circle around the camp commander. Soon, they backed away and started walking toward their barracks, each leaving behind his rifle stacked upright with all the others.

It would take several more minutes for the camp commander to confirm to the barracks leaders that the war was indeed over. As word spread through the camp, members of the *Grenadier* crew came to the Death Hut to share an embrace with Bob.

Bob smiled, the first time he'd done so in months.

Ten days after the emperor had announced the Japanese surrender, Bob hobbled across the camp, steadying himself with a tree limb Len Clark had crafted into a crutch. He was heading toward a large box. It had just been dropped in the center of camp by a low-flying F4U, which had come swooping down out of the sky with its pilot canopy open and wheels down.

This wasn't the drop of supplies. Immediately after the surrender, the prisoners had painted a large POW sign on top of one of the barracks and had spelled out POW in white rocks in the middle of the compound. One of the drops had included Army-issued clothes, with more than enough to go around.

Bob was one of the first to reach the new box. He had been feasting on packages of Canadian Red Cross food that the prisoners had found in a storage room after most of the Japanese guards had fled the camp. For the last three days Bob had been splurging on bacon–Hershey bar sandwiches. He'd also been getting heavy doses of vitamin B_1, likewise found with the Red Cross food. Although he'd gained 5 pounds and his physical condition had improved enough that he'd moved out of the Death Hut back to the barracks, he was still easily confused. He'd been told that he could try to contact Barbara when he reached Guam in a few more weeks. "What's Guam?" he asked.

Bob and the other prisoners quickly opened the box; it was full of Viceroys. Wrapped around the cartons was a handwritten note. "Frank Sinatra #1."

Bob furrowed his brow. "Sinatra is president?" he asked.

The next day several POWs met and made a list of Japanese mineworkers who had treated them nicely. They rounded up as many of these men as they could find and brought them to the center of the camp, where they presented them with supplies that had been dropped from planes. Every one of the mineworkers cried when given their gift of American food and clothing. So did the ex-prisoners.

On the morning of September 5, 1945, thirty days after the dropping of the atomic bomb on Hiroshima, Bob limped out of the Ashio prison camp, using a newly carved tree limb as a cane. Along with the other prisoners, he walked two miles to the train station and boarded a train for the Yokohama-Tokyo area. The tracks had been repaired. At the station, he saw no civilians, only members of the *kempeitai* posted menacingly around the station.

Climbing aboard the train, Bob felt an overwhelming sense of joy and relief. Over the twenty-eight tortured months as a POW, he'd survived on less than a cup of rice a day, received more beatings than he could remember, spent nine months in solitary confinement, performed slave labor in a smelter, watched other prisoners die, lost half his body weight, had no contact with the outside world, and battled beriberi, amoebic dysentery, and dengue fever. And now he was heading home.

Despite his sense of liberation, he knew one hard truth still remained. "I'm not capable of a logical decision," he admitted.

That did not, however, stop him from asking when he'd be allowed to try to contact Barbara. In Guam, he was told. He could barely wait.

Part Eight

GOING HOME

42

Tim "Skeeter" McCoy

Texas

In the days immediately following the end of the war, Tim was practically coming unglued waiting to leave Fukuoka #3. There were promises of B-29s dropping in supplies, but so far, nothing had arrived. There were also daily threats of a court-martial to anyone leaving camp.

"I'm not sticking around much longer," he vowed.

Some men had bribed the posted guards to let them out of camp so they could walk around the town or go down to the ocean for a swim. A few even talked about going out and killing some random Japs. As much as he hated the Japanese, Tim didn't want any part of that. He was, however, interested in making a raid on the nearby sake plant. For his first unguarded venture outside the camp, he and Chuck walked a mile to the sake plant and traded a Red Cross parcel for a couple of bottles, and then came back to the camp and got drunk.

Top military officials in all branches had determined that POWs would return to America and be assigned to a hospital, and then be reassigned to a base. Tim had it all figured out; as soon as he got home he would bring Valma to America with the help of the War Brides Act and then get married. He'd buy her a one-way ticket with the back pay that all the POWs were rumored to be getting.

As for a career after the Navy, he wasn't sure. Maybe he'd talk to his uncle about going into the insurance business. Or maybe he'd stay in the Navy. Either way, he figured he'd have plenty of time to make a decision.

There was a rumor that all the POWs would be getting a ninety-day leave once they were stateside and had been checked out at a hospital.

He was looking forward to seeing his mom again, too. As for his father, he wasn't sure if he'd even bother to see him. Being a POW hadn't healed that wound.

With each day that passed without a food drop or word about when they would be able to start their journey back home, Tim's frustration and impatience grew. He talked to Chuck about joining him in escaping. He said he'd wait one more week and then he was leaving.

Approaching the main opening of the prison camp, Tim whispered to his two accomplices, Elwood O'Brion, a *Grenadier* crew member from Fort Dodge, Iowa, and Chuck. "Don't look suspicious."

They were sneaking out of camp dressed in Army uniforms and hats that had been dropped into camp. On their sleeves they wore black armbands on which was printed MP in large white letters. Their plan was to catch a train to Tokyo and, crazy as it seemed, find General MacArthur and get him to expedite their return home.

Despite the leaflets that had been dropped into camp advising POWs not to leave and that they would soon be repatriated by the Army, Tim's impatience had gotten the best of him. It didn't matter that B-29s had finally dropped multiple cases of food, candy, Pall Malls, gum, and medicine.

Passing one of the posted sentries, they all saluted and kept walking down the dusty street that led to the train station. Tim was surprised at how calm he felt.

The three men were feeling fit for their journey. Food had indeed arrived at last, packed inside 55-pound drums that floated gently to earth under multicolored parachutes. It had been a beautiful sight and the men had gorged themselves. A few of the prisoners had cut out pieces of a lavender parachute and crafted them into elegant coverings with fringed edges to be draped over the boxes containing the ashes of the men who had died. The covered boxes would be shipped home to the families of the deceased prisoners.

At the station, they were surprised not to see any Japanese soldiers, and even more surprised to see a large pile of rifles stacked on a platform. "Maybe we should each grab one," suggested Tim.

"There are three of us and millions of them," countered Chuck, and he reminded Tim that Emperor Hirohito had instructed the military to put down their arms and treat the Americans with dignity and respect.

None of the three men had any money, so without tickets they boarded a train bound for Tokyo, located about 400 miles to the north. The train was standing room only; all the other passengers were Japanese. The relentless bombing by the Americans had displaced millions of civilians, and now many of them were on the move, hoping to relocate with family or friends elsewhere in the country.

Three Japanese men got up from their seats, bowed, and offered the seats to the men of the *Grenadier*, who returned the bow and took the seats. A few minutes later, another person offered bowls of rice. Tim and his companions accepted this goodwill gesture graciously, although Tim saw the irony of being given a bowl of rice as a peace offering when they had existed on nothing but rice for more than two years.

The train continued rolling northbound, stopping in Hiroshima. Tim looked out the window at the devastated city. It looked pretty much like all the other cities and towns they'd passed.

It was after midnight when the train arrived in Tokyo. The men walked to the temporary Army headquarters, arriving at 4:00 a.m.

"We're here to see General MacArthur," Tim announced.

MacArthur wasn't there, but the next day, General William Curtis Chase paid them a visit, assuring them they would get anything they wanted.

For the next twenty-four hours they were treated to beds with clean white sheets, beers, and huge amounts of mashed potatoes and pork chops. Then they were driven to Yokohama and taken to a hospital ship, where Army nurses greeted them.

"Y'all are just about the prettiest sight I've ever seen," offered Tim.

After being deloused and given Navy dungarees to wear, the men waited to be taken to the airport to catch a transport plane bound for

Guam. During their wait, Tim and Chuck spotted Commander Barney Siegal, under whom they'd briefly served aboard the submarine tender USS
Pelius. Siegal pulled out his wallet and handed each of them $10.

"I'll repay you, I promise," Tim told him. The $10 was more than he'd
made during his eighteen months of labor in the steel mill at Yawata.

Getting off the C-147 transport plane in Guam, Tim was greeted by warm
tropical air and a large sign that proclaimed: "GUAM—WHERE AMERICA'S
DAY BEGINS."

The largest and southernmost of the Mariana Islands, Guam was the
only American-held island in the region before the war. Occupied by Japan
from December 1941 until July 1944, it was also the only U.S. soil ever to
be occupied by a foreign military power. Its recapture had been crucial in
establishing the Marianas as a launching site for the B-29 raids on Japan.

For the next two weeks, Tim and the many POWs who had been sent to
the American hospital in Guam were examined by doctors and questioned
about their experience in captivity. They were also given large amounts of
food.

"I've never seen so much ice cream," observed Chuck.

For Tim it seemed like every time he turned around, he was filling out
another form. One asked him to detail his treatment at each of the places
where he'd been imprisoned: Penang, Singapore, and Fukuoka. Another
was to authorize a request of the Japanese government for compensation
for labor performed as a prisoner, a request Tim figured would never be
honored. He also filled out a form agreeing not to talk to any representa-
tives of the media or to allow his photo to be taken for publication without
first receiving authorization from the military. Somebody told him that it
was because General MacArthur didn't want to get the American public any
more riled up about Japan than they already were; he and President Truman had figured out that it would be the Russians and Chinese who would
be America's most formidable challenge in the years ahead, and America
would eventually need Japan as an ally to help stop Communist expansion.

"I'll sign whatever they want if it'll help me get home," said Tim.

He spent a lot of time in the recreation center with the other men, sharing stories and talking about what they were going to do when they got home, as well as drinking copious amounts of beer. The more beer he drank, the less he dwelled on the hell he had just survived.

Tim sent two telegrams—one to Valma in Perth and another to his mother in Dallas. Because his name had shown up on a POW list after he'd been transferred to Fukuoka #3, they both knew he was alive. He wrote Valma that he would check into the War Brides Act to bring her to America as soon as he got back home.

His mother sent him a return cable in response: she and his father were back together, and they had been corresponding with Valma. Tim wasn't sure what to make of this, but his first reaction was that it was good.

The next day, he was on a ship, heading home to America.

43

Gordy Cox
Yakima, Washington

His tray heaped with food, including a large T-bone steak, Gordy sat alone at a table in the empty mess hall at the Navy hospital in Pearl Harbor. It was September 5, 1945, and tomorrow he was leaving for America and the homecoming he'd been dreaming about.

He glanced up and spotted an attractive young woman carrying a tray into the mess hall. Her presence startled him. By her uniform, he knew she was a Wave (Women Accepted for Volunteer Emergency Service). When he'd first joined up, there were almost no women in the Navy, but now at war's end, there were almost 90,000, 2.5 percent of the Navy's total strength.

"Mind if I join you?" she asked.

Gordy nodded okay, suddenly feeling awkward and uncomfortable. He hadn't talked to an American woman since 1941, and he wasn't exactly the smoothest of operators back then.

As she sat down, he stared at his steak. The past three weeks had been a whirlwind. For Gordy, the first realization that the war was truly over was when he walked out of the barracks in Fukuoka #3 and surprised a Japanese guard, who quickly turned and ran away. A week earlier that same guard probably would've hit him for failing to bow or salute. A few days after that he'd sat in the barracks listening to several POWs talking about going in search of guards to hang. He said no thanks, believing the greater punishment would be to let the guards continue living in "this godforsaken hell."

In the last month his health had dramatically improved. The swelling from the beriberi had gone down, and after the food drops began, he'd gained almost ten pounds and regained some of his energy. In fact, when one of the drums had landed fifty yards out in the ocean, he swam out and pushed it back to shore.

"Where are you from?" asked the woman.

Gordy contemplated his answer. Should he tell her he was a POW just returning from a living hell in Japan?

"Yakima," he muttered.

Two other Waves entered the mess hall and sat down at his table; he didn't greet them. Taking a small bite of his steak, he was suddenly not hungry.

Like everyone else in Fukuoka #3, Gordy had become impatient to leave the prison camp and start his journey home. A few days after Tim and Chuck took off on their own, he and two other crewmates did the same, catching a train to Yokohama. He wore the tattered dungarees in which he'd been captured, wanting to leave the country the same way he'd arrived. On the train ride, he was surprised by the large number of Koreans on board, including women who'd been forced to work as "comfort women," providing sexual services for the Japanese troops.

At Yokohama, Gordy had been one of the lucky ones to be flown to Guam. There he finally learned that the twenty-nine men who'd been separated from the rest of the crew when they'd first landed in Japan, including Captain Fitzgerald, had survived. Along with all the other POWs, he was asked to fill out a war-crimes report against the guards who had tortured him. He declined, saying that as much as he hated them, he didn't want to have to return to Japan to testify at a trial.

After ten days of physical exams, clean clothes, and heaping mounds of food in Guam, he'd gotten lucky again and been put aboard a transport plane to Pearl Harbor. Most of the men, including Tim, Chuck, and Bob, would have to make the journey home aboard a ship.

"You stationed here at Pearl?" asked one of the Waves.

Gordy shook his head. He took another bite of his steak, but now it was hard to chew.

"Did you serve in the war?" asked another.

Without answering, Gordy picked up his tray and left the table, dumping the half-eaten steak and the rest of the food into a trash can as he left the mess hall.

Sitting at the bar in Bimbo's 365 Club on Market Street in San Francisco, Gordy stared into his beer, feeling out of place. It was two days after his return to America, and so far, it wasn't quite the joyous return he'd envisioned. There'd been no bands or parades to greet him, although two men from a submarine relief organization had met him when he got off the plane and took him into San Francisco, offering to treat him to anything he wanted. He turned down the offer, explaining he hadn't done anything that thousands of other POWs hadn't done. They drove him to Oak Knoll Hospital in Oakland, where POWs were taken for more physicals and reassignment.

Gordy's biggest disappointment upon returning home was that his mom and dad weren't there to greet him. He'd sent them a telegram from Pearl, letting them know he was coming to the naval hospital in Oakland but so far he hadn't seen them. He'd concluded that his mother wasn't well enough to travel. Unbeknownst to him, his parents had driven the 900 miles from Yakima to Oakland but had gone to the wrong hospital, and were now frantically trying to find him.

Gordy had taken a bus into San Francisco on a twelve-hour liberty pass from Oak Knoll, and come to Bimbo's because he'd heard it was a hangout for Navy men. Indeed it was, but when he got there everyone was sitting in groups, laughing and having a good time. He tried making conversation with a sailor at the bar, but it went nowhere and the sailor got up and left, leaving Gordy to stare into the last sip of his beer.

He quickly headed for the exit. On the sidewalk in front of the bar, a wino approached him. "Hey, sailor, how about buying me a bottle of wine?"

"Sure, why not?" Gordy replied.

Using money the Navy had advanced him on his back pay, he bought a bottle of the cheapest rotgut he could find at a nearby liquor store and handed it to the wino.

"Wanna swig?" asked the wino.

"Sure," answered Gordy.

For the next hour, he and the wino sat on the curb, passing the brown-paper-bag-wrapped bottle back and forth, barely saying a word. When it was empty, Gordy stood up, thanked the man for his time, and then caught a bus back to Oakland.

The next day he was awarded a Purple Heart.

Gordy beamed as he drove his shiny '41 Buick down Main Street, accompanied by his brothers Willie and Larry and a friend, Ray Vanderver. It was October 1945 and he was back home in Yakima. He'd paid the pretty penny of $1,500 for the Buick, using up almost a third of the back pay he'd gotten from the Navy.

To Gordy, it seemed everyone back home had changed, especially his mom. Her hair had turned completely gray; having three of her four sons in the war had taken its toll. They'd all received Purple Hearts. When the brothers picked Gordy up at the bus depot upon his return, he barely recognized them. They were grown men, not the boys he remembered.

Since he'd been home, his routine was pretty much the same every day—sleep late, eat a big breakfast, and then go cruising in his new Buick with his brothers and friends. In the evenings they'd usually end up at Dopey's, a restaurant and hangout for young people; if they were lucky they'd meet some girls. With his back pay in his pocket and a nice car, he had lots of new friends. He rarely talked about the nightmare he'd been through.

Once, a woman asked him what it was like in prison camp, but when Gordy started to tell her about the starvation, beatings, and death, she screamed: "Stop, stop! I don't want to hear about that." After that he decided to stop talking about it, concluding that most people would rather ignore the fact that people could act that way or hope that it never really happened.

Gordy wasn't sure what he wanted to do with his life after his leave was up. One option was the Navy. He'd started dabbling with taking pictures, so maybe he could try to be a photographer's mate. But he wasn't confident that he was good enough or that the Navy would agree to it. Staying in the submarine service was another possibility, but that seemed unlikely, too, given that he hadn't been able to pass the qualification tests prior to the sinking of the *Grenadier*.

Going to college was another option. The passage of the GI Bill in June 1944 now made it possible for returning servicemen to have their entire education paid for. It was being hailed as one of the most significant pieces of social legislation of the century, for its positive impact on both the economy and its recipients. Many economists were predicting a post–World War II economic depression as the country tried to convert its wartime production levels to those of peacetime. Gordy went to Yakima High to check his transcripts, but left discouraged. For one thing, he learned he was still a year and a half short of getting his diploma. But what dissuaded him even more was seeing all the high-school kids in the halls. He was only twenty-two, but after what he'd been through, he felt decades older.

The prospects of finding a job didn't look too rosy either. With so many returning GIs flooding the market, jobs were scarce. Gordy's previous work history was unimpressive—jobs in high school delivering papers, picking fruit, and cleaning an ice rink weren't likely to impress potential employers, and four years in the submarine service without learning any real marketable skills wasn't likely to have employers lining up either. He figured he couldn't count the two years he'd spent slaving in the steel mill in Yawata. He laughed at the thought of writing them for a recommendation.

On this day, he was content to do a little joyriding. Heading north out of town, Gordy had no real destination other than to be back in town that evening to go to Dopey's.

Suddenly a Chevy coupe coming in the opposite direction turned left immediately in front of him. Gordy slammed on the brakes, but it was too late. The cars collided, launching Larry through the front windshield and

Gordy into the steering wheel (laws requiring seat belts were many years in the future).

Gordy staggered out of the car to survey the damage. The other car was crushed, and its young driver and his girlfriend appeared seriously injured. Larry was bleeding profusely from the cuts to his head; Willie and Ray, although badly shaken, appeared okay. But Gordy's Buick, his pride and joy, was beyond repair, and he had a stabbing pain in his side. Plus, a witness was accusing him of driving drunk.

Gordy sat at the side of the road, watching the ambulance speed away with the injured couple. Adding to his problems was the fact that he was driving with no insurance. This was not the homecoming he'd dreamed about.

44

Chuck Ver Valin

Sodus, New York

Before Chuck left prison camp, he wrote Gwen a letter using a pencil and lined paper he found in the abandoned Japanese officers' quarters. In the nearly two and a half years he'd been held captive, he'd written her several times, but she had not received any of the letters. Gwen had read a story in the Perth newspaper about the *Grenadier* being missing in action, and although she tried to be optimistic, she assumed the worst. She began dating again, eventually getting engaged to another American sailor, Adolph Cornberg from Chicago.

Chuck gave the letter to Arthur King, an Aussie POW from Perth whom he'd met in camp. King promised to deliver it to Gwen in person.

Darling Gwen,

As I sit here outside my so-called home, or what has been my home for twenty eight months, which also seemed to me a lifetime, I am taking my first opportunity to write to you and try to tell you just why we have been away from each other so long. After we parted that night of March 19, 1943, which has been a long time but never did I once quit thinking of you because I knew that some day the war would end and I only prayed I would make it.

On the morning of the twentieth–43 March we did not leave Fremantle Harbor until 11:30 a.m. and as we went out of the channel I got one

*of the fellows to stay in the engine room so I could take my last good look
at the barracks where you were. I never thought it would be such a long
time before I could see you again. Also I got a good look at the Ocean
Beach Hotel and Leighton Beach, where we had gone several times. My
buddy said take your last good look so I then went below saying to myself
I sure will be glad to get back.*

*After many days of patrol on the morning of April 21 we were bombed
by a Jap divebomber and sunk off Pilgrim Island. We were captured on
the 22nd and taken to Penang. We arrived in Japan on the 9th of October. I have worked in a factory here at the town called Yawata on the
island of Kyushu. We worked hard and worked right up until the 16th of
August when we heard that the war was over. It came as a very sudden
surprise and as yet it is quite hard to believe.*

*I will not tell you my hardships during this time but you can imagine
they were not easy. It sure seemed good to watch the B-29s come over and
give these people hell because that was the only way we knew it was getting close to an end.*

*I understand that there is a battleship and transports just outside the
channel awaiting the word to come in. It cannot be too soon for me. I am
writing this letter now to give to Arthur King to bring to you. He is one of
only three Aussies in camp. I was sure glad to see them when I first came
to this camp as they are all swell fellows.*

*The only thing I had when I was captured was a pair of pants, a shirt
and that Catholic medal. I still have the medal and as I told you I would
keep it always. Do you remember me saying on that last night that I had
a feeling that something was going to happen? I believed it because once
I had found the one I loved I knew something would happen. But all
that time I have not changed my mind and I want you to write and tell
me just how you feel and what you did while I was away. How did those
pictures you had taken turn out? Please send me one as soon as possible
because I am very anxious to get it. I will also do the same as soon as my
hair grows out. Right now I have none. I now weigh about 150 but at*

one time I only weighed 105 and when I left Australia I reached 160.
All I need to get my strength and weight back is some good steak and eggs
and Aussie bread. I sure hope some how to get home by September 25th.

Well, Gwen, I will have to say goodbye, but not for such a long time as
before. So many thanks to Arthur King to take this letter to you, but he is
like all Aussies willing to do a good turn for a Yank. Please send photos
and write as soon as possible.

Love, Charlie

Returning POWs from the war in the Pacific were required to spend
two weeks at the Navy's Oak Knoll Hospital in Oakland, California. Chuck
sat in a doctor's office at Oak Knoll; he'd been back in America two weeks,
and this was supposed to be the last exam before getting discharged and
heading home to see his parents in New York. It had been over a month
since he and Tim McCoy had walked out of Fukuoka #3, and he was anxious to get home.

He and Tim had been the only Navy men on an Army transport ship
carrying 900 soldiers on the long ride across the Pacific. Chuck spent a lot
of the trip drinking beer and playing poker; he won over $1,200, money
he planned to use to bring Gwen to America, if she'd come. He hadn't received a reply to his letter yet.

Aside from not hearing from Gwen, his first two weeks in America
had gone well. He and Tim had been topside when the ship sailed under
the Golden Gate, their arrival greeted by huge white letters on the Marin
side of the bay that spelled out WELCOME HOME. He got goose bumps. At
the pier at Hunter's Point in San Francisco, the men were welcomed by a
large contingent of Wacs, Waves, and a handful of female Marines. After
a few dockside speeches, they were taken to Oak Knoll to begin their two
weeks of debriefing, which to Chuck just seemed like more of the same
that he'd been through in Guam. For the first time he was allowed to call
home. He talked to his sister Yvonne and his mom, who both cried at the
sound of his voice. They told him about the article that appeared in the
local paper headlined DUNDEE BOY LOST IN ACTION, about the memorial

service that had been held in his honor, and how happy and hopeful they were when his name later showed up on a POW list.

Chuck had no complaints about Oak Knoll Hospital, commissioned by the Navy in 1942. It consisted of twenty-five wooden barracks built on the site of the Oak Knoll Golf and Country Club in the Oakland Hills, and was the primary regional hospital for handling battle casualties returning from the Pacific war and naval personnel requiring specialized care. The best part of Oak Knoll was that he received a pass almost daily. He and Tim had found plenty of opportunities to chase fun in San Francisco and Oakland, doing their best to make up for lost time.

The debriefing and examinations had been mostly physical in nature, poking and probing, lots of blood tests, urine samples, blood pressure monitoring, and making sure that the beriberi was under control. Chuck met with a psychologist, briefly, who asked if he was having any nightmares or negative effects from his twenty-eight-month imprisonment. Chuck reported that other than some pain in his back he was doing fine. He did mention that he was pissed off that the Navy charged him $5 for the phone call he'd made home.

Chuck was ready to get on with his life. On the fourteen-day voyage home, he'd been asked about his imprisonment by the soldiers on board. "The Japs treated us like shit every day," he replied. Beyond that, he didn't go into many details. He preferred talking about the upcoming 1945 World Series between the Detroit Tigers and Chicago Cubs, and whether the Tigers' Hank Greenberg would be rusty coming back from serving in the Army.

The doctor had summoned Chuck to his office for this last exam primarily to make sure his leg was healing properly. On the voyage home, he had slipped off a steel ladder and injured his leg, the one that had bothered him since getting pounded with the stairway railing on the *Asamu Maru*. The doctor had diagnosed a hairline fracture and put Chuck's leg in a wraparound cast, but that had done little to slow him down.

The doctor reexamined him and authorized his release. Back in his barracks, Chuck found Tim sitting on the edge of his bunk, head in his hands. He'd seen Tim the previous night at Sweets Ballroom in Oakland, a popular spot for dancing, music, and drinking with returning servicemen and local young women. When it had come time to leave, Chuck, with an attractive nurse from Oak Knoll on his arm, went looking for Tim and finally found him passed out on a bench in the upstairs VIP mezzanine. Chuck tried to rouse him, but when Tim didn't stir, Chuck took off with his new friend.

"I've got a huge favor to ask," said Tim, glancing up through bloodshot eyes. "I need to borrow three hundred dollars."

"What happened to all your back pay?" asked Chuck.

"I wired a lot of it home, and you're not going to believe what happened to the rest," replied Tim. He then explained that while he was passed out at Sweets, somebody had taken a knife and cut open the pocket of his pants and stolen his wallet.

"I'll pay you back," promised Tim.

Chuck counted out $300. "I know you're good for it," he said.

Chuck and his friend Buck Dekum sat in Buck's car in front of Irene Damien's apartment building. Buck was Irene's cousin, and he'd been the one to encourage Chuck to pay her a visit—against the advice of Chuck's mom.

"I'll knock on her door," said Buck. "If she's there, I'll signal you to come up."

"Okay," Chuck replied, nervously.

He'd finally made it back home, hitchhiking the last leg of his long journey to Sodus, New York, where his parents had moved after he'd joined the Navy. Sodus, a small town on the shore of Lake Ontario between Rochester and Syracuse, prided itself in being the birthplace of Arbor Day. For the Ver Valins, Chuck's homecoming was a joyous reunion. His mom and sisters all cried; his dad wanted to know what his plans were for the future. Chuck wasn't sure yet; right now all he wanted to do was just relax and hang out. When pressed, he talked about making a career in the Navy and becoming an officer. His dad thought that was a good idea. Chuck still had dreams of being involved in harness racing, but that just didn't seem practical. He was going to need steady employment, especially if he was, as he was hinting, going to bring Gwen over from Australia and get married.

A letter from Gwen had been waiting when he got home, and it gave him hope. Arthur King had delivered Chuck's letter to her just as he'd promised, and it had turned Gwen's world upside down. Until she received it, she'd assumed Chuck was dead, although she admitted to him that she had never given up hope or stopped thinking about him. Her fiancé, Adolph Cornberg, had returned to America after the war, and hoped to bring her over and get married under the War Brides Act, but when she received Chuck's letter she started to have second thoughts. In the three weeks Chuck had been home, he'd received three more letters from her. He'd also received a letter from King, telling him how lucky he was to have found someone so pretty as Gwen. "You Yanks have all the luck," he said. To his mom, Chuck extolled Gwen's Aussie charm, and he told her that he was thinking about proposing. "Then why do you want to go see Irene?" she countered.

Good question. Irene was his high-school sweetheart, the girl he'd sent his buddy to pick up on dates, and in the first few months after he'd joined the Navy, she had written regularly, sometimes three or four times a week, signing every letter with "All my love forever." But the letters started coming further and further apart until they eventually stopped altogether. At first it had been hard to deal with, but at least it was better than getting the Dear John letter like so many of his friends.

Of all the Dear John stories he'd heard, the worst involved his crewmate George Stauber, the guy who'd been on watch the morning they went down. Stauber thought about his fiancée constantly when they were in the camp. When Stauber got back stateside, she came to visit him in the hospital—with her new husband. Stauber ended up having to be restrained in a straitjacket—at least that's the way Chuck heard it.

Chuck watched Buck climb the stairs to Irene's apartment. He knew that Irene had married and had a child while he was gone, but still, he wanted to see her. She was his first brush with love. He remembered how pretty she was. Did she know he'd been a POW?

Heart pounding, Chuck peered around a corner of the building and watched Buck knock on her door. What if her husband answered? The door opened. "I have somebody I want you to meet," he heard Buck say.

Irene stepped outside and Chuck moved to the bottom of the stairs in full view. Irene stared in disbelief, her hand covering her mouth. "Chuck! Chuck!" she exclaimed, running down the stairs. "I thought you were dead. You're alive . . . you're alive!"

She threw her arms around him, tears streaming down her face. Chuck hugged her, and they embraced for what seemed like forever to Chuck, as her tears turned to joyful sobs.

Finally, Irene took him by the hand and led him back up the stairs and into the apartment. Toys covered the living room floor. She quickly explained that her two-year-old son was asleep in a back room, and that her husband was at work. As Chuck sat down on the couch, he let his eyes wash over her. She was just as pretty as he remembered—and she was pregnant.

Buck excused himself, saying he'd be back in a couple of hours to pick up Chuck.

The two hours sped by. Irene told him that she'd stopped writing because she'd met her husband and just couldn't make herself write a Dear John letter, figuring that Chuck would eventually figure it out. Her husband had been in the Army Reserve but didn't see combat and was now selling insurance. She talked about what a nice, considerate man he was, and how hard he worked to support her and their son. When the boy woke up from his nap, Chuck held him on his knee while Irene fixed lunch.

Buck returned to pick up Chuck. Hearing Buck come up the stairs, Irene grabbed Chuck's hand and clutched it tight. "I really did love you, Chuck," she said, tears filling her eyes.

Two weeks later, Chuck sat across from his mother, holding a letter from Irene. "What should I do?" he asked.

"You're a grown man, Chuck," she replied. "I can't tell you what to do. But I hoped I raised you well enough so that you know what's right."

Chuck glanced down at Irene's letter. It had caught him completely off guard. In it she confessed that she had never stopped loving him, and had gotten married because her husband was just so nice and promised he would take good care of her, but it was Chuck who truly owned her heart. But what took him totally by surprise was that she said that she would leave her husband and marry Chuck if he would still have her and her children. She said that she wanted to have more children with him.

"I thought you wanted to marry the Australian girl," said his mom.

"I thought I did," replied Chuck.

45

Bob Palmer
Medford, Oregon

B ob stood on the deck of the transport ship, staring out at the ocean. He couldn't remember if they'd been sailing for ten or eleven days—a lot of things were still fuzzy to him—but he did know they'd be arriving in San Francisco in a couple of days. He hoped his beloved wife Barbara would be there to greet him.

Before leaving Guam, he'd sent a telegram to the apartment on Pine Street where she'd lived when they got married on December 16, 1941. He didn't know if she still lived there, but he was counting on the telegram being forwarded if she didn't. He'd also sent a telegram to his dad and stepmother in Medford, telling them to make sure Barbara knew he was coming home.

When he'd walked out of the Death Hut, he weighed barely 80 pounds; now a month later, he'd already gained back about 30 pounds, although he still had little muscle tone. His various physical ailments, including the beriberi, were greatly improved, but he was still struggling psychologically. On a couple of the days aboard the ship, he'd been so depressed that it was all he could do to get out of his bunk to go for chow. He kept reminding himself not to let his mind go to the dark places, to keep it positive, to think about holding Barbara in his arms once again, but it was a struggle.

Barbara tried to digest the news. "What should I do?" she asked.

"You know what I want," replied Robert Kunhardt.

They were sitting in a motel room in Escanaba, Michigan, on the shores of Lake Michigan in the state's Upper Peninsula, the latest stop on the USS *Mero*'s goodwill tour of the Great Lakes. Barbara had just received the telegram from Bob; Edna, her former roommate back in San Francisco, had forwarded it to her. His ship would be arriving in San Francisco in seven days.

For over two years, Barbara had not known whether her husband was dead or alive. She had repeatedly tried to get information from the Navy Department, without success. When other names of *Grenadier* crew members showed up on the Red Cross's list of POWs, but not his, her hopes sunk even lower. When Barbara initially started dating Kunhardt, eight months after the *Grenadier* went down, she wondered whether she'd waited long enough and if she'd been persuaded to start dating again because of the package of Bob's belongings that she'd received from the woman in Australia.

Barbara was, of course, greatly relieved to find out Bob was still alive. But now she was almost two years into a relationship with Kunhardt and in love with him.

The next day, with the wife of another *Mero* officer as her passenger, she took off for San Francisco in Kunhardt's '41 Ford. She was going to do the right thing and be there to meet Bob when he got off that ship. Beyond that, she wasn't sure.

Barbara heard the knock on the door and groggily rolled off the couch. It was 11:00 a.m. on September 29, 1945, and she was in her former apartment on Pine Street in San Francisco, where her friend Edna now resided. She'd arrived at 3:00 a.m. after driving straight through from Salt Lake City and dropping off the other wife at a friend's house. Bob's ship was due in in four hours.

She opened the door, surprised to find her father standing there. He'd taken a Greyhound bus from Medford and then a cab to the apartment. Before leaving Michigan, she had sent her parents a telegram telling them she was going to meet Bob.

She recognized the look on her father's face: it was the same one he'd worn when he and her mother told her back in high school that they didn't want her dating Bob.

"Your mother and I don't think you should meet that ship. Don't get me wrong. We're happy to know that Bob is still alive. But we just think you'd be making a big mistake if you show up to greet him. It'll send the wrong message. The truth is, your lot in life will be infinitely better with Robert Kunhardt. We don't even know what Bob will be like. I've seen some of these returning GIs, and most of them have battle shock. They're not the same as they were before the war. That's probably going to be the case with Bob."

Barbara looked overwhelmed.

"I think you and I should drive home to Medford," said her father.

When Bob stepped off his ship, finally back in America after all those months, nobody was there to greet him.

Bob handed the bus driver a $100 bill. "I can't change this," the driver said. "Don't you have a dime?"

Bob shook his head. At Oak Knoll, he'd received over $3,000 in back pay, paid in $100 bills. He was trying to catch a bus from Oak Knoll to San Francisco. He needed to get to the Navy outfitter; all he had was the Army uniform he'd been given in Guam.

He had been back in America for over a week. He was glad to be back home, but his state of mind wasn't good. Every day in prison camp he had fantasized about what it would be like when Barbara greeted him when he stepped off the ship, even down to the clothes she'd be wearing; when she wasn't there when he walked down the gangway, he was crushed. He stood on the pier for minutes, shoulders sagging, hoping she would appear. He wondered if maybe she hadn't gotten his telegram, so he took a cab to the Pine Street apartment, where he talked with Edna, the woman now living there. After several awkward moments, she explained that Barbara had met another man, an Annapolis grad from a prominent family back east, and was now up in Medford with her parents. He thanked Edna for the information and left. The next day, he reached Barbara by phone, telling her that when he was released from Oak Knoll in a couple of days, he would be transferred to Camp White near Medford and hoped to see her. She said nothing about Kunhardt; he said nothing about being a POW. She did, however, agree to meet.

The bus driver handed Bob back the $100 bill. "Did you serve overseas?" he asked.

Bob nodded.

"Then you're a hero in my book. And heroes ride for free."

Barbara's father opened the door and let Bob inside, shaking his hand. "We were so happy to get the news that you were alive," he said. "How are you doing?"

"Fine, thank you, sir," replied Bob, turning to also greet Barbara's mother. Then he caught his first glimpse of Barbara.

She was even cuter, shapelier than he remembered. Tears welled in his eyes; his knees felt as if they would surely buckle. He tried to speak, but the words stalled, his long-rehearsed speech vanishing back down his throat. He just stood and stared.

Tears also rushed to Barbara's eyes. Bob looked so much older. The last time she'd seen him he was a young twenty-one-year-old, bright-eyed and sure of himself even as he was about to go off to war. Now, standing there in his new blue Navy uniform, he looked tired, puffy, uncertain.

She giggled nervously, and then moved to give him a hug. Bob hugged her back, but the moment was stiff, uncomfortable. In his dreams of this moment, he never saw Mr. and Mrs. Koehler standing two feet away. Nor did he imagine seeing another man's engagement ring on his wife's finger, a ring that probably cost twenty times more than the one Barbara had bought just before they got married.

They all sat down in the living room, and Barbara sensed his discomfort. "Shall we go for a drive and look around the old town?" she offered.

Soon they were driving south of town on Highway 99, through Ashland and up into the Siskiyou Mountains, Bob just staring at the road.

"What happened to you?" asked Barbara. "What happened to your ship? How come you were never on any Red Cross POW list I saw?"

"Don't know."

"How did they treat you? Did they beat you?"

He didn't answer and just kept driving on the narrow road up Mount Ashland in silence. He lit another cigarette, flicking the ashes out the window.

"Are you okay?" she asked.

"Fine," he answered.

But clearly he wasn't. His silence and his refusal to tell her anything about what had happened scared Barbara. She didn't think that he was going to hurt her physically, but she was afraid that he had come back so emotionally scarred that he would never be the same.

The last three weeks had moved so fast: the telegram that he was alive, the decision to meet his ship, the cross-country drive, the intervention by her father, the return to Medford, the cables from Kunhardt, and now seeing the shell of a man who was still her husband.

"You just seem, er, um . . ." she stuttered.

"Seem so what?"

"I guess 'sad' is the word I'd use."

"Can you blame me?" he said. "I survived by thinking about you. And I come home and find you've run off with somebody else."

"Bob, I thought you were dead."

"Well, I hear this is the age of gold diggers, so I guess that's what I can expect."

"That's not fair."

"So what do you want to do?" he asked. "Do you want a divorce?"

She hesitated, and then replied softly: "I suppose."

He turned the car around and drove back to Medford in silence.

Two weeks later, Barbara parked Kunhardt's Ford in front of the Medford Hotel and went inside, heading directly for the bar. A friend had told her that Bob had been spotted drinking there the past couple of nights.

Barbara had also heard from mutual friends that at one point Bob had been put in a very small hospital room, almost like a cage, and spent most of the next forty-eight hours curled in the fetal position in a corner. A nurse had come into the room and Bob proposed to her. Despite this behavior, Bob had improved enough that he was regularly given twelve-hour leaves, which he used to go to the Medford Hotel bar and get drunk.

One of the reasons Barbara wanted to talk to Bob was to tell him that she was driving back to Michigan the next day to rejoin Kunhardt. She also wanted to tell him that her father had offered to pay the $200 necessary for them to get a divorce in Reno. And she just wanted to see how he was doing. She truly cared about him, even though she was worried that what he'd been through was just too hard for him to cope with, and would be for her as well.

Entering the dimly lit bar, Barbara spotted Bob sitting alone on a stool at the end of the bar. "Mind if I sit down?" she asked.

"I hear it's a free country," he slurred.

She quickly told him she was leaving the next day. He awkwardly put his arm around her. "Does this mean I'll never see you again?" he asked.

"Who knows what the future holds?" she said.

"Well, if we aren't ever going to see each other again, then how's about let's get a room here . . . and . . . you know. For old time's sake?"

The offer completely surprised Barbara. She studied him to see if he was serious. He was—at least he was to the extent he could be after drinking for three hours. She saw those beautiful blue eyes and the hint of that devilish smile she'd loved so much as a teenager.

Taking his hand, she led him out of the bar to the front desk.

There was a knock at the door. "I'll get it," said Barbara, getting off the couch. It was mid-December 1945, and she was visiting with Edna in the apartment on Pine Street in San Francisco. After leaving Medford, she'd driven back to Michigan and rejoined Kunhardt. They'd traveled to New Orleans, where the *Muro* was temporarily stationed prior to shipping off to Pearl Harbor for several months. From New Orleans, she had driven back to San Francisco; Kunhardt would join her there in the early spring, when they planned to marry.

She opened the door, surprised to find Bob standing there. She hadn't talked to him since the night at the Medford Hotel in October, a night that had not gone well. Whether it was the alcohol, or performance anxiety, or not having been with a woman for so long, Bob was not able to perform.

Barbara was amazed at how much better he looked. He was no longer puffy, his eyes bright and clear, his smile back. "You look great," she said.

"So do you."

He was still on his ninety-day leave, on his way to Reno to get a divorce with the $200 that Mr. Koehler had given him. He had taken a big detour to San Francisco. In truth, he'd come to the apartment to ask Edna out for a drink. But not now.

"Why don't you come to Reno with me?" he asked.

Barbara thought for a moment. "Sure," she answered.

The snow was still falling when they awoke. For Bob, everything seemed perfect. The drive from San Francisco to Reno in Kunhardt's car had been so romantic, a light snow falling the last few miles. Along the way, Barbara had scooted across the front seat and snuggled up next to him, her hand on his leg, kissing his neck and cheek. By the time they checked into the hotel, they were in full heat. This time, Bob was able to finish what he hadn't been able to in Medford—four times—although they interrupted their lovemaking long enough for Barbara to send a telegram to her parents letting them know where she was. They also went out dining and dancing, stopping at several places and each time requesting the band play "The Anniversary Waltz." It was December 16, 1945, four years to the day that they got married.

"Let's just stay in bed all day," suggested Bob.

Barbara sat up. If Bob was not 100 percent the man she'd fallen in love with, he was certainly better. His spark and his humor were back, reminding her of what had attracted her to him in the beginning; she found him so damn cute. She was attracted to Kunhardt too, but the sexual chemistry she had with Bob was not there.

"We can't stay in bed all day," she replied.

"Why not?"

"First of all, you wore me out. Second of all, we have to go file for divorce."

Bob's mouth fell open. She couldn't be serious. They'd made love all night long and she still wanted a divorce?

Barbara's heart was telling her to stay with Bob. There was passion there, and history. She had cried on her pillow for months after she received the telegram telling her he was missing in action. And when he finally got back, he'd confessed that he'd survived his nightmarish imprisonment only because of the hope of seeing her again. With all of that (not to mention the incredible sex), how could she not be with him?

But her brain was telling her something else. She was convinced her parents would never accept Bob and would surely disown her if she chose him. Kunhardt would obviously provide a more secure future. He talked about how he was going to make admiral one day and she loved the thought of being an officer's wife and the prestige that went with it. Bob, on the other hand, didn't seem to have a clue where his life was heading other than to the next bar. Kunhardt's family had been so warm and welcoming, something that she'd never felt with Bob's. And as affectionate and passionate as he'd been last night, there was something that told her he still wasn't whole. He had not said one word about what had happened to him, brushing off every attempt she made to get him to open up with either "You wouldn't want to know" or "You couldn't possibly understand."

"Bob, I know this is hard for you to understand," she said, "but I still want to go through with the divorce."

An hour after getting their divorce, they headed west out of Reno on US 50. Bob eyed a hitchhiker up ahead. "Barbara, I'm asking you one last time," he said. "Let's turn around and get remarried."

"I can't do it, Bob."

"But how can you tell me you love me like you did last night and not want to be married? I thought people who were in love were married. Or did that all change while I was away?"

"I don't understand all of this myself, but I just think I'm doing the right thing."

He swerved to the side of the highway, motioning for the hitchhiker to climb aboard, instructing the man to sit in the middle, between him and Barbara.

For the rest of the way to San Francisco, Bob talked occasionally to the hitchhiker, but not to Barbara, six hours of icy silence between them.

Back at the apartment, Barbara read the brief-but-to-the-point telegram from her parents: "Your recent escapade leaves much to be desired in the way of comportment."

She set it down and took a deep breath. She was twenty-four years old, but her parents' opinion still meant everything to her. Her parting with Bob in front of the apartment building had been as silent as the ride home, but in some ways, that had been for the best.

As Barbara put the telegram in a drawer, the phone rang. It was Kunhardt, calling on a two-way radio from Pearl Harbor. Yes, she reassured him, she really missed him and still loved him. "I can't wait for us to be married," she said.

The next day, Bob boarded a bus and headed back to Medford, and an uncertain future.

46

Tim "Skeeter" McCoy

of Texas

Tim peeked out the blinds of his parents' house in Chula Vista, California, a growing suburb in southern San Diego County. He was impatiently waiting for Gordy Cox, who'd called to say he was visiting from Yakima and needed to see him. They hadn't talked since prison camp.

After his release from Oak Knoll, Tim had been transferred to the Balboa Naval Hospital in San Diego, although he was spending most of his time in Chula Vista with his parents. During his imprisonment, Harrell and Cappy McCoy had begun talking to each other for the first time since they'd divorced when Tim was in ninth grade. His dad had divorced his second wife, remarried Cappy, and moved to California for the climate. He seemed devoted to Cappy and proud of Tim. This was all good news to Tim, especially how happy his mom seemed. Tim was doing his best to forgive his dad.

Tim was trying to keep a positive attitude, not just about his dad but about everything. On the days he had to go to Balboa Naval Hospital for tests, however, it was tough. Located next to scenic Balboa Park in San Diego, the hospital had become the primary care provider for thousands of military families in Southern California, and now housed nearly 20,000 war wounded; a walk down a hallway could be depressing. The facility was so short-staffed that on some rotations young doctors were overseeing as many as a thousand patients. For Tim, who was born impatient, the waits seemed endless.

He glanced out the window again, hoping to see Gordy arrive; there was still no sign of him. Bulldozers and contracting crews worked on a new subdivision across the street. Chula Vista was on the front edge of suburban expansion in southern California, and with the return of thousands of servicemen who wanted to stay in the area, the lemon tree orchards that once covered the landscape were now giving way to low-cost housing developments soon to be financed by the GI Bill.

Tim spotted the postman and his hopes soared, just as they did every day. Maybe there would be another letter from Valma. Since his release, he had reconnected with her by mail, telling her that he'd thought about her every day in prison camp and that he still wanted to marry her. To his great relief and happiness, she'd written back, telling him how she'd never taken off the engagement ring he'd given her the last day they were together in Perth. He was also happy to learn that she and his parents had been exchanging letters for over a year while he was in prison camp. She'd even sent them a picture of herself, which was now framed and sitting on a shelf in the living room. But Tim was even happier when she agreed to his proposed plans. He'd already sent her the money for the trip to the States; she had said that she wanted to get married in Los Angeles. She'd never been to America, but she'd read about LA in magazines and seen it in movies, and it seemed so romantic, the perfect place to be married. LA was fine by Tim. Now he just had to wait for the red tape to be removed. According to reports, Congress was about to pass the War Brides Act, which would make it easier for servicemen to bring their foreign girlfriends to America to wed. There was still a lot of paperwork they would have to complete before it could happen, but Tim was impatiently counting the days.

On this day, however, there was no letter from Valma, for the tenth day in a row.

Finally, a car arrived and Gordy stepped out, accompanied by a woman. At first glance, Tim figured his crewmate had gotten married, but upon closer examination, Tim saw the gray hair and wrinkles. It was Gordy's mom.

Tim ushered them into the living room and introduced his parents.

Gordy explained that he and his mother and youngest brother, Willie, had driven down from Yakima to deliver Willie to Navy boot camp. "But that's not why we came to see you," added Mrs. Cox, looking first at Tim, then at his mother.

She paused, choking back tears, and pointed toward Tim. "Young man," she said, "as a mother I want to thank you for what you did for my son. He tells me you saved his life."

Tim remembered smuggling portions of rice back into the barracks to feed Gordy when he was close to death. "We all did what we had to do to survive," he said.

Mrs. Cox turned to Tim's parents. "Your son's a hero," she said.

"They're all heroes," said Tim's dad, beaming.

Tim checked the mailbox again, hoping for a letter from Valma. This time there was a nice thick one.

He was nearing the end of his ninety-day leave, and soon he'd have to make a decision on what he wanted to do next. He'd always admired his uncle's success in the insurance business and considered the possibility of going to work for him. But his uncle was back in Texas, and with his parents now living in California, that might be a harder transition. It was more likely that he would stay in the Navy and try to become an officer. Before he had been captured, he really liked the life—the camaraderie, structure, job security, and feeling of being part of something special, especially as a submariner. But he didn't know whether he could qualify for training as a naval officer. He hadn't completed high school, and although the Navy would count the time he'd spent as a POW toward a commission, he didn't feel confident that he'd learned the skills necessary to advance, at least not yet. His second, and bigger, concern was Valma. It would be hard enough on her coming to a new country and culture without knowing anyone, but to have her husband away from home and out to sea for long periods of time seemed a truly daunting way to start a marriage.

He opened the envelope, smelling the letter as he pulled it out. He liked the way her letters always were written on scented stationery.

Congress had just passed the War Brides Act, and Tim was just one of tens of thousands of U.S. military personnel now involved in bringing their potential mates across the Atlantic and Pacific to marry. America was now experiencing an unusual new wave of immigrants, dubbed "petticoat pilgrims" by the press, women who'd first met American servicemen during a time of war and chaos. These women were now arriving daily on converted warships. It wasn't an easy transition; prior to leaving, they had to fill out mountains of forms in triplicate and endure sometimes humiliating physicals. They were also often the target of anger and scorn from returning servicemen in their own countries, who were resentful that the women were chasing after a romanticized version of love in America. And now these war brides were quickly encountering difficulties for which love in wartime hadn't prepared them. They stepped off the ships and discovered men much different from the ones they'd met during the war. Some were battle-scarred. Some had gone from romantic to abusive. Some were broke. Some were jobless. Some were drinking too much. And now, on top of all that, these women were far from home and incredibly lonely, with no money for return passage.

But unfolding Valma's letter, Skeeter wasn't worried about any of that. What he knew was that she was the prettiest girl he'd ever met, with an accent so sweet and lilting that he would never get tired of listening to her. In his eyes, for her to be willing to give up everything she had to come halfway across the world to be with him . . . well, she certainly had to love him an awful lot.

He began to read:

Dear Tim,
It is with the deepest sorrow that I am returning your engagement ring
and the money you sent for my trip to America.

He stopped reading. "No, no," he gasped; it felt like someone had sucked all the air out of his lungs. How could this be true? His mind flashed to their last night together, and how he'd shouted for joy when she accepted his proposal. And all those nights in prison camp when he lay in his bunk and thought about her and dreamed of their life together. It didn't matter that they had probably spent less than ten days together, or that they had never made love. This couldn't be happening.

Maybe he'd misread that first line. But no, it was true. He continued reading: Valma's mother had cancer and Valma needed to be there for her. His first thought was that Valma had just made up the story to let him down easy. His second thought was that maybe her mother would die soon and Valma could come to the States then.

But the more he reread the letter and the more he thought about it, the more hopeless it felt. Nothing he'd suffered in prison camp—the starvation, the days in the bunker, the constant battle with the guards—had ever caused him to lose hope. But this was pushing him to the edge.

Part Nine

SIXTY YEARS LATER

47

Chuck Ver Valin

Concord, California

As far as Las Vegas buffets go, it was pretty pathetic: skinny chicken thighs, lumpy mashed potatoes, soggy green beans. But the tasteless food didn't matter to the *Grenadier* survivors, men familiar with eating rice one grain at a time. It was December 2000, and they were gathered for their annual reunion within the Sub Vets Reunion at the Imperial Palace, a low-rent hotel on the Vegas strip.

Chuck Ver Valin was holding court, his deep voice rising above the low din of slot machines and gamblers on the other side of the wall. Of the dozen survivors at the reunion, he seemed the most robust, a cross between Ernest Borgnine and Ed Asner.

"Has anyone heard from Johnny Johnson?" he asked, inquiring about his bunkmate at Fukuoka #3.

For Chuck, seeing Johnny Johnson had been a big incentive to attend this reunion. They had not seen each other since the day in 1945 when Chuck and Tim walked out of camp. They'd each sent a few Christmas cards over the years, but there had been no other contact. Johnson lived in Winston-Salem, North Carolina; Chuck in Concord, California.

Since Bob Palmer organized the first *Grenadier* reunion in 1975, Chuck had been to all but one. Now, with most of the survivors in their early eighties, there was a greater sense of urgency; fewer and fewer men attended each year, their ranks depleted by death and illness. A bottle of

Dom Perignon was being held in safekeeping by a son of one of the crew, to be delivered to and shared by the last two remaining survivors.

During dessert Bernie Witzke, who now lived in San Diego, brought up the subject of reparation. He had recently written Senator Orrin Hatch of the Armed Services Committee, inquiring about the status of a proposed bill to make restitution to all former POWs. He pulled a sheet of paper out of a folder.

"I got this form letter back telling me the same old bullshit they've been telling us for years," said Witzke, passing around the letter. "It's funny how our government has been able to somehow pay $25,000 to all those Japs that had to go into internment camps but has never given us a dime. I'm not saying those Japs didn't deserve compensation, it's just that we were the ones fighting for our country."

As Chuck pushed back from the table, ready to call it a night, he glanced across the room and spotted a handsome, elderly man with thinning silver hair entering the room, escorted by an elegantly dressed elderly woman. Chuck studied the man, trying to place him. Suddenly a light of recognition went on, and he quickly headed toward the couple.

"Johnny!" he exclaimed, his voice cracking.

The two men walked toward each other, meeting in the center of the room. They paused ten feet apart, each trying to peel away five decades. It was Chuck who spoke first.

"You old blanket hog," he said.

"Friend," drawled Johnson, "I do believe it was you who hogged the blanket."

Chuck and Johnny embraced, tears rolling down their cheeks.

After his visit with Irene Damien, and her letter telling him that she wanted to get a divorce and be with him, Chuck wrote back and gently told her that he just couldn't do it. Instead, he continued exchanging love letters with Gwen in Australia, and in May 1946 he brought her to America on the War Brides Act. Three days after her arrival, they were married in a small wedding ceremony in Chicago, where Chuck was first stationed after deciding to pursue a career in the Navy. His best man was Eugene Lutz, the Marine he'd met at Fukuoka #3. At Gwen's request, Chuck converted to Catholicism.

Their wedding night at the Blackstone Hotel was a disaster. Like many young men who'd gone off to war, Chuck had not yet learned a more gentle approach to lovemaking. For Gwen, a virgin, the experience was painful and traumatic. She screamed so loudly for him to stop that hotel security came to the room to make sure everything was okay. Chuck assured them that it was, but it was an inauspicious start to the marriage.

Over the next couple of months, Chuck tried to introduce Gwen to life in America, taking her to a Cubs game at Wrigley, midget auto racing, a Sinatra concert, and even an opera, but for Gwen, the transition was difficult, and she had serious doubts about her decision to move to America. Chuck took her to parties with other Navy personnel and their wives, but she didn't drink and found it hard to fit in.

Six months after they were married, Chuck was transferred to Pensacola, Florida. By this time, Gwen was pregnant, so she stayed behind in Chicago, living in a $30-a-month, one-room hotel studio, sleeping on a Murphy bed. With no friends or family for support, one lonely day passed into another. When their son, John, was born in July 1947, Chuck did not return to Chicago, and Gwen became deeply depressed.

She thought about getting a divorce, but she couldn't reconcile that with her strict Catholic upbringing. For the next twenty-five years, while Chuck traveled the globe with the Navy, including a stint in Vietnam, and climbed to the rank of lieutenant commander, Gwen stayed home and raised their children: John and a daughter, Marilyn, born in 1954. Chuck's career took him out to sea for months at a time, and Gwen resented his long absences. After thirty-eight years, they divorced in 1984. Neither remarried.

It was June 2002, and Chuck was at his daughter Marilyn's house on a cul-de-sac in Walnut Creek, a suburb twenty miles east of San Francisco. His car, a Japanese-made Toyota with a "WWII POW and Submarine Vet" license frame, was parked in front. Marilyn was at work at her job as an insurance adjuster, and her two children, Paige, a fifth grader, and Jonathon, an eighth grader, were at school. Chuck, who lived five miles away in nearby Concord, was at the house to supervise the installation of new windows, for which he was paying. Chuck's son-in-law had died of a stroke three years earlier at the age of forty-two. That same night, Chuck suffered a heart attack after he rushed over to Marilyn's house; he spent a week in intensive care and missed his son-in-law's funeral. Adding to the family's grief, his son John died a year later at the age of fifty-three.

Wearing khaki pants and an Old Navy T-shirt, Chuck sat outside in the sun-splashed backyard, proudly pointing out the deck that he had built.

"I wasn't the best husband or father," he admitted. "I was never around when my kids were growing up. I guess I'm trying to make up for it now with Marilyn and her two kids."

He pointed toward a new flat-screen TV he'd just bought for his daughter. "I pulled a groin muscle trying to unload that damn thing," he said. "But I did a good job negotiating down the price. The salesman was Jewish. They know how to deal."

Over the sound of hammers and Skilsaws in the background, Chuck talked about his life over the last sixty years. When he talked about Gwen, he was gruff and surly, but when talking about Marilyn and his grandkids, he was thoughtful and borderline sweet. He also showed signs of the devilish sense of humor that had repeatedly gotten him into trouble as a child, and despite being in his eighties and having suffered a number of physical setbacks, he was clear-minded. When the conversation turned to his time in prison camp, he furrowed his brow and stiffened.

"Those little bastards were fuckin' evil," he said, almost snarling. "I'll never forget what they did to us." He paused, considering his next words carefully. "But I can forgive them. A few of the guards and pushers were actually nice to me. When you think about it, they were just doing what they'd been trained to do. It was all that Bushido bullshit. It's like the Palestinians today. They don't know any other way."

*   *   *

Chuck planned well for his retirement; he was collecting a Navy pension, Social Security, disability compensation, and another pension from the fifteen years he worked for the Contra Costa Humane Society after retiring from the Navy. In total, his income was almost $6,000 a month, plus his house was paid off and he was making a little money from investments in the stock market. He claimed he broke even on his regular excursions to the racetrack. In addition to being able to contribute to remodeling and other household expenses for Marilyn, he still made monthly support payments to Gwen, even though they'd been divorced for nearly twenty years. He co-owned her condo in Concord a few miles away.

Chuck vividly recalled the details of the sinking of the *Grenadier* and how Captain Fitzgerald had been waterboarded.

"That's one thing I can't forgive 'em for," he bristled. "That was inhuman. Believe me, Fitzgerald was one tough sonuvabitch."

Chuck was interrupted again, this time by a phone call from Gwen. They still talked on the phone or saw each other almost daily. Perhaps it was because of a shared grief over the loss of their son, or because they were both deeply involved in the lives of their daughter and grandkids, or because they had met and fallen in love in the frenzy of wartime. Whatever the reason, the connection was still there. When Chuck was sick the previous week, Gwen had brought him meals and done his laundry. The day before, he had gone to her condo to fix a leaky kitchen faucet and help get her car repaired. Although hard-pressed to say anything nice about Gwen, even about her parenting skills, he generously gave her his time and provided a big part of her financial support.

"Two weeks ago is a perfect example," he said. "I spent almost the whole day taking her to get her medicine up at Travis Air Force Base because it's cheaper there, but when I asked her for three dollars for bridge fare, she acted as if I was some sort of serial killer.

"And I'll tell you something else that pisses me off about her. From the day we got married, she has constantly told me how I ruined her life. If you listen to her, I practically kidnapped her from her beloved Australia.

Well, if that's the case, why didn't she move back? I'll tell you why . . . she'd rather stay here and bitch at me and remind me what a bad father and shitty husband I was.

"I've tried to be nice, but it doesn't work. I tried not talking to her and that didn't work either. She just keeps complaining. Just once I'd like to talk with her when she doesn't complain about something. She goes to church every week, but as far as I can tell, it doesn't do her any good."

The final straw that destroyed their marriage was when Gwen found out Chuck was having an affair. She picked up a pitcher of orange juice and dumped it on him, then tried to slap him. Chuck flew into a rage and grabbed her, he explained, partly because of all the times he'd been slapped as a POW and a vow that he'd never let anybody slap him ever again. Gwen called the police, who ordered Chuck to pack his suitcase and leave. He did as ordered, bringing his golf clubs as well. For the next two weeks he slept in the back of his car in the parking lot of the Humane Society, where he was working at the time. When he finally went to rent a room in a cheap motel, he discovered that she'd wiped out their joint checking account.

When the topic changed to his career in the Navy, however, he talked with pride. "I was a real hard-ass, by-the-book kind of officer," he said. "My men liked to call me 'Big V,' although not to my face. Looking back, I think the Navy and the government treated me fairly. They didn't originally give me combat disability for the injuries I received as a POW, but overall, I can't complain."

One tough time in his career was when he got home from Vietnam. He'd volunteered to go, and served in the Mekong Delta supplying riverboats. He injured his neck in a helicopter accident, and when he came home, the sight of hippies from Berkeley and San Francisco, with their long hair and protest signs, didn't sit well with him. Neither did Jane Fonda.

"But what was I going to do about it?" he said. "Tell them I was an ex-POW and convince them how much I sacrificed for this country?"

It was during the mid-1960s that John started acting out. Chuck was trying to be a good father, even joining a father-son bowling league when they were stationed in Hawaii, but it was hard to make up for all the lost time. The low point came when Chuck slammed John against a wall for staying out all night. Later, when John married and had a child, Chuck did not have a good relationship with his daughter-in-law, which further limited the time he spent with his son.

"I wouldn't give her a nickel to blow her ass to hell," he scowled.

Eventually, John separated from his wife, and then a year after that, he died. According to Chuck, it was cancer. "It just spread through his whole body," he said.

Chuck left Marilyn's house to run errands, and while he was out, Gwen stopped by to check on the progress the contractor was making. In her eighties now, it was easy to see the beauty that made Chuck fall in love all those years ago.

Gwen wasted little time before complaining about her lot in life. "My whole life has been a wreck," she claimed. "And it's his fault. And now I have emphysema and he's to blame. All those years he smoked and I had to breathe it all in. He knew I had asthma—I almost died from it—and yet it didn't stop him from smoking two packs a day. He was inconsiderate. But at least he finally quit.

"When I first met him during the war, he wasn't that way. He looked like Gary Cooper, and was very gentlemanly and well behaved. I thought he carried himself well and looked great in his uniform. He took me to movies and skating. We'd go to Leighton Beach and just sit on the beautiful white sand and talk. I was proud to point to him and say he was with me. Because of the war there was rationing, and new clothes were hard to come by, so most of the time I'd wear my military uniform, and if I do say so myself, I looked quite good in it. I still have that uniform, and it still fits."

She struggled to recall her fondest memory of their marriage. "I don't have any," she finally said. "During our marriage he never took me out to dinner, or movies, or anywhere. He never got me anything for my birthdays or gave me a Mother's Day card. I gave him a Saint Christopher's medal just before that last patrol and he said he'd wear it forever. Well, he lost it and didn't even care.

"He didn't know how to show affection. He was like his dad, gruff, a man's man but not easy for me to be around. He was always bossing me. He still does.

"We were married thirty-eight years and he was home maybe five of those years. He was married to the Navy. But I'll say this about him, he never hit me. He still ruined my life, and it started right from our wedding night. He was rough. He didn't know he was doing anything wrong, and he just didn't care. Years later we were watching a video of the movie *Ryan's Daughter* and there was a scene where a man was forcing himself on a woman. Chuck turned to me and said, 'I did that to you.' At least he admitted it.

"Not even my family understands how hard it's been for me. My sisters fall all over him and think he's wonderful. I have to admit he's very likable and has a fabulous personality, but he never saw me for who I was.

"We were strangers when we wed—hadn't seen each other in four years. We had no business getting married. We're just too different: He likes to drink; I've never touched a drop. I'm a Republican; he's a Democrat. I'm a strict Catholic; he never goes to church. About the only thing we had in common, other than our children, was that we both have bad tempers. It was the Irish in me that made me always yell at him."

She told the story of how she met and got engaged to Adolph Cornberg, after Chuck's ship was reported lost at sea. "I probably made a mistake by not marrying Adolph," she said. "Chuck was always jealous of him. He found a picture I had of him and tore it up. Adolph's the reason he doesn't like Jews."

Despite her age, she still wanted to return to Australia. "I've lived too long apart from my family," she said. "In my heart, I'm Australian. I don't want to die here. Nor do I want to die with it being on my soul that I was mean to Chuck. He told me many times that he survived prison camp because he was so determined to marry me."

Even when she talked about the death of her son, her anger and resentment were unmistakable. "Chuck likes to tell everyone that John died of cancer," she said. "That's not true. Our son died of AIDS and Chuck knows it. He's just too ashamed to admit it.

"It was so hard to watch John waste away," said Gwen. "The nurse told me that he was afraid he wasn't loved, so every time I came to see him I told him I loved him. Two hours before he died, he opened his eyes and looked at me and nobody else. I left to go home, and then after Marilyn called to tell me he had passed, I came back, and when I saw Chuck I put my arms around him and he just stood there like a statue. I didn't get any comfort from Marilyn either. I'd just lost my son and nobody cared about me. It broke my heart. John was my life. Then I had to watch him die the way he did. He said to me at one point, 'Mom, I'm dying in shame.' After he died I was at bingo one night and told a woman there that my son died of AIDS and she said, 'He deserved to die.' Can you imagine saying that to the mother? But John didn't get AIDS like people suspect. He was married and had a child. He told me he got it from a prostitute."

It was a scorching summer day in Concord in 2004. The surrounding hills were parched, as were most of the lawns on Chuck's street in a working-class neighborhood of modest houses built in the 1960s. But his lawn was green and the sprinkler was beating out a rat-tat-tat, disturbing the stillness. Answering the door, he was shirtless, his breathing labored. A scar from his open-heart surgery ran down the middle of his chest from his neck to his belt line.

"I feel like shit today," he said.

His doctor had him on a special liquid diet in preparation for an exam tomorrow for a new intestinal pain. He had to drink a phosphate-sodium solution and a bottle of water every hour. In the past twelve years he had endured a heart attack, stomach cancer, kidney stones, high blood pressure, open-heart surgery, bad knees, an operation to fuse two vertebrae, loss of feeling in a couple of fingers, and a pacemaker implant. When he was diagnosed with stomach cancer, his doctor told him he most likely had six months to live. That was seven years ago.

"Thank heavens for the outstanding medical coverage I have through the Navy and VA," he said.

Over the years he'd also taken medication to help him cope with the nightmares and flashbacks from his POW experience. In the mid-1970s, he also took part in group therapy sessions at the VA with fifteen POWs from World War II and Vietnam. "It was a tough time for me," he recalled. "I was still having nightmares, plus my marriage was falling apart and I didn't want anyone to know. I was depressed. They put me on Valium, and I was chasing it with stiff bourbon and water. I'd wake up the next morning feeling funny. This went on for six or seven months.

"The shrink was this Jewish guy. He classified me with post-traumatic stress, although I don't think he called it that at the time. At one point these other guys in the group were all complaining that they'd been treated poorly and the doctor was reinforcing them. I went off. 'Uncle Sam don't owe you nothing,' I told them. I almost hit that sonuvabitch of a doctor. They kicked me out of the group."

Chuck sat in a well-worn easy chair, watching the San Francisco Giants on TV, berating Barry Bonds. On the fridge in the kitchen was an Oakland Raiders magnet, his favorite team. The phone rang. It was Gwen calling to tell him that there was a piece on Fox News right then about World War II submarines. He thanked her, but by the time he switched to Fox, the story was over. He continued to watch the game. "At least I have to give her credit for trying," he said.

Clearly, his grit helped him survive prison camp. "I took what they dished out and accepted it the best way I knew how," he explained. "I try not to think about it too much because I'd go nuts if I do, but there probably hasn't been a day that's gone by since then that I don't revisit it. Gwen said to me once that it was like being married to a guy with a mistress, only worse because I took the POW thing with me everywhere I went, even to bed. But you know, when I was in prison I always believed that one day we'd get to go home. If you didn't believe that, you wouldn't make it."

The doorbell rang; it was a couple of Jehovah's Witnesses. Chuck told them no thanks, but they persisted. He politely but firmly interrupted their spiel. "I spent three years in prison camp to give you the right to preach whatever you want," he said. "But that doesn't mean I have to listen to you. Good-bye." And then he closed the door.

Chuck was busy helping Marilyn get ready for a car trip the next day; she was taking Gwen, Jonathon, and Paige to Disneyland and then on a cruise to Mexico. His list of tasks was long: fix the weird noise in Marilyn's van; help Paige count her nickels and dimes for the trip; coerce Jonathon into cutting the lawn. He also had no shortage of tasks for when they'd be gone: take care of the dog and cat; water the plants; feed the gecko; wash and fold the laundry.

"I don't mind doing it," he said. "Anything to get Gwen out of town."

Nothing in his life brought him more joy than his grandkids. Almost every day, he chauffeured Paige, a cute quintessentially California sixth grader with blond hair, blue eyes, and freckled cheeks, to ballet or other after-school activities. Jonathon, a middle-schooler, regularly tested him. Today, Jonathon, wearing a Metallica T-shirt, was refusing to clean his room, including the gecko's cage, or pick up his skateboard off the kitchen floor.

"His dad's death has been hard on him," said Chuck. "John was his Little League coach, and since he died Jonathon hasn't picked up a base-ball. Gwen claims I spend so much time with the grandkids because I'm trying to relieve my guilt for not being around as a father. Maybe there's some truth to that.

"I worked my ass off for all those years trying to support Gwen and the kids," he continued. "But it's like none of that mattered to her. She'd rather whine, and that makes it hard for Marilyn to want to be around her. I just hope Marilyn and the kids don't want to kill her by the end of this trip."

* * *

Despite his guilt for being a less-than-perfect father and husband, Chuck took great pride in other endeavors. "For a guy who didn't finish high school, I think I've done all right for myself," he said.

He talked about the handyman projects he'd done at his house, as well as Marilyn's, and described his role in getting the Contra Costa Humane Society to provide a more humane form of euthanasia for its animals. He could recall the exact cards he'd held sixty years ago when he won the big pot in the poker game on the trip home from Guam, and he puffed out his chest when he told of bumping into Commander Barney Siegal in 1965 and repaying him the $20 Siegal had given to him and Tim when they were leaving Japan after the war. He honored the promise he made to himself in prison camp to apologize to his teachers for causing so much trouble, and laughed when he told how finally, twenty-five years later, Tim paid him back the $300 he'd loaned him after he was robbed at Sweets Ballroom.

He even took pride in the one time he had smoked pot. He had promised his son that when he retired from the Navy he would give it a try, so when John invited him to join a couple of friends on a boat trip up the California coast to a cove near Mendocino, Chuck agreed to go. After anchoring, the young men fired up a joint and passed it to Chuck. He took only a couple of hits.

"I saw the way the other guys were twisting and scrunching up their faces when they took a drag, and I thought, 'That doesn't look like fun,'" he said. "But at least I kept my word and tried it."

Standing in his garage, he showed off a model submarine that John had made for him and pulled down from a shelf a bowling trophy John had won as a boy when they participated in the father-son league in Hawaii. He paused, trying to stay composed.

"You really never get over losing a child," he acknowledged.

Chuck reluctantly admitted the truth when told that Gwen and Marilyn had both said John died of AIDS. It was not an easy admission, but once the burden of secrecy was removed, he spoke candidly about his son's final year.

In 1995, Chuck accompanied John to a farmers' market in Stockton to help him set up a table to sell Dungeness crabs that he'd caught. At the time, John was making a living catching and selling abalone and crab. As they were setting up, John turned to his father and, with tears rolling down his cheeks, said there was something he had to tell him.

"I've got AIDS," he revealed.

John was certain he'd gotten it when he and two friends spent the night with three prostitutes in San Francisco. He was still married at the time. His two friends were lucky and didn't get it. Neither did his wife.

Eventually, as John's condition deteriorated, Chuck volunteered to provide hospice care in his own house, buying a hospital bed, hiring a part-time nurse, and fixing all John's meals. John spent the last six months of his life at his dad's, except for one three-day period at Christmas when he insisted on going to Half Moon Bay for one last abalone dive before he died.

"He could barely walk," recalled Chuck. "He loved the ocean, and I figured he was going to just dive down and never come back up. But he came back home."

One of the hardest parts of the final weeks of John's life was the tension in the house when Gwen came to visit. At one point, John had gotten so frustrated at his mom that he ordered her to leave.

"He couldn't take her constant whining," said Chuck. "He just wanted to die in peace."

Shortly after returning from Half Moon Bay, John started going downhill fast, getting out of bed only to eat. To help ease the constant pain, he'd grown a small crop of marijuana in Chuck's backyard, and smoked a couple of joints each day for relief. Chuck learned to roll the joints for him.

During his last month, John's cat spent most of each day sleeping on his chest. "It was weird," Chuck mused. "That cat slept on John's chest every day, but in the two days before he died, the cat wouldn't go into his room. It knew."

48

Gordy Cox

Culver, Oregon

It was 2003 and another Submarine Vets Reunion, this one held at the Hilton in Reno. Gordy Cox leaned against his walker, taking in the scene. The place was swimming in octogenarians, underwater heroes filling the lobby, lounges, and elevators with their camaraderie and liver spots. There must have been over a thousand men, many with canes, walkers, and a slap on the back for a long-lost crewmate. Many of them proudly wore a blue vest embroidered with patches and insignia denoting the ships served on and hometown. It was a gathering of the tribe, a confirmation of belonging to a special fraternity. The crew of the *Grenadier*, or what was left of it, was just one part of the gathering. Since the previous reunion in Las Vegas, two more survivors had died.

Gordy pulled a pack of Pall Malls from the pocket of his blue vest and lit a cigarette. He flicked the ash into an ashtray he'd customized into his walker, and blew the smoke into the stale air of the hotel.

"Little bit late to try to quit now," he observed.

Indeed. He'd been smoking two packs a day since he'd first started during the war. The previous week his doctor had discovered a growth the size of a baseball on one of his lungs. He was scheduled for more tests the following week, but now he was enjoying the reunion and the idea of being one of the dozen *Grenadier* survivors. His frail, sallow appearance belied his feisty demeanor.

Standing next to him, his wife Janice, equally feisty, lit up her own cigarette. Twenty-two years younger than he, they were married in 1968, not too long after she interviewed for a job as a bartender/waitress at the tavern Gordy owned in a working-class neighborhood on the east side of Portland, Oregon. He gave her the job, and now, almost forty years later, they were rarely out of each other's sight.

The view from Highway 97 approaching Gordy and Janice's house just outside of Culver, in central Oregon, is spectacular. To the west sits Mount Jefferson and the Three Sisters, and to the east are rolling hills, alfalfa fields, red barns, and giant stacks of hay. The irrigation sprinklers work hard to keep it lush.

Gordy's blue prefab house sits alone on the ten-acre parcel of land he owns, a former mint farm. Eight of those acres are rented out to a local farmer to grow alfalfa. He and Janice moved here in 1981 and were now both retired. A sign greets visitors: TWO PEOPLE LIVE HERE—ONE NICE PERSON AND ONE OLD GROUCH.

Indeed, Gordy, in his eighties, could be a bit of a grouch when he talked about reparation for POWs or "the lazy shits who don't know anything about an honest day's work." For most of his adult life, he was a loyal, punch-the-clock employee for a host of manufacturing companies in Washington and Oregon. On this warm summer afternoon, however, he sat in his living room, lighting up one Pall Mall after another and recalling his work history since the war. By his recollection, he'd had well over a dozen employers, not counting the jobs that lasted only a week or two, or his time spent in the tavern business. As he talked, Janice was in the kitchen, preparing lasagna for dinner. She too was smoking, and the house reeked of cigarette smoke. They had both enrolled in a stop-smoking clinic fifteen years ago, shelling out $600 each, money that went straight out the chimney when they quit the clinic after the first session.

Janice is Gordy's second wife. He met his first wife, Jeanne, at Dopey's, the drive-in restaurant popular with Yakima's young people after the war. She was an attractive nineteen-year-old telephone operator—5 feet 2 inches, brunette, dark brown eyes, one-eighth Indian. When he first asked her out, she turned him down, choosing to go out with one of his friends instead. On a double date, however, she decided she'd rather be with Gordy and the switch was made. Soon they began seeing each other regularly, although she put the brakes on when it came to "going all the way." He asked her to wait for him when he went off to Seattle to check into reenlisting. Gordy wasn't gung ho about a career in the Navy—he was still a seaman first class—but without a high-school diploma, his job prospects were limited. He'd thought about becoming a cop, but when he applied to the Yakima Police Department they told him that at 5 feet 5 inches he was too short. He'd been fooling around with photography, and hoped that if he reenlisted he could be assigned as a photographer's mate, but at the Navy office in Seattle, he was told they wanted him to work shore patrol for two years, and then possibly move up in rank. He didn't like the officer's attitude, so he asked for his discharge and headed back to Yakima, eager to get back to partying. He had no clue what he would do for work.

The first thing he did back in his hometown was drive to the telephone company to see Jeanne. As he wheeled into the parking lot, she was getting into a car with another guy. Impulsively, Gordy angled his car to block their way, a move that impressed Jeanne. She hopped out of the other guy's car and climbed in with Gordy, signaling him to drive away. A couple of weeks later, they eloped to Lewiston, Idaho, consummating their relationship on their wedding night. The next day he learned that she'd lied about her age: she was seventeen, not nineteen. When they returned to Yakima, he discovered that her father was looking for him, possibly with a shotgun. Jeanne was able to calm her father down, and soon she and Gordy moved into a dumpy one-bedroom apartment.

Desperate for work, Gordy returned to a job he'd had as a kid: picking fruit. With Jeanne now pregnant, he knew he needed to do better, so taking advantage of the newly enacted GI Bill, he enrolled at Perry Trade School in Yakima, focusing on aircraft maintenance. Upon completing training in late 1947, he, Jeanne, and their infant son, Ron, moved to Ellensburg, Washington, where Gordy got a job painting aircraft parts for $1.25 an hour. A couple of months later, everyone at the plant got laid off, but Gordy got lucky and was hired as a mechanic by United Airlines in Seattle for $1.55 an hour.

At United, he worked the graveyard shift; Jeanne stayed home with the baby. To help make ends meet, Gordy also worked days, selling vacuum cleaners door-to-door, or at least trying to sell them. He quickly learned that being a salesman wasn't his thing. Between the two jobs, plus his beer drinking, he was often exhausted, sometimes falling asleep on the job or in the middle of a conversation. He also suffered from nightmares, usually about being trapped or unable to move. He'd wake up kicking and flailing. Jeanne was having problems, too, trying to cope with severe headaches, the cause of which doctors couldn't pinpoint. In 1948 they had a second child, Sharon.

Gordy continued to work as a journeyman mechanic until the spring of 1953, when he packed up the family and moved to California, where he heard that Douglas Aircraft in Santa Monica was hiring.

On the drive south they stopped in Portland to visit with Jeanne's sister and husband. They all got to drinking and partying, and pretty soon Gordy's money for the move was gone, so he had to go out and find a job in Portland. For the next several years he worked jobs in manufacturing, including one for a plastics company that took him to Houston to work on the project to build skylights for the Astrodome. He tried looking up Tim McCoy but was not successful; he learned later that his old shipmate was on a ten-day bender at the time.

Gordy was likewise doing quite a bit of drinking during those years. He and Jeanne were spending so much time at the Rockwood Tavern that they thought maybe they should look into buying a tavern of their own.

The kids were now in school and Jeanne was restless. Their marriage was shaky. Jeanne had a bad temper, especially when she'd been drinking. Her headaches had not gone away, not even after she had surgery on her nose in an attempt to open up her sinuses. Eventually, they found another couple—their drinking buddies—to go in half with them on a tavern. After shopping around for months, they finally found one in a working-class neighborhood on the east side of Portland. Gordy scrounged up the $1,000 for their share of the down payment, but then the other couple bailed. Jeanne insisted that they go through with the deal, so they refinanced the fixer-upper home they'd recently purchased. During the day, Jeanne ran the tavern while Gordy continued his job as a supervisor at the plastics company. At night and on the weekends, they both worked behind the bar. There was a side room where the kids slept while they worked. At closing time, they'd bundle up the kids and head home. Neither Gordy nor Jeanne was shy about having a drink on the job.

In the summer of 1962, Jeanne had to be hospitalized for her headaches. She wasn't the easiest patient, throwing tantrums, berating the staff, and physically attacking other patients. Gordy wasn't sure if it was because of the headaches, the alcohol, or just her personality. Because she was unable to work at the tavern, Gordy convinced Jeanne that they should sell it. In October of that year, her condition worsened. Gordy and his fourteen-year-old daughter, Sharon, took turns staying home during the day to take care of her. But within a few days Jeanne suffered a seizure and died on the way to the hospital. The doctor listed the cause of death as a swelling of the brain caused by acute alcoholism. She was thirty-three. Gordy was now a widower, responsible for raising a fifteen-year-old son and a fourteen-year-old daughter, a task for which he knew he was completely ill-equipped.

It was another beautiful day in central Oregon. Gordy reached for the remote control. Most days he sat in his easy chair, switching channels and smoking. Not much of a sports fan, he preferred the History Channel or old movies.

He got up to let his Australian sheepdog into the house, then sat back down in his chair, waiting for a coughing jag to pass before lighting another Pall Mall. On shelves behind him sat dozens of Avon beer steins that Janice had collected over the years. "My motto was: 'I drink it, she saves it,'" he said. "But that was before I sobered up. My drinking was at its worst after Jeanne died. I pretty much went on a five-year drunk. Probably had something to do with why I wasn't a very good parent."

The mementos of his war experience sat in a small display case: his POW photo, eight medals, including a Purple Heart and a Prisoner of War Medal, and several photo albums with pictures of his old war buddies. "It's depressing to look at those now. So many are dead."

For thirty years after the war he didn't see any of his *Grenadier* crewmates, but in 1975 he attended the crew's first reunion, held in Nashville, Tennessee. Twenty-two men showed up, including Captain Fitzgerald, who was thinking about writing a book about his experiences. At the reunion, Fitzgerald tried interviewing several of the men, but his tape recorder kept malfunctioning and he ended up with nothing.

During the reunion, Gordy overheard several men talking about Fitzgerald, and he realized that some of the men had changed their attitude about the captain since the war. They still held him in high regard for the torture he endured as a POW, but they now questioned his decision to take the ship to the surface in daylight.

Late one night during that reunion weekend, Gordy was walking back to the hotel and encountered Captain Fitzgerald on the street. Gordy couldn't recall having ever talked to the captain while he was on the sub, but on this night Fitzgerald was in a talkative mood, perhaps loosened up by the large amount of alcohol everyone had been consuming. He asked Gordy if the men blamed him for their getting captured. It seemed almost sad to Gordy that this man, whom he respected so much, and who had gone on to reach the rank of rear admiral, was still tormented by guilt that he might have been responsible for his crew's fate. Gordy decided to tell the captain that wasn't the case, and the two men walked amiably through the Tennessee night back to the hotel.

Following Jeanne's death, Gordy struggled to raise the kids. Sometimes his mother or father traveled to Portland to lend a hand, but for the most part the responsibility of fixing the meals and keeping the house in order fell to Sharon. In school and at home, she was never a problem. The same couldn't be said for Ron.

Soon after Jeanne's death, Ron started acting out—skipping school, drinking, hanging with the wrong crowd. Every time he'd get in another scrape, Gordy would bail him out, rationalizing it by conceding that Ron had been close with his mother, maybe even a bit of a mama's boy, and her death was especially hard on him.

The tavern and Jeanne's spending had put Gordy in debt; life was a constant financial struggle. When Sharon was sixteen, she came into the tavern where Gordy was drinking one evening and announced that she and her boyfriend were eloping. Gordy had no choice but to wish them good luck. Ron had dropped out of school several years before. Gordy warned him that he was on a path that would surely end up in prison.

Gordy was in a grumpy mood. It was an overcast, dreary day in Portland and he'd spent the morning at the VA Medical Center for a follow-up visit to the doctor who had diagnosed him with lung cancer several months earlier. It wasn't the diagnosis that had him in a bad mood as much as it was dealing with the VA bureaucracy. He and Janice were grabbing a bite to eat at a Denny's before the return three-hour drive to Culver, on the other side of the Cascades. As usual, Janice would do the driving in their Dodge Caravan.

"At least the VA and Navy aren't as bad as they used to be," he said.

He was referring to the difficulties he and other *Grenadier* crew members, as well as vets in general, had had in collecting benefits. Despite being plagued with back pain ever since being beaten on the *Asama Maru*, he did not receive any compensation until 1974. And not until he was diagnosed with post-traumatic stress disorder (PTSD) in 1999 was he able to receive 90 percent disability compensation, even though he'd been haunted for decades by nightmares and physical problems relating to his imprisonment.

But it wasn't just his lack of compensation from the Navy or VA that he was venting about. A registered Democrat, he was blasting away at whatever came to mind:

George Bush: "He made me want to move back to Canada."

Government: "I haven't trusted our government since LBJ had Kennedy killed."

Shrinks: "Now, that's another good way to make a living without working. When I got examined in 1999, the guy asked if I had any friends to go fishing or do other things with. I said no. He said, 'That's it, you have PTSD.' I said, 'Whatever you say.'"

POW speaking engagements: "One time my daughter's teacher asked me to come to the school and talk about my experiences. I said that I would but I wouldn't sugarcoat it. I'd tell them about the starvation, beatings, death, and torture. The teacher said she didn't want her students to hear all that, so I decided I'd never speak publicly about it."

Osama bin Laden: "Bush let him escape because it gave him another reason to be over there trying to steal their oil."

God: "I don't believe in a heaven above and a hell below. If you get to go to heaven, does your dog get to go with you? Your horse? If there was a God, why has he made so many errors?"

Death: "I believe there's a big pool of energy that invades everything. It's what makes the grass grow, the trees, people. Our bodies and spirits become part of that energy. We become dust, but that becomes part of the soil, and that supports life. My theory is you do what you have to do for as long as you do and that's the end of that."

Barbara Palmer: "She claims that she didn't know Bob was a POW and still alive. But if he wasn't reported as a POW, he was the only one out of the entire crew of seventy-six who wasn't. I've talked to a lot of people about this, and it's true that the prisoners who went to Ofuna, including Fitzgerald, didn't get reported, but they eventually all got transferred from there to Omori or Ashio, and all those prisoners got reported."

Whatever Gordy tried, it did little to straighten out Ron's miscreant ways. He was constantly in and out of trouble. When he turned twenty-one, Gordy put him to work in the tavern, which he'd reacquired, but that proved to be a mistake. Ron borrowed money from the till and conveniently forgot to pay it back. He instigated fights. In one barroom brawl with members of a motorcycle gang, he lost two teeth and then tried to recruit his father and friends to help him get even. Gordy and the friends turned down that offer.

When Ron stole a Corvette Stingray and got caught, Gordy reluctantly bailed him out. But it was hard for him not to get discouraged. Ron stole his tools and sold them; he started using drugs; he couldn't keep a job, even when Gordy pulled strings to get one for him. Gordy concluded that his son was one of those guys who thought it was easier to steal than work for a living. It bothered Gordy that every time Ron got into another scrape, he conveniently used his mom's death as an excuse. But there was also a part of Gordy that felt guilty that maybe his own shortcomings as a parent contributed to his son's behavior.

When Gordy married Janice in 1968, she was a single mother with a five-year-old daughter. Janice seemed to have a steadying influence on him. He got out of the bar business and continued his work in plastics manufacturing, and he and Janice acquired all the burdens of a typical blue-collar, working-class couple in the late 1970s and 1980s—debt, blended families, and disaffection with a government they felt had not properly supported Gordy for his sacrifice during the war. His emotional and financial load was lightened when Ron drifted to the Bay Area and moved in with a girlfriend and her child.

In 1980, Gordy and Janice left Portland and moved to central Oregon, and two years later they purchased the ten acres and prefab home near Culver. When they first moved in, there was no plumbing or electricity, but Gordy's handyman skills helped build them a comfortable home. They were, however, $91,031.18 in debt, the big majority of it owed on the house. Within ten years, though, they paid off their loan and became debt-free, owning their land and house outright. In 1991, Gordy retired and started collecting Social Security, which supplemented his VA compensation. Janice retired in 1997.

Ron's move to the Bay Area did not solve his problems. He spent a couple of years in prison on a drug charge, and then was busted again on charges of fixing cars with stolen parts. As badly as Ron's life had gone,

Sharon's was a success story. She was still married to the man she eloped with at sixteen. They had raised a family and made good money running a storage-tank business in Sandy, Oregon, with nice cars, boats, and a big house to show for it.

Then, in October 1991, Gordy got a call from Ron's ex-girlfriend saying that Ron was in a hospital and close to death. When Gordy got to the hospital, he learned that Ron was infected with HIV. According to Ron, he had gotten infected from a shared needle.

Gordy stood next to his son's bed, holding his hand; he felt Ron squeeze back. Gordy felt it was as if Ron was letting his father know that everything would be okay.

Ron died later that day. Gordy had him cremated and then brought his ashes back to Portland, where he buried him in the cemetery next to Jeanne.

Gordy and Janice had made the trip back to the Portland VA Medical Center again for another series of tests. Vets filled the waiting room; every seat was taken by men waiting to be called for their appointments. There were canes, walkers, wheelchairs, and oxygen tanks, but no smiles. One man was so fat that he couldn't button his pants, leaving his belly exposed. Most of the men looked like they had served in Vietnam, maybe a few from Korea. In the cancer ward, where as an inpatient Gordy shared a room with a Vietnam vet, he was the only World War II vet.

The tumor in his chest had continued to grow, but the doctors had decided not to operate. They said that Gordy's lungs weren't in good enough shape. But it was now over two years since he'd been diagnosed, already doubling the doctor's prognosis for survival, and Gordy was nowhere close to throwing in the towel.

He stepped outside to a courtyard to smoke. Leaning against his walker, he looked frail and sickly, but he'd clearly lost little of the orneriness that had served him well during his hardscrabble life. Over the past few months, he had poured his energy into writing a detailed account of his life in longhand. Janice entered the text on a computer and assembled the pages—including photos, maps, and statistics on American prisoners of war—in an 8x10 spiral-bound notebook with a powder blue cover. The narrative began with an apology: "Knowing that flunking English in school does not qualify for great writing, I'll proceed." On the final page was a drawing of a pelican with a squirming frog hanging out of its mouth. The caption read: "It Ain't Over Till It's Over."

Gordon Cox was that squirming frog. Toward the end of his account of his life, he wrote this: "It irritates me when I hear someone from Viet Nam complaining today that they had no parade when they came home like the World War II vets did. There were no parades for most of the soldiers and sailors that fought that war. The celebrations were over by the time we got home.

"How long did it take to get over the effects of prison camp? My answer is that you never get over it. You just live with it. Any man who served in a war on the front lines, where men are killed, shelled, blown to bits, whether he is doing the shelling or the dying, will never get over it. These things change a person. You just live with it in your changed condition.

"My injury is a constant reminder of what happened and where. I got it on the *Asama Maru* in 1943, and it still plagues me six decades later. As the body gets older, these old injuries make their presence known.

"I have always believed that the government should have done more for the returning soldiers, sailors, and other fighting men. It spends a fortune to make them into killers, and then when they returned, they were just turned loose on society. I guess what gripes me is how our government tried to sneak out from under its responsibility to returning vets, and especially the POWs.

"We as POWS had in our mind that once we got out of prison camp, everything would be all right. All our ills would clear up. The doctors had to know that wasn't so."

49

Tim "Skeeter" McCoy

Austin, Texas

Although he was physically absent from the last two *Grenadier* reunions, there was no shortage of conversation and speculation about Tim McCoy. Over the years, he had taken on an almost mythical status with his old crewmates. One story had it that he got court-martialed for punching another sailor through a portal. Another one said he'd given away over a million bucks to his church.

It was hard to know what to believe.

Like many of his crewmates immediately after the war, Tim felt uncertain about what to do next. He'd dropped out of high school, and because the war had broken out shortly after he enlisted, he had never really had the time to learn a trade. So he reenlisted. Until he retired in 1965, he spent his entire Navy career assigned to some form of submarine-related duty, including submarine rescue vessels, submarine tenders, and submarine support activities of the Pacific Fleet. By the time he left the service, he had reached the grade of full lieutenant.

Tim had first thought about an insurance career as a teenager in Dallas; he had even moonlighted selling fire and casualty insurance in Chula Vista during his last couple of years in the service. After his retirement from the Navy in 1965, he moved to Austin, Texas, and became the director of the military division for National Western Life Insurance before being promoted to director of all its marketing divisions.

Tim's financial star started to skyrocket in 1973 when he founded NEAT (National Employees Assurance Trust), a niche insurance company specializing in policies for seniors, specifically to cover burial costs, cancer care, Medicare supplement, and supplemental support for current and retired military personnel. Although he turned the running of the company over to his son Tim Jr. when he retired in 1999, he continued to serve as chairman of the board and showed up at the office every morning at seven thirty.

In the entryway at NEAT Management Group in Austin hangs a ten-foot-high painting of Tim McCoy, the old-time cowboy movie star; it's impossible to miss. Tim, now in his early eighties, pointed to the painting with a self-satisfied grin. "Tim McCoy, larger than life," he said with a big ol' Texas accent. "That's me."

In his ready-for-inspection office, the phone rang. It was his wife, Jean. He spoke to her briefly, then stood up and excused himself.

"She has an appointment at the beauty parlor today and it's my job to get her there," he said, smiling, pleased with his assignment. "I'm a honey-do husband."

He met Jean in San Diego in December 1945, three months after returning from the war and after Valma had returned his engagement ring and money for the trip to America. He had moped around for a couple of weeks after he received her letter, but quickly decided to move on. Like so many returning vets, he was drinking pretty hard and searching for love. He and Jean were set up (their parents knew each other in Texas), and for their first date Tim took her ice skating, figuring he could impress her with his slick moves on the ice. For him it was pretty much love at first sight—Jean had light brown hair, a great smile, and a nice figure. In his eyes, she was the marrying kind. But there was a problem: she was only fourteen years old.

Patience was never Tim's strength, but he and Jean did wait a year and married on December 27, 1946. She was fifteen; he was twenty-two. A year later they had a son, Chuck. Five years later, they had another son, Tim Jr.

Tim spent much of his Navy career on sea duty. Jean was the quintessential Navy wife, staying home to raise the boys and support her husband, while Tim gained notoriety for his athletic skills, hot temper, and drinking.

On the base football team, he played defensive back, earning a reputation as one of the most hard-nosed players in a league that included many former college stars. He took up handball and within a couple of years won the Pacific region all-service championship. He traveled to Washington, D.C., to take part in the Navy's deep-sea-diving training and soon became known as one of the best divers around Hawaii. To keep fit, he regularly went on ten- and fifteen-mile runs, long before the jogging craze struck. To help earn extra cash, he worked at a roller rink, and was never shy about demonstrating his fancy spins and jumps. When Chuck reached Little League age, Tim took on coaching duties, and in 1960 he led the Pearl Harbor team all the way to the Little League World Series in Williamsport, Pennsylvania. They didn't win the championship, but it wasn't because they hadn't been drilled in the fundamentals.

Tim put as much energy into boozing as he had into outmaneuvering the guards in prison camp. He often overindulged, either blacking out or staying out all night. The carousing took a toll on his family. On several occasions, Jean warned him that if he didn't quit she was leaving. He'd be contrite and promise never to do it again, but then he would.

With his sons, he was a demanding, gruff, no-nonsense, intimidating disciplinarian. He wouldn't tolerate lying and maintained strict rules. If the boys didn't come home by the assigned time, day or night, there was a good chance they were going to get their butts beat with a belt. From their mom they heard a lot of "Wait until your dad gets home."

But the one thing the boys always knew was that he loved them. He could be fiery mad one day but over it a day later. They came to understand that it was just the way he was—passionate about everything he undertook. When he was coaching Little League, Tim was famous for getting the team pumped up with his motivational pep talks. He could be tough on his players, especially Chuck, who was an excellent shortstop and catcher. But he would also give him or the other players a hug when he thought they needed it. He wasn't afraid to tell his sons he loved them. On long drives, he often reached into the backseat and affectionately tugged on their legs.

He required that they go to church every Sunday and take part in family prayer. He also demanded a strong work ethic. He'd worked hard as a boy, learning the value of a nickel, and he was determined they would too. He didn't give them an allowance, and by the time they were teens they were expected to earn their own money, whether it was by mowing lawns or by flipping burgers. If they went out on dates, they were expected to use their own money to pay for the evening and behave like perfect gentlemen.

Tim frequently lectured them; the subject might be money, or manners, or morals, the talks often taking the form of mini-sermons. There could be no back talk. He demanded respect, something he'd learned from this father and in the military. He was the commanding officer of the house, and his orders were not to be questioned.

After an afternoon visiting the National Museum of the Pacific War in Fredericksburg, Texas, Tim eased his big new Cadillac onto Highway 290 and headed east toward Austin and home. He swerved to miss an oncoming car that he hadn't seen.

"No fear," he offered. "We're as safe as if we're in the hands of Jesus."

Located on a six-acre site in the heart of the Texas Hill Country, the museum is "dedicated to perpetuating the memories of the Pacific Theater of World War II in order that the sacrifices of those who contributed to our victory may never be forgotten." Tim had come to the museum to tour its many exhibits, but he was even more interested in seeing his new plaque embedded on a wall next to the Veterans Walk of Honor. Donated by his family, it included a picture of him in his dress whites and commemorated his Purple Heart, Silver Star, and service on the USS *Trout* and *Grenadier*.

The visit had put him in a reflective mood. "I'm a better man for having been a POW," he claimed. "It taught me so much about myself, primarily that I possessed the inner strength to survive real adversity. When I lost my oldest son, I think I was able to call on that same inner strength.

"I'm sure some of my crewmates thought I didn't always do the smartest thing in camp. But I was not going to cut the guards any slack. I was not going to be intimidated by them, nor was I going to let them break my will. If anyone was going to return from a Japanese prison camp, it would be me."

Unlike many of his fellow survivors, he said he held no grudge against the Japanese. "At the time I kept thinking that if this was another time and place I'd kick your ass," he continued. "But at some point after the war, I made a decision. As much hate and resentment as I'd built up against those people, I knew I had to do something or I would never get over it. I prayed a lot for guidance. Most of the Japanese were extremely cruel to me, but a few actually tried to help me, despite risking serious punishment by their superiors if they got caught. To some extent they were victims, too.

"When I was going to deep-sea-diving school I met a Japanese man who was a little younger than me. I asked him what he remembered most about the war and he told me that on his fourteenth birthday in 1944 his mom gave him a full bowl of rice. He hadn't had a full bowl in over a month. That was his most vivid memory of the war. That drove home the fact that they had also truly suffered. When I left prison camp and headed for Tokyo, I saw the damage our bombs had inflicted. Total devastation.

"I came to realize that we're all prisoners in one way or another. We might be trapped by cancer, or financial hardship, or a bad relationship. I knew that to forgive would be to set the prisoner in me free, and that all the hate I had for those people—and trust me, nobody hated them more than I did—could only keep me a prisoner of my own thoughts. So I forgave them. I could do it because I was a Christian. I simply forgave them and put it all behind me as best I could and got on with my life."

He also held no negative thoughts regarding his treatment by the Navy. "I receive a generous pension and benefits," he said. "I had a wonderful career in the Navy, and when I retired they honored me with a special ceremony. Men whom I'd served with all wore dress whites and formed an arc with crossed swords. It was very emotional."

He disagreed with his shipmates who felt the U.S. government had not done enough in pursuing the Japanese companies that used brutal and exploitive practices in building postwar fortunes on the slave labor of American POWs. "That's another one I had to let go," he acknowledged. "I could go nuts thinking about all the injustice."

When asked about Captain Fitzgerald, his tone and posture shifted. He sat up straight behind the wheel. "It's easy for all the Monday morning quarterbacks to question the captain's decisions that led to our capture, but that doesn't change a thing as far as I'm concerned," he said, his voice now choked with emotion. "That man was as fine a captain as I ever met. Nobody endured more punishment than he did. It was inhuman. As far as I'm concerned, he deserves the Congressional Medal of Honor."

As we reached the outskirts of Austin, the topic changed again, this time to his fight with Trigg in prison camp. The more he talked about it, the more worked up he got, his tone and voice peeling away the years and the Christian tolerance he'd been espousing a few minutes earlier. "He was a sonuvabitch," he concluded.

Trigg stayed in the Navy after the war, eventually receiving a dishonorable discharge when he was caught stealing morphine from a base hospital. After that he moved to Dallas, found religion, and became a Baptist minister. In the early 1990s he was diagnosed with terminal cancer and moved to Austin, his hometown, to be with a daughter. He'd heard that Tim lived in town and called him.

"It was a surprise to get a call from him," said Tim. "He told me he was a changed man and had been for a long time. He'd confessed his sins and accepted Christ as his personal savior. I told him what a wonderful thing that was. He admitted what he'd done in camp and apologized. I asked if I could take him out to lunch and he said yes. But when I called back a couple days later, his daughter told me he'd passed. I was sorry I didn't get to see him."

Tim waved a greeting to an acquaintance as he entered his favorite lunch spot, Rudy's "Country Store" & Bar-B-Q. Located a few blocks from his office, Rudy's is famous for its collegial atmosphere, friendly staff, and big slabs of beef served on butcher paper and in Coke crates. Tim ordered the brisket.

"By golly, this is the best brisket in the good ol' U.S. of A.," he informed a lady standing behind him.

Sliding his tray down to the young woman at the cashier's stand, he gave her a wink. "Dad gum it, y'all must have the prettiest smile in Texas," he said, handing her a twenty. "Keep the change."

Known by his friends as a terminal flirt, he carried his lunch to one of the communal picnic tables and offered a greeting to anyone within range.

Taking a sip of his iced tea, he scanned the room, looking for familiar faces, and spotted a local car dealer. He shouted a greeting across the room. "He's a good man," he said, pointing toward him. "A deacon at our church."

The Baptist Church had become a large part of Tim's life, just as it had been when he was a child growing up in Lubbock. It wasn't that he just showed up every Sunday to pray—he became involved in a variety of community projects: he donated money; he gave the church two houses; he set up a scholarship fund for disadvantaged students; he mentored. Although he claimed not to impose his religious beliefs on others—"I'm no Holy Joe; I try to let my actions speak for me"—he certainly took to heart one of the basic tenets of the Baptist religion as stated in Mark 16:15: *"Go ye into all the world, and preach the gospel to every creature."*

In the past twenty years, he had given countless motivational speeches at business conferences, seminars, conventions, and schools. His most often delivered speech was titled "One Moment of Glory—Then What?"

"I believe that if you don't believe in God and a future existence, then you are bound for hell," he asserted, taking a last bite of brisket. "I guess that's what helps me behave better as an adult. I'm dumbfounded by people who are agnostic. Where do they go when they need a higher voice to tell them what to do? Like Bob Palmer. Every time I saw him after the war, he seemed so disconnected, not just to the people around him but to any sense of life and spiritual guidance."

It was this moral rectitude that directed him to seek out Doug Graham, one of his former crewmates on the *Trout*, the sub that had transported the Philippine treasure to safety. For fifty years he held the memory of Graham taking coins out of one of the bags of silver and slipping them into his pocket. When Tim learned that Graham now lived in Houston, he tracked him down and called him to tell him he didn't think what he did was right.

"He admitted that he'd done it, but told me he'd given the coins to his daughter," said Tim. "He said he'd call her and get the coins back, and then mail them to me. I would donate them to the museum in Fredericksburg. Well, I waited and waited, and he never sent them to me. Guess that's something he'll have to deal with on Judgment Day."

Tim McCoy Jr., Tim's younger son and the CEO of NEAT, sat behind the desk in his office. In comparison to his father, he is far more laid back. A small framed picture of his older brother Chuck hung on the wall behind him.

"I'm sure it was my dad's faith that allowed him to get through what happened to my brother," he said. "He was devastated."

Chuck died in 1994 at the age of forty-seven. The cause of death was listed as a heart attack, although friends of the family have sometimes wondered if there wasn't something else involved. At the time, Chuck was going through some difficulties—a divorce, business failure, and dependence on alcohol and prescription drugs. Years earlier, Tim Sr. had gotten him involved in NEAT, but that didn't work out.

Maybe the father had pushed the son too hard for too many years, some people speculated, and in the end the stress of trying to live up to a war hero/self-made millionaire father just caught up with him. By Tim Jr.'s account, Chuck was never quite able to meet his father's high standards. In high school, Chuck challenged his dad to a footrace and lost. As a young adult he got into drugs, a vice few parents from Tim's generation could understand. The more Chuck's personal life fell into disrepair, the greater the tension between them.

"My brother and I had a good childhood," said Tim Jr. "Yes, Dad was a disciplinarian and pretty strict. But really, there weren't many tough times. At the time [of Chuck's death] he didn't really go into a deep, dark depression. His faith got him through, and he also threw himself into his work. He never took a day off. He stayed focused, pouring himself into his job rather than sitting at home and dwelling on it."

Tim Jr.'s relationship with his father now was good. "For a long time I felt like I lived in his shadow, especially here at work," he explained. "But he's let me come into my own. Now I feel like I stand in his light. He's been one hell of a mentor.

"I think one of the things that helped me through some of the tough times is that I have hobbies. I play golf and I've played guitar in rock 'n' roll bands around town. Dad's even come to see me play. But he doesn't have any hobbies of his own. It's work and being with my mom. Well, I guess you could count the church as a hobby. And he's been a Mason for over fifty years."

Perhaps it was the lack of a physical outlet that contributed to Tim's health issues after his son's death. He suffered a case of vertigo, and on a business trip to Atlanta he had an anxiety attack and had to get off an airplane just before it took off. But with each setback, he fell back on his faith to help him through.

"There are quite a few sides to his personality," Tim Jr. continued. "He can be gruff, giving to a fault, or deeply religious. And he's definitely a big teaser, especially with his grandkids. He's a fantastic grandparent, very involved in those kids' lives. He likes to take them on trips with him—it could be to the zoo in San Antonio or snorkeling in Hawaii. He's a big hugger. But maybe the thing I notice most about my dad is that he's really mellowed out. Maybe it was my brother's death, or maybe it's just age, but he is definitely a lot calmer."

Maureen Bright, or Mo as she's known to friends, has an office down the hall from Tim Sr. She has worked for him for over twenty years, starting as a secretary and working her way up to senior VP. Outside of his family, probably nobody knows him better, although in some ways they are very different. She speaks with a British accent; he has a thick Texas drawl. She's divorced; he's been married for over sixty years. He was a vigorous George W. Bush supporter; she thought Bush was "a fool." But over the years, they have forged a deep mutual respect.

"He's an up-front kind of guy," she said. "Honest. Full of integrity. Big heart. Levelheaded. Great family man, completely devoted to his wife. Just an all-around nice guy. As a boss, he was demanding. Very no-nonsense, very forceful. He ran the business like a ship. Everything had to be tidy and shipshape. He'd walk around picking up staples off desks. He couldn't tolerate clutter. And he wanted it done yesterday. He also can't tolerate people being late. He fired his own grandson because the kid thought he could keep getting away with showing up late. Yes, he was tough, but he always treated his employees really well, although he kept a professional distance.

"He's as generous as anyone I know. I've watched him loan employees money. He bought one man a set of dentures. And I can't even begin to estimate how much he's given to the church. He bought new Dell computers for the office and gave all the old ones to the church. He set up a foundation. And it's not just money he gives. It's also his time and energy."

For all the success and money Tim earned in business, he also suffered setbacks. In the late 1980s, his company encountered significant financial problems. He lost his office, agents, just about everything. But he converted the bottom half of the split-level house in which he was living at the time into office space. He didn't draw a salary for over a year, getting by on his Navy pension. He and Mo diligently worked the phones and sent out mailers, and in time they rescued the business and built it back up bigger than ever.

"I think his attitude during that difficult time and with the loss of his son was that if he could survive being a POW, he could get through anything," Mo concluded.

* * *

Tim steered his customized van into the driveway of his million-dollar home in an Austin suburb and flipped a switch under the dash, activating a lift for the side rear door. He hurried around the car and waited for the lift to fall into place, then stepped into the van to lend a hand to Jean. Since being diagnosed with multiple sclerosis in the mid-1990s, she has been confined to a wheelchair. During that time, Tim has dedicated his life to providing her care—shopping, running errands, making sure she gets to lead as full a life as possible. It's payback, he said, for all the years she took care of him. On this evening, they had just returned from dining out at a local steakhouse, Tim working the room like he was the newly elected mayor—a wave, a slap on the back, a quick visit to a table of suits, with Jean smiling all the while, well accustomed to her husband's big-as-Texas style.

He followed her motorized wheelchair into the house and pushed the button to the elevator he'd had installed to make it easier for her to navigate the large house. As she headed upstairs, he walked to his office, a room with an expansive view of the rolling mesquite hills to the south. If this office was a testimonial to the life he had led, with plaques and pictures of his careers in the Navy and insurance, one memento stood out—a framed, handwritten letter to him from Chuck, written a couple of months before he died. Its last sentences read: "You've always been there for me, Dad, even through the hard times. Thanks. I love you."

50

Bob Palmer

Ocean Pines, Maryland

Eighty-one-year-old Bob Palmer sat in an easy chair in the living room of his modest home in Ocean Pines, Maryland. Slowly, arduously, he got up to get himself a drink of water, his breathing labored. His body might have been a little wobbly, but his mental acuity was still sharp.

"When Barbara and I drove up to Reno after I got back from the war," he said, sitting back down, "I thought we would get back together, especially after we spent that night dancing to 'The Anniversary Waltz' and making love. Didn't work out that way."

He stared wistfully off into space, thinking of what might have been if the love of his life hadn't deserted him. Dressed in slacks and a white golf shirt, he was still a handsome man despite his failing health, with clear blue eyes and a thick shock of silver white hair. Peeking out just beneath the right sleeve of his shirt was a tattoo of a sailing ship riding the waves of a red reef. He got it back when tattoos were the province only of military men and convicted crooks.

"I was a little drunk when I got it," he admitted. "Okay, I was real drunk."

Bob regained his physical health after the war and decided to make a career of the Navy. His mental health slowly rebounded, too, although rarely an hour went by that he didn't think about Barbara, who married Robert Kunhardt on March 2, 1946. His primary coping mechanism was alcohol.

In late 1947, while stationed at Treasure Island in the Bay Area, he met Jean Towne, a divorcée who worked as a secretary in the same naval office he did. She did little to hide the fact that she was looking for a husband. She wore her reddish-brown hair in pigtails and had a personality 180 degrees away from Barbara's. Spirited and independent, she loved sports, especially baseball; she had worked as an usherette at Seals Stadium in San Francisco for the city's Pacific Coast League team and liked to boast of seeing Joe DiMaggio before he got famous. Her quick temper and sassy mouth often got her in trouble. On a previous job when she was told to take her hair out of pigtails, she responded by telling her boss to "kiss my ass" and walked off the job.

She brought this impertinence to her relationship with Bob. From the very beginning, they argued, often over his flirty ways with other women. She shared his fondness for alcohol, and she wasn't afraid to start an argument. Bob's usual way of coping was to head off to the nearest bar. Nevertheless, they married in 1948, and a year later, while stationed in Saipan, they had a son, Marty.

Like many POWs after the war, Bob filled out an affidavit detailing his imprisonment—prison conditions, torture, medical care, food, exercise, and Red Cross supplies—taking great care to provide an accurate account of his time in the four camps—Penang, Singapore, Ofuna, and Ashio—where he had been held. He made little effort to hide his hatred for his captors, and whenever possible he provided names or descriptions of the guards at each of the sites.

Bob's affidavit would become part of the mountain of evidence compiled by the U.S. Investigative Group to assist in the prosecution of Japanese war criminals in what would become known as the Tokyo War Crimes Trials, which stretched from 1946 through 1948. He did not testify in person, although Captain Fitzgerald did, specifically regarding the brutality at Ofuna. Other POWs, among them Gordy Cox, had no desire to participate. The past was the past, and all they wanted to do was get on with their lives and not dredge up those painful memories.

In the end, 920 Japanese military personnel were executed, including officers responsible for ordering waterboarding and other excessive torture. Another 475 received life sentences, and another 2,944 drew prison time, with 1,018 being acquitted. Tojo, the prime minister and war minister, was executed, but General MacArthur ordered that Emperor Hirohito be exonerated. It was a decision second-guessed by many who believed it distorted the Japanese understanding of what it was to lose a war in which the country's supreme commander went unpunished.

Bob was particularly interested in the sentences handed down to the thirty-three officers and enlisted men from Ofuna who were put on trial. Three officers received death sentences, one committed suicide; the rest were given prison sentences of various lengths.

In some small measure the war crimes trials and punishments they meted out helped Bob feel like his treatment had been avenged, but it did not erase the memory of all those horrible days and nights when he was convinced he was going to die. For that, alcohol was a better eraser. But even more than a case of beer, what helped him move forward with his life the most was his son, Marty.

The same wasn't so true with his feelings about Jean. The first year of their marriage went well enough, but after that their relationship rapidly deteriorated. Bob was drinking and running around with other women, Jean was constantly yelling and screaming about his miscreant ways, each blaming the other for their behavior. They not only slept in separate beds, they moved into separate rooms. But they both felt a sense of obligation to stay married because of Marty.

As bad a husband as Bob was, he was as good a father, wrapping his life around Marty. He took him everywhere with him; he even welded a special seat for him into the backseat of his Navy-issued jeep.

Marty looked up to his dad, admiring the way he looked in his Navy uniform and the way he could fix just about anything. How many times did he hear Bob repeat his little mantra for getting things done: "Do it now while you're thinking about it." In the Philippines, Bob bought and rebuilt an old sailing junk and took Marty sailing with him. He also bought and tinkered with motorcycles, and with Marty riding behind him, he loved to go for rides in the countryside. When Marty was old enough to drive a motorcycle, Bob always encouraged him to let out the throttle. To Marty, it seemed that everyone loved to be around his dad except his mother. Once, while Bob was stationed at Pearl Harbor, Jean woke Marty up in the middle of the night and brought him out on the front porch and pointed to his father passed out on the front lawn. "I want you to see what a drunk your father is," she said. On Marty's eighteenth birthday, Bob took him to a bar in the Philippines. After a few beers, Bob confessed that he hadn't always been faithful to Jean, an admission that didn't surprise Marty but one he still wished he hadn't heard.

But the one thing Bob rarely talked about with his son was his experience in the war. Marty knew very little about what had happened to his father and didn't ask. Bob made it clear that he believed that it had been his patriotic duty and honor to serve his country, no matter how badly it turned out for him.

Nor did Bob talk to Marty about Barbara.

Bob eventually became a chief warrant officer 4 (CWO-4). Primarily, he served on the office staffs of commanding officers throughout the Pacific; his duties included overseeing motor and boat pools, controlling correspondence throughout the staff, coordinating VIP tours, and maintaining personnel records. He consistently received high grades from his commanding officers.

With each new transfer or assignment, he checked the duty rosters and phone books looking for Barbara's name. He knew that her husband was a Navy officer on track to become an admiral, and that she'd had two children, a boy and a girl. They both ended up stationed in Hawaii, where Bob was careful to avoid situations where they might run into each other. But once, after a night of heavy drinking, he drove to their house at 3:00 a.m. and parked across the street. He just sat behind the wheel, staring at the house, tears rolling down his cheeks. After an hour, he drove away.

Most of the time, he felt like he was just going through the motions, with no purpose to his life. Barbara was always a ghostly presence in his marriage. In the heat of an argument, he told Jean he would do anything to get back with Barbara and would never be happy without her. "I'd crawl back to her on my hands and knees if she'd take me," he blurted out, effectively ending what little affection Jean had left for him. Still, they stayed together for Marty.

In 1967, Bob suffered a heart attack. He was convinced that it was related to the stress and physical toll his years as a POW had taken on him, but the Navy didn't see the connection and refused to give him disability compensation. He soon retired and settled in San Mateo, south of San Francisco. Bob wasn't bitter; he was immensely proud of his nearly thirty years of service and the stack of letters of commendation. Although he hadn't gone to college, he felt that the education and travel he'd experienced during his career had served him well.

With the war in Vietnam escalating rapidly, Marty enrolled at Sonoma State College and received a college deferment, but he flunked out after his first year and was immediately reclassified 1-A. To avoid getting drafted into the Army, he followed his dad's advice and enlisted in the Navy, eventually volunteering for the Riverine Forces, a joint U.S. Army and U.S. Navy force that helped transport troops and saw combat in the Mekong Delta. The boats often came under heavy fire from Vietcong units dug in behind trees and foliage along the riverbanks that ran through the delta. For Marty, being part of such a dangerous assignment was a way to show his dad that he was every bit as brave and tough.

Marty survived his tour of duty, but like many returning Vietnam vets, he struggled with reentry into civilian society, falling into the grips of dope, including heroin, and a deep depression. Bob struggled to understand, and he and his son began to drift apart, the closeness they shared during Marty's childhood giving way to an uneasy tension. Bob suspected Marty of stealing from him; Marty believed that Bob was not sympathetic to the difficulties he was experiencing in readjusting after Vietnam. In one heated argument, he blamed Bob for his problems.

In 1970, Bob's marriage to Jean finally disintegrated. He packed his few belongings, took their two small dogs, and moved back to southern Oregon where he'd grown up, renting a single-wide mobile home in the hills west of Jacksonville near Medford. He got by on his Navy pension and small savings. He dabbled with the idea of writing a book about his POW experience, but whenever he sat down to work on the project, he was overwhelmed with the enormity of the task and soon abandoned the idea. Mostly, he drank beer and did nothing. He rarely talked to Marty. Even the task of taking care of the two dogs seemed too much to handle, and he returned them to Jean in California.

It was January 1971 and Bob was sitting in the living room of his mobile home, trying to get a fix on how to spend the day, when the phone rang.

"This is Barbara," the voice on the other end said.

"Who?" he responded.

"Barbara Kunhardt. You know, Barbara Koehler. Barbara Palmer. Your ex-wife."

Bob hesitated, trying to match the voice with the memories. "Is this somebody playing a joke?" he asked.

"No, it's really me," she said.

She had come home to visit her mom, who was recuperating in the hospital following surgery, and her father had told her where Bob was living.

"God, it's great to hear your voice," he said. "How'ya doing?"

Barbara told him that she was still married to Kunhardt, who had retired from the Navy in 1966 and now worked as a consultant for the government. She had two children in their early twenties and lived in a large house in McLean, Virginia, an upscale suburb near Washington, D.C. She and Kunhardt liked to entertain and go sailing on his yacht.

Bob and Barbara talked nonstop for two hours, both admitting that they had regularly checked the duty rosters in search of the other's name at each new assignment. "It'd sure be nice to see you," Bob finally offered.

They agreed to "accidentally" bump into each other the next day at a market in Central Point.

What Barbara didn't mention in their conversation was that she'd made the decision to call Bob (her courage bolstered by a couple of stiff drinks) after her husband had called to demand that she cut short her visit with her parents and come back home "where you belong." He ended the conversation by hanging up on her.

The reality was that Barbara's marriage had not been a happy one for years. Robert Kunhardt, as Barbara had learned soon after they were married, was not an easy man to live with. He had a notoriously short fuse and kept a tight rein on her and the children. A gun collector, he kept five loaded pistols and eight shotguns in the house. He demanded his dinner be served every night precisely at 1800 sharp (6:00 p.m.) and often graded Barbara on the quality of the meal, or their sex. They took family vacations every year at the same time and to the same place—to visit his parents in Connecticut. He kept her on a tight budget and had to approve of every expense. At one point, their daughter, Lynn, told him to "stop trying to run the family as if you're commanding a ship."

His naval career had not gone the way he'd hoped. After rising to the rank of commander, he was passed over for promotion to captain and the admiralship he'd wanted. He alternately blamed it on being discriminated against because he was short or because he'd married an enlisted man's wife. He'd always been a big drinker, but after being passed over, he began drinking even more heavily. Barbara usually kept pace.

He was a strict and controlling parent, rarely showing affection to his two children. He hand-selected the classes Lynn took in high school so that she could qualify for Annapolis. He repeatedly told his son, Bobby, that he was worthless and a loser and beat him with a belt.

Kunhardt's drinking had gotten so bad that one of his friends advised Barbara that if she was to have any chance of saving the marriage, she needed to lock the liquor cabinet. There was a part of her that was afraid of him and wanted to leave, but over the years she'd grown comfortable in their material world. She liked her big diamond ring. She remained faithful in the marriage.

Lynn heard Kunhardt's tirade ordering Barbara to return from Oregon. "It would serve you right if she never came home," she said.

At the market the next day, Bob had a six-pack of beer in his shopping basket when he came around the aisle and spotted Barbara. As he approached, tears filled his eyes. "Oh, my God, you're as beautiful as ever," he said.

"You look pretty darn good yourself," she replied.

Their old chemistry was instantly ignited. They got into Bob's pickup and started south on I-5, past Medford and Ashland, and up into the Siskiyous toward Mount Ashland. It was the same route they'd taken the day they first saw each other after Bob's return from the war. To Barbara, on that day Bob had been a shadow of the man she'd married. Now he was robust and full of life, barely able to stop talking or casting lustful sidelong glances in her direction.

They turned around and headed back north. In his bed in his single-wide, they made love for five hours.

The next three days were a whirlwind of sex, reminiscing, and feelings of guilt. Every evening Robert Kunhardt called and demanded that Barbara come home, and every time she told him she couldn't leave until her mother was better. She even took Bob to visit her mom in the hospital. When her father learned that she'd seen Bob, he was disapproving, just as he'd been back when they dated in high school.

"See where you'd be if you'd ended up with him?" he demanded. "You'd be living in a trailer. What kind of life would that be?"

As the time neared for Barbara to head back home to Virginia, she and Bob agonized over what to do next. As intense as the sparks had been, she wasn't ready to leave her marriage. "Maybe we can just have a long-distance love affair," she suggested.

"I want more," Bob insisted.

He remembered when they went to Reno in 1945 to get a divorce and ended up making love all night long, only to have Barbara dash his hopes of getting back together. But this time it felt as if renewing their relationship might be possible. She'd told Bob how unhappy she was in her marriage, and that she'd never loved her husband with the same passion and intensity that she'd loved him.

For Bob, being with Barbara again had been the best thing that had happened to him since their wedding day back in 1941. All the years that had intervened had done nothing to diminish his passion or desire to be with her. It was as if he'd just been treading water while she was away, treading water for twenty-five years.

"I'll do whatever it takes to get you back," he vowed.

On their last night together, they bid each other a tearful farewell. "I don't think we should contact each other," she proposed. "It would just be too painful."

"I don't know if I can promise that," he responded.

After he watched her walk back into her parents' house, he drove away, but instead of heading home, he headed south toward California. He drove all night, and the next morning when her plane landed at San Francisco Airport, he was waiting to greet her when she headed for her connecting flight.

"You got away from me once," he said. "I can't let it happen again."

Her heart told her to get in his pickup and head back to Oregon with him. "All I thought about on the flight down here was being with you," she admitted. "But I can't do it. At least not now. I have to go home and see if there's anything to be saved in my marriage."

Once again they said a tearful good-bye. Bob headed back to Oregon and Barbara flew east to her husband.

"Bobby, I want you to meet me at the Holiday Inn in Georgetown tomorrow at six o'clock," said Barbara. She sat nervously across the family room

from her twenty-two-year-old son. A senior at the University of South Carolina, he was home on vacation.

"Why?" he asked

Barbara cleared her throat. "Because I'm going to introduce you to
the man I'm going to leave your father for," she replied.

Bobby stared in disbelief. Had he heard her right? She'd always been
high-spirited, a bit of a kidder. "Say that again," he said.

Barbara took a deep breath and repeated the words. "This is for real,"
she added.

Bobby studied her face. Clearly, she was serious. But she'd always been
the dutiful wife and good mother, living in her husband's world and by his
rules. "Who is this guy?" he asked.

Barbara paused. Bobby vaguely knew that his mother had been married before, but how could she possibly explain to her son the history she
shared with Bob Palmer and the passion that had been reignited? "I want
you to meet him and see for yourself who he is," she answered.

When she'd first returned from Oregon, she initially tried to brush
her rekindled feelings for Bob into a back corner of her mind and heart.
She had lived her whole life doing what others expected of her and she saw
too many barriers in the way—they lived on opposite sides of the country;
she couldn't imagine giving up her life to go live in a single-wide trailer; she
didn't think she could ever get up the courage to confess to her husband.

But the pull to be with Bob was relentless. Barbara had decided to
enlist her daughter's support. She invited Lynn upstairs to her bedroom,
where she went into a closet and pulled out a shoe box. Inside the box
was another box, and inside that box was still another locked box. Barbara
opened it to reveal pictures of her and Bob, as well as other little mementos. Lynn had never seen her mother look so happy or excited. It had always been a mystery to her why she'd stayed with her father. Lynn was no
longer living at home, and she volunteered her address as a place where
Bob could write to Barbara. In the months ahead there was a steady stream
of letters back and forth, as well as phone calls. Once, when Barbara's

husband was out of town on business, Bob got in his car and drove forty-six hours straight through across the country to see her. They spent five days in a motel room. When he went for a physical shortly after returning home, he still had rug burns on his knees and elbows. The doctor inquired how he got them, and when Bob confessed, the doctor shook his hand.

Sitting across from his mother in the family room, Bobby had never seen her look so resolved, so self-assured.

"Does Dad know about all this?" he asked.

Her smile disappeared. Yes, she had told him. At first, she'd just told him how unhappy she was and she was considering leaving. He responded by telling her he wanted to save their marriage, and asked for a month and promised to make changes. He took her out to dinner, bought her gifts, and treated her nicer than he had in years. But it was too little, too late. She called Bob and asked him if he'd marry her if she left Kunhardt. "Yesterday," he responded.

"I told your dad last night while we were out on the boat that I was leaving him to go back to Bob Palmer," she said.

"What did he say?"

"The first thing he said was, 'Who's going to help me with the boat?'"

Bobby rolled his eyes. "What about the house and boat and all of that?" he asked.

"I'm giving everything to your dad," she replied. "I just want out."

"Wow, this guy must have money," Bobby ventured.

"Not at all."

"You guys must be really in love."

Barbara smiled. "I can't wait for you to meet him tomorrow. He's special. You'll see."

"I'm staying at the house tonight," said Bobby. "I don't trust Dad with all those guns."

In July 1971, Bob flew across the country to bring Barbara back to the West Coast. Despite his nerves, the meetings with Bobby and Lynn went well, both of them giving their blessings to the relationship.

Some of Barbara's friends thought she was nuts to run off with a man who couldn't afford an engagement ring. "I can't imagine leaving someone who won a national sailing championship," said one friend. They also thought she was being naive; she had not hired a lawyer and she had signed everything over to Kunhardt. "I admitted to him that I'd slept with Bob and he was going to charge me with adultery if I tried going after property," she explained.

For Barbara, physically leaving had not gone as badly as she'd feared. All she was taking were a couple of suitcases packed with clothes and an old sewing machine, which she put in the backseat of a five-year-old Chevy Nova. The morning she left, Kunhardt rode with her to the Holiday Inn, stopping a block from the motel. As he got out of the car, he threw two $100 bills at her and then walked away. She and Bob didn't even get out of the state before they stopped at a motel and made love the rest of the day.

They stopped at a drugstore in Ohio, where Barbara bought two imitation gold wedding rings until they got something more permanent. Instead of returning to Oregon, they rented a small one-bedroom apartment in San Mateo, south of San Francisco. Bob took a job working three and a half days a week for a drywall company that installed movable partitions in buildings. Barbara stayed home and clipped coupons and decorated the apartment. For her, the romance and affection Bob gave her more than made up for the material things she'd left behind. She felt that for the first time in her life, she had a say in decisions. She had money, though not much, to spend however she wanted. When Bob wasn't at work, they spent almost every possible moment together.

They held hands everywhere they went; Bob opened doors for her and wrote her love notes and cards. His manners were almost Victorian. He regularly told friends that his main purpose in life was to make Barbara happy. Because she'd been an officer's wife and lived in a big house, he worried that he wouldn't be able to measure up financially, so he took a part-time job selling lawn mowers for Sears. Barbara constantly reassured him how happy she was. It wasn't unusual for them to make love in the morning

before he went to work, then when he came home, and then again before
they went to sleep. They remarried on August 12, 1972.

One of the things that impressed Barbara the most was how handy and
practical Bob was. He could fix anything. If he was driving down the street
and heard the engine ping, he'd pull over and fix it on the spot. If a door
squeaked, he'd take off the door and replace the hinge. For Christmas, he
bought her son a screw gun.

The only gray cloud in their life came from Marty, who had married
his high-school sweetheart and was now living in the Bay Area too. It wasn't
that Marty didn't like Barbara, it was just that she was stealing such a big
part of his father's heart and time. Marty's long hair and his being stoned a
lot didn't help his relationship with his father.

Bob was constantly amazed at Barbara's positive attitude. He marveled
at the way she started singing as soon as her feet hit the floor every morning and the fact that she kept separate envelopes of money for furniture,
dishes, bedding, clothes, and other expenses, just as she'd done when they
were first married in 1941. When he got home from work she'd excitedly
show him her purchases for the day. It might be a salt-and-pepper set or
a TV tray. She told him that when she was married to Kunhardt, she'd go
shopping with no intent to buy because she already had everything she
needed. They traveled frequently to Oregon on long weekends to visit old
friends.

In 1977, Bob and Barbara moved back to Medford. He wanted to be
closer to the mountains and rivers he'd loved so much as a kid. With his
Navy pension and the disability pay he was now collecting, he figured they'd
have enough money to live comfortably, especially after he started receiving Social Security in a few years. Plus, every time he drove through the
Hunter's Point neighborhood in San Francisco and saw all the blacks, he'd
usually say the same thing: "I hate those people." Medford was a lily-white
community.

Soon after moving back to Oregon, Bob suffered his second heart attack. The cardiologist told him he needed to slow down, so he and Barbara

started to play golf regularly and bought a camper to take trips. Barbara was a faithful follower of *All My Children*; so that she wouldn't miss any episodes while they were on the road, Bob hooked up an antenna on the camper and always made sure they stopped in a place with good reception.

It wasn't too long after the heart attack that Bob received a jolt of another kind—Barbara's father apologized to him. For almost forty years Mr. Koehler had held firm to his belief that Bob wasn't good enough for his daughter, but after seeing how happy Barbara was now, and the adoration, love, and respect that Bob lavished on her, he pulled Bob aside.

"I was wrong," he admitted.

Because the war was responsible for his long separation from Barbara, he wanted to be able to show her a part of that experience, so in 1988 he took her to Penang to the place where he'd spent the first four months of his imprisonment—the Convent on Light Street. After the war, it became a highly respected school for girls again. For several months he'd been exchanging letters with Sister Francis de Sales, the director of the school. He'd even made a charitable contribution to the convent. It was an emotional return as he visited the classroom where he had been held and saw all the names of the crew memorialized on a plaque. He cried as he listened to Sister de Sales introduce him to the students, teachers, alumni, and local dignitaries:

> *This is no ordinary day for us here in Light Street Convent. We have as our guest someone who came here, metaphorically in chains, forty-five years ago. He was a prisoner of war then; today he has freely come of his own accord to visit what he often calls "the old school."*
>
> *Some of you once studied in the classroom near the laundry, generally known in school as the "Grenadier Sanctuary." I regard it as a sacred place, a monument to the love and loyalty to one's country and fellow men that inspired, strengthened, and goaded on the* Grenadier *men to a superhuman endurance that could take the beatings, the clubbings, the bayonet pricks, and the physical weakness caused by near starvation and*

intense hunger. We here have long sensed the mystery that surrounded these gallant men.

Mr. Palmer edits and circulates the Grenadier Newsletter. *I have been receiving a copy of it monthly for almost six years. I wish to pay tribute not only to Mr. Palmer's outstanding writing ability but also to the splendid work he's doing in keeping the men together. He was the ship's writer before that fateful day in April 1943. He is still that today in fact, but he is more than that because of the part he plays in strengthening the bond between the men. They are a unique bunch of men, sharing one another's interests, plans, joys, and sorrows, all the nitty-gritty of daily life.*

Someone has said that of all the fighting men of World War II, the submariners lived in the closest confinement and therefore forged the closest companionship of all. That seems particularly true of the Grenadier *men, and that such close and constant companionship has not only weathered the passing of time but has been strengthened in an unbreakable bond is due in no small measure to Mr. Palmer's efforts.*

That brings me to the Grenadier's *bond with us, a strange one in a way, since our school was the crucible of their sufferings. Mr. Palmer tries to explain it this way in a newsletter dated September 1983: "For some there are definite ties with the old school, it seems. I cannot really understand that except that young men are impressed by everything that happens, and it must be remembered that the first blows struck by the Japanese with bayonet, or fist, or club were the first real physical hurts some of us had ever received. Little wonder we remember and attach significance to the school of 1943 and the lovely school of today."*

Elsewhere in a personal letter to me, Mr. Palmer wrote: "Why we hover over the painful or the unusual is a mystery to me, but what is clear is that a small group of very young boys encountered their first real and genuine confrontation with life within the walls of your school. It would seem that they have profited much by that experience."

In 1990, Bob and Barbara moved to Ocean Pines, Maryland. Bob wasn't all that keen on moving to the East Coast, but he went along with it because he knew that Barbara wanted to be closer to her two children and four grandkids. Making her happy continued to be the most important thing in his life. He often expressed this love in writing, as he did in a letter to friends in 1998:

> Twenty-six years have passed since Barbie and I reconnected. She is 77 and I am 78. To put into words seems beyond me. We have traveled, both in the United States and overseas, and have felt the touch of the other's hand all this time. Our hearts quicken at each other's return home from an errand. To watch her walk across the room arouses those urges present in a much younger man. She excites me and I am so proud of her. She line dances and started to tap dance at the tender age of 75. She plays bridge, gardens and maintains a household environment of cleanliness along with three square meals each day. Our bills are paid on time, no birthdays are forgotten and I have been privileged to count her children and theirs as "very close." I heard that a man has only six chances in this world of finding a completely suitable mate. Considering the billions of women in the world, I count myself as lucky beyond belief in not only getting her in the first place but in being able to recover her a second time. My cup runneth over.

Bob's health continued to decline slowly over the next few years. He had a triple bypass, an aneurysm, a ruptured appendix, restless leg syndrome, gout, and failing kidneys, and his gallbladder had to be removed. He had stents implanted and a new aorta made from a vein in his leg. The doctors marveled that he was still able to stay semiactive. He took to calling himself "the Gray Ghost from the West Coast."

His relationship with Marty, who had recently divorced, also continued to deteriorate. Marty had moved briefly to Atlanta to try to reconcile with his ex-wife and children, but soon moved back to the Bay Area and started hanging out with the meth crowd. He found a new girlfriend, but he was arrested and sentenced to a five-year prison term in San Quentin for having sex with her sixteen-year-old daughter. He finally got up the courage to write his father, apologizing for his drug use and the way he had burned bridges behind him. He admitted to having attempted suicide four times, but said he had now found religion and hoped to qualify for PTSD compensation upon his release. "The shrinks say I have double PTSD because of your history and mine." He closed the letter with "I want to shake your hand again, Dad, and hug Barbara. I love you, Dad."

Bob received the letter and, after considering his response for a week, sent this reply:

Well, Marty, who is to blame for this one? You can put away the whitewash. It just doesn't sell anymore. I cannot imagine what you told your doctor about me and my experiences. You know nothing about them. You never asked and all you have, if anything, is fabrication. You are good at that!

You have blamed me for so many years for all your failings. I cannot imagine your ending your letter with "I love you Dad." You have a wall of hate so very high and thick. I don't think you can see over it. I guess you could blame your mother for awhile. You managed to call her enough foul names these past years.

I almost overlooked your Post Traumatic Syndrome. There's a good scapegoat. Strange, there were none from WWII or Korea, only Vietnam. I rode the A Frames of a submarine through women, kids, dogs, all screaming and drowning right after we torpedoed their ship. I spent a day on the bottom of the ocean in a sunken submarine that was on fire. The Japs beat me for months. I spent nine months in a solitary cell. What do I have to show for it? A stack of commendation letters from admirals and flag rank captains, years of fitness reports all marked in the 4.0 column written by high-ranking officers. No Post Traumatic Syndrome! How come? You have been "near death" four times—no kidding!

I have been confined to the house and a chair for two years and sit all day with a hose up my nose. I am almost eighty years old and have a very short time left, so do not bother with the "handshake" when you get out.

I probably will not be here. Please do not bother Barbie—she has nothing
of value to give you to throw in the corner to gather dust and forget. She
will have no extra money and her family will be helping her. Just do not
bother her!

   You are past fifty now, Marty. Not much time to join the human
race and start carrying your own load. You cannot live on the 50%
service-connected disability.

   I wish you well.

   Your father

Marty wasted little time in responding, saying he was sorry if Bob mis-
understood the intent of his first letter. He said he felt ashamed and knew
he'd been "a piece of crap" the last few years and didn't expect forgiveness,
including from his two children. He closed this letter with "I remember
who was there while I was growing up and I love you for it."

Bob stuck the letter in a drawer. He wanted to believe his son's words;
he wanted to believe that Marty could somehow turn his life around. He
remembered riding on a motorcycle together and how proud he was to
have such a tall and handsome son. He remembered how happy he was
when Marty got accepted into college. So how did it go so wrong? There
was a part of him that wanted to reach out again, like he'd done so many
times. But at what cost? He felt betrayed. Marty's behavior ran so contrary
to his own sense of right and wrong, strength and weakness. Drinking two
six-packs of beer, he believed, was a far cry from the dope-smoking of Marty
and his generation. As much as it pained him, he thought it was too late in
his life to spend the emotional capital to repair the wounds.

The one thing that kept Bob from becoming depressed over his son
was the continued fountain of love and joy he gained from Barbara. On the
occasion of her birthday in 1997, he wrote this to her:

Barbara, my debt to you grows by the day. I try all I can to pay it but just
cannot seem to catch up. Seventy-five years is a long time to remain as
beautiful as you were when you were born.

In spite of my constant sores and complaints, I think of you every waking hour, and everything I do is, for the most part, for you!

You are very loving and loyal to those around you. You look straight ahead and are arrow-like in your flight to your targets.

You have provided me with so many thrills through the years with your sensuous touch and your loving look.

Mostly, I think, I love to touch and hold you. These moments are the most precious and are never repetitive! Each one is a new thrill. I always feel a little pang when we separate.

I look to you for so much and appreciate all the many things you do for me. Thanks, Barbie, for all of the above and for the beauty and thrills I know are in store for the future! Happy Birthday.

Epilogue

There were moments in interviewing each of the men when I was brought either to tears, or laughter, or complete amazement. On my penultimate interview with Chuck, he told me he had recently flown to Florida for a heartwarming visit with Irene Damien, his high-school sweetheart. She was still married to the man she met after Chuck joined the Navy, but she was now totally paralyzed. Chuck had gone to visit her after her husband had called to tell him Irene wanted to see him one last time before she died.

Every time I met with Chuck, I was impressed with the strength of his determination. He'd suffered a lot of physical setbacks in the last twenty years, but he was resisting slowing down. He seemed almost obsessed with being the best grandparent he could possibly be to somehow make up for being an absent father. Thinking back on all the time I spent with him, two things stand out. The first was when he told me about providing hospice care for his son when he was dying of AIDS. He had kept that fact from me for over two years, even though Gwen and Marilyn had already told me. He was reluctant to have me include it in his story. But what he did for his son while he was dying, I think, redeemed whatever shortcomings he'd had as a father.

The second was a conversation we had the last time I saw him. It was just before the presidential election of 2008, and it spoke volumes about his generation. Chuck was a lifelong Democrat, and I asked him if he was going to vote for Obama. "I'll be go-to-hell if I'm going to vote for that goddamn Muslim," he replied.

In interviewing Tim McCoy, I was regularly struck by his almost evangelical approach to life. Financially, he was far and away the most successful of the four men and the one with the most braggadocio. But every time

I would get to thinking that this guy was too full of himself, out popped a sign of his kindness and consideration, like his total devotion to his wife, Jean, who was confined to a wheelchair. When I asked him to name his greatest accomplishment, he didn't hesitate: "Taking care of my wife."

When I first met Gordy Cox in 2001, I figured he had six months to live, tops. He already looked like a cadaver. But the little bantam rooster somehow kept hanging in there, feisty as ever. This was a guy who by all rights should have died several times in prison camp.

But of all the interviews and research I conducted for this book, nothing came close to matching what happened on my visit with Bob Palmer. At that point, I had not talked to any of the other men. I had traveled across country to the Maryland shore from my home in Oregon to meet with him and Barbara. They had generously offered to let me stay in a spare bedroom. In return for their hospitality, I was prying into all the dusty neglected corners of their lives.

During our interview, Bob sat in the pink easy chair in his living room, his voice animated and full of energy, his blue eyes as clear as the water in Crater Lake, where he'd spent countless hours as a boy. Barbara sat in a nearby chair.

Shortly after I arrived, he reached out and placed his hand on my forearm. I noticed his little finger, bent and discolored, like that of a catcher who'd absorbed too many foul tips, only I knew that's not how it got so crooked.

"I'm glad you're here," he said, tears welling in his eyes. "I've wanted to tell this story for a long time. People need to know what happened to us in those prison camps."

Barbara got up to bring him a glass of water. As she passed his chair, he reached out and let his fingers trickle across the side of her leg. In return, she slid her hand over his shoulder, letting it linger for an extra moment. I thought of my own parents, people from the same generation, and even though I never doubted their love and devotion to each other, I couldn't remember a similar display of affection, at least not publicly.

As I waited for Barbara to return from the kitchen, my eye caught a flat, brightly colored box sitting on the lamp table next to Bob's easy chair.

"What's this?" I inquired.

"A Passion Wheel," he answered.

I got up to examine it. It had a plastic spinner and a dozen multicolored sections, each with a sexy title: Cop a Feel . . . French Kiss . . . Dance Naked.

"It's a game, sorta like spin the bottle," he says. "My stepdaughter Lynn gave it to me last Christmas."

Barbara walked back into the room. Actually, it was more of a bounce than a walk. At eighty, she was amazingly fit, a chorus-line member of the Happy Hoofers, a tap-dance team that performed around the state. I eyed her smiling at Bob, one of those secret little glances couples do. It occurred to me that I was in a room with two octogenarians, husband and wife, who were still physically in love: real, honest, hands-on love. Maybe their generation wasn't as sexually and emotionally repressed as my contemporaries believed. She pulled out a copy of his 1938 high-school yearbook and pointed to a quote next to his class picture: "His favorite saying, 'Where is Barb?' will remind us of him always."

It was nearing the end of the second day of my visit. Bob looked tired, but in my thirty years of interviewing people about their lives, I'd never had anyone so appreciative or eager to tell his story. "Thank you for being here," he repeated.

I've heard it said many times that we need to let the men and women of Bob's generation know that we applaud and appreciate the sacrifices they made in order that future generations could enjoy the many freedoms and benefits our society has to offer.

"It's what we had to do," he said. "We didn't have any choice."

Slowly, he rose from his chair, ready to call it a day. It was past his bedtime. "We'll start going through the box tomorrow," he promised, referring to a seventy-pound box of memorabilia he kept in his closet. It contained photos, patrol logs, POW documentation, *Grenadier* newsletters, love letters, transcripts from the 1946–1948 war crimes trials.

"Wait," I said, pointing at the Passion Wheel. "Before you say good-night, let me give this thing a spin for you."

I spun the wheel. It made a couple of quick revolutions before skidding to a halt, the arrow pointing directly at "Feel Above the Waist." Bob winked at Barbara, then headed down the hall toward the bedroom. He would shower before turning in, just as he did every night. On his list of priorities, cleanliness was near the top; two years without a shower in prison camp can do that to a guy.

Barbara got up to follow him to the bedroom. She stopped and clasped my hand. "Every day before you arrived he'd say, 'I wish that writer guy would hurry up and get here.' This means so much to him."

She walked down the hall and turned into the bedroom. Behind her, I gathered my notebook and reached for the light.

Then I heard Barbara scream. "Bob's collapsed. Help!"

It took me only a second to reach the room. Barbara was standing at the end of the bed, frantically pointing to the floor. Stripped to his Skivvies, Bob was splayed across the carpet. I knelt next to him, cradling his head in my hands.

"Bob! Bob!" I shouted.

"Check his pulse," urged Barbara.

I eased his head back to the floor and felt for a pulse in his neck. All I felt was the blood rushing through my own fingers.

"Is he dead?" cried Barbara.

I'd never seen a dead person, let alone touched one, but I had no doubt Bob was already dead, probably gone before he hit the carpet.

"Call 911!" I instructed.

I looked down at him; his face was already turning a purplish blue. His eyes and mouth were open. He gasped slightly, like a fish that's been lying on the dock for several minutes.

I stroked his forehead, and then felt for a pulse again. Nothing.

Barbara knelt down next to him, gently touching his lips. "Don't die, Bob, please don't die," she whispered. "I love you, I love you."

I had never seen anything so tender.

It took less than two minutes for the paramedics to arrive. They quickly pulled out the shock paddles, but just as quickly put them back in the case. It was already too late. Bob Palmer was gone.

At Barbara's request, I stayed at the house for three more days, doing what I could to comfort and support her and the family. I helped write Bob's obituary, met with neighbors and friends, and listened to Barbara's stories. A month later she flew out to Oregon with his ashes, and as she put it, "I kept them right between my legs the whole flight." With her daughter, Lynn, we drove to Crater Lake National Park, where Bob had spent much of his youth, and we scattered his ashes, surrounded by the deep blue water and the wind whistling through the conifers.

In the years that it took me to finally finish this book, there wasn't a day that went by that I didn't think about Bob and that moment when I cradled his head in my hands as his life slipped away.

A year after Bob's death, I met Marty. He had been released from San Quentin and was living in a mobile home in Novato, north of San Francisco. He was off of drugs, but clearly fragile and, by his own admission, fighting a "horrible battle" with depression. "Vietnam and prison can do that to a guy," he said. A tall, slender, good-looking man, with deep blue eyes like his father, he talked softly, breaking into tears on several occasions, clearly saddened by the lack of reconciliation with his dad. He showed me poetry he'd written about his experiences in Vietnam and pictures of his mother, who died a couple of months after Bob; he admitted to thoughts of suicide. Several times during the conversation he repeated his mantra: "I'm okay today, and that's the best I can expect. I'll deal with tomorrow when it comes."

Leaving our meeting, I drove across the Golden Gate Bridge into San Francisco. I wanted there to be a happy ending to my story. Looking back,

I realize that I wanted this to be a story of resiliency and of how these four men had survived the Great Depression, gone off to war, and suffered through the unthinkable, but returned to America and ultimately left that darkness behind. But what I found were four men who came back from war and, although they did live out lives of differing degrees of quiet nobility, strength, and resiliency, carried with them the deep scars of a "good war" not only that never went away but that they passed on to their sons.

I guess one lesson from the stories of these men is that they offer further testimony, not that any is really needed, that there are no winners in war, only survivors.

In 2010, World War II veterans were dying at a rate of over a thousand a day. In late 2009, I found out Gordy Cox finally passed away, six years after the doctor had given him six months to live. Then I got a call from Chuck. I could tell from his voice he wasn't well. In the past several months, lung cancer had racked his body. He'd just completed six weeks of radiation. He had lost forty pounds.

"More pain than anything I've ever experienced, including prison camp," he said. "But guess what? I got married."

"To whom?"

"Gwen. We got remarried. Sixty-three years after the first time. We're not living together or anything, but I figured she wouldn't get anything from my Navy pension when I finally croak. Now she will."

Chuck died a few weeks later.

I've always been a little confused about what constitutes a hero. Is it hitting sixty or seventy-four home runs? Inventing a vaccine? Serving your country? Maybe. Probably. But I've also got to include a man who, despite his flaws, gives hospice care to his dying son and then makes sure that his ex-wife is taken care of financially. I'd also include a millionaire on that list, a man who listed his greatest accomplishment as the care he's given his invalid wife. The fact that these men also gave so much in service to their country pretty much seals the hero deal.

Author's Notes

When I started researching this book in 2001, I couldn't wait for each day, each new discovery. I knew that I had stumbled on a story that went to the heart of America—love, war, loss, history, failure, courage, and redemption. But something happened along my journalistic way. My journey broke down.

Maybe it goes back to my second research trip. I traveled to Florida to talk with a Navy buddy of Bob Palmer's. The morning I arrived at his house was September 11, 2001. We sat in his living room and together we watched in stunned disbelief as the image on the television screen framed the twin towers crashing down.

"It's like Pearl Harbor all over again," he said.

Two days later I traveled to Georgia to interview Robert York, one of a handful of men still living out of the original crew of seventy-six. He was a nineteen-year-old electrician's mate second class when the ship went down; now he was seventy-seven. Along with the rest of the nation, he was trying to make sense of what had just happened. I figured that his experience in World War II and the fact that he had been at Pearl Harbor and had suffered unimaginable torture as a prisoner of war would provide patriotic insight that I couldn't possibly feel. We watched Billy Graham try to bring a measure of peace to the televised hysteria. When a flag flying at half-mast filled the screen, York stood up and saluted.

"I don't think people in this country fully understand what that flag represents," he said, his voice quivering.

"Did you vote for President Bush?" I asked.

"I've never voted," he answered. "What good would it do?"

How could I ever unscramble the paradox of such a contradiction?

The deeper I probed into these men's stories, the more my focus kept shifting; I felt as if I was standing on quicksand. For example, the more details I learned about how the *Grenadier* sank, the more I believed that Captain Fitzgerald had screwed up royally, but how could that be the case when every man I talked to under his command steadfastly called him a hero?

These were men of the so-called Greatest Generation, and for the longest time America had been falling all over itself gushing over the way this generation had endured the depths of the Great Depression, performed heroic deeds against truly evil aggressors, then somehow found the strength to bounce back and rebuild a postwar utopia.

Yet in almost every interview, I regularly heard the "N" word tossed around like kindling and women referred to in terms that negated every advance for women's rights over the past fifty years. How could I paint these men as the "Greatest Generation" when so much of the evidence I was gathering seemed to draw a picture of a racist, xenophobic, and misogynistic generation?

I would read about the treatment of prisoners at Abu Ghraib and Guantánamo, and then sit down and try to write about the torture the Japanese inflicted on the men in these pages. I wondered what would have happened if somebody had photographed the degradation in the Japanese camps. Would there have been a greater public outcry against the Japanese after the war? Would President Bush, Dick Cheney, and Donald Rumsfeld still believe that waterboarding was okay or that due process didn't apply? Did our leaders know that in the war crimes trials in Tokyo following the war, many of the Japanese military men directly responsible for the torture inflicted on our POWs were sentenced to death by American military tribunals? None of the men portrayed in this book believed such torture would accomplish anything other than lower our standing in the world. If these guys didn't crack under the torture inflicted upon them (and I included only a portion of those descriptions on these pages because writing about it was difficult and I assumed reading about it would be equally hard), what would make anyone believe it would work against our captured enemy?

*   *   *

For research I beat a regular path to Google, as well as read books, official Navy documents, and firsthand accounts I found in the National Archives. But perhaps the best document I had for my research was from Gordy Cox, the guy who supposedly flunked first grade because he'd been kicked in the head by a horse. To help me in my research, he wrote a seventy-five-page account of what happened to him, stunning in its details and honesty. Captain Fitzgerald's written testimony submitted during the Tokyo War Crimes Trials in 1947 was also very useful, as was Bob Palmer's twenty-page autobiography titled "A Rather Unusual Story."

Bob, Tim, Gordy, and Chuck weren't just subjects for my book; we forged special connections. In sharing such intimate details of their lives, they put their trust in me. It was impossible not to feel a closeness, a responsibility. I visited their homes; sat in their living rooms; talked to their wives, ex-wives, and children; and dug through old letters. We met in restaurants, at a hospital, and rode in cars together. I attended two of their reunions, one in Las Vegas and the other in Reno—reunions that at times were so drenched in memories that it brought these men to tears. Always, the subjects understood the purpose of my visit. In most cases, I used a tape recorder, and if that was not possible, I took notes. All transcriptions were done by me.

By the time I showed up, these men were old, liver-spotted, hard of hearing, and sometimes slow to remember. Yet at times they told tales from sixty years ago as if it was yesterday morning. They showed me telegrams to their parents from the Department of the Navy that declared them missing in action. I listened to their anger over their treatment by their own government—and Japan's—and the callous disregard for their right to reparation. I spent time with a psychiatrist who specializes in post-traumatic stress disorder, a term that wasn't even coined until 1985. These men were all textbook cases, but they were all reluctant to admit that they suffered from it.

Scenes in this book were reconstructed from the memories of those involved, and are subject to the inaccuracies that the decades might have brought. When dialogue is directly quoted, at least one of the participants

is the source. With but a few exceptions, the real names of the people involved are used. In the few instances where I have changed the name of a
minor character, it was to protect his or her privacy.

The "true story" was often hard to pinpoint. In some cases, the recol-
lections of different individuals of the same event varied—e.g., the *Grenadier*'s sinking. In that specific case, as well as others, I recounted the story that
made the most sense to me in terms of the published facts. If there was an
account recorded within a couple of years of the incident, I relied more on
that. With regard to the ship's sinking, I interviewed ten men who experienced it and they all had different accounts. Four men believed the *Grenadier*
fired two torpedoes at the freighters, yet there was nothing about any torpedoes in Captain Fitzgerald's official report immediately following the war.

In the letters and journals that are included, they are reprinted exactly
as they were originally written, although sections might have been omitted
for brevity.

At times I cringed at the stories I was hearing. Combined, I was told
over one hundred torture stories. But these were men who had to be
tough. They had endured hardscrabble childhoods and withholding fathers. Every time they pulled out of the harbor to patrol enemy waters, they
didn't know if they were coming back. A submarine is no place for a loner,
and these men grew to know each other better perhaps than anyone they'd
meet the rest of their lives and forged a bond they found hard to explain,
stumbling on words such as "respect" and "affection."

When the war was over and liberation finally came, they returned to
a country much different from the one they'd left five years earlier. All of
them were married within a couple years of their return. Was it because it
was an era when that's what young people did, or because their imprisonment had made them all starved for affection and female companionship?
I'll leave that for the shrinks to determine.

Another thing the four men had in common was that they rarely, if
ever, talked about what they'd been through, or spent time indulging in
introspection. For the most part, they lived veiled lives. Until this book.

What was it that gave each of these men the mettle to survive a POW experience almost unimaginable in its brutality? What gave them the strength to endure? Most days I felt inadequate to the task of figuring it out. In the end I could only conclude that they were all very tough sons of bitches, not just because they survived their captivity, but also because they endured the lifetime burden of war.

For whatever reason, Bob, Chuck, Gordy, and Tim were ready to talk when I came to visit. Maybe it was because they knew that this was likely their last chance to tell the world what happened to them. They talked freely about their childhoods, Navy careers, and years as POWs. They bristled at the handling of Iraq. They made dark jokes about living long enough to read this book. They were not pleased that I was past my dead-line . . . by several years.

For all their honesty and candor about the past, most of them drew tight when talking about their relationships with their sons. I had to won-der. Had their experiences in World War II directly or indirectly impacted their kids? Three of their sons preceded them in death, and a fourth was in prison. There were stories of drug addiction, disease, and deep depression. But I didn't initially learn any of that from these men.

I knew that to tell their stories, I needed to include the parts they would rather not discuss, if only in a final chapter. But to do so would surely cause them pain, a pain they didn't deserve at this late moment in their lives. I wondered if there was a part of me that was waiting for them to die so as to spare them any pain this book might cause, or me the pain of thinking I may have betrayed them. As I write this, only Tim is still alive.

For months at a time, it seemed too daunting a story for me to try to tell. I'm not a historian or a psychologist, and yet it felt like I needed to be those things to somehow make sense of it all.

But perhaps nothing paralyzed me more than the day in December 2006 when I opened a Christmas card from Chuck Ver Valin, of whom I'd grown especially fond. He wrote a little note on the inside: "I am 84 years old. I have read ten books in my life. I hope to live long enough to read the eleventh."

I let him down. But I hope I still did him justice.

Appendix 1

Sailing List

USS *Grenadier* (SS210) March 17, 1943

Officers

John Critchlow	Washington, D.C.
John Fitzgerald	Vallejo, California
Kevin Hardy	River Edge, New Jersey
Arthur McIntyre	Bessemer, Alabama
Harmon Sherry	La Mesa, California
Al Toulon	Washington, D.C.
John Walden	Portsmouth, New Hampshire
George Whiting	Quaker Hill, Connecticut

Enlisted Men

Ralph Adkins	Whitsburg, Kentucky
Norm Albertsen	Edgewater, Michigan
David Andrews	Oswego, New York
Clyde Barrington	Orlando, Florida
Lesly Baker	Brownsville, Texas
Lynn Clark	Los Angeles, California
Thomas Courtney	Wyandotte, Michigan
Gordon Cox	Yakima, Washington
William Cunningham	New York, New York
Charles Doyle	Weymouth, Massachusetts
Jewell Embry	Rosine, Kentucky
Charles Erishman	Quaker Hill, Connecticut
Rex Evans	Muskogee, Michigan
Robert Evans	Weber, Nebraska
Ben Fulton	San Angelo, Texas
Glen Fourre	Shelton, Washington
Randolph Garrison	Brooklyn, New York
Justiniano Guico	Los Angeles, California

John Gunderson	Lincoln Park, Michigan
Carlisle Herbert	Johnstown, Nebraska
Richard Hinkson	Modesto, California
Joe Ingram	Pharr, Texas
Johnny Johnson	Cartersville, Illinois
William Keefe	Waterbury, Connecticut
Riley Keysor	Modesto, California
Joseph Knutson	San Diego, California
James Landrum	Richmond, Virginia
Charles Leskovsky	Bellaire, California
Raymond Leslie	Dover, Massachusetts
Charles Linder	South Cambrian, Michigan
Irving Loftus	Minneapolis, Minnesota
John McBeath	Bronx, New York
Charles McCoy	Dallas, Texas
Dempsey McGowan	Charlotte, North Carolina
Joseph Minton	Jacksonville, Florida
Elwood O'Brion	Fort Dodge, Iowa
Virgil Ouillette	Ypsilanti, Michigan
Robert Palmer	Medford, Oregon
John Pianka	San Diego, California
Miner Pierce	Arlington, California
Edgar Poss	Anson, Texas
Joseph Price	Brooklyn, New York
Carl Quarterman	Macon, Georgia
Thomas Rae	Franklin, Texas
Warren Roberts	Des Moines, Iowa
Charles Roskell	Brooklyn, New York
Albert Rupp	Philadelphia, Pennsylvania
Paul Russell	Saint Louis, Missouri
Henry Rutkowski	Bridgeport, Connecticut
Lyle Sawatzke	Crofton, Nebraska
John Schwartzly	Saginaw, Michigan
Lee Shaw	San Antonio, Texas
Dean Shoemaker	Philadelphia, Pennsylvania
John Simpson	Omaha, Nebraska
George Snyder	Phillipsburgh, New Jersey
George Stauber	Buffalo, New York
Orville Taylor	Grand Rapids, Michigan
Thomas Trigg	Austin, Texas
Charles Ver Valin	Sodus, New York
Charles Westerfield	Danielson, Connecticut

Charles Whitlock	Rock Mills, Alabama
Charles Wilson	Santa Ana, California
William Wise	Los Angeles, California
William Withrow	Goshen, Virginia
Bernard Witzke	Saint Paul, Minnesota
Robert York	Port Chester, New York
Peter Zucco	Santa Barbara, California
Fred Zufelt	Portland, Oregon

Appendix 2

Because this is a nonacademic narration, I don't feel it is necessary to footnote or provide a comprehensive bibliography of sources. But I do want to include the names of authors who were essential in my research:

David Creed, *Operations of the Fremantle Submarine Base 1942–1945*; Anthony Barker and Lisa Jackson, *Fleeting Attraction: A Social History of American Servicemen in Western Australia During the Second World War*; Lynne Cairns, *Fremantle's Secret Fleets*; Beth Bailey and David Farber, *The First Strange Place: Race and Sex in World War II Hawaii*; Time-Life Books, *War Under the Pacific*; Robert Stern, *U.S. Subs in Action*; Antony Preston, *Submarines*; Clay Blair Jr., *Silent Victory: The U.S. Submarine War Against Japan*; Richard Perry, *United We Stand: A Visual Journey of Wartime Patriotism*; Life, *Our Finest Hour: Voices of the World War II Generation*; Donald De Nevi, *The West Coast Goes to War 1941–1942*; Stan Cohen, *To Win the War: Home Front Memorabilia of World War II and V for Victory: America's Home Front During World War II*; Bert and Margie Webber, *The Lure of Medford*; Doug Stanton, *In Harm's Way*; Carl Lavo, *Back from the Deep*; Rear Admiral Corwin Mendenhall, *Submarine Diary: The Silent Stalking of Japan*; Jonathan McCullough, *A Tale of Two Subs*; John Burton, *Traveling Life's Twisting Trails*; Albert Rupp, *Threshold of Hell*; Terence Kirk, *The Secret Camera*; Linda Goetz Holmes, *Unjust Enrichment: How Japan's Companies Built Postwar Fortunes Using American POWs*; Gavan Daws, *Prisoners of the Japanese: POWs of World War II in the Pacific*; Tom Mathews, *Our Father's War*; Hampton Sides, *Ghost Soldiers*; Stephen Ambrose, *Comrades*; Tom Brokaw, *The Greatest Generation*; James Bradley, *Flyboys* and *Flags of Our Fathers*.

Acknowledgments

This list must start with Barbara Palmer. I appreciate her candor, support, and patience.

From the beginning, there was my agent, Richard Pine, who initially believed in the project and never gave up despite all the setbacks.

Editorially, I appreciate Rachel Klayman's patience and significant input, and then the way that Sydny Miner at Crown Publishers brilliantly picked up the ball.

In Portland, David Kelly was such a friend and mentor.

I can't give enough thanks to Gordy Cox, Tim McCoy, Bob Palmer, and Chuck Ver Valin, not only for what they endured during the war but also for the trust they afforded me. I apologize again for taking so long. And a big thanks to their families, and to all the other crew members of the *Grenadier* who shared their stories.

I also appreciate the sound advice I got from early readers—Tim Boyle, John Strawn, and John Norville.

And to all the many people who gave their time, money, passion, and energy to the projects—Wordstock and Community of Writers—that diverted me from finishing this book, especially Peter Sears, Greg Netzer, Jan Smith, Eden Bainter, Tom McKenna, Shelley Washburn, Sydney Thompson, Rich Meyers, and Erin Erginbright. Thanks also to all the writers and teachers in supporting the mission.

My sister Barbara Colton Juelson, the world's nicest person, was always there for me. So were my daughters, Sarah and Wendy.

And to Stacy Bartley, who offered so much encouragement, I owe so much.

And special thanks to Greg Dufault, Kerry McClanahan, Regina

Perata, Laure Redmond, Steve Duin, Gail McCormick, Arlene Schnitzer, Katie Merritt, Storm Large, Katherine Dunn, Terry and Val Holberton, Todd Houlette, Kelly Burke, Don and Wendy Cobleigh, Rebecca Burrell, Shel Buch, Kate Finn, Rick Weiss, Brian Herman, Week 10 campers, Jill Spitznoff, Lodi Rice, Trudi Morrison, Maria Ponzi, Teresa DiFalco, Shirley Williams, Jim Swaisgood, COW teachers, the Boys of Bandon, and all the book clubs who listened to this story.

Index

A

acupuncture, 255–256
air raid alerts, 261–263
alcohol, torpedo fuel as, 96
alcohol and drinking, 54, 85–86, 91, 93, 96
ambulatory sick, 239
America
    anti-Japanese sentiment, 115–116
    Australian attitudes about, 109–110, 125
    as segregated country, 127
Asama Maru, 186
Ashio copper mine, 252–253
Asiatic fleet, 59, 92
Asiatic sub force, 98, 99
atomic bomb, 279
Austin, Linley, 121, 122
Australia
    America's cultural influence on, 110
    fearful of Japanese invasion, 105–106
    looking to America for defense, 106
    tolerance for Americans beginning to wane, 125

B

Babe, 249
Bataan Death March survivors, 266
bathhouse conditions, 237
batteries, 58
B-29 (bomber), 234–235
    diverted to capture Iwo Jima, 262
    pilot prisoners, 243
    raids, 241–242
Beck, Fred, 25–26
bedbugs and lice, 238
beriberi, 186, 214, 254–255
Bick's Car, 279
Big Stoop (guard), 212

Bimbo's 365 club, 296
Black Sheep Squadron, 220
Blair, Clay Jr., 98, 121
bombing raids, 241–242, 261–263, 270–271
Boyington, Greg "Pappy," 220–221
Boyle, Joe, 87
breadfruit, 178
Bright, Maureen (Mo), 358–359
brothels, 54–56, 86, 108
Bulkeley, John, 82, 85
Bungo Suido, 63
Bureau of Ordnance, 121
"Burping Betsy" (siren), 276
Bushido (national code), 209, 281–282
Butcher (guard), 212

C

California after Pearl Harbor, 70–71
Carolina Islands, 58
Carr, Bruce, 117–118
the Castle, 192
censorship, 107, 119, 123, 245
Chappell, Lucius Henry, 93, 98
Chase, William Curtis, 291
Chinese prisoners, 256–257
cigarette smoking, 96–97, 249
Clark, Len, 118, 285
code breakers, 65
Collins, Ripper, 225–226
comfort women, 295
Congressional Medal of Honor winners
    Greg "Pappy" Boyington, 220
    James Doolittle, 115
    John Bulkeley, 85
Convent on Light Street, 153–154, 373
Cornberg, Adolph, 301
Corregidor, 81–83, 266

Courtney, Tom, 173, 268–269, 272, 279–280
Cox, Gordy, 48–49
  assigned to USS *Grenadier*, 119
  assigned to USS *Pelius*, 122
  assigned to USS *Sculpin*, 92
  attacked by Dave Megeson, 195
  attacked by Japanese guard, 154
  automobile accident, 298–299
  awarded Purple Heart, 297
  boot camp, 88
  Communications School, 88–92
  declines to fill out war-crimes report, 295
  drinking years, 342–343
  early days back home, 297–299
  enlists in the navy, 48–49
  first horse, 41–42
  graduates from polliwog to shellback, 99
  hears about bombing of Pearl Harbor, 93
  kicked by a horse, 40, 47
  letters from home, 196, 197, 199
  letters home, 88–92, 119–124
  makes seaman first class, 119
  marries Janice, 338–339
  marries Jeanne, 339–342
  moves to the United States, 45–46
  nightmares, 341
  opinions about a number of things, 344–345
  physicality, 47, 88
  postwar work history, 339–342
  prisoner #528, 165–168, 193
  problems with son Ron, 345–347
  Quartermaster Signalman's Radio School, 90–91
  regretted submarine assignment, 102
  reunites with James Fitzgerald, 343
  school years, 46–48
  seasickness, 97–98
  shares coconut with mates, 178–179
  as single parent, 343–344
  suffers dysentery, 271
  transferred to USS *Holland*, 119–120
  volunteers for submarine service, 90–91
  works in Yawata steel mill, 194–195
  writes account of experiences, 387
  youth, 40–49
Cox, Julian (Shorty) (father), 43–44, 45
Cox, Nellie (mother), 40; 42–43
crabs, 238
cremation, 210
Cromwell, John, 257

D
Dalhart, Texas, 34
Damien, Irene, 17, 18, 304, 305, 380
Dear John stories, 305
Death Hut, 254–255, 274–275
deaths, 208, 266
deathwatch, 203
debriefing and examinations, 303
Dekum, Buck, 304
dental care, 204, 205
Depression years, 28, 154, 159, 240
  Bob Palmer, 22–31
  Chuck Ver Valin, 11–21
  Gordy Cox, 40–49
  Tim McCoy, 32–39
DeTar, John, 73–74, 75, 76
DeWitt, James, 116
dysentery, 222, 244, 271, 272, 286
dives, requirements for, 64
Doolittle, James, 115
Dornin, Dusty, 105
Dorris, W. O., 282–283
Doyle, Charles, 203, 208, 209
Dragon (guard), 162
Dullin, Dr., 255–256
Dumar, Preston, 18–19

E
Enola Gay, 279

F
faking illness, 197, 248
Fat Boy (bomb), 279
Fenno, Frank, 80, 81, 85
Fitzgerald, John
  accepts blame for desperate situation, 135
  assigned to USS *Grenadier*, 118
  considers abandoning ship, 139
  crew's respect for, 127, 190, 213, 354
  defiant message to crew, 167

destroys vital equipment on *Grenadier*, 140

grateful for rice ball, 220

interred at Ofuna transit camp, 212

journal entries, 229–230, 233

leads crew to save sunken *Grenadier*, 128–131

lies to Japanese about American casualties, 214–215

orders ship abandoned, 144

reputation, 112

tortured with waterboarding, 156, 160

written testimony, 387

food shortages, 204, 248

foot race challenge, 204–205

Formosa, 94

Freemantle, Australia, 106

Freemantle Sentinel

"The Anglo-Saxon Race-America and Australia Unite," 107

Fukuoka Camp #3

B-29 bombing raid, 276–277

conditions, 192–193

new site, 201–202

G

gambling and poker, 205–206

Geneva conventions, 173, 198, 213

GI Bill, 298, 340

Goldtooth Maizie (guard), 157, 160

gonorrhea, 157–158

Graham, Doug, 83–84, 87, 356

Gray, Valma, 126, 293, 318, 319–321

Greatest Generation, 386

Grenadier Newsletter, 374

Grenadier Sanctuary, 373

Grenfell, Joe, 61

Guadalcanal, 122

"Guam-Where America's Day Begins," 292

Guico, Justiniano, 208

guidance system, 63

H

"happy feet," 246

Hardy, Kevin, 140, 146, 275

Hart, Thomas, 92

Haughey, Gwen, 109–113, 111–113, 300–302, 326–327, 384

Hawaiian Islands under martial law, 80

health problems, common POW, 173, 176, 186, 200–201, 214, 220, 222, 254

heat rash, 95–96

Hell Ships, 186

heroes, definition of, 384

Hir Maru (freighter), 179

Hirohito, 284, 362

Hiroshima, 279

Honolulu, conditions, 85–86

"Humor in Uniform," 146

I

I-173 (Japanese warship), 65–66

Imperial Cabinet, 270–271

Imperial Iron and Steel Works, 194

Imperial Marines, 187, 189

incendiary bombs, 262, 270–271

internment camps, 115–116

J

Jane's Fighting Ships, 215

Japan, 58

Japanese Americans, 70–71, 115–116

Japanese Army Air Force, 242

Japanese civilians

behavior toward prisoners of war, 189

deaths, 270–271

deprivation, 353

displaced, 291

Japanese codes, 65

Japanese Hell Ships, 186

Japanese medical treatment, 255–256

Japanese strategy, 93–95

Japanese War Crimes Trials, 361–362

Java, 99–100

Javanese Dutch, 275

Johnson, Johnny, 205, 325–326

"Join the Navy and See the World," 100

Joyce, Allen, 117

K

kamikaze (divine wind), 197

kangaroo hunting, 108

Katoku (Kato), 255–256

Keep Your Trap Shut, 115

Keller, Ed, 257

kempeitai (Japanese "Gestapo"), 211

killing flies, 219

King, Arthur, 301
King, Ernest, 99, 121
Kitamura Cognochyo, 220
Koehler, Barbara, 27–31, 68–69, 72. *See also* Palmer, Barbara
Korean comfort women, 295
Kublai Khan, 197
Kunhardt, Robert, 231, 308–309, 366–367, 371

L
"laborer hunting," 256–257
Last Man Club, 34
latrines, 202–203, 246, 247
LeMay, Curtis, 262, 270–271
letters from home, 245
lice, 238
Light, Francis, 154
Linder, Charles, 208
Liver Lips (guard), 212, 219–220
Lockwood, Charles, 119–120, 121
Loose Lips Sink Ships, 114–115
Lutz, Eugene, 245, 247, 326–327
Luzon, military setback at, 99

M
MacArthur, Douglas
    anticipates future alliance with Japan, 292
    exonerates Emperor Hirohito, 362
    unprepared to protect the Philippine Islands, 94
magnetic exploders, 64, 73, 76
Malang, 100
malnutrition, 214, 222, 248
Manila, 93, 99
Marianas Islands, 58
Marines in Fukuoka #3, 206
Markowitz, Herbert, 223, 270–271
Mark VI magnetic exploders, 64, 73
Mark XIV torpedoes, 64, 98–99, 121
Marshall Islands, 58
martial law, Hawaiian Islands under, 80
McCoy, Capitola Boatwright (mother), 32–33, 34
McCoy, Chuck (son), 356–357
McCoy, Harrell (father), 32–33, 34, 35
McCoy, Tim
    acquires nickname "Skeeter," 82
    assigned to USS *Grenadier*, 125–126
    assigned to USS *Pelius*, 80, 125
    attacks guard, 163–164
    baptism, 35
    bonding with Gordy, 266
    boot camp, 79
    child of divorce, 36
    cultural awakening on board USS *Trout*, 81–82
    decks petty officer, 87, 125
    disinterest in brothels, 86
    early days after return home, 317–321
    early employment, 37, 38
    encounter with poisonous sea snakes, 141–142
    enlists in Navy, 39
    Gordy and his mother visit, 318–319
    insurance career, 349–350
    learning to speak Japanese, 225
    meets and marries Jean, 350–351
    as a parent, 350–352
    physicality, 32–33, 37, 264
    postwar perspectives on Captain Fitzgerald, 354
    postwar perspectives on Japanese people, 352–354
    postwar re-enlistment, 349
    prisoner #526, 161–164, 193
    protector of Sidney Segal, 38–39
    racial attitudes, 235
    reasons for enlisting, 79–80
    school days, 36–37
    showdown with Rooster Boy, 263–264, 265
    sobriety and religion, 355–356
    steals to survive, 222–223, 227–228
    teaching English, 225
    tortured, 161, 188
    trades Red Cross parcel for sake, 286
    turns to scriptures and imagination, 175–176, 191
    and Valma Gray, 126, 224, 293, 318–321
    volunteers for USS *Trout*, 80
    walks away from POW camp, 290
    youth, 32–39
McCoy, Tim Jr. (son), 356–358
Megeson, Dave, 194–195
Midway Island, 65, 105
Murray, Sunshine, 94–95

N

Nakajima Aircraft Company, 261–262
naval code breakers, 65
Naval Submarine School, 56–57
NEAT (National Employees Assurance
    Trust), 350
New London Naval Treaty, 61–62
nightmares and flashbacks, 334

O

Oak Knoll Hospital (Oakland), 296, 302,
    303
O'Brion, Elwood, 290
Ofuna crouch, 214
Ofuna transit camp, 211–216
Operation Matterhorn, 234

P

Pacific Fleet, 59
    on high alert, 59
    Japanese plan to bomb, 93–95
    stationed in Honolulu, 55
Palmer, Barbara. *See also* Koehler,
    Barbara
    announces pregnancy, 74–75
    considers abortion, 77–78
    divorces Bob, 312
    father apologizes to Bob Palmer, 373
    informed USS *Grenadier* is lost, 216–217
    notified of Bob's return, 308–309
    parents object to Bob Palmer, 28–29,
        69, 72, 76, 310, 315, 316
    receives Bob's wallet and dog tags, 218
    receives notice Bob is unreported
        prisoner of war, 253–254
    reports miscarriage, 114
    reunites with Bob Palmer, 365–372
    and Robert Kunhardt, 219, 231–232,
        360, 370
    sees Red Cross missing list, 217–218
    volunteers for Red Cross Emergency
        Team, 71–72
Palmer, Bob
    agrees to divorce Barbara, 312
    assigned to USS *Tuna*, 68
    assigned to USS *Wright*, 67
    autobiography, 387
    boot camp, 67
    considering a transfer, 74

continuing desire for Barbara, 68–69,
    114–115, 215–216, 311, 313–316,
    363–372
and Death Hut, 274–275, 284
death of mother, 23–24
declared unreported prisoner of war,
    253–254
dies at home, 382–383
displays Passion Wheel, 381
forges weekend pass, 69
going home, 286
health conditions, 186, 375
hears news of war's end, 284–285
learns that Barbara has not waited,
    310–311
makes rice ball gift for Fitzgerald, 213
marries Jean Towne, 361
meets and marries Barbara Koehler,
    27–31, 72–73
meets Leslie Phillips, 118
moves to Maryland with Barbara,
    374–375
physicality, 27, 160, 214
postwar re-enlistment, 363–364
prepares to be boarded, 139–140
prisoner of war, 157–160
reacts to first direct hit, 76–77
reasons for enlisting, 67
relationship with son, 375–377
remarries Barbara, 371
school years, 28–29
struggling with depression, 308
suffers heart attack, 364, 372
takes Barbara to Penang, 373
tortured, 157, 187–188
youth, 22–31
Palmer, Cora (stepmother), 24, 25–26
Palmer, Martin (father), 22–23
Palmer, Marty (son), 362–365, 372, 375–
    376, 383
Palmer (grandfather), 22–23
Passion Wheel, 381
peacetime conscription, 20
Pearl Harbor
    announcement of attack, 60
    Pacific Fleet depleted by shift to Asiatic
        Fleet, 59
    personal plans changed by bombing,
        69–70

Penang, 153, 184–185, 213, 236, 373
Philippine Islands
    anticipated Japanese attack on, 58–59
    essential to control of western Pacific,
        80–81
    failed submarine defense of, 98
    strategic location, 93–95
    unprepared for hostilities with Japan,
        94
Phillips, Leslie, 118, 217–218
Photo Joe (plane), 239
Pink Ladies (torpedo fuel alcohol), 96
Plan Orange, 58–59, 61
The POW Cookbook, 257
POW Information Bureau, 201
Prisoner of War Camp #3, 192–193. See
    also Fukuoka Camp #3
prisoners of war
    aboard the Asama Maru, 185
    cared for and debriefed, 292
    conditions on Hir Maru, 183
    deaths, 197–198
    decorate cremated remains, 290
    encouraged by American planes,
        238–239
    first night of freedom, 282
    forced to assault each other, 167–168
    forced to stand naked in snow, 208
    and Geneva conventions, 198
    health problems, 173, 176, 186, 200–
        201, 214, 220, 222, 254
    identify their location and receive
        supplies, 285–286
    inadequate food and water, 178–179
    killing flies, 219
    kindness to Japanese mineworkers,
        286
    lack of fraternization among
        nationalities, 244–245
    lack of training, 166
    moved to Ofuna transit camp, 211–212
    moved to Shimonoseki, Honshu, 189
    at new Fukuoka Camp #3 site, 202–207
    offered goods by Japanese civilians,
        291
    rations, 204
    response to POW situation, 157–160
    self-preservation and survival, 209
    in Singapore, 184–185

sleeping under the stars, 282
stunned by announcement of war
    ending, 281–282
trucked to Penang, 149, 153
work routine, 204
prostitution, 54–56, 86, 108
provisions, 213
PTSD (post-traumatic stress disorder),
    344
push-up contests, 163–164

Q
the Quack (doctor), 220
Quiz Kids, 214

R
racial attitudes, 91, 107, 115–116, 235–236
racial conflict, 55, 86
racial segregation in the Navy, 127. See also
    Trigg, Thomas
rash relief, torpedo fuel as, 95
Red Cross parcels, 198–199, 229, 240–241
Remember Pearl Harbor, 115
rice, 213, 249, 291, 353
Roosevelt, Franklin Delano
    building up Naval fleet, 57
    death announced, 267
    running for third term, 19–20
Rooster boy, 263–264, 265
rules of combat, 61–62
rumors, 100–101, 250, 279–280
Rupp, Al, 197

S
saboteurs, paranoia about, 114–115
sand fleas, 239–240
seasickness, 97–98
sea snakes, 141–142
Segal, Sidney, 38–39
sexual liaisons, 108
Sherry, Dick, 170
Shimonoseki, Honshu, 189
Siegel, Barney, 292
silver dolphin insignia, 58
Sister Francis de Sales, 373
smoking, 96–97
smuggling, 223
Snake (Japanese guard), 161, 166
solitary confinement, 212

spooning for warmth, 205
Stauber, George, 128, 142, 305
stealing, 206, 222–223
Strevous, Wesley, 53
submariners
    behavior on leave, 108
    camaraderie, 68, 101
    feeling of frustration, 99
    high morale, 229, 230
    literacy, 68
    relaxed attitude of, 54
    wartime pay, 107
submarines
    conditions aboard, 62, 68
    as main naval defense, 98
    medical services aboard, 62–63
Submarine Vets Reunion, 338–339
Superfortress (B-29), 234–235
Surabaya, Java, 99–100
survival, motivations for, 244
Sweeney, Charles, 279
Swivel Neck (guard), 212

T
Taylor, Charles, 157–158, 163–164, 173
Taylor, Otis, 93
Termite (guard), 212
toilet conditions, 202–203, 246, 247
Tojo, Prime Minister, 59
Tojo soup, 248
torpedoes
    failure, 98, 101–102, 121
    mistrust of defective, 64, 73
    part of new ships design, 57–58
    shortage of, 61–62, 73–74
torpedo fuel cocktails, 96
torpedo performance tests, 121
torpedo spread, 63–64
torture, 170–172, 175, 190, 211
    aboard the Asama Maru, 186–188
    and uncertainty, 158
    waterboarding, 156, 362, 386
Toulon, Al, 112, 137, 139, 143
Towne, Jean, 361
transit camp, 211–212
Trigg, Thomas, 127, 146, 207, 235–236,
    354
Truitt, George W., 34–35
Truman, Harry, 292

U
U.S. submarine forces, 57–58
USS Goldfish, 148, 166
USS Grenadier. See also prisoners of war
    attacked by torpedo plane, 128–131
    in battle with freighter, 126
    capsizes, 145–146
    crew moved to Ofuna transit camp,
        211–212
    crews attempts to rig a sail, 138–139
    crew taken aboard Japanese merchant
        ship, 147–149
    design and history, 117
    in firefight with diving plane, 142–144
    mining Haiphong harbor, 117–118
    onboard condition after attack, 136–
        137
    survivor's reunion, 325–326, 338–339
USS Gudgeon, 53–66
    destroys I-173, 65–66
    first U.S. warship on offensive strike, 61
    performance records, 105
    sinks first enemy ship, 64
    survives Pearl Harbor attack, 59–60
USS Holland, 92, 106, 120–121
USS Maryland, 53, 54, 60
USS Sculpin, 92, 95–96, 99, 100–102, 106
USS Trout, 80, 82, 83–84
USS Tuna, 73–76

V
Vanderver, Ray, 297
Varner, Byron, 35, 38
venereal disease, 86, 93, 157–158
Ver Valin, Art (father), 12, 13–14, 15
Ver Valin, Beulah (sister), 11–12
Ver Valin, Chuck
    abusive family life, 12
    applies for submarine service, 54
    apprehension about assignment, 61–62
    approach to adversity, 169–170
    assigned to USS Gudgeon, 58
    attacked by Japanese guard, 154
    boot camp, 53
    in a brothel, 53–56
    changing attitudes toward Japanese and
        war, 243
    and Civilian Conservation Corps, 19
    daughter and grandchildren, 328, 335

death of sister, 11–12
difficulties with son John, 330–331
divorces Gwen, 327–330
early days back home, 302–304
enlists in Navy, 19–21
fires on diving plane with rifle, 143
generosity of, 16–17
health conditions, 333–334
hears end of war announcement,
    281–282
homecoming with family, 304–305
and Irene Damien, 17, 304–306, 326,
    379
letter to Gwen, 300–302
loans money to Tim, 304
meets and marries Gwen Haughey,
    109–111, 326–327
in Naval Submarine School, 56–57, 58
nightmares and flashbacks, 334
physicality, 16–17, 20
playing catch with Babe, 249–250
popularity of, 13, 16
prepares to be boarded, 140
and race horses, 18
receives letter from Gwen, 305
receives Saint Christopher medal from
    Gwen, 112–113
relationship with Gwen, 111–113, 301,
    331–332
remarries Gwen, 384
response to first strike, 66
reunited with Johnny Johnson, 325–
    326
as rice server, 247–248
riding the rails, 18–19
second class chief petty officer goal,
    111–112
smokes pot, 336

son John dies of AIDS, 332, 336–337
toothache, 200–201, 203, 204, 205
tortured, 170–171
traded Red Cross parcel for sake, 286
transferred to USS Pelius, 109
volunteers for Vietnam, 330
walks away from camp, 290
witnesses B-29 bombing raid, 276–277
writing to Gwen, 245
youth, 11–21
Ver Valin, Florence (mother), 12, 14
Ver Valin, Ynez (sister), 16
Veterans Administration benefits, 344
"V" for Victory signs, 115

W
war, harbingers of, 38
War Brides Act, 293, 318, 320
waterboarding
    James Fitzgerald tortured, 156
    Japanese executed for, 362
    practiced by Americans, 386
Water Snake (Japanese civilian), 237, 240
WAVES (Women Accepted for Volunteer
    Emergency Service), 294
Wayne, Alberta, 44–45
Whiting, George, 139
Whitling, 213
whorehouses, 54–56
Withers, Thomas, 59, 73–74
Witzke, Bernie, 142, 143, 166, 326
women, shortage in Honolulu, 86
World War II veterans, 384
World War I submarine forces, 57

Y
Yellow Peril, 107
York, Robert, 166, 385

About the Author

Since his days as a pitcher for the Philadelphia Phillies, Larry Colton has taught high school, worked for Nike, and written three books. Between 1976 and 2000, his articles appeared in the *New York Times Magazine*, the *Boston Globe*, *Sports Illustrated*, *Ladies' Home Journal*, *Esquire*, and elsewhere. His previous books are *Idol Time*, *Goat Brothers* (a main selection for Book of the Month Club), and *Counting Coup*, which in 2000 won the Frankfurt eBook Award (FeBA) for nonfiction. He is also the founder of Wordstock, the Portland Book Festival.